SPORT STADIUMS AND ENVIRONMENTAL JUSTICE

This book explores the local environmental impact of sports stadiums, and how that impact can disproportionately affect communities of color. Offering a series of review articles and global case studies, it illustrates what happens when sport organizations and other public and private stakeholders fail to factor environmental justice into their planning and operations processes.

It opens with an historical account of environmental justice research and of research into sport and the natural environment. It then offers a series of case studies from around the world, including the United States, Canada, Kenya, South Africa, and Taiwan. These case studies are organized around key elements of environmental justice such as water and air pollution, displacement and gentrification, soil contamination, and transportation accessibility. They illustrate how major sports stadiums have contributed positively or negatively (or both) to the environmental health of the compact neighborhoods that surround them, to citizens' quality of life, and in particular to communities that have historically been subjected to unjust and inequitable environmental policy. Placing the issue of environmental justice front and center leads to a more complete understanding of the relationship between stadiums, the natural environment, and urban communities.

Presenting new research with important implications for practice, this book is vital reading for anybody working in sport management, venue management, mega-event planning, environmental studies, sociology, geography, and urban and regional planning.

Timothy Kellison is Associate Professor and Director of the Center for Sport and Urban Policy at Georgia State University, USA. His research is primarily focused on sport in the urban environment, with special emphasis in sport ecology, urban and regional planning, public policy, and politics. He is coeditor of the *Routledge Handbook of Sport and Sustainable Development* and the *Routledge Handbook of Sport and the Environment*.

Routledge Research in Sport, Culture and Society

Training the Body
Perspectives from Religion, Physical Culture and Sport
Edited by David Torevell, Clive Palmer and Paul Rowan

Indigenous Sport and Nation Building
Interrogating Sámi Sport and Beyond
Eivind Å. Skille

Sport, Identity and Inclusion in Europe
The Experiences of LGBTQ People in Sport
Ilse Hartmann-Tews

Social Innovation, Entrepreneurship, and Sport for Development and Peace
Edited by Mitchell McSweeney, Per G. Svensson, Lyndsay M.C. Hayhurst and Parissa Safai

Sport and Physical Activity in Catastrophic Environments
Edited by Jack Black and Jim Cherrington

Social Issues in Esports
Edited by Anne Tjønndal

Sport, Physical Activity and Criminal Justice
Politics, Policy and Practice
Edited by Haydn Morgan and Andrew Parker

Sport Stadiums and Environmental Justice
Edited by Timothy Kellison

For more information about this series, please visit: www.routledge.com/routledgeresearchinsportcultureandsociety/book-series/RRSCS

SPORT STADIUMS AND ENVIRONMENTAL JUSTICE

Edited by Timothy Kellison

LONDON AND NEW YORK

Cover image: Dustin Chambers Photography

First published 2023
by Routledge
4 Park Square, Milton Park, Abingdon, Oxon OX14 4RN

and by Routledge
605 Third Avenue, New York, NY 10158

Routledge is an imprint of the Taylor & Francis Group, an informa business

© 2023 selection and editorial matter, Timothy Kellison; individual
chapters, the contributors

The right of Timothy Kellison to be identified as the author of the editorial
material, and of the authors for their individual chapters, has been asserted in
accordance with sections 77 and 78 of the Copyright, Designs and Patents
Act 1988.

The Open Access version of this book, available at www.taylorfrancis.com,
has been made available under a Creative Commons Attribution-Non
Commercial-No Derivatives 4.0 license.

Trademark notice: Product or corporate names may be trademarks or
registered trademarks, and are used only for identification and explanation
without intent to infringe.

British Library Cataloguing-in-Publication Data
A catalogue record for this book is available from the British Library

Library of Congress Cataloging-in-Publication Data
Names: Kellison, Timothy, editor.
Title: Sport stadiums and environmental justice / edited by Timothy
Kellison.
Description: Abingdon, Oxon ; New York, N.Y. : Routledge, 2023. |
Series: Routledge research in sport, culture and society | Includes
bibliographical references and index. |
Identifiers: LCCN 2022034085 | ISBN 9781032201818 (hardback) |
ISBN 9781032201825 (paperback) | ISBN 9781003262633 (ebook)
Subjects: LCSH: Sports facilities--Environmental aspects. |
Sports facilities--Environmental aspects--Case studies. |
Sports facilities--Social aspects. | Sports facilities--Social aspects--Case
studies. | Environmental justice. | Environmental justice--Case studies. |
Urban ecology (Sociology) | Urban ecology (Sociology)--Case studies.
Classification: LCC GV415 .S67 2023 | DDC 796.06/8--dc23/eng/20220830
LC record available at https://lccn.loc.gov/2022034085

ISBN: 978-1-032-20181-8 (hbk)
ISBN: 978-1-032-20182-5 (pbk)
ISBN: 978-1-003-26263-3 (ebk)

DOI: 10.4324/9781003262633

Typeset in Bembo
by MPS Limited, Dehradun

CONTENTS

List of Figures	*vii*
List of Tables	*ix*
List of Contributors	*x*
Foreword	*xiii*
Acknowledgments	*xv*
List of Abbreviations	*xvii*

PART I
Overview   **1**

1   Considering Environmental Justice in Sport: Green Fields,
Gray Skies   3
Timothy Kellison

2   Stadiums, Gentrification, and Displacement: A
Comparative Overview of U.S. Cities   20
John Lauermann

3   Indigenous Environmental Justice in U.S. and Canada
Sport Stadiums   32
Alisse Ali-Joseph, Kelsey Leonard, and Natalie M. Welch

4   Environmental Impacts of Shadow Stadia   55
Taryn Barry, Daniel S. Mason, and Lisi Heise

5   Stadiums and State Environmental Policy Acts   71
Kellen Zale

vi Contents

PART II
Case Studies 89

6 Stadiums, Race, and Water Infrastructure: Flooding on
Atlanta's Southside 91
Marni Davis, Richard Milligan, and Andy Walter

7 Intracity Team Relocation and Environmental Justice in
Baltimore 105
Jessica R. Murfree and Walker J. Ross

8 Old and New Stadium Development in Miami 118
Laura Sivels

9 Stadia and Community Stewardship: Community Benefits
and Public Finance for New York's Yankee Stadium 129
Austin H. Thompson and Kyle S. Bunds

10 The Anacostia Waterfront Initiative, Nationals Park, and
Environmental Justice in Washington, D.C. 143
Michael Friedman

11 Cape Town's 2010 FIFA World Cup Stadium Location
and Its Spatial and Environmental Justice Implications 158
Aadil Engar and Jacques du Toit

12 Settler Colonialism as Environmental Injustice: Rogers
Place and Edmonton 172
Chen Chen and Judy Davidson

13 Micro Land Grabbing of Sporting Grounds in Nairobi: A
New Form of Environmental Justice at Play 188
Stephanie Gerretsen

14 Politics and Decision-Making in the Taipei Dome
Complex Project 211
Chun-Chieh Lin

15 Seattle and Climate Pledge Arena: A Progressive and
Sustainable Arena that Must Integrate Equity and Increase
Accountability 230
Alex Porteshawver

Index *249*

FIGURES

2.1	Geographic profile of major sports venues in the United States	25
3.1	Expansion of professional sport stadiums across the United States and Canada from 1900 to 2021	36
3.2	Historical Indigenous Nations within each state/province where a professional sport stadium is located	39
4.1	Maple Leaf Gardens in Toronto, pictured in 2016	61
4.2	The Houston Astrodome, pictured in 2004	66
6.1	Detailed view of Atlanta's southside neighborhoods in 1892	93
6.2	Present-day sewer lines, stadium footprints, and interstate highway corridor overlaid on 1930 Atlanta map of roads and buildings	97
6.3	Staging of the 1996 Paralympic Games at Centennial Olympic Stadium	99
7.1	Baltimore Memorial Stadium	106
7.2	Oriole Park at Camden Yards	107
8.1	loanDepot Park	122
9.1	Yankee Stadium and Macombs Dam Park in 2011	132
9.2	Satellite imagery of the Yankee Stadium site in 2004 (top) and 2020 (bottom)	133
9.3	Comparison of greenspace near the Yankee Stadium site in 2004 (top) and 2020 (bottom)	137
9.4	Joseph Yancey Track and Field at Macombs Dam Park	138
10.1	Nationals Park	144
10.2	Nationals Park, under construction in 2007	150
10.3	Sustainable design at Nationals Park	151
11.1	Aerial view of Cape Town	160
11.2	Athlone Stadium	163

viii Figures

11.3	Cape Town Stadium	167
12.1	Rogers Place and the Edmonton Ice District in 2016	174
12.2	Portrait from *Pillars of the Community* mural collection	184
13.1	Map of Nairobi County	202
13.2	Front façade of Kirigiti Stadium in Kiambu County, under construction in January 2022	205
13.3	Interior of Kirigiti Stadium, under construction in January 2022	206
14.1	Songshan Tobacco Factory historic site and Taipei Dome Complex under construction in June 2015	217
14.2	Construction of Taipei Dome Complex in April 2015	222
15.1	Construction of the Space Needle and Coliseum (later KeyArena and ultimately Climate Pledge Arena) in 1961	231
15.2	Climate Pledge Arena	236

TABLES

2.1	Major Sports Venues in the United States, by Geographic Situation	25
2.2	Neighborhood Class Characteristics near Urban Stadiums	27
2.3	Neighborhood Racial and Ethnic Characteristics near Urban Stadiums	27
3.1	Principles of Indigenous Environmental Justice across Sport Teams and Stadiums	34
3.2	Frequency of Professional Stadium/Team Land Acknowledgment across the United States and Canada, 2022	38
3.3	Frequency of Professional Stadium Community Engagement across the United States and Canada, 2022	38
3.4	Frequency of Professional Team Partnerships with Indigenous Nations Across the United States and Canada, 2022	38
5.1	Stadium Projects Receiving Legislative Exemptions from the California Environmental Quality Act	80
5.2	Stadium Projects Using Ballot Box Loophole	83
13.1	Sample of Nairobi County's Wards and Their Areas' Population and Size	198
14.1	Square Footage of Taipei Dome Complex Plan at Selected Stages of Environmental Impact Analysis Review	220

CONTRIBUTORS

Mustafa Santiago Ali is Vice President of Environmental Justice, Climate, and Community Revitalization for the National Wildlife Federation. A renowned thought leader, international speaker, policymaker, community liaison, trainer, and facilitator, Dr. Ali is also founder of Revitalization Strategies, a business focused on moving our most vulnerable communities from "surviving to thriving."

Alisse Ali-Joseph is an Applied Indigenous Studies faculty member at Northern Arizona University, USA, and specializes in the importance of sports and physical activity as a vehicle for empowerment, cultural identity, health, and educational attainment for American Indian people.

Taryn Barry is a Ph.D. student in the Faculty of Kinesiology, Sport, and Recreation at the University of Alberta, Canada. Her research interests include safe and inclusive sport, sport ecology, and the sustainable design of sport facilities.

Kyle S. Bunds is Associate Professor of Sport and Sustainable Community Development at North Carolina State University, USA, where his research examines the connection between sport, the environment, and equitable development.

Chen Chen is Assistant Professor in the Department of Educational Leadership at the University of Connecticut, USA. He takes an interdisciplinary approach to studying sport and settler colonialism. He is interested in mobilizing sport, education, and movement spaces to be more just and equitable, facilitating meaningful community-building and actions toward collective liberation.

Judy Davidson is Associate Professor in the Faculty of Kinesiology, Sport, and Recreation at the University of Alberta, Canada. Her research interests include queer and feminist approaches to sport and leisure phenomena. She has published on homonationalism, the international LGBT sport movement, and arena gentrification projects as forms of settler colonialism.

Marni Davis is Associate Professor of History at Georgia State University, USA. She is currently writing about immigration, race, and urban development in Atlanta's southside neighborhoods.

Jacques du Toit is Senior Lecturer in Town and Regional Planning at the University of Pretoria, South Africa. His critical interest is in social sciences methodology to improve the rigor and relevance of built environment research, while his epistemic interest is in People-Environment Studies, particularly in terms of planning sustainable built environments that help facilitate human well-being and pro-environmental behavior.

Aadil Engar is a professional planner with a master's degree in Town and Regional Planning. His interest lies in strategic master planning, airport planning, investment planning, and development facilitation.

Michael Friedman is Lecturer in Physical Cultural Studies in the Department of Kinesiology at the University of Maryland, College Park, USA. His research focuses on the relationship between public policy, urban design, and professional sports.

Stephanie Gerretsen is a Postdoctoral Research Scholar at Arizona State University's Global Sport Institute, USA, and works as a consultant for the United Nations. Her research interests lie in the intersection of sport, urban planning and development, and public policy.

Lisi Heise holds a Master of Community and Economic Development and works with the City of Edmonton, Canada in Urban Planning and Economy. Her research interests include the economic impacts of public-private partnerships between municipalities and professional sports franchises and the role of sport social identity theory on local politics and policymaking.

John Lauermann is Associate Professor and Director of the Spatial Analysis and Visualization Initiative at the Pratt Institute, USA. He is a geographer who researches the environmental and social impacts of large real estate developments.

Kelsey Leonard is Canada Research Chair in Indigenous Waters, Climate and Sustainability in the Faculty of Environment at the University of Waterloo, Canada, where her research focuses on Indigenous environmental and water justice.

Chun-Chieh Lin is a Ph.D. candidate in the Moray House School of Education and Sport, University of Edinburgh, UK. His research interests focus on the field of sport and international relations, sport for development and peace and the capability approach, and the intersection of the sport industry, stadium projects, and urban planning.

Daniel S. Mason is Professor in the Faculty of Kinesiology, Sport, and Recreation at the University of Alberta, Canada. His research focuses on the business of sport

xii Contributors

and the relationships between its stakeholders, including all levels of government, sports teams and leagues, the communities that host teams, agents, and players' associations.

Richard Milligan is Assistant Professor of Geosciences at Georgia State University, USA. He is a nature-society geographer whose research on the intersections of racism and colonialism with environmental issues contributes to scholarship on political ecology, environmental justice, and water governance.

Jessica R. Murfree is Visiting Assistant Professor in Sport Management and an Accountability, Climate, Equity, and Scholarship Fellow at Texas A&M University, USA. Her research examines the effects of climate change on sport, namely the social and legal implications of extreme weather and climate risks, and environmental injustices faced by minoritized groups in sport and recreation.

Alex Porteshawver is passionate about working at the local level to address climate change and equity. She is a skilled program manager, policy wonk, and trained facilitator.

Walker J. Ross is Lecturer of Sport Management and Digital Marketing in the Moray House School of Education and Sport at the University of Edinburgh, UK. His research focuses on sport ecology with emphasis on the Olympic Games, FIFA World Cups, and venue management.

Laura Sivels is a graduate student at the German Sport University in Cologne, Germany. Her research is at the intersection of equitable resilience and access to sport participation.

Austin H. Thompson is a Ph.D. student in the Parks, Recreation, and Tourism Management department at North Carolina State University, USA, and Ph.D. Research Assistant at the Environmental Finance Center at the University of North Carolina at Chapel Hill, USA. Thompson's research has focused on how and why local governments make environmental finance decisions and how those decisions affect the distribution of community benefits from environmental projects.

Andy Walter is Professor of Geography and Director of the Center for Interdisciplinary Studies at the University of West Georgia, USA. He is an economic geographer who examines the geographical dimensions of the professional sports industry.

Natalie Michelle Welch is Assistant Professor of Sport Management and program coordinator in the School of Business at Linfield University, USA. Her research primarily focuses on Native American sport and decolonizing research methods.

Kellen Zale is Associate Professor at the University of Houston Law Center, USA, where she researches and teaches in the areas of property, real estate, land use, and local government law.

FOREWORD

Mustafa Santiago Ali

In this transformational moment in our country, when we are facing impacts from pollution, climate change, racial and civil unrest, and a myriad of other issues, I am reminded of the words of Dr. King when he said, "The time is always right to do the right thing." To do the right thing, we need proverbial north stars to guide us, hard lessons learned, and examples of pathways forward. This book can help us on our journey toward justice.

As a young boy, my north star was my grandfather. He shared with me his daily experiences with racial injustice, which came in many forms. One of his solutions to confront injustice was to inspire men and women of good conscious to work together to address the challenges facing them. His generation fought segregation policies that forced Black people to the back of buses and policies that refused to allow Black people the dignity of eating at a food counter. His generation also struggled with the impacts of redlining and restrictive covenants that pushed Black and Brown people into the least desirable areas and then disinvested, creating ghettos, barrios, and hollers. Finally, but equally as destructive, were the restrictive job opportunities and relegation of Black people to the dirtiest, most dangerous, low-wage occupations. These examples may seem antiquated and out of touch with today's reality, but far too many are still trapped in the quicksand of generations of oppression, failed policies, systemic inequities, and economic injustice.

Today, we still see and feel the remnants of those past and present economic policies that continue to impact public health and economic sustainability of our most vulnerable. Black and Brown communities disproportionately suffer from toxic air and water pollution at alarming rates, increasing mental health stressors and creating sacrifice zones across America. Many young athletes from these polluted areas are challenged to reach their full athletic and academic potential because of what they breathe and drink.

xiv Foreword

These sacrifice zones, once considered disposable and unusable, have become prime real estate in some areas of the country for development opportunities. Once again, Black, Brown, and low-wealth communities are the ones who have to carry the environmental, economic, and climate burden unless we begin to implement a 21st-century paradigm shift toward centering people. Twenty-first-century actions must be centered on knowing that "communities speak for themselves." Twenty-first-century development cannot add additional burdens and must understand the historical impacts of toxic loading in Black, Brown, and low-wealth communities.

Sport has an opportunity to play a significant in healing our society. This book elevates significant challenges while placing a spotlight on the opportunities of transforming this moment into a movement—a movement where the voices, experiences, and ingenuity of the unseen and unheard can be uplifted, infused, valued, and implemented with real authenticity. One of the 17 principles of the Environmental Justice movement "mandates the right to ethical, balanced and responsible uses of land and renewable resources in the interest of a sustainable planet for humans and other living things." By integrating fundamental actions in the design and placement of stadiums and other structures, we can honor and support existing cultures in an area, protect human health, safeguard wildlife, and create new economic opportunities that are not damaging to those who have lived in our communities for decades.

My grandmother said, "When you know better, do better." We now know how to mitigate and even eliminate air, water, and land pollution in vulnerable communities. We know that if we incorporate equitable development and environmental justice principles, we can limit gentrification and displacement. We also know how to help our most vulnerable communities move from surviving to thriving. The lessons shared throughout this important book help us all have a better understanding of how we can play a role in creating healthier and more sustainable communities. After reading *Sport Stadiums and Environmental Justice*, it will be time to take action, because once you know better, it's our collective responsibility to do better together!

ACKNOWLEDGMENTS

In 2021, the annual meeting of the North American Society for Sport Management was planned for Minneapolis. After the murder of George Floyd, the society's Executive Council adopted a conference theme, "Race Forward," in which sport scholars and educators were encouraged to "more fully explore [their] role in advancing racial justice through ... research, teaching, and practice." As part of this charge, conference participants were asked to consider the "ways that race, racism, and social justice efforts have affected the management and marketing of sports." This book is an outcome of that call, and I am grateful for the bold leadership of those who championed the conference theme. In particular, I thank Jacqueline McDowell, chair of the ad hoc conference theme committee, and fellow committee members Leeann Lower-Hoppe and Eric MacIntosh. The theme was developed in collaboration with NASSM's Diversity and Inclusion Committee, comprised of co-chairs Drew Pickett and Cindy Veraldo and members Laura Burton, Alexandra Fairchild, Lauren Hindman, Tiesha Martin, NaRi Shin, Sarah Stokowski, and Robert Turick. I extend my thanks to these individuals for their direct influence on this project and, more broadly, for their work fostering a more equitable and just academy and industry.

Many other colleagues and friends were instrumental in the creation of this book. In particular, I appreciate the continued support of Simon Whitmore and the staff at Routledge, who are steady sources of expertise and encouragement. For the same reasons, I thank my colleagues at Georgia State University, the Sport Ecology Group, and the Sports Venues Education and Research Group.

Each of this book's contributors deserves special mention. I called upon them during an extraordinary time, and despite being pulled in many professional and personal directions, they remained steadfast in their commitment to this project. I owe an immense debt of gratitude to Mustafa Santiago Ali, Alisse Ali-Joseph, Taryn Barry, Kyle Bunds, Chen Chen, Judy Davidson, Marni Davis, Jacques du

xvi Acknowledgments

Toit, Aadil Engar, Michael Friedman, Stephanie Gerretsen, Lisi Heise, John Lauermann, Kelsey Leonard, Chun-Chieh Lin, Dan Mason, Richard Milligan, Jess Murfree, Alex Porteshawver, Walker Ross, Laura Sivels, Austin Thompson, Andy Walter, Natalie Welch, and Kellen Zale. I also thank Dustin Chambers, whose talented work is featured on the book cover.

Finally, I am grateful to my spouse, Rosemary, for her love and tireless encouragement. And for my children, Felix and Ozzie, who keep me grounded every day.

ABBREVIATIONS

COVID-19 Coronavirus Disease 2019
FIFA   Fédération Internationale de Football Association
GHG   Greenhouse gas
LEED   Leadership in Energy and Environmental Design
LULU   Locally unwanted land use
MLB   Major League Soccer
MLS   Major League Soccer
NBA   National Basketball Association
NFL   National Football League
NHL   National Hockey League
NIMBY   Not in my backyard
$PM_{2.5}$ Particulate matter with a diameter $\leq$ 2.5 μm
PM_{10} Particulate matter with a diameter $\leq$ 10 μm
WNBA   Women's National Basketball Association

PART I
Overview

1

CONSIDERING ENVIRONMENTAL JUSTICE IN SPORT: GREEN FIELDS, GRAY SKIES

Timothy Kellison

The relationship between sport and the environment is cyclical: sport both affects and is affected by the natural (e.g., land, air, water) and built (e.g., neighborhoods, homes, streets) environments. One tangible expression of this connection is the sport stadium.[1] Building stadiums, holding events, and indulging fans are often extractive processes, and these energy- and resource-intensive operations can profoundly impact the environment around a venue (McCullough et al., 2020a). Conversely, climate-related threats like extreme heat and sea-level rise may prompt sport organizations to implement strategies that reduce their climate vulnerability (Kellison & Orr, 2021). It is on the former premise that this book is primarily situated. In prosperous times, the economic benefits,[2] civic pride, and euphoric feelings produced at a stadium can be broadly enjoyed by a city's residents. But those living in the shadow of a stadium experience the venue differently, in ways—good and bad—that are more intimate, less trivial, and entirely inevitable.

As more and more sport stadiums are constructed in urban spaces (e.g., downtown, city centers; Kellison, 2021), any environmental harms produced by a stadium may intensify existing problems such as poor air quality, urban flooding, and scarce greenspace. Historically, these problems—and the poor health outcomes and economic inequality that result—disproportionately imperil communities of color. As discussed by Taylor (2014), these disparities are the legacy of environmental racism, because of which "minority and low-income communities [have faced] disproportionate environmental harms and limited environmental benefits" (p. 2). In response, environmental justice activists and community organizers have led efforts to unburden those communities affected most by ecological degradation. To support the claim that sports venues contribute positively to their communities, sport federations, organizations, and developers may argue that their venues can enhance the livability and desirability of urban neighborhoods.

DOI: 10.4324/9781003262633-2

In this introductory chapter, I illustrate how sport can be an effective setting to study the concept of environmental justice. To support this argument, I first provide an overview of environmental justice, both as a social movement and a multidisciplinary area of scholarship. Next, I explain how it may be applied to critical analyses of sport stadiums. As part of this discussion, I draw parallels between the heavy industrial facilities typically found in the environmental justice literature and the stadiums central to this book. Additionally, I identify similarities in the political challenges encountered by environmental justice activists and opponents of major stadium developments. I conclude with an outline of the book and the chapters that follow.

Environmental Justice as a Movement and a Frame

Definitions of the term *environmental justice* are manifold, but they all share a common understanding that communities of color experience relatively high rates of exposure to environmental hazards while receiving relatively low levels of environmental benefits.[3] In the academy, this imbalance may also be labeled *environmental racism*, or "the disproportionate effects of environmental pollution on racial minorities" (Sze, 2007, p. 13). The terms may be used complementarily: environmental racism produces harm, and environmental justice is realized when those harms are undone (Holifield, 2001). As Holifield et al. (2018a) observed, environmental justice and environmental racism can be framed around several similar ideas:

> They can serve as descriptive terms for observable or measurable states of affairs, as normative terms condemning present conditions and naming desired outcomes for the future, or as political terms deployed to name substantive problems and antagonists, mobilize activism, and justify advocacy for particular policies and laws. (p. 4)

Thus, environmental justice has been used to describe either an activist aspiration or an academic approach. However, despite the different applications of the term, they both are born from the problems of environmental inequity (Čapek, 1993).

A sample of recent studies illustrates how environmental racism manifests in communities of color today. Liu et al. (2021) found that despite improvements to air quality in the United States overall since 1990, Black, Hispanic, and Asian populations faced higher levels of exposure to various air pollutants[4] than White populations and concluded their "findings on 'which group was most exposed over time?' (on average, nationally) varied by pollutant, but in all six cases the most exposed group was a racial/ethnic minority group" (p. 12). Similarly, Tessum et al. (2021) noted that exposure to $PM_{2.5}$ "disproportionately and systemically [affects] people of color in the United States" (p. 1). According to the researchers, this current issue was at least partially artifactual of historical redlining, the racist system of denying loans and mortgage insurance for homes in predominately Black neighborhoods (Coates, 2014; Rothstein, 2017). Segregated by redlining and other economic and physical barriers (e.g., highway systems; Schindler, 2015), communities of color in urban neighborhoods face other environmental hazards beyond air pollution, including extreme heat events that disproportionately affect places where "there are fewer and smaller parks than nearby neighborhoods that are predominantly White, and natural shade from trees is also lacking" (Van Dam & Brink, 2021, para. 22; cf. Billaudeau et al., 2011).

Environmental justice may also be understood as a social movement (the origins of which predate scholarship on the subject; Bullard, 1993) of organizers, advocates, and activists working to overcome the harms of racist planning and policymaking (Sze, 2020). Scholars have pointed to several historical examples of environmental justice activism, including Martin Luther King, Jr.'s support of striking sanitary workers in Memphis in 1968 (Bullard, 2001). Elsewhere, in 1979, homeowners from a predominately Black neighborhood in Houston organized to block a planned landfill near the local public school. While ultimately unsuccessful, the resulting lawsuit, *Bean v. Southwestern Waste Management, Inc.*, was the "first of its kind to challenge the siting of a waste facility under civil rights law" (Bullard, 2001, p. 151). From this case emerged some of the earliest and most influential academic studies of environmental racism, including Bullard's (1983) examination of solid waste sites in Houston, and later, his groundbreaking book, *Dumping in Dixie: Race, Class, and Environmental Quality* (Bullard, 1990). In 1982, the environmental justice movement gained widespread attention after civil rights leaders and residents staged a protest against a plan to designate land in the predominately Black community of Warren County, North Carolina, as a toxic waste landfill (Mohai et al., 2009). More than 500 protesters were arrested, including members from the United Church of Christ (UCC). The Warren County protests led to a landmark study conducted by the UCC Commission for Racial Justice entitled *Toxic Wastes and Race in the United States*. Based on their analysis of 415 commercial hazardous waste facilities and more than 18,000 uncontrolled toxic waste sites, the authors concluded, "Race proved to be the most significant among variables tested in association with the location of commercial hazardous waste facilities" and that this result "represented a consistent national pattern" (Chavis & Lee, 1987, p. xiii).

As indicated in these examples, many justice-seeking organizations form at the grassroots, originating from community activists (and sometimes bolstered by established civil rights groups) in response to a local environmental issue. Efforts to confront environmental racism at a more systemic, institutional level have also grown. In a key example, in 1991, delegates representing myriad groups in the environmental justice movement assembled in Washington, DC, for the First National People of Color Environmental Leadership Summit, signaling that the environmental justice movement "had arrived as a force to be reckoned with on the national level" (Cole & Foster, 2001, p. 31). There, delegates affirmed and adopted the *Principles of Environmental Justice*, 17 statements that laid out the fundamental ideals and demands of the environmental justice movement.[5] Since a

1994 Executive Order detailing the U.S. government's actions to "address environmental justice in minority populations and low-income populations," federal protections have waxed and waned with changing administrations (Buford, 2017; McCausland, 2021).

Despite these compelling cases, many have expressed frustration with the lack of progress in the environmental justice movement (e.g., Whyte, 2020). Citing the environmental advocacy inhered in "many, if not all" Indigenous traditions, McGregor et al. (2020) argued that international and nation-state protections have fallen short of their goals: "Not only do current global, national and local governance and legal systems fail Indigenous peoples, they fail all life" (p. 35). This inertia is underscored by Pellow and Brulle (2005), who asked (and answered):

> … What can be said about the state of the movement for environmental justice? The outlook is not positive. The production of toxic chemical waste continues to increase exponentially; the level of cancers, reproductive disorders, and respiratory illnesses is on the rise in communities of color; environmental inequalities in urban and rural areas have remained steady or increased during the 1990s and the 2000s; the gap between the wealthy and the poor is the greatest seen in several decades; and the labor movement continues to lose ground as corporate power has usurped the ability of ordinary citizens and politicians to ensure that basic sovereignty remains intact in the United States. (pp. 11–12)

They continued by arguing that this inaction should be unsurprising, given that "the movement's founding was largely premised on a challenge to the mainstream, white-middle class environmental movement and its lack of attention to the crises occurring in communities of color" (p. 16).

In addition to defining environmental justice, its cognates, and its outcomes, scholars have studied the processes that lead to environmental inequity. Early discussions of environmental justice focused on toxic and hazardous siting, but they have since expanded to include other areas, including air pollution, water justice, flood hazards, energy systems, transportation, food justice, and urban parks (Holifield et al., 2018b). Taylor (2014) identified seven broad categories of theories that have been applied "to explain unequal exposure to environmental hazards" (p. 34) in minority and low-income communities:

1. Disproportionate siting and discrimination
2. Internal colonialism
3. Market dynamics[6]
4. The legal, regulatory, and administrative context
5. Manipulation, enticement, and environmental blackmail
6. Unique biophysical characteristics
7. Zoning and residential segregation

Taylor (2000) also demonstrated the breadth of ways environmental inequity may play out in communities, some of which are direct and obvious, like facing higher levels of exposure to environmental hazards and being deliberately targeted for the siting of noxious facilities. Other processes are less obvious, like segregation (i.e., of ethnic minority workers in dangerous and dirty jobs; of the environmental workforce; of housing and communities; of facilities and public services such as parks and transportation), lack of access to environmental amenities such as parks and playgrounds, disproportionate negative impacts of environmental policies (e.g., slower rates of cleanup in communities of color), inequality in the delivery of services like garbage removal, and expulsion of peoples from their Indigenous homelands (and appropriation of that land). Additionally, environmental inequity may be analyzed based on how environmental racism is not exclusively the result of "discriminatory facility siting and malicious intent" but also "less conscious but hegemonic form of racism, white privilege" (Pulido, 2000, p. 12).

Those familiar with the literature on sport, stadiums, and urban development will notice striking parallels between it and Taylor's (2000, 2014) descriptions of environmental inequity. In the next section, I make these connections more explicit. I begin by tracing past work linked to sport, the environment, and racism. I then present the central thesis of this book: that the design, construction, and operation of sport stadiums have contributed directly to the problems of environmental inequity and the principles of environmental justice.

Why Stadiums? Situating Environmental Justice in Sport

Environmental justice scholars have advocated exploring the effects of racism and inequity outside of the typical hazards associated with landfills, polluting factories, and other heavy industrial facilities. For instance, while recognizing some facilities (e.g., nuclear plant, uranium dump) carry more risk than others (e.g., landfill for household trash), Taylor (2014) identified "a plethora of small facilities such as dry cleaners, gas stations, and garages that have impacts on nearby residents worth studying" and contended that "more effort should be put into understanding the impact that different types of facilities have on health, property values, jobs, host-community compensation, and so on" (pp. 279–280). Pellow (2018) similarly suggested that scholars consider ways that environmental inequity may surface more broadly: "Environmental justice struggles are also evident—*if* we are paying close attention—within spaces of conflict and collaboration that are not always typically defined as 'environmental'" (p. 3).

Some scholars have responded to these calls by applying environmental justice themes to the sport context. For example, Sze (2009) established a clear connection between sport and environmental justice in her examination of the Atlantic Yards project, the multibillion-dollar project in Brooklyn anchored by the Nets (then New Jersey Nets) NBA team, in which she argued:

> In one sense, stadiums, recreational facilities, and open space represent the seeming "reflection" or opposite to the polluting facilities that have been the

8 Timothy Kellison

focus of the vast majority of environmental justice research that addresses harms, specifically racial disparities in exposure to noxious facilities (the definition of open space is contested, used by some opponents to mean public parks, and by the developer to mean nondeveloped land that is privately owned but publicly accessible). However, my analysis suggests that the development and siting of so-called positive amenities follows a similar cultural and political trajectory as that of noxious facilities. (p. 112)

Other work has shown how the sports venue, particularly as it is used as part of a larger entertainment district, "(re)produces social inequalities, shreds social fabric, and eliminates public spaces and culture by sanitizing and isolating groups and individuals of different race and ethnic backgrounds, age, gender and sexual orientation, physical ability, life experiences, and social standing" (Mincyte et al., 2009, p. 108).

Building on the work of these scholars, below, I explain the connection between sport stadiums and environmental justice. This argument is presented in two forms. First, sport stadiums and the events that occur within them can come with direct and significant environmental risks for their surrounding neighborhoods. Second, efforts by residents and local activists to block major stadium developments have played out in ways that are similar to the political battles that occur when siting traditional environmental hazards such as landfills and polluting facilities in communities of color.

Stadiums as Environmental Hazards

Sporting events attract tens of thousands (or more) of fans to stadiums, and the money spent in and around those stadiums is often used to evidence stadiums are engines of economic development and urban regeneration. Stadium boosters such as team owners and local policymakers often argue that stadiums create jobs, generate tax revenues, and revitalize neighborhoods.[7] But as civic leaders tout these benefits, they need not look hard to also recognize crosscurrents of environmental harm. Consider, for example, the possible consumption patterns of a stadium user at a sporting event (McCullough et al., 2020b). First, they may reach the stadium by foot, bike, or public transportation, taxi, or rideshare—but they are more likely to arrive via their own personal vehicles (after, depending on the scope of the event, traveling some distance to reach the city). Coupled with the return trip home, this travel can produce significant levels of CO_2 emissions (Triantafyllidis, 2018). Second, during the event, they may purchase individually packaged foods and beverages served in plastic cups, which may later be disposed of either in trash bins or as wastewater, placing added stress on municipal services like garbage collection and sewage treatment (Bagli, 2004). Third, producing the event requires water to irrigate the field and electricity to power the lighting, audiovisual, and ventilation systems. Collectively, this basic hypothetical demonstrates the significant demands a stadium may place on local resources.[8]

Some of these effects are felt outside of the stadium's immediate proximity. For instance, Humphreys and Pyun (2018) found that travel among those attending MLB games contributed to nearly 28,000 hours of traffic delays and $7 million in social costs annually in host cities. These costs were associated with "traffic congestion, wear and tear on roads, and greenhouse gas emissions that affect the climate" (pp. 870–871). In light of this potential environmental impact, Locke (2019) estimated the impact of MLB games on local air pollution and found the effect, while statistically significant, was unlikely to cause "an increase in local air pollution levels large enough to create a public health concern" (pp. 242–243). On the other hand, Casper and Bunds (2018) have suggested that tailgating activities and idling vehicles produce unhealthy microenvironments for those in close proximity to a stadium.

Other disamenities are similarly limited to those in the immediate vicinity of the stadium. In an early study of stadium nuisances, Bale (1990) surveyed residents across 37 Football League grounds and found that those living closest to the venue (i.e., within 0.5 km) were more likely to "perceive football-related nuisances" (p. 326) such as traffic, noise, and hooliganism. With respect to crime, Pyun (2019) estimated that the arrival of the Nationals MLB team in Washington, D.C., led to an increase in reported assaults by 7–7.5% annually, representing a yearly increase in cost from $20 to $35 million. It is unlikely that the victims of these crimes are only fans; in a study of crime reports around Wembley Stadium, Kurland et al. (2013) concluded that events at the stadium "[contribute] to levels of crime in the area that surrounds it" (p. 5). The link between crime and sporting events underscores the need for an efficient emergency response, but there is evidence that congestion and activity near sporting events may lead to delays in emergency services. In Propheter's (2020) study of the Golden 1 Center (home of the NBA's Sacramento Kings), he found events at the arena added approximately 33 seconds to police response times. There is also evidence that the so-called dead zones created by stadiums on non-event days "may be conducive to criminal activity because of the lack of activity around the venue" (Jakar & Gordon, 2022, p. 366).

Some hazards are unavoidable for stadium users, and as a result, annoyances such as traffic and long queues may be subsumed as part of the eventgoing experience. Others can ignore these issues entirely by staying away from the stadium whenever events are taking place. But, what about those who live in the area around a stadium? Using the context of football, Bale (1990) observed it "generates certain 'bads' (for example, noise, crowds, traffic, parking, etc.) which are necessary for the production of a football match but whose costs are borne by local residents, not the football" (p. 325). In other words, some hazards are inescapable for residents. This point is emphasized in Hyun's (2022) study of Gwangju-Kia Champions Field in South Korea: "In this regard, the new stadium may have simply been an amenity as a landmark for the city and its citizens as a whole, but instead become a disastrous and extremely harmful living condition for those residing in close proximity of the facility" (p. 616).

People who live close to a stadium face additional environmental hazards that those elsewhere in the city can avoid. As Humphreys and Ruseski (2019) illustrated, some of this negative interaction occurs in the earliest stages of stadium development. Comparing venue construction and natality data, they found that infants born in counties with new sports venues had lower birth weights. Based on their observation that "the concentration of airborne particulate matter was higher in counties during these construction projects," they reasoned that the result was "evidence of a direct mechanism at work since we know that airborne [particulate] matter easily passes through a placenta" (p. 3). Other nuisances uniquely experienced by those living near a stadium include reduced greenspace (Chan, 2006; Lavine & Oder, 2010) and increased exposure to various forms of pollution related to litter, light, noise, and vibration (Bertero et al., 2013; Hyun, 2022). For instance, in a *Baltimore Sun* interview of locals during the opening of the Ravens' NFL stadium, a neighborhood resident of 56 years said, "I can't remember seeing this much trash before. It makes you want to throw up your hands" (Mathews, 1998, para. 4). While litter was a significant source of frustration among residents, the majority of complaints focused on noise pollution "from the advertising planes and news helicopters that circled the stadium" (para. 11).

Once a stadium opens, exposure to these environmental hazards is unavoidable for those who live, work, and play in the neighborhoods around it. For that reason,[9] community members may reject plans to construct a stadium project in their neighborhood and organize a public campaign to stop it. But those who oppose stadium projects often face an uphill battle against a city's powerful political leaders, well-established civic institutions, and wealthy business elite. As discussed below, in many ways, these challenges mirror those faced by environmental justice activists.

The Politics of Urban Stadium Developments

Despite the environmental risks they present to nearby neighborhoods, sport stadiums offer a lot of appeal for their cities more broadly. They may be used for image building, signaling a city's entrepreneurial status (Mason et al., 2015). Additionally, when it houses a major professional or collegiate sport team, stadiums may provide fans with profoundly meaningful emotional experiences (Delia et al., 2022); conversely, when a team relocates to another city, fans may express feelings of loss and sadness (Mitrano, 1999). Still, for the communities around a stadium, these benefits may feel out of step with the problems that can emerge. For that reason, individuals may support a stadium development in principle but oppose its placement near their homes; this attitude reflects a "not in my backyard" (NIMBY) ideology. In the environmental justice literature, NIMBY-related opposition sometimes surfaces when considering sites for "locally undesirable land uses" (LULUs). Despite the fact LULUs are "considered beneficial to society at large, and many agree that they should be located somewhere"[10] (Been, 1993, p. 1,001), residents may see them as unwelcome nuisances. As a result, affected residents may campaign to shift a planned site outside of their neighborhood (for this application in a stadium-related context, see Ahlfeldt & Maennig, 2011).

Environmental justice activists mobilize in many different ways, including writing official complaint letters, petitioning, waging public campaigns, organizing street protests and marches, and developing networks for collective action (Martinez-Alier et al., 2016). These strategies are consistent with the political tools employed in past stadium-related debates, which include campaigning and voting, canvassing and petition-signing, contacting elected officials, attending and speaking at public meetings, and participating in rallies and protests (Kellison et al., 2020). Communities that fight against stadium sites in their neighborhoods face numerous obstacles, including limited opportunity to participate in the decision-making process (Kellison & Mondello, 2014) and inadequate resources to challenge powerful growth coalitions made up of the city's business elite and political leadership (Delaney & Eckstein, 2007). These obstacles may be even more pronounced in predominately Black neighborhoods, as Bullard (1990) observed: "White communities (middle- and lower-income areas) have been more successful than [Black] communities in defending against unwanted industrial encroachment and outside penetration" (p. 45). These issues are hardly new; in her recounting of the history of public parks in the United States, Taylor (2009) described how, early in the 19th century, "wealthy urbanites, unwilling to continue building private parks at their own expense, successfully convinced cities to subsidize private gated parks that only that would have access to," while "attempts to develop public parks in working-class neighborhoods failed" (p. 231).[11]

Various reasons explain why communities of color face additional barriers to environmental justice (e.g., Taylor, 2014), many of which are similar to the problems experienced by anti-stadium groups. For instance, corporate interests and lobbyists actively seek, and then take advantage of, what they perceive to be the path of least resistance. Additionally, minority and low-income communities may be incentivized with promises of new jobs, additional tax revenues for schools, and improved municipal services, but "the compensation packages do not include strict environmental protection for current and future generations" (p. 144). These assurances also often fail to include mechanisms to protect housing and property values (from decreasing because of LULUs, or from increasing and pricing residents out of their own homes; Humphreys & Nowak, 2017; Mara & Immergluck, 2016). Third, the use of eminent domain—a common practice in past stadium cases (Chen, 2013)—disproportionately affects Black communities, which "have often been described as slums regardless of the quality of the housing" (Taylor, 2014, p. 229).

Environmental inequities can also be explained more broadly by imbalances in power between policymakers, business leaders and corporate interests, and ordinary citizens. Similar imbalances are prevalent in the sport industry. Recognizing "a great number of asymmetrical power relations exist within sport," Sartore-Baldwin et al. (2017) argued "over time, these power relations have established cultural norms that produce and reproduce deeply embedded standards that

12 Timothy Kellison

promote inequality and injustice across social groups" (p. 367). As discussed further in the next section, in this book, we explore how power imbalances have been exploited to construct sport stadiums, providing cities as a whole with new centers of commerce, entertainment, and pride, while leaving their communities of color to shoulder the environmental burdens that follow.

About This Book

Much has been written about sport stadiums, but to date, discussions of their environmental justice implications have only occurred superficially. Such connections are important as most professional sport teams in the United States have moved from suburban stadiums to replacement venues in central cities, increasing their likelihood of interaction with urban communities. The desuburbanization of sport stadiums has led some to suggest that major stadium developments are inerrant catalysts for urban regeneration and neighborhood revitalization. Throughout this book, we aim not to downplay the positive impacts sport stadiums can have on their cities but instead to explore the environmental and human costs that may also result. As I have argued in previous work, sports venues—particularly those with eco-friendly designs—"undoubtedly deserve praise, but it is equally important to recognize the legacy of the land, neighborhoods, and communities on which a stadium is built" (Kellison, 2022, p. 269).

In *Sport Stadiums and Environmental Justice*, we explore the relationship between sport stadiums and environmental justice from an interdisciplinary perspective, as reflected in contributors' diverse theoretical and methodological approaches to environmental justice research. The book is arranged in two parts. Part I contains an overview of key environmental justice issues and broad discussions of the ways in which they are relevant. Following this introductory chapter, John Lauermann shows in Chapter 2 how gentrification is a direct environmental justice issue and analyzes the relationship between stadiums and gentrification in 169 U.S. cities. In Chapter 3, Alisse Ali-Joseph, Kelsey Leonard, and Natalie Welch explore the relationship between North American stadiums and Indigenous environmental justice, focusing specifically on land acknowledgments, community engagement, partnerships, and ownership stakes. Taryn Barry, Daniel Mason, and Lisi Heise follow in Chapter 4, where they introduce the concept of "shadow stadia," venues left behind when major professional or amateur sports teams have moved elsewhere. Kellen Zale completes the first section in Chapter 5; there, she recounts how stadium projects in California have legally circumvented their state's environmental policy act and considers the environmental justice consequences.

Every major-league city represents a unique case study, and its historical, cultural, and political landscape may be explored to understand the extent to which sport stadiums contribute to environmental justice. Part II contains a collection of case studies from which some common threads can be found. In Chapter 6, Marni Davis, Richard Milligan, and Andy Walter discuss the history of flooding problems in Atlanta's southside neighborhoods and explain how several generations of stadium projects have exacerbated these—and other—issues.[12] Jessica Murfree and Walker Ross follow in Chapter 7, where they explore how the move of Baltimore's professional teams out of historic Memorial Stadium mirrored societal inequities visible elsewhere in the city. Next, in Chapter 8, Laura Sivels investigates the recent—and still evolving—stadium cases in Miami, where city officials are grappling with the threats of sea-level rise and climate gentrification. Chapter 9 centers on New York City; Austin Thompson and Kyle Bunds analyze the impact of the New York Yankees' stadium project on greenspace in the Bronx and discuss its public health implications. Chapter 10, by Michael Friedman, traces the history of Washington, D.C.'s Anacostia Waterfront Initiative and describes the role Nationals Park has played in the District's major urban redevelopment project.

The second set of case studies expands the section's scope beyond American cities. In Chapter 11, Aadil Engar and Jacques du Toit consider the spatial and environmental justice implications of Cape Town's 2010 FIFA Men's World Cup location. Chen Chen and Judy Davidson follow in Chapter 12, where they use the case of Rogers Place in Edmonton to highlight how contemporary sport stadiums and entertainment districts contribute to the enduring problem of displacement or removal of Indigenous community members. In Chapter 13, Stephanie Gerretsen examines how the practice of land grabbing sporting grounds has produced social and environmental justice issues in Nairobi, at a time when the Kenyan government is embarking on ambitious plans to grow its legacy as a sporting nation. Chapter 14 focuses on Taipei Dome Complex; as Chun-Chieh Lin explains, the venue has been mired in more than 30 years of political battles. The book concludes in Chapter 15 with some hope provided by Alex Porteshawver, who, returning to the United States, focuses on the great potential of stadiums to contribute to environmental justice and challenges leaders to realize that potential.

Scholarship related to sport and the environment (i.e., sport ecology) continues to grow. Furthermore, environmental justice—particularly its absence from many urban neighborhoods—is attracting more public and scholarly attention. To date, however, these issues have been studied largely in isolation from one another. While a strong foundation of academic work has pointed out some of the positive and negative effects of urban stadiums on their communities, very few have been framed around environmental justice. This book represents a comprehensive examination of the extent to which sport stadiums respond (or contribute) to the problems of neighborhoods and communities. In particular, we focus on the places and people that have historically been subjected to unjust and inequitable environmental policy. Recognizing that environmental justice is not solely a study of outcomes, we also recount the struggles and actions of environmental justice activists working in communities affected by stadium developments. Placing the issue of environmental justice front and center enables a better understanding of the direct relationship between stadiums, the natural environment, and urban communities.

14 Timothy Kellison

Notes

1 Throughout this book, *stadium* is used to refer to all major sporting venues, including, but not limited to, indoor and outdoor arenas, ballparks, and speedways.

2 Or the economic costs (Bradbury, 2022; Coates & Humphreys, 2008).

3 In the United States, these communities of color may include majority Black, Hispanic, Asian, or Indigenous peoples, and their exposure to environmental hazards are measured against those of majority White neighborhoods. As discussed elsewhere in this book, outside of the US, a wide range of other diverse communities may be affected.

4 Liu et al. (2021) investigated exposure to six pollutants: carbon monoxide (CO), nitrogen dioxide (NO_2), ozone (O_3), particulate matter with diameters $\leq$ 2.5 and 10 μm ($PM_{2.5}$ and PM_{10}), and sulfur dioxide (SO_2), all of which can contribute to numerous health and environmental problems. For example, $PM_{2.5}$ has been linked to health effects (e.g., premature death in individuals with heart or lung disease, irregular heartbeat, aggravated asthma, decreased lung function, and increased respiratory symptoms), visibility impairment, environmental damage (e.g., acidifying lakes and streams, depleting soil nutrients, damaging sensitive forests and farm crops), and materials damage (Environmental Protection Agency, 2021).

5 See http://www.ejnet.org/ej/principles.pdf.

6 *Market dynamics* includes, among others, the so-called Chicken or Egg and the Minority Move-In Hypothesis, which focuses on whether a hazardous facility is purposely sited in a predominately minority and low-income community or that facility was in place before a neighborhood's modern-day demographic characteristics had been established (see also Mohai and Saha [2015] on "disparate siting" vs. "post-siting demographic change").

7 These supposed benefits have—time after time—been empirically disproven by a choir of peer-reviewed economic studies (Bradbury et al., 2022; Coates & Humphreys, 2008).

8 Increasingly, however, some sport organizations and stadium operators have begun championing environmental causes and supporting the delivery of events in more sustainable ways. In Chapter 15, Alex Porteshawver highlights one such example.

9 And others, including opposition to publicly financing the cost of construction or the lack of a referendum (Kellison & Mills, 2021).

10 Though I present LULUs as an analog to sport stadiums, I acknowledge that between the two, a much stronger case can be made for the societal benefits of LULUs like "homeless shelters, drug or alcohol treatment centers, and waste disposal facilities" (Been, 1993, p. 1,001).

11 Recently, scholars have documented neighborhood resistance to so-called green LULUs because of fear that initiatives like tree plantings could lead to gentrification and displacement (Anguelovski, 2016). As Checker (2011) explained, "These challenges face a pernicious paradox—must they reject environmental amenities in their neighborhoods in order to resist the gentrification that tends to follow such amenities?" and furthermore, "What happens to environmental justice activism when it meets state-sponsored sustainable urban development?" (p. 211).

12 Davis, Milligan, and Walter focus on Atlanta-Fulton County Stadium, Centennial Olympic Stadium, and the Peoplestown and Summerhill neighborhoods. A companion chapter could have easily focused just two miles to the northwest, where the historic Vine City neighborhood shares a similar past. Vine City is adjacent to several downtown destinations, including the CNN Center, the Georgia World Congress Center, and until recently, the Georgia Dome, itself entangled in problems of displacement and environmental injustice (see Blau, 2019). These developments are a key source of Vine City's troubles, as Samuel (2017) reported: "All the pavement ... the subterranean-feeling roads and parking lots near the Georgia Dome, lead to issues with flooding, erosion, and pollution downstream" (para. 10). In 2002, rainfall from Tropical Storm Hanna overwhelmed Proctor Creek and Vine City sewer system, resulting in "a toxic mixture of stormwater and untreated sewage" to flood the neighborhood, damaging

"hundreds of homes, many beyond repair" (Faulkner, 2021, p. 56). Ultimately, "city leaders decided the cost of rebuilding the flooded homes was too great—and the likelihood of future flooding was too high" (p. 56), so residents from more than 60 homes were permanently relocated, and their homes were razed by the city. In 2017, the Georgia Dome was replaced by Mercedes-Benz Stadium, the $1.6-billion venue pictured on this book's cover. As part of its water management program, the new stadium features a 680,000-gallon rainwater cistern and 1.2-million-gallon vault to "reduce stormwater runoff and flooding in the neighborhoods to the west of the stadium" (Fennessy, 2017, para. 5).

References

Ahlfeldt, G. & Maennig, W. (2011). Voting on a NIMBY facility: Proximity cost of an "iconic" stadium. *Urban Affairs Review, 48*(2), 205–237. 10.1177/1078087411423644

Anguelovski, I. (2016). From toxic sites to parks as (green) LULUs? New challenges of inequity, privilege, gentrification, and exclusion for urban environmental justice. *Journal of Planning Literature, 31*(1), 23–36. 10.1177/0885412215610491

Bagli, C. V. (2004, July 25). Stadium could send sewage into river, lawmaker says. *The New York Times*, 27.

Bale, J. (1990). In the shadow of the stadium: Football grounds as urban nuisances. *Geography, 75*(4), 325–334. http://www.jstor.org/stable/40571880

Been, V. (1993). What's fairness got to do with it? Environmental justice and the siting of locally undesirable land uses. *Cornell Law Review, 78*, 1001–1085. https://scholarship.law.cornell.edu/clr/vol78/iss6/1

Bertero, R. D., Lehmann, A., Mussat, J., & Vaquero, S. (2013). Vibrations in neighborhood buildings due to rock concerts in stadiums. *Journal of Structural Engineering, 139*(11), 1981–1991. 10.1061/(ASCE)ST.1943-541X.0000756

Billaudeau, N., Oppert, J.-M., Simon, C., Charreire, H., Casey, R., Salze, P., Badariotti, D., Banos, A., Weber, C., & Chaix, B. (2011). Investigating disparities in spatial accessibility to and characteristics of sport facilities: Direction, strength, and spatial scale of associations with area income. *Health & Place, 17*(1), 114–121. 10.1016/j.healthplace.2010.09.004

Blau, M. (2019). Lightning, struck. *The Bitter Southerner*. https://bittersoutherner.com/lightning-the-atlanta-community-lost-to-super-bowl-dreams

Bradbury, J. C. (2022). Does hosting a professional sports team benefit the local community? Evidence from property assessments. *Economics of Governance*. 10.1007/s10101-022-00268-z

Bradbury, J. C., Coates, D., & Humphreys, B. R. (2022). *The impact of professional sports franchises and venues on local economies: A comprehensive survey*.

Buford, T. (2017, July 24). Has the moment for environmental justice been lost? *ProPublica*. https://www.propublica.org/article/has-the-moment-for-environmental-justice-been-lost

Bullard, R. D. (1983). Solid waste sites and the Black Houston community. *Sociological Inquiry, 53*(2–3), 273–288. 10.1111/j.1475-682X.1983.tb00037.x

Bullard, R. D. (1990). *Dumping in Dixie: Race, class, and environmental quality*. Westview Press.

Bullard, R. D. (1993). Race and environmental justice in the United States. *Yale Journal of International Law, 18*(1), 319–336.

Bullard, R. D. (2001). Environmental justice in the 21st century: Race still matters. *Phylon, 49*(3/4), 151–171. 10.2307/3132626

Čapek, S. M. (1993). The "environmental justice" frame: A conceptual discussion and an application. *Social Problems, 40*(1), 5–24. 10.2307/3097023

Casper, J. M. & Bunds, K. S. (2018). Tailgating and air quality. In B. P. McCullough & T. B. Kellison (Eds.), *Routledge handbook of sport and the environment* (pp. 291–300). Routledge.

Chan, S. (2006, August 17). Groundbreaking for Yankees draws politicians and protest. *The New York Times*, B2.

Chavis, B. F., Jr. & Lee, C. (1987). *Toxic wastes and race in the United States: A national report on the racial and socio-economic characteristics of communities with hazardous waste sites.* United Church of Christ Commission for Racial Justice.

Checker, M. (2011). Wiped out by the "greenwave": Environmental gentrification and the paradoxical politics of urban sustainability. *City & Society, 23*(2), 210–229. 10.1111/j.1548-744X.2011.01063.x

Chen, S. (2013). Keeping public use relevant in stadium eminent domain takings: The Massachusetts way. *Boston College Environmental Affairs Law Review, 40*(2), 453–485.

Coates, D. & Humphreys, B. R. (2008). Do economists reach a conclusion on subsidies for sports franchises, stadiums, and mega-events? *Econ Journal Watch, 5*(3), 294–315.

Coates, T.-N. (2014). *The case for reparations.* The Atlantic. https://www.theatlantic.com/magazine/archive/2014/06/the-case-for-reparations/361631/

Cole, L. W. & Foster, S. R. (2001). *From the ground up: Environmental racism and the rise of the environmental justice movement.* New York University Press.

Delaney, K. J. & Eckstein, R. (2007). Urban power structures and publicly financed stadiums. *Sociological Forum, 22*(3), 331–353. 10.1111/j.1573-7861.2007.00022.x

Delia, E. B., James, J. D., & Wann, D. L. (2022). Does being a sport fan provide meaning in life? *Journal of Sport Management, 36*(1), 45–55. 10.1123/jsm.2020-0267

Environmental Protection Agency. (2021). *Health and environmental effects of particulate matter (PM).* https://www.epa.gov/pm-pollution/health-and-environmental-effects-particulate-matter-pm

Faulkner, T. (2021). Before & after. *Land + People, Spring/Summer*, 54–61.

Fennessy, S. (2017, November 15). It's official: No other sports facility in the world is as eco-friendly as Mercedes-Benz Stadium. *Atlanta Magazine.* https://www.atlantamagazine.com/news-culture-articles/official-no-sports-facility-world-eco-friendly-mercedes-benz-stadium/

Holifield, R. (2001). Defining environmental justice and environmental racism. *Urban Geography, 22*(1), 78–90. 10.2747/0272-3638.22.1.78

Holifield, R., Chakraborty, J., & Walker, G. (2018a). Introduction: The worlds of environmental justice. In R. Holifield, J. Chakraborty, & G. Walker (Eds.), *The Routledge handbook of environmental justice* (pp. 1–11). Routledge.

Holifield, R., Chakraborty, J., & Walker, G. J. (Eds.). (2018b). *The Routledge handbook of environmental justice.* Routledge.

Humphreys, B. R. & Nowak, A. (2017). Professional sports facilities, teams and property values: Evidence from NBA team departures. *Regional Science and Urban Economics, 66*, 39–51. 10.1016/j.regsciurbeco.2017.06.001

Humphreys, B. R. & Pyun, H. (2018). Professional sporting events and traffic: Evidence from U.S. cities. *Journal of Regional Science, 58*(5), 869–886. 10.1111/jors.12389

Humphreys, B. R. & Ruseski, J. E. (2019). *Geographic determinants of infant health: The impact of sports facility construction projects.* https://papers.ssrn.com/sol3/papers.cfm?abstract_id=3467702

Hyun, D. (2022). Proud of, but too close: The negative externalities of a new sports stadium in an urban residential area. *The Annals of Regional Science, 68*(3), 615–633. 10.1007/s00168-021-01095-6

Jakar, G. S. & Gordon, K. O. (2022). Dead spaces: Sport venues and police stops in a major league, upper midwestern city in the United States. *Journal of Sport Management, 36*(4), 355–368. 10.1123/jsm.2021-0080

Kellison, T. (2021). Enduring and emergent public opinion in relation to a suburban stadium district: The case of Truist Park–Battery Atlanta. *Journal of Global Sport Management*. Advance online publication. 10.1080/24704067.2021.1886685

Kellison, T. (2022). An overview of Sustainable Development Goal 11. In B. P. McCullough, T. Kellison, & E. N. Melton (Eds.), *The Routledge handbook of sport and sustainable development* (pp. 261–275). Routledge.

Kellison, T. & Mills, B. M. (2021). Voter intentions and political implications of legislated stadium subsidies. *Sport Management Review, 24*(2), 181–203. 10.1016/j.smr.2020.07.003

Kellison, T. & Mondello, M. J. (2014). Civic paternalism in political policymaking: The justification for no-vote stadium subsidies. *Journal of Sport Management, 28*(2), 162–175. Article. 10.1123/jsm.2012-0210

Kellison, T. & Orr, M. (2021). Climate vulnerability as a catalyst for early stadium replacement. *International Journal of Sports Marketing and Sponsorship, 22*(1), 126–141. 10.1108/IJSMS-04-2020-0076

Kellison, T., Sam, M. P., Hong, S., Swart, K., & Mondello, M. J. (2020). Global perspectives on democracy and public stadium finance. *Journal of Global Sport Management, 5*(4), 321–348. 10.1080/24704067.2018.1531680

Kurland, J., Johnson, S. D., & Tilley, N. (2013). Offenses around stadiums: A natural experiment on crime attraction and generation. *Journal of Research in Crime and Delinquency, 51*(1), 5–28. 10.1177/0022427812471349

Lavine, A. & Oder, N. (2010). Urban redevelopment policy, judicial deference to unaccountable agencies, and reality in Brooklyn's Atlantic Yards project. *The Urban Lawyer, 42*(2), 287–374.

Liu, J., Clark, L. P., Bechle, M. J., Hajat, A., Kim, S.-Y., Robinson, A. L., Sheppard, L., Szpiro, A. A., & Marshall, J. D. (2021). Disparities in air pollution exposure in the United States by race/ethnicity and income, 1990–2010. *Environmental Health Perspectives, 129*(12), 127005. 10.1289/EHP8584

Locke, S. L. (2019). Estimating the impact of Major League Baseball games on local air pollution. *Contemporary Economic Policy, 37*(2), 236–244. 10.1111/coep.12404

Mara, K. & Immergluck, D. (2016). *Preserving affordability and preventing displacement in Vine City and English Avenue in the face of major neighborhood investment initiatives: A report to the Westside Communities Alliance*. Georgia Institute of Technology.

Martinez-Alier, J., Temper, L., Del Bene, D., & Scheidel, A. (2016). Is there a global environmental justice movement? *The Journal of Peasant Studies, 43*(3), 731–755. 10.1080/03066150.2016.1141198

Mason, D. S., Washington, M., & Buist, E. A. N. (2015). Signaling status through stadiums: The discourses of comparison within a hierarchy. *Journal of Sport Management, 29*(5), 539–554. 10.1123/jsm.2014-0156

Mathews, J. (1998, September 8). Stadium's neighbors less than thrilled: Trash, noise, crowds mar their Sunday. *Baltimore Sun*. https://www.baltimoresun.com/news/bs-xpm-1998-09-08-1998251041-story.html

McCausland, P. (2021, August 5). *Cut in infrastructure money for communities hurt by highways disappoints advocates*. NBC News. https://www.nbcnews.com/politics/politics-news/cut-infrastructure-money-communities-hurt-highways-disappoints-advocates-n1275986

McCullough, B. P., Orr, M., & Kellison, T. (2020a). Sport ecology: Conceptualizing an emerging subdiscipline within sport management. *Journal of Sport Management, 34*(6), 509–520. 10.1123/jsm.2019-0294

McCullough, B. P., Orr, M., & Watanabe, N. M. (2020b). Measuring externalities: The imperative next step to sustainability assessment in sport. *Journal of Sport Management, 34*(5), 393–402. 10.1123/jsm.2019-0254

McGregor, D., Whitaker, S., & Sritharan, M. (2020). Indigenous environmental justice and sustainability. *Current Opinion in Environmental Sustainability, 43*, 35–40. 10.1016/j.cosust.2020.01.007

Mincyte, D., Casper, M. J., & Cole, C. (2009). Sports, environmentalism, land use, and urban development. *Journal of Sport and Social Issues, 33*(2), 103–110. 10.1177/01937235 09335690

Mitrano, J. R. (1999). The "sudden death" of hockey in Hartford: Sports fans and franchise relocation. *Sociology of Sport Journal, 16*(2), 134–154. 10.1123/ssj.16.2.134

Mohai, P., Pellow, D., & Roberts, J. T. (2009). Environmental justice. *Annual Review of Environment and Resources, 34*(1), 405–430. 10.1146/annurev-environ-082508-094348

Mohai, P., & Saha, R. (2015). Which came first, people or pollution? A review of theory and evidence from longitudinal environmental justice studies. *Environmental Research Letters, 10*(12), 125011. 10.1088/1748-9326/10/12/125011

Pellow, D. N. (2018). *What is critical environmental justice?* Polity.

Pellow, D. N. & Brulle, R. J. (2005). Power, justice, and the environment: Toward critical environmental justice studies. In D. N. Pellow & R. J. Brulle (Eds.), *Poewr, justice, and the environment: A critical appraisal of the environmental justice movement* (pp. 1–19). MIT Press.

Propheter, G. (2020). Do urban sports facilities have unique social costs? An analysis of event-related congestion on police response time. *International Journal of Urban Sciences, 24*(2), 271–281. 10.1080/12265934.2019.1625805

Pulido, L. (2000). Rethinking environmental racism: White privilege and urban development in southern California. *Annals of the Association of American Geographers, 90*(1), 12–40. 10.1111/0004-5608.00182

Pyun, H. (2019). Exploring causal relationship between Major League Baseball games and crime: A synthetic control analysis. *Empirical Economics, 57*, 365–383. 10.1007/s00181-018-1440-9

Rothstein, R. (2017). *The color of law: A forgotten history of how our government segregated America*. Liveright.

Samuel, M. (2017, June 18). *The trouble with Atlanta's Proctor Creek*. WABE. https://www.wabe.org/the-trouble-with-atlantas-proctor-creek/

Sartore-Baldwin, M. L., McCullough, B., & Quatman-Yates, C. (2017). Shared responsibility and issues of injustice and harm within sport. *Quest, 69*(3), 366–383. 10.1080/00336297.2016.1238769

Schindler, S. (2015). Architectural exclusion: Discrimination and segregation through physical design of the built environment. *The Yale Law Journal, 124*(6), 1934–2024. http://www.jstor.org/stable/43617074

Sze, J. (2007). *Noxious New York: The racial politics of urban health and environmental justice*. MIT Press.

Sze, J. (2009). Sports and environmental justice: "Games" of race, place, nostalgia, and power in neoliberal New York City. *Journal of Sport & Social Issues, 33*(2), 111–129. 10.1177/0193723509332581

Sze, J. (2020). *Environmental justice in a moment of danger.* University of California Press.

Taylor, D. E. (2000). The rise of the environmental justice paradigm: Injustice framing and the social construction of environmental discourses. *American Behavioral Scientist, 43*(4), 508–580. 10.1177/0002764200043004003

Taylor, D. E. (2009). *The environment and the people in American cities, 1600s–1900s: Disorder, inequality, and social change.* Duke University Press.

Taylor, D. E. (2014). *Toxic communities: Environmental racism, industrial pollution, and residential mobility.* New York University Press.

Tessum, C. W., Paolella, D. A., Chambliss, S. E., Apte, J. S., Hill, J. D., & Marshall, J. D. (2021). PM2.5 polluters disproportionately and systemically affect people of color in the United States. *Science Advances, 7*(18), eabf4491. 10.1126/sciadv.abf4491

Triantafyllidis, S. (2018). Carbon dioxide emissions research and sustainable transportation in the sports industry. *Journal of Carbon Research, 4*(57), 5. 10.3390/c4040057

Van Dam, E. & Brink, H. (2021, October 2). *'Hotlanta' is even more sweltering in these neighborhoods due to a racist 20th-century policy.* CNN. https://www.cnn.com/2021/09/18/weather/extreme-urban-heat-environmental-racism-climate/index.html

Whyte, K. (2020). Too late for indigenous climate justice: Ecological and relational tipping points. *WIREs Climate Change, 11*(1), e603. 10.1002/wcc.603

2
STADIUMS, GENTRIFICATION, AND DISPLACEMENT: A COMPARATIVE OVERVIEW OF U.S. CITIES

John Lauermann

Stadiums have long been viewed as anchors for urban regeneration, around which cities can build districts for entertainment, consumption, and tourism (Bale & Moen, 2012; Gaffney, 2008). This kind of stadium-led development is especially common in the United States, which hosts hundreds of stadiums, primarily in urban neighborhoods. In theory, this spatial strategy enables urban regeneration in historically under-invested neighborhoods and spurs growth for economically languishing post-industrial cities. But it also has costs, particularly where stadium development catalyzes gentrification and contributes to the displacement of marginalized populations. In many cities, disadvantaged neighborhoods are often the only places with sufficient vacant or low-cost land to enable such large-scale developments. By default, the most vulnerable communities—working-class, majority-minority neighborhoods—are thus also the most vulnerable to displacement, despite having the most need for urban regeneration benefits.

Sportswriter Dave Zirin (2015) goes so far as to classify this model of stadium-led urban regeneration as "sports-driven apartheid." Writing about Black Lives Matter protests at Oriole Park in Baltimore—and more broadly about stadiums, urban planning, and systemic racism in U.S. cities—he argues:

> These stadiums were all built with the promise of an attendant service economy that could provide jobs and thriving city centers, with restaurants mushrooming around the fun and games … [T]his sports-centric urban planning has been a failure. It's been an exercise in corporate welfare and false political promises. What the stadiums have become instead are strategic hamlets of gentrification and displacement. They have morphed into cathedrals to economic and racial apartheid, dividing cities between haves and have-nots, between those who go to the game to watch and those who go to the game looking for low-income work. (para. 4)

DOI: 10.4324/9781003262633-3

In this sense, stadiums are both symptoms of systemic inequality and drivers of more geographically-specific gentrification patterns. But the problem is not the stadium per se. The urban benefits of stadiums are real (though typically smaller than promised by boosters), and the idea of stadium development (but not the reality of paying for it) has long been politically popular among city leaders (Kellison & Mills, 2021; Lauermann, 2022). Rather, the problem lies in the spatial strategy underlying stadium-led urban regeneration: it lies in the process of bulldozing "disadvantaged" neighborhoods, replacing them with large-scale redevelopment, and populating that redevelopment with real estate targeting tourism rather than residents.

The result is a neighborhood planned—to paraphrase Zirin's quote—primarily for those who go to the game to watch rather than long-term residents or displaced former residents. The strategy creates neighborhoods that cater to tourists and other temporary users, like suburbanites who visit for an afternoon but otherwise have minimal interaction with the inner city. This is an environmental justice issue for three reasons: First, stadiums are—as Kellison's introduction to this volume outlines—locally unwanted land uses: desirable for cities in general, but presenting environmental hazards for the host neighborhood (e.g., transit-related emissions, traffic and noise pollution, and the voluminous waste generated by large crowds). Like many examples of environmental justice politics, stadium development is filtered through the lens of NIMBYism, such that the most marginalized communities are the least able to resist unwanted land uses. Second, gentrification impacts communities' access to environmental amenities, since displacement from a neighborhood obviously limits one's ability to benefit from environmental improvements that neighborhood receives through urban regeneration. Stadium development often does generate new greenspace, more efficient buildings, and better public transit options, but not necessarily for the historical communities who find themselves priced out of the new neighborhood. Third, gentrification limits the ability of marginalized communities to shape the urban landscape—architecture, infrastructure, and public spaces. Stadium landscapes are oriented around tourism and consumerism, not around the needs of long-term, economically diverse, socially integrated residential communities.

The chapter proceeds by first reviewing literature on the link between stadiums, gentrification, and displacement. Broadly, these conversations explore two sides of the same coin: what looks like stadium-led urban generation to some stakeholders may very well look like stadium-led gentrification to others. To clarify the terms of debate, I also define an empirical framework for differentiating gentrification from other kinds of neighborhood change. Using that framework, the chapter then analyzes empirical evidence from U.S. cities. I draw on a GIS analysis that compares the locations of 472 urban stadiums to common indicators of gentrification. The areas near stadiums do exhibit some clear indicators of gentrification (e.g., above-average increases in household income and new residents) and have higher rates of displacement among some racial and ethnic minorities. The chapter concludes by

22 John Lauermann

summarizing implications for urban planning and policy and identifying new directions for future research on stadiums and gentrification.

Stadiums, Gentrification, and Displacement

There are two broad conversations about stadiums and urban development: research on stadium districts as catalysts for urban regeneration, and research on the role of stadiums in state-led gentrification. Urban regeneration approaches emphasize the multiplier and legacy effects of stadium districts. There are, of course, multiplier effects associated with stadiums, for instance, through job creation in related industries or tourist spending at other local businesses (Long, 2013; Santo, 2005). However, much research questions whether these benefits are large enough to justify public subsidies for stadiums (Matheson, 2019; Noll & Zimbalist, 2011). There are also legacy effects over the lifespan of a stadium. These are especially important for analyzing the costs and benefits of stadiums built for a narrow purpose such as hosting a mega-event (Gold & Gold, 2008). Drawing on comparative research on sports mega-events, Smith (2012) argues that stadiums can create legacies through both "event-led regeneration" like new or renovated venues, and "event-themed regeneration" with broader-based effects like growth in the tourism industry, physical regeneration of the surrounding landscape, improved social engagement and civic participation, and institutional capacity building within government agencies. Preuss and Plambeck (2021) identify 12 legacy values of stadiums, including "stadium as venue" for tourism at sport and non-sport events; "stadium as catalyst" for developing surrounding areas and stimulating local economic activity and attracting future events; "stadium as exhibition piece," where cities can highlight state-of-the-art architecture, engineering, or technologies, or create future historical landmarks; and "stadium as iconic building," which serves as a symbolic capital for the nation, for politicians, or for national identity.

Comparatively speaking, there is relatively less research on the gentrification impacts of stadiums (van Holm, 2018), and much of it focuses on broader neighborhood change rather than the stadiums themselves. Framed this way, stadiums are not just "catalysts" for urban regeneration, but also tools of "state led gentrification" (Stein, 2019) and "touristification" (Sequera & Nofre, 2018) of the city for outsiders at the expense of residents. Regeneration and gentrification are, of course, logically correlated: what looks like regeneration to one stakeholder group may look like gentrification to another. Thus, some definitions are in order to clarify the terms of debate. Gentrification, traditionally defined, is a process of neighborhood class upgrading from predominantly working class to predominantly middle class (Lees et al., 2013). It has both demographic and environmental impacts. In the U.S. context, there are strong racialized effects on neighborhood demographics, especially displacement of Black and Hispanic households (Rucks-Ahidiana, 2020). There are several varieties of displacement such as direct (e.g., eviction), exclusionary (e.g., being priced out of a housing market), and more diffuse kinds of displacement pressure (e.g., losing social and commercial ties within a neighborhood as the old community is replaced by newcomers; Easton et al., 2020). The environmental impacts include renovation of existing buildings, new development, and remediation or even expansion of environmental amenities like green space (Amorim Maia et al., 2020). Indeed, there is a large literature on "green gentrification," the notion that sustainability policy can induce displacement by zoning out working-class jobs (e.g., loss of industrial land) and that environmental amenities are used to bid up real estate prices (Rigolon & Németh, 2018).

Stadium development can, of course, lead to direct displacements when residents are removed to make way for new development. This is especially of concern for populations with precarious housing tenure, for instance, the homeless (Saito, 2019; Suzuki et al., 2018) or residents of public housing (Gaffney, 2016; Vale & Gray, 2013). Exclusionary displacement is more common, however, as residents are more gradually priced out of nearby housing markets. van Holm (2018) finds that stadiums are associated with increases in income and slower than average *growth* in minority populations in U.S. cities but have less direct effect on rent costs and residential turnover. This suggests that even if there is not a net decline in a population (as would be expected under direct displacement), future growth of minority communities is precluded by gentrification-induced real estate appreciation and speculation (a pattern associated more closely with exclusionary displacement). Finally, there is also more indirect displacement pressure, for instance, when legacy promises are viewed as a "trojan horse" for gentrification (Panton & Walters, 2018; Weber-Newth et al., 2017) or when long-term residents feel the new development is "not for us" (Danley & Weaver, 2018; Watt, 2013). Others have noted a displacement of the working class from the stadiums themselves, as corporatization and an upscaling of stadium amenities have priced out low-income fans (Dinces, 2016; Palvarini & Tosi, 2013).

A recurring theme is the way in which stadiums distribute gentrification effects geographically within a city. Activists note the diverging fortunes of stadium districts—which receive lavish public subsidies—and other inner-city neighborhoods—which do not. One activist interviewed by Doucet (2020) described this problem regarding Little Caesars Arena in Detroit:

> Many of us say that there are two Detroits developing now. There are areas where tremendous amounts of capital are being poured into. But in this neighbourhood there is no capital being poured in … We see public subsidies for this gentrification; the new hockey arena that's being built is essentially being publicly subsidized with the idea that if we can create this huge development that somehow that's going to create some prosperity for the rest of Detroiters. (p. 645)

That is, the concern is less about *what* stadium-led regeneration entails than about *where* it occurs and *who* it impacts in those places. The reason for this is, in part, because there is much consensus on what stadium development does to a city. The differences lie in evaluation of whether those effects are positive or negative, and for whom. One particularly relevant—and contentious—effect is the impact on nearby real estate values. On the one hand, stadiums often improve property values in surrounding neighborhoods, to the benefit of property owners (Ahlfeldt & Maennig, 2007) in what some have called "positive" (Cameron & Coaffee, 2005) or "good" gentrification (Balletto et al., 2018). On the other hand, it is not always clear whether stadiums are creating property value or merely redistributing it within the city. van Holm (2019) analyzed residential development near minor league stadiums in smaller U.S. cities, finding that while there is a positive re-development effect in nearby neighborhoods, the stadiums concentrate the effect in particular neighborhoods rather than spurring growth overall in a city's property values. And, of course, higher property values are only a boon to some class groups: for lower-income renters, this trend creates exclusionary displacement pressures either way.

Evidence from U.S. Cities

There are extensive debates over how to measure gentrification, both due to the methodological challenges of analyzing complex processes like class identity (Clerval, 2020) or displacement (Easton et al., 2020) and due to theoretical dis-agreements over causality (Zapatka & Beck, 2020) and covariance (Preis et al., 2021) among indicators. In the U.S. context, however, most studies of gentrification-related displacement start with proxies for class (e.g., Census vari-ables like household income, educational attainment, or employment in white-collar occupations) and then compare class transitions to residential indicators such as racial and ethnic composition, housing tenure and costs, or physical changes in the built environment (e.g., demolition, new construction; Halasz, 2018; Podagrosi et al., 2011; Rucks-Ahidiana, 2020; Sutton, 2020). I will use a similar strategy here: comparing the geographic location of stadiums to tract-level Census data on local class and racial demographics.

One place to start is the Department of Homeland Security's (2021) *Homeland Infrastructure Foundation-Level Data*, which includes historical and contemporary geospatial data on various North American infrastructure, including major sports venues. The initial sample used here included 649 venues classified as "promoters of arts, sports, and similar events with facilities," a category that primarily includes open-air stadiums and sports-oriented arenas. Descriptive analysis of that sample reveals two important patterns in the geography of stadiums in the United States. The first is that while stadium capacity generally mirrors population distribution (e.g., populous states such as California, Texas, and New York also have the most stadium capacity), there are important regional variations due to university sta-diums in less populous states (e.g., in college towns of the Southeast and Midwest).

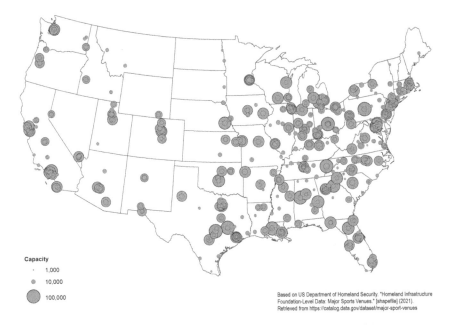

FIGURE 2.1 Geographic profile of major sports venues in the United States

The second pattern is that stadiums are predominantly located in urban settings. This can be assessed by comparing the location of stadiums to the *National Center for Education Statistics* locales map, which classifies the entire country into various urban, suburban, and rural categories based on Census place definitions (NCES, 2021). Of the sample venues, 73% (472) are located in cities, and most of the rest are located in suburbs (Table 2.1). Delving further into geographic classification, 265 of the "urban" stadiums are located in large cities (defined as cities with populations over 250,000), 112 are located in mid-sized cities (between 100,000 and 250,000), and 95 in small cities (less than 100,000). Many of these urban stadiums anchor larger commercial districts, with extensive infrastructure for parking, transit, and commercial land use. The broader implication is that these

TABLE 2.1 Major Sports Venues in the United States, by Geographic Situation

	# venues	*Average Seating Capacity*
Rural areas	71	13,079
Suburbs	106	20,327
Cities	472	23,976
Large cities	*265*	24,642
Midsize cities	*112*	25,608
Small cities	*95*	20,192
Total	**649**	**22,188**

Note: Data from Department of Homeland Security, 2021.

urban stadiums have sizeable environmental footprints, both locally within their respective neighborhoods and nationally across hundreds of metropolitan regions (169 metropolitan areas host one or more sampled venues, to be specific).

These urban stadiums were then compared to changes in neighborhood class characteristics. This can be measured with tract-level data from the *National Historical GIS* (Manson et al., 2020), a platform that synthesizes various editions of the Census into time-series datasets to allow longitudinal comparison. Likewise, a working definition of "neighborhood" is needed so that the areas near stadiums can be compared to their surrounding cities. I define the stadium "neighborhood" as all census tracts with their centroids located within 1 km of a stadium. Geographic centroids were calculated rather than using original tract boundaries to include only those tracts that are primarily within the 1-km zone (excluding, for example, tracts that intersect the 1-km zone but lie primarily outside it). Likewise, tracts with less than 100 residents in the most recent year of data availability were also excluded to avoid sparsely populated areas such as parks or airports. This definition is of course somewhat arbitrary, but it was chosen to approximate the sort of walkable distance thresholds that define many neighborhoods.

Gentrification trends are measured with four indicators: per capita income, the percent of adults with a bachelor's or higher degree, the poverty rate (all measuring class transitions in general), and the proportion of households who have lived in their current home for less than 10 years (a more direct measure of newcomers in a neighborhood). Sutton (2020) includes two of these indicators (education and share of newcomers) as part of a composite gentrification index used to model displacement effects, while the other two indicators (income and poverty) are widely used in quantitative analysis of gentrification patterns in U.S. cities (Halasz, 2018; Podagrosi et al., 2011). Since the theoretical definition of gentrification is based on the middle class, we can use city-wide averages as proxies for "middle" class status (e.g., "middle class" income in any given city is, presumably, somewhere near the metropolitan mean).

Using those definitions, it is clear that the class profile of areas near stadiums exhibits stronger indicators of gentrification in comparison to other urban tracts (Table 2.2). Tracts within 1 km of stadiums have higher rates of educational attainment and proportions of neighborhood newcomers. They have also changed faster than other urban areas over time, again consistent with gentrification patterns. They have steeper declines in poverty over time and higher-than-average increases in income and educational attainment. All of this is to say that areas near stadiums have changed faster than urban averages, in ways that are consistent with middle-class upgrading.

Similar analysis can help illustrate patterns in racial demographics. Here, too, we can use National Historical GIS data to assess longitudinal changes in census tracts, with the same definition of a stadium "neighborhood" (tracts with their centroid located within 1 km of a stadium, and with at least 100 residents). In the U.S. context, displacement is often proxied using indicators of neighborhood transitions in racial and ethnic groups as measured by the Census: with the percentages of residents identifying as Asian, Black or African American, White, other

TABLE 2.2 Neighborhood Class Characteristics near Urban Stadiums

	Tracts near Stadiums	Other Urban Tracts	t-tests
	Mean (SE)	Mean (SE)	t(p)
Per capita income, 2019	$37,685 (1136.4)	$34,989 (154.2)	2.35
Δ Per capita income, 2000–19	$7,671 (613.9)	$2,123 (68.7)	8.98***
% Bachelor's degree or more, 2019	47.77 (1.01)	34.22 (.16)	13.29***
Δ % Bachelor's degree or more, 2000–19	12.81 (.59)	7.90 (.07)	8.21***
Poverty rate, 2019	20.55 (.42)	13.91 (.06)	15.62***
Δ Poverty rate, 2000–19	−8.96 (.46)	−1.91 (.06)	−15.06***
% New residents, 2019	67.38 (.68)	53.05 (.10)	20.79***
Δ % New residents, 2000–19	−7.31 (.42)	−12.59 (.08)	−12.32***
# Tracts	659	19,884	

Note: Data derived from National Historical GIS. Analysis based on 472 stadiums in 169 core-based statistical areas. * p < 0.05, ** p < 0.01, *** p < 0.001.

races, multi-racial, and Hispanic (an ethnicity category which can overlap with any of the preceding racial categories). These indicators are commonly used in quantitative analysis of gentrification and racial displacement in U.S. cities (Rucks-Ahidiana, 2020; Sutton, 2020).

Using those definitions, there are also differences in the racial demographics of areas near stadiums and differential rates of displacement (Table 2.3). The areas surrounding the stadiums have significantly higher concentrations of Asian and White

TABLE 2.3 Neighborhood Racial and Ethnic Characteristics near Urban Stadiums

	Tracts near Stadiums	Other Urban Tracts	t-tests
	Mean (SE)	Mean (SE)	t(p)
% Asian, 2020	10.34 (.37)	8.63 (.09)	4.47***
Δ % Asian, 2000–20	3.14 (.21)	2.63 (.04)	2.36
% Black, 2020	23.28 (.87)	22.28 (.19)	1.12
Δ % Black, 2000–20	−6.14 (.49)	−.67 (.08)	−11.10***
% White, 2020	48.82 (.85)	44.91 (.19)	4.52***
Δ % White, 2000–20	−4.45 (.56)	−13.77 (.10)	16.52***
% Other, 2020	8.05 (.38)	11.81 (.10)	−9.56***
Δ % Other, 2000–20	3.26 (.31)	3.06 (.08)	.62
% Multiple races, 2020	8.80 (.20)	11.33 (.05)	−12.28***
Δ % Multiple races, 2000–20	6.01 (.18)	8.2 (.05)	−11.95***
% Hispanic (any race), 2020	16.61 (.63)	24.2 (.17)	−11.69***
Δ % Hispanic (any race), 2000–20	2.46 (.27)	5.8 (.07)	−11.99***
# Tracts	837	19,541	

Note: Data derived from National Historical GIS. Analysis based on 472 stadiums in 169 core-based statistical areas. * p < 0.05, ** p < 0.01, *** p < 0.001.

28 John Lauermann

populations than the surrounding city and lower rates of Hispanic populations. This would be expected in areas that have experienced prior waves of gentrification, especially if that gentrification was led by White middle-class migration. The differences are more apparent when considering rates of change in these categories: In particular, tracts near stadiums had greater declines in Black residents and slower-than-average declines in White residents, a pattern consistent with Black displacement and White replacement common in gentrifying neighborhoods (Sutton, 2020), within the broader national context of a shrinking White population and a trend toward moderately less-segregated White residential geographies (Ellis et al., 2018).

These racial and class indicators do not, of course, in themselves prove that stadiums have a displacement effect. Questions of causality and sequences of household migration are far beyond the scope of a survey chapter and would require both more fine-scaled data and statistical techniques such as difference-in-difference modeling (Hess, 2020) or cross-lagged regression (Zapatka & Beck, 2020). But they do show patterns consistent with gentrification and related displacements: Areas near stadiums are now more affluent than other urban neighborhoods, but those neighborhoods were less affluent in the past and have experienced more dramatic class and racial transitions over time.

Conclusion

To summarize, this chapter explored the relationship between stadiums, gentrification, and displacement. Academic literature on the subject tends to focus on the role of stadiums in urban regeneration, or the way in which stadium development is imbricated in state-led gentrification agendas. The key point of contention is not necessarily the stadiums themselves but their geographically uneven impacts and the spatial strategies that anchor regeneration around elite stadium districts. Urban regeneration premised on stadium districts tends to prioritize the needs of tourists and commuters over inner-city residents. The result is a geography of neighborhoods reshaped by gentrification, as vulnerable communities are displaced and the landscape is rebuilt for a more affluent clientele. An empirical review of stadiums in U.S. cities demonstrates this pattern. The chapter analyzed 472 urban stadiums spread across 169 metropolitan regions, finding that areas near stadiums have more affluent class profiles today but also experienced more dramatic class upgrading—and declines among some racial groups—over time.

This suggests two implications for urban regeneration planning and policy. The first is that the urban regeneration benefits of stadiums—while real—may not be large enough to justify the costs of gentrification and displacement. Much sports economics literature argues that economic impacts rarely live up to promised expectations and warns against public subsidies for stadium construction (Matheson, 2019; Noll & Zimbalist, 2011). Similarly, much urban studies literature questions the design and planning of stadium districts and challenges the legacy narratives promoted by sports and mega-event boosters (Lauermann, 2019;

Stewart & Rayner, 2016). Future research might prioritize ex-ante and long-itudinal analysis of these costs and benefits to more systematically analyze both boosterish and critical narratives that predominate in media and popular discourse.

The second implication is that cities need to consider not only *what* a stadium does to a region but also *where* those impacts are concentrated within the region. The creation of "strategic hamlets of gentrification and displacement" (Zirin, 2015, para. 4) starts with a spatial planning strategy that concentrates enormous investment in a relatively small area, on the assumption that benefits will diffuse outward into the wider metropolitan region. This is the geographic equivalent to trickle-down economics—that preferential treatment for the few will somehow benefit the many through some combination of multipliers and legacies. And just like trickle-down theory, the idea has been widely challenged with empirical evidence to the contrary (Clark, 2020), yet curiously remains prominent in some policy circles (Krugman, 2020). Future research might integrate more geographic elements into analysis, consider impacts within and between neighborhoods, and interpret the socio-spatial interactions of stadium development and neighborhood demographic change.

References

Ahlfeldt, G. M. & Maennig, W. (2007). The role of architecture on urban revitalisation: The case of Olympic arenas in Berlin-Prenzlauer Berg. *Hamburg Contemporary Economic Discussions, 1*, 1–29.

Amorim Maia, A. T., Calcagni, F., Connolly, J. J. T., Anguelovski, I., & Langemeyer, J. (2020). Hidden drivers of social injustice: Uncovering unequal cultural ecosystem services behind green gentrification. *Environmental Science & Policy, 112*, 254–263. 10.1016/j.envsci.2020.05.021

Bale, J. & Moen, O. (Eds.). (2012). *The stadium and the city*. Edinburgh University Press.

Balletto, G., Borruso, G., Tajani, F., & Torre, C. M. (2018, May 2–5). *Gentrification and sport: Football stadiums and changes in the urban rent* [Paper presentation]. International Conference on Computational Science and Its Applications, Melbourne, VIC, Australia.

Cameron, S. & Coaffee, J. O. N. (2005). Art, gentrification and regeneration—From artist as pioneer to public arts. *European Journal of Housing Policy, 5*(1), 39–58. 10.1080/14616710500055687

Clark, J. (2020). *Uneven innovation: The work of smart cities*. Columbia University Press.

Clerval, A. (2020). Gentrification and social classes in Paris, 1982–2008. *Urban Geography, 43*(1), 34–58. 10.1080/02723638.2020.1826728

Danley, S. & Weaver, R. (2018). "They're not building it for us": Displacement pressure, unwelcomeness, and protesting neighborhood investment. *Societies, 8*(3), 74. 10.3390/soc8030074

Department of Homeland Security (2021). *Homeland infrastructure foundation-level data: Major sports venues* [Data set]. https://catalog.data.gov/dataset/major-sport-venues

Dinces, S. (2016). The attrition of the common fan: Class, spectatorship, and major league stadiums in postwar America. *Social Science History, 40*(2), 339–365. 10.1017/ssh.2016.6

Doucet, B. (2020). Deconstructing dominant narratives of urban failure and gentrification in a racially unjust city: The case of Detroit. *Tijdschrift voor economische en sociale geografie, 111*(4), 634–651. 10.1111/tesg.12411

Easton, S., Lees, L., Hubbard, P., & Tate, N. (2020). Measuring and mapping displacement: The problem of quantification in the battle against gentrification. *Urban Studies, 57*(2), 286–306. 10.1177/0042098019851953

Ellis, M., Wright, R., Holloway, S., & Fiorio, L. (2018). Remaking white residential segregation: Metropolitan diversity and neighborhood change in the United States. *Urban Geography, 39*(4), 519–545. 10.1080/02723638.2017.1360039

Gaffney, C. (2008). *Temples of the earthbound gods: Stadiums in the cultural landscapes of Rio de Janeiro and Buenos Aires* (1st ed.). University of Texas Press.

Gaffney, C. (2016). Gentrifications in pre-Olympic Rio de Janeiro. *Urban Geography, 37*(8), 1132–1153. 10.1080/02723638.2015.1096115

Gold, J. & Gold, M. (2008). Olympic cities: Regeneration, city rebranding and changing urban agendas. *Geography Compass, 2*(1), 300–318. 10.1111/j.1749-8198.2007.00080.x

Halasz, J. R. (2018). The super-gentrification of Park Slope, Brooklyn. *Urban Geography, 39*(9), 1366–1390. 10.1080/02723638.2018.1453454

Hess, C. L. (2020). Light-rail investment in Seattle: Gentrification pressures and trends in neighborhood ethnoracial composition. *Urban Affairs Review, 56*(1), 154–187. 10.1177/1078087418758959

Kellison, T., & Mills, B. M. (2021). Voter intentions and political implications of legislated stadium subsidies. *Sport Management Review, 24*(2), 181–203. 10.1016/j.smr.2020.07.003

Krugman, P. (2020). *Arguing with zombies: Economics, politics, and the fight for a better future.* WW Norton.

Lauermann, J. (2019). The urban politics of mega-events: Grand promises meet local resistance. *Environment and Society, 10*(1), 48–62. 10.3167/ares.2019.100104

Lauermann, J. (2022). The declining appeal of mega-events in entrepreneurial cities: From Los Angeles 1984 to Los Angeles 2028. *Environment and Planning C: Politics and Space.* Advance online publication. 10.1177/23996544211066101

Lees, L., Slater, T., & Wyly, E. (2013). *Gentrification.* Routledge.

Long, J. G. (2013). *Public/private partnerships for major league sports facilities.* Routledge.

Manson, S., Schroeder, J., van Riper, D., & Ruggles, S. (2020). *IPUMS National Historical Geographic Information System: Version 15.0.* 10.18128/D050.V14.0

Matheson, V. (2019). Is there a case for subsidizing sports stadiums?. *Journal of Policy Analysis and Management, 38*(1), 271–277. 10.1002/pam.22096

National Center for Education Statistics (2021) *Locale boundaries: Entire U.S.* [Data set]. https://nces.ed.gov/programs/edge/Geographic/LocaleBoundaries

Noll, R. G. & Zimbalist, A. (Eds.). (2011). *Sports, jobs, and taxes: The economic impact of sports teams and stadiums* (2nd ed.). Brookings Institution Press.

Palvarini, P. & Tosi, S. (2013). Globalisation, stadiums and the consumerist city: The case of the new Juventus stadium in Turin. *European Journal for Sport and Society, 10*(2), 161–180. 10.1080/16138171.2013.11687917

Panton, M. & Walters, G. (2018). "It's just a Trojan horse for gentrification": Austerity and stadium-led regeneration. *International Journal of Sport Policy and Politics, 10*(1), 163–183. 10.1080/19406940.2017.1398768

Podagrosi, A., Vojnovic, I., & Pigozzi, B. (2011). The diversity of gentrification in Houston's urban renaissance: From cleansing the urban poor to supergentrification. *Environment and Planning A: Economy and Space, 43*(8), 1910–1929. 10.1068/a43526

Preis, B., Janakiraman, A., Bob, A., & Steil, J. (2021). Mapping gentrification and displacement pressure: An exploration of four distinct methodologies. *Urban Studies, 58*(2), 405–424. 10.1177/0042098020903011

Preuss, H. & Plambeck, A. (2021). Utilization of Olympic stadiums: A conceptual stadium legacy framework. *International Journal of Sports Marketing and Sponsorship, 22*(1), 10–31. 10.1108/IJSMS-06-2020-0110

Rigolon, A. & Németh, J. (2018). "We're not in the business of housing:" Environmental gentrification and the nonprofitization of green infrastructure projects. *Cities, 81*, 71–80. 10.1016/j.cities.2018.03.016

Rucks-Ahidiana, Z. (2020). Racial composition and trajectories of gentrification in the United States. *Urban Studies, 58*(13), 2721–2741. 10.1177/0042098020963853

Saito, L. (2019). Urban development and the growth with equity framework: The National Football League stadium in downtown Los Angeles. *Urban Affairs Review, 55*(5), 1370–1401. 10.1177/1078087417751216

Santo, C. (2005). The economic impact of sports stadiums: Recasting the analysis in context. *Journal of Urban Affairs, 27*(2), 177–192. 10.1111/j.0735-2166.2005.00231.x

Sequera, J. & Nofre, J. (2018). Shaken, not stirred: New debates on touristification and the limits of gentrification. *City, 22*(5–6), 843–855. 10.1080/13604813.2018.1548819

Smith, A. (2012). *Events and urban regeneration: The strategic use of events to revitalise cities.* Routledge.

Stein, S. (2019). *Capital city: Gentrification and the real estate state.* Verso.

Stewart, A. & Rayner, S. (2016). Planning mega-event legacies: Uncomfortable knowledge for host cities. *Planning Perspectives, 31*(2), 157–179. 10.1080/02665433.2015.1043933

Sutton, S. (2020). Gentrification and the increasing significance of racial transition in New York City 1970–2010. *Urban Affairs Review, 56*(1), 65–95. 10.1177/1078087418771224

Suzuki, N., Ogawa, T., & Inaba, N. (2018). The right to adequate housing: Evictions of the homeless and the elderly caused by the 2020 Summer Olympics in Tokyo. *Leisure Studies, 37*(1), 89–96. 10.1080/02614367.2017.1355408

Vale, L. & Gray, A. (2013). The displacement decathlon. *Places Journal.* 10.22269/130415

van Holm, E. J. (2018). Left on base: Minor League Baseball stadiums and gentrification. *Urban Affairs Review, 54*(3), 632–657. 10.1177/1078087416663003

van Holm, E. J. (2019). Minor stadiums, major effects? Patterns and sources of re-development surrounding Minor League Baseball stadiums. *Urban Studies, 56*(4), 672–688. 10.1177/0042098018760731

Watt, P. (2013). "It's not for us": Regeneration, the 2012 Olympics, and the gentrification of East London. *City, 17*(1), 99–118. 10.1080/13604813.2012.754190

Weber-Newth, F., Schlüter, S., & Helbrecht, I. (2017). London 2012: "Legacy" as Trojan horse. *ACME: An International Journal for Critical Geographies, 16*(4), 713–739. https://www.acme-journal.org/index.php/acme/article/view/1455

Zapatka, K. & Beck, B. (2020). Does demand lead supply? Gentrifiers and developers in the sequence of gentrification, New York City 2009–2016. *Urban Studies, 58*(11), 2348–2368. 10.1177/0042098020940596

Zirin, D. (2015). *Apartheid games: Baltimore, urban America, and Camden Yards.* The Nation. https://www.thenation.com/article/archive/apartheid-games-baltimore-urban-america-and-camden-yards/

3

INDIGENOUS ENVIRONMENTAL JUSTICE IN U.S. AND CANADA SPORT STADIUMS

Alisse Ali-Joseph, Kelsey Leonard, and Natalie M. Welch

Environmental justice requires fairness, equity, and participation in environmental decision-making (Jarratt-Snider & Nielsen, 2020). However, Indigenous Environmental Justice (IEJ) recognizes that given the specific types of injustice experienced by Indigenous Peoples linked to settler colonialism, there is a need to empower Indigenous legal orders and conceptualizations of justice for environmental protection of planetary health (McGregor et al., 2020). This presents distinct frameworks by which to pursue justice that go "beyond the human dimension" (McGregor et al., 2020, p. 36) to acknowledge ecological injustice and the agency of the Earth itself as a living being with rights. Within this understanding, the agency of land and water is central to the efficacy of Indigenous justice movements—a recognition of the inherent rights of nature as living and recipient of reciprocity and care across the human–environment nexus. These multifaceted and complex relationships between Indigenous Peoples and nature underscore the deep connections to place held by many Indigenous communities.

Indigenous Environmental Justice

In their groundbreaking text *Indigenous Environmental Justice*, Jarratt-Snider and Nielsen (2020) note three pillars of IEJ set it apart from traditional conceptualizations of environmental justice: (1) Indigenous Nations are sovereign governments; (2) "connections to traditional homelands"; and (3) ongoing impacts of settler colonialism (p. 10). In this chapter, we argue that these three pillars shape the environmental injustices experienced by Indigenous Nations and communities with respect to professional sport teams and stadiums. In particular, the activities of the professional sport industry that have disenfranchised Indigenous Peoples from decision-making in their traditional homelands and promoted Indigenous land

DOI: 10.4324/9781003262633-4

theft unconsciously or consciously constitute sport colonialism that has grown exponentially across the industry since the 1990s largely through sport stadium expansion. McGregor (2018) highlights that IEJ:

> requires an examination not only of the power relations among peoples that tend to result in a disproportionate burden being shouldered by less-dominant segments of society, but also of the colonial legacy that continues to play out in laws, court cases, and policies that systematically enable ongoing assaults on Indigenous lands and lives. (p. 2)

Embedded within IEJ are processes toward the realization of justice, including recognition justice, procedural justice, and distributive justice (Fitzgerald, 2022).

Within this chapter, *recognition justice* explores the processes and policies employed by professional sport teams and stadiums to consider Indigenous Nations and communities in their shared history of place and ways of knowing. Pathways for recognition justice may include land acknowledgments, heritage nights, and youth programming. The construction of stadiums across the United States and Canada is an act of "white possession" (Fortier & Hastings, 2019). Within these spaces of white possession, settler colonialism is expansive. Territorial integrity of U.S. and Canadian nationalism through sport is socialized among generations of sport enthusiasts. Indigenous ceremony, land acknowledgments, heritage nights, and so on serve as public acts of disruption that reshape and rematriate Indigenous narratives of place and ways of knowing diverse geographies of sport (Fortier & Hastings, 2019).

Procedural justice explores how professional teams and stadiums include Indigenous Nations and communities as decision-makers through creative and financial partnerships. According to McGregor (2018), IEJ strives for "meaningful involvement" of Indigenous Peoples in environmental decision-making that would impact their lands and lives. Lastly, *distributive justice* examines the ways in which professional sports teams and stadiums can address legacies of environmental racism through the redistribution of benefits to Indigenous Nations and communities through ownership (McGregor, 2018). Across the ecological sport justice literature, key themes emerge on principles for realization of IEJ across stadiums including acknowledgment, community engagement, partnership, and ownership (see Table 3.1).

This chapter focuses on professional sport venues and excludes intercollegiate and interscholastic facilities, as well as Olympic and primarily individual sports such as tennis and golf. Professional team sports facilities are often the face of many major cities and states, areas where Indigenous Peoples are often overlooked due to colonialism and attempted erasure. By focusing on these areas, we can shed light on the Indigenous communities that have historically been removed and forgotten from these sportscapes.

TABLE 3.1 Principles of Indigenous Environmental Justice across Sport Teams and Stadiums

Principle	Definition	Sources
Acknowledge	Professional sports stadiums and affiliated team franchises develop land acknowledgment recognizing local Indigenous nations or communities whose traditional territories the stadium or team now occupy.	Blenkinsop & Fettes, 2020; Fitzgerald, 2022; Fraser & Komarnisky, 2017; McGregor, 2018; McGregor & Nelson, 2022
Community engagement	Professional sports stadiums and affiliated team franchises work to address community concerns and build relationships through community events such as Indigenous heritage nights, special clothing, and signage.	Campbell et al., 2021; Forsyth, 2016; Fortier & Hastings, 2019; McGregor, 2018
Partnership	Professional sports stadiums and affiliated team franchises establish partnerships with Indigenous nations or communities such as sponsorships or naming rights as mechanisms for redistribution of benefits and/or to increase Indigenous visibility.	Hawley, 2020; McGregor, 2018; Miller & LaBlanc, 2009
Ownership	Indigenous nations or communities reclaim land, power, visibility, and community well-being through ownership of professional team franchises and/or stadiums.	Hawley, 2020; McGregor, 2018; Miller & LaBlanc, 2009

Indigenous Land Loss and the Expansion of Professional Sport and Stadia in North America

There are 574 American Indian Nations (legally called federally recognized tribes) in the United States. There are 638 First Nations across what is currently known as Canada, as well as Inuit and Metis peoples. Indigenous Nations and communities have a sacred land base, cultures, languages, religious beliefs, and governments distinct from western peoples. Indigenous Nations are sovereign Nations with unique legal histories across the United States and Canada (Porter, 2005). The U.S. and Canadian governments have a government-to-government or Nation-to-Nation relationship with Tribal Nations and First Nations, respectively, exemplified in the over 400 years of policymaking from the U.S. Constitution to the Indian Act and the hundreds of treaties with Indigenous Nations. The principles of Indigenous self-determination and sovereignty are inherently grounded in place, where Indigenous Nations hold a fundamental right to govern themselves within a land base and, with few exceptions, have the same rights as state, provincial, and federal governments to regulate their internal affairs. As sovereign Nations, Indigenous Nations determine their own citizenship, employ their own political system, and ascertain policies and practices around education, health, economic development, culture, and language for the enhancement and future of their people (Porter, 2005).

As sovereign Nations, Indigenous Nations and communities continue to contend with the ongoing impacts of settler colonialism and the historical implications of U.S. and Canadian federal policies rooted in racism. Despite centuries of stolen land, colonization, assimilation, racism, and destructive policies, Indigenous Nations are still present and continue to honor their reciprocal relationship with land and place. For Indigenous Peoples, land is relational. This means that rather than merely living "on" land, Indigenous Peoples live "with" land and acknowledge an abundant relationship often tied to emergent stories, language, and ceremony. The space-centered epistemologies that form the bases of Indigenous relationships with land demonstrate that land has always been the foundation of Indigenous existence (Blu Barnd, 2017).

Indigenous rights to land and territory are protected under international law. The United Nations Declaration on the Rights of Indigenous Peoples (UNDRIP), signed in 2007, supported by the United States in 2010, and adopted for domestic implementation in Canada in 2021, also provides an international framework for addressing environmental injustices facing Indigenous Peoples (McGregor, 2018). While Indigeneity and space/land are mutually exclusive and dependent on one another, since the beginning of European contact, land has been the focal point of contention throughout the settler-colonial experience. Indigenous Nations have experienced removal from land, allotment of land, and numerous movements and policies that extract natural resources and implement foreign obstructions such as oil pipelines. While these colonial experiences continue to impact some Indigenous Peoples' ability to physically live on their inherent land base, it no less devalues the necessity and relationship between land and Indigenous lifeways. In fact, today, the re-centering and reclaiming of space are crucial acts of sovereignty, self-determination, and cultural continuity (Blu Barnd, 2017).

Embedded within Indigenous Peoples' ancestral connections to place are millennia-old lifeways that are threatened and continually reshaped through loss of land and water due to sport stadium expansion across what is currently known as the United States and Canada. Professional stadiums have contributed to the "intensification of colonialism" by controlling Indigenous lands and territories to the exclusion of the regions' Indigenous Peoples (McGregor et al., 2020; Whyte, 2017). In this way, the rapid growth of professional sport stadiums over the past century has unequivocally reshaped Indigenous landscapes (see Figure 3.1).

In some instances, Indigenous Nations have also been revictimized through sport colonialism subsidies. For example, in 1995, the Detroit Tigers received

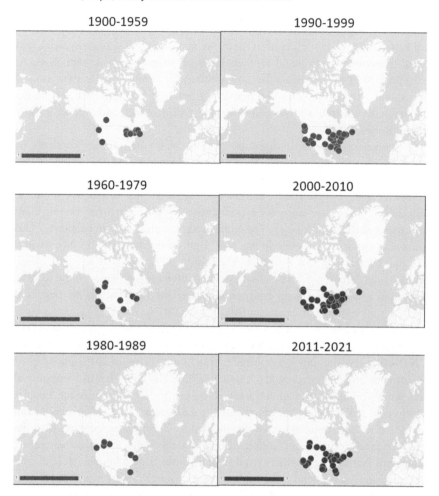

FIGURE 3.1 Expansion of professional sport stadiums across the United States and Canada from 1900 to 2021

more than $26 million in funds toward a new ballpark from seven Michigan Tribes who had paid settlement fees on a gaming compact negotiated with the state of Michigan for revenue from Tribal casinos in the state (Bordson, 1997). The Tribes had been making payments to a Michigan Strategic Fund created for community revitalization projects. One year later, the funds from payments made by the Tribes had been earmarked by the Downtown Development Authority to help fund Comerica Park, the new $300-million home of the Detroit Tigers (Miller & LaBlanc, 2009). Many might assume Indigenous land loss occurred centuries prior, but the exponential growth of stadiums from 1990 to 2021 shows that Indigenous land loss is ongoing across professional sports. Moreover, as seen in the case of the Detroit Tigers, many of these injustices have been subsidized by Indigenous

Nations and citizens through settler-colonial capitalist structures that seize Indigenous wealth through gaming and or taxation.

This chapter explores professional stadiums, arenas, and other sports venues in the present-day United States and Canada and their relationship to IEJ. As previously mentioned, land is a critical piece of the Indigenous ethos, and therefore the facilities that occupy a significant part of the United States and Canada are of particular importance. The chapter aims to elucidate the pathways of recognition, procedural, and distributive justice undertaken by professional sport teams and stadiums to address Indigenous environmental injustice through principles of acknowledgment, community engagement, partnership, and ownership. By investigating the ecosystem in which professional sports facilities operate, we can better understand the legacy of environmental injustice for Indigenous Peoples in these sportscapes.

Acknowledgment: Land Acknowledgments and Reclaiming Visibility

Given the current height of social and racial injustice within the United States and Canada, the necessity of recognizing Indigenous Peoples through not merely a historical lens but, more importantly, through contemporary existence has come to the forefront. Moreover, recognizing Indigenous Peoples as stewards of land solidifies both this political and cultural importance and symbiotic relationship. Recognition justice understands that acknowledging a legacy of past harms is pivotal to addressing environmental injustice (Fitzgerald, 2022). Professional sports stadiums and affiliated team franchises will often *acknowledge* these past harms by developing land acknowledgments recognizing local Indigenous Nations or communities whose traditional territories the stadium or team now occupies. While the abundant relationship that Indigenous Peoples have with land is well known within Indigenous communities, the "land acknowledgment" movement has recently become an accepted way to honor land through a "western" lens. Land acknowledgments are most notably seen in universities and land-grant institutions in the United States, and in expression of the Truth and Reconciliation process in Canada. So, what is a land acknowledgment?

As discussed by the Native Governance Center (2019), land acknowledgments are being instituted because:

> it is important to understand the longstanding history that has brought you to reside on the land and to seek to understand your place within that history. Land acknowledgments do not exist in past tense, or historical context: colonialism is a current, ongoing process, and we need to build our mindfulness of our present participation.

Land acknowledgments are not only meant to honor the traditional homelands of Indigenous Peoples but also call for the allyship of non-Indigenous peoples.

Fitzgerald (2022) highlights how major cities in the United States have adopted land acknowledgments to address past harms—a form of recognition justice. Many of the cities included in the study, such as Austin, Texas, are also home to major professional stadiums. As cities begin processes of reconciliation to address environmental injustices facing Indigenous Peoples, professional sport franchises and stadiums are becoming more integrated into overall practice and outcomes. While acknowledging the land expresses gratitude for the territory one resides on, it also must emphasize the need for non-Indigenous peoples to learn Indigenous history, recognize the ongoing impacts of settler colonialism and contemporary policy, and be mindful of their responsibility within that history and contemporary Indigenous communities.

Table 3.2 identifies the number of stadiums and teams that have implemented land acknowledgments in the United States and Canada. Although smaller in total numbers, Canada has a much higher proportion of teams and stadiums utilizing land acknowledgments. These data (and those presented in Tables 3.3–3.4) are based on Google searches for every professional stadium in conjunction with "land acknowledgment," and for every professional team in conjunction with "land acknowledgment." Data documents were identified inclusive of news articles,

TABLE 3.2 Frequency of Professional Stadium/Team Land Acknowledgment across the United States and Canada, 2022

		United States	*Canada*
Stadium land acknowledgment	No	147	22
	Yes	**5**	**11**
Team land acknowledgment	No	188	34
	Yes	**5**	**12**

TABLE 3.3 Frequency of Professional Stadium Community Engagement across the United States and Canada, 2022

	United States	*Canada*
No	106	15
Yes	**46**	**18**

TABLE 3.4 Frequency of Professional Team Partnerships with Indigenous Nations across the United States and Canada, 2022

	United States	*Canada*
No	161	40
Yes	**32**	**6**

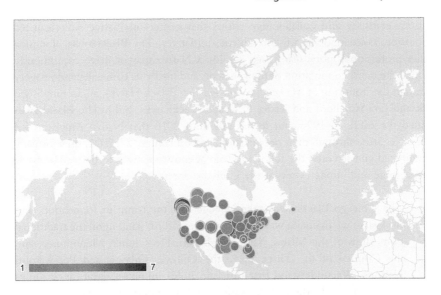

FIGURE 3.2 Historical Indigenous Nations within each state/province where a professional sport stadium is located. (Map data: Government of Canada, Native Land Digital.)

team or sports arena websites, and social media. These data were compiled into a database and categorized based on the absence or presence of a land acknowledgment. Any mention of territorial or Indigenous land was also noted.

Despite the recent growth in land acknowledgments as a form and practice of recognition justice across sport colonialism and environmental injustice, many stadiums have yet to fully acknowledge the Indigenous Nations and communities' territories their facilities now occupy (see Figure 3.2).

All stadiums across the United States and Canada occupy the traditional lands and territories of Indigenous Nations. The contemporary land tenure status of places stadiums occupy, from treaty lands to unceded to aboriginal and non-abrogated lands, is complex and multifaceted. In fact, the unique history of the terrestrial and marine environments encompassing U.S. and Canadian stadiums is localized and context-specific. Thus, presenting even more reasons why acknowledging the unique history of each stadium's geography is ever more important for environmental justice.

United States

In the past decade, land acknowledgments have become more common in the U.S. sports world. They can be heard across college campuses, during championship games, and to some extent, within the professional arena. The Chicago Blackhawks, a professional hockey team with a controversial history with the local and national Native American community, utilizes a land acknowledgment to express gratitude and collaborative efforts that center on Native American-led education, contemporary art, and athletics initiatives. The ~~Blackhawks~~, alongside other professional sports teams that employ a Native mascot, have continuously denied the racial connotation of their mascots and justify its namesake and imagery through the honoring of *Ma ka tai me she kia kiak* (Black Hawk), an accomplished Sak and Fox war hero and leader (Chicago Blackhawks, n.d.). The ~~Blackhawks~~ joined the NHL in 1926, but it was not until 2010 that Native American-led initiatives arose through their organization, and on January 22, 2021, they formally announced and devoted the following land acknowledgment to be read at every home game and public events at the United Center:

> The Chicago Blackhawks acknowledge that the team, its foundation, and the spaces we maintain work and compete within, stand upon the traditional homelands of the Miami, Sauk, Meskwaki, Ho-Chunk, Menominee, and the Council of the Three Fires: the Ojibwe, Odawa, and Potawatomi Nations. We understand that this land holds immense significance for its original stewards, the Native Nations and peoples of this region.
>
> We would also like to recognize that our team's namesake, Sauk War Leader Black Hawk, serves as a continuous reminder of our responsibility to the Native American communities we live amongst and draw inspiration from.

Despite the land acknowledgment, the ~~Blackhawks~~ are still a professional sports team that faces controversy due to their team name and imagery. While the organization has made efforts to provide historical background and education around honoring the Indigenous communities they are wearing and utilizing in their name, the ~~Blackhawks~~ corporation is still at the forefront of the Native mascot discussion. The team has signified strong partnership and programming with the local Indigenous communities. Yet, Native mascots tend to erase contemporary Native experiences and dehumanize Indigenous Peoples and have shown to show negative psychological impacts on Native youth (Fryberg et al., 2008). Sports teams that utilize Native imagery and names have a responsibility to acknowledge the land they are playing on and, more importantly, listen to the Indigenous Nations they supposedly serve and represent.

A newer facility that has pushed the envelope in terms of what's possible for modern sports stadiums is Climate Pledge Arena in Seattle, Washington (see additionally Chapter 15). The roof of the old Key Arena, which was inspired by a local tribe's customary hat when it was built in 1962, was preserved during the arena's recent renovation (McCormick, 2021). Over two years before the arena's reopening, CEO Tod Leiweke and Vice President of Community Engagement and Social Impact Mari Horita met with local Indigenous leaders to see how they could best support and engage the Native community. Following those initial meetings, the Seattle Kraken hired Pyramid Communications' Indian Country group to help turn ideas and aspirations into action (Condor, 2021). Among the outcomes was crafting a Land and Peoples Acknowledgment, developed over six months, with input from a number of Coast Salish Tribal leaders, including Leonard Forsman, chairman of the Suquamish Tribe since 2005. That land acknowledgment reads as follows:

> Climate Pledge Arena acknowledges that we are on the homelands of the Coast Salish peoples, who continue to steward these lands and waters as they have since time immemorial. We recognize Washington's tribal Nations and Native organizations, who actively create, shape and contribute to our thriving communities.
>
> Climate Pledge Arena is committed to doing our part to engage with, and amplify the voices of, Native peoples and tribes.
>
> *(Condor, 2021, paras. 20–21)*

Pyramid Communications director of the Indian Country practice, Temryss Lane (Lummi), noted, "The statement needs a call to action. We have the opportunity to extend this message beyond [from Climate Pledge Arena and Kraken Community Iceplex] to digital spaces. One priority is to engage Native youth" (Condor, 2021, para 22). In comparison, the political context in Canada following the investigation of the horrific residential schooling system reshaped much of the landscape for acknowledging past harms to Indigenous Peoples and lands.

Canada

In Canada, land acknowledgments have grown in recent years following the Truth and Reconciliation Commission (TRC) of Canada's (2015) *Calls to Action Report* that documented the horrific Indigenous residential school system and forced removal of Indigenous children from their families and communities (Paraschak, 2019). Although land acknowledgments have been customary for many Indigenous societies for centuries prior to colonization, today, non-Indigenous entities are adopting this practice as a form of reconciliation. These actions have also moved beyond educational institutional initiatives to be inclusive of the professional sporting community. On a global scale, territorial acknowledgments in Canadian sport were widely documented during the 2010 Winter Olympic and Paralympic Games in Vancouver, British Columbia. However, as seen with the Salt Lake City Games in 2002, there were concerns among Indigenous Peoples as to whether Indigenous representation in opening ceremonies for Olympic events was authentic or pageantry of Indigenous tokenism to meet the demands of settler gaze and desire (O'Bonsawin, 2010). The Vancouver Olympics faced distinct challenges in attempting to host an international event on unceded stolen Native land. Although an acknowledgment is one step in recognizing the status of land tenure and its complexity across geographies, it does not relinquish state responsibility to repair injustices against Indigenous Peoples or provide a mechanism for returning the land. Indigenous scholar Janice Forsyth argues that, in large part, the Vancouver Games worsened Indigenous Olympic relations despite greater recognition of Indigenous Peoples in the programming (Forsyth, 2016). These attempts at inclusion and recognition of land justice for Indigenous Peoples across the professional sport industry have led to a new era of Indigenous inclusion activities informed by these past missteps and the TRC *Calls to Action*—namely, that major sporting venues across Canada have adopted their own land acknowledgments for their facilities. Two venues in particular highlight the challenges and opportunities facing professional sports venues attempting to promote environmental justice through land acknowledgments: Scotiabank Arena in Toronto and Tim Hortons Field in Hamilton.

Scotiabank Arena is the home venue for the Raptors (NBA) and Maple Leafs (NHL). Both teams are owned by Maple Leaf Sports and Entertainment (MLSE), which announced in 2021 that all pregame activities held at Scotiabank Arena would include a land acknowledgment (MLSE Foundation, 2022). The announcement also followed the inaugural commemoration of National Orange Shirt Day, the first national holiday for Truth and Reconciliation held in remembrance of residential school survivors (Orange Shirt Day, n.d.). The MLSE land acknowledgment notably not only acknowledged the Indigenous Nations whose land the organization and its teams work and play on, including the Anishinaabe, Wendat, and Haudenosaunee, but also recognized distinct treaties with Indigenous Nations. Specifically, MLSE acknowledged their responsibility as treaty inheritors under the Dish With One Spoon Wampum Belt, Williams Treaty, and Treaty 13. MLSE developed the land acknowledgment in consultation with Anishinaabe Elder Philip Cote and explicitly stated a commitment to the recommendations of the TRC.

However, there are also examples of land acknowledgments that have gone awry. Unfortunately, this was the case for the Hamilton Tiger-Cats and Tim Hortons Field, hosts of the 2021 Grey Cup. The Grey Cup is the championship game of the Canadian Football League (CFL). The 2021 championship followed a horrific year in Canadian history, not only marked by the COVID-19 pandemic but also by the uncovering of thousands of child graves and remains at sites of former residential schools across Canada. In light of these genocidal reckonings, the federal government held the first national Orange Shirt Day on September 30, 2021, and the day now marks an annual holiday to commemorate Indigenous victims and survivors of residential schools. As national consciousness rose, so did calls for greater acknowledgment of Indigenous presence across the Canadian public sphere including in sport. As mentioned earlier, one action undertaken by many professional sport organizations included utilizing land acknowledgments. The Grey Cup organizers accordingly opened the championship game by inviting a local Indigenous Nation dignitary secretary, Leroy Hill of the Haudenosaunee Confederacy Chiefs Council (3Down Staff, 2021). Unfortunately, the land acknowledgment only recognized the Haudenosaunee presence in the region and did not include recognition of the City of Hamilton as located on the traditional treaty lands and territories of the Missaugas of the Credit First Nation (MCFN;

Hristova, 2021). There was a significant negative response from MCFN after being left out and calls for the TiCats and the Grey Cup organizers to apologize and ensure this type of erasure never happened again. After failing to adequately include all the region's Indigenous Nations, the TiCats formed a committee of Six Nations and Mississauga leadership to develop a more inclusive land acknowledgment for future use.

Together, these examples provide a set of wise practices other professional sport organizations and venues may adopt:

1. Acknowledge the Indigenous Peoples of the territory the organization now occupies.
2. Build community partnerships with Indigenous knowledge holders and elders to develop language for public land acknowledgment.
3. Recognize Indigenous treaty responsibilities in the area.
4. Commit to action to address injustice(s) facing Indigenous Peoples today.

When these wise practices are not followed, an ill-conceived land acknowledgment can have detrimental consequences for sport organizations and the Indigenous communities it is meant to empower.

Community Engagement: Empowerment over Appropriation and Mascotry

In recent decades, some professional sport teams and stadiums have developed community relations programs to bolster engagement with Indigenous Nations and communities and reconcile a legacy of harm due to offensive team mascotry. The majority of engagement has come from teams with Native nicknames, mascots, or imagery such as the Chicago ~~Blackhawks~~, Edmonton ~~Eskimos~~, Kansas City ~~Chiefs~~, and Atlanta ~~Braves~~. Other engagements, such as Indigenous heritage nights, have often served the limited purpose of the teams' marketing and public relations aspirations. That is, few teams have built meaningful, long-lasting relationships with Indigenous Nations or communities. Community engagement initiatives build upon efforts to acknowledge Indigenous People's lands and territories and provide meaningful pathways for addressing Indigenous environmental injustices. Professional sports stadiums and affiliated team franchises work to address community concerns and build relationships through *community engagement* events such as Indigenous heritage nights, wearing special clothing, and signage displays. Following the 2015 Truth and Reconciliation Commission Report findings, there have been increased attempts at community engagement activities by stadiums across Canada in comparison to facilities located in the United States (see Table 3.3). However, across both countries, the most action taken by stadiums to address Indigenous environmental injustices has occurred under the auspices of community engagement.

United States

In 2021, the MLB World Series shined a spotlight on the Atlanta ~~Braves~~, not only because of their play on the field but also how they presented their relationship with the Native American community. Before Game 1, MLB commissioner Rob Manfred said, "It's important to understand that we have 30 markets around the country. They aren't all the same. The ~~Braves~~ have done a phenomenal job with the Native American community" (as cited in Yates, 2021, para. 1). When questioned about the inappropriateness of the ~~Braves'~~ tomahawk chop, he went on to say, "The Native American community in that region is wholly supportive of the ~~Braves~~ program, including the [tomahawk] chop. For me, that's kind of the end of the story. In that market, we're taking into account the Native American community" (para. 3). This statement was highly covered and criticized in the media. Manfred gave the ~~Braves~~ a free pass because they relied on one marginal relationship with one tribe in the Southeast, ignoring the protests from the public about the racist behavior exhibited by the tomahawk chop at Atlanta ~~Braves~~ games. The ~~Braves~~ engaged the Eastern Band of Cherokee in a consultation relationship that appeared to serve their public relations interests. This case shows the complications of having a single tribal community grant permission to use generic Native American-inspired names, imagery, and rituals.

In women's professional sports and sports with more obvious traditional Native roots, such as lacrosse and hockey, there has been more investment in the Indigenous community. The Professional Women's Hockey Players Association (PWHPA) participates in regular training and education around social justice issues, and Dr. Courtney Despa-Szto called on coauthor Welch to speak with the PWHPA about the Indigenous community. The PWHPA would go on to commission Native artist Tracey Anthony (Delaware [Lenni Lenape] from Six Nations of the Grand River Territory) to create land acknowledgment helmet stickers for the league's 2021 Secret Dream Gap Tour.

In April 2021, the Premier Lacrosse League (PLL) released their season schedule alongside a land acknowledgment by Indigenous lacrosse legend Lyle Thompson. In the tweet alongside the land acknowledgment, they noted, "Together we recognize that our games will be played on lands that have been inhabited, cared for and respected by Indigenous people for centuries. They are the originators of lacrosse" (Premier Lacrosse League, 2021a). Just a few months later, the league implemented an initiative to raise awareness and drive education around the multiple, tragic discoveries of unmarked graves at the sites of former Indigenous residential and boarding schools. Players had the option to wear orange helmet straps, and fans, viewers, youth organizations, and partners were able to purchase the straps with all proceeds donated to the National Native American Boarding School Healing Coalition (Premier Lacrosse League, 2021b). Additionally, while on tour in Minnesota, the PLL games featured local tribes and the traditional stick lacrosse game and emphasized the game's roots in Indigenous culture (Olson, 2021).

One of the longest known relationships between a sports team and a tribal community can be found between a minor league baseball team, the Spokane Indians, and the Spokane Tribe of Indians in Washington state. Back in 2006, the team went to the tribe with "everything on the table, including the team name, in conversations about rebranding" (Caputo, 2020, para. 5). The team developed two versions of a logo, one in English and the other in the tribe's language, Salish. The team also posted signs in the ballpark in both English and Salish. The team was the first to use a Native American word on their uniforms in 2014. In 2017, the team introduced an alternative identity to raise awareness and promote conservation of Redband trout, one of the first foods of the Spokane Tribe (Caputo, 2020). In addition to the commitment to protecting the wild Redband trout, called the "Redband Rally Campaign," the time also began a "zero waste" project in the stadium (Nichols, 2020).

Canada

In June 2021, the Edmonton ~~Eskimos~~, a CFL team with a stadium located in Edmonton, Alberta, changed their team name from a long recognized racial slur toward Inuit Peoples to the Edmonton Elks (Appel, 2021). This process underwent extensive community engagement to address concerns Indigenous community members had with the legacy of harm caused by the violent racial slur team name. However, community engagement has also worked to address other legacies of harm and advance recognition of justice, such as National Truth and Reconciliation Day nights hosted in 2021 by professional teams such as the Ottawa Senators (2021). NLL teams all wore orange stickers reading "Every Child Matters" on their helmets the entire 2021 season to honor the lives of Indigenous children killed at residential schools and in recognition of the National Day for Truth and Reconciliation ("NLL Teams," 2021).

Teams have also recognized National Indigenous Peoples Day in June with special game nights. Other forms of community engagement included programs to support Indigenous youth with access to sport such as the Toronto Blue Jays Rookie League and James Bay Girls at Bat program. The Jays Care program states:

> We believe in on-going collaboration and reconciliation with Indigenous peoples. This means working with Indigenous communities to create inclusive programs that promote the health and well-being of children, youth and families. We use baseball to engage hard to reach children and youth through inter-generational events and tournaments that involve elders, partners and community leadership.
>
> *(Jays Care Foundation, 2022)*

Many Indigenous athletes come from urban Indigenous communities. Building connections with professional sports franchises and teams is a pathway toward addressing environmental injustice and building community engagement. It is

46 Alisse Ali-Joseph, Kelsey Leonard and Natalie M. Welch

also a way to reclaim space and community in urban environments because the city is also Indigenous space. To capture these challenges, the Toronto Raptors highlight Indigenous athletes who are leaders in addressing the legacy of harm, such as Michael Linklater, a Nehiyaw (Cree) from Thunderchild First Nation, located on Treaty 6 Territory (Toronto Raptors, n.d.). Community engagement is necessary to address environmental injustices, and it can build authentic relationships and trust with Indigenous Nations and communities that experienced over a century of land loss due to sport colonialism. However, beyond recognition justice is the need for procedural justice whereby Indigenous Nations and communities are sport decision-makers with access to redistribution of benefits from professional sport teams and stadiums such as through partnerships.

Partnership: Naming Rights and Performative #LandBack

Working toward IEJ can also be achieved by developing a *partnership* with Indigenous Nations and communities. Professional sports stadiums and affiliated team franchises establish partnerships with Indigenous Nations or communities, such as sponsorships or naming rights as mechanisms for redistribution of benefits or to increase Indigenous visibility. Indigenous Nations and communities may view partnership schemes as an opportunity to combat erasure in their homelands. The increased visibility not only has societal benefits but is often linked to increased visibility of the Indigenous Nation brands and economic development ventures. Partnerships between Indigenous Nations and professional sports teams have occurred more frequently in the United States than Canada (see Table 3.4). Further research is needed to determine whether access to capital, particularly connected to the gaming industry, contributes to the expansion of Indigenous purchasing power for naming and sponsorship partnerships in professional sport sectors.

Sports sponsorship is one of the most lucrative and fastest-growing forms of advertising in the 21st century (Delia, 2014). An element of sports sponsorship that is highly utilized is the acquisition of naming rights for facilities by corporations. For example, the banking and financial services company, Barclays, purchased the naming rights to a New York City NBA arena for 20 years for $200 million. More recently, Staples relinquished its naming rights to Crypto.com for Los Angeles' famous NBA arena for $700 million over 20 years in what is believed to be the largest naming rights deal in sports history ("Staples Center," 2021). The concept of purchasing naming rights, signaling "ownership" of a facility, has become widely accepted. However, these partnerships are mere "signals of ownership," and in reality, they do not amount to ownership and the associated benefits for Indigenous Nations as owners and beneficiaries. These deals can be seen as an extension of the problematic privatization and colonization of sports at the expense of communities and obstruction of IEJ.

United States

Naming rights deals have caused controversy between communities and sports teams for multiple reasons, for instance, when fans' values do not align with the industry connections of sponsors. For example, in Minnesota, protestors hung a sign from the rafters of U.S. Bank Stadium during an NFL game to urge U.S. Bank to withdraw its support of the Dakota Access Pipeline (Chiari, 2017). The protesters hung next to a 40-foot-high vertical sign with U.S. Bank's logo from the start of the second quarter until the end of the game and even took calls from the press about their demonstration (Murphy, 2017). The pipeline project violated treaty rights but also posed environmental threats. The pipeline was originally planned to pass upstream of Bismarck, North Dakota, but it was rerouted due to citizens' concern for the safety of the water supply. One of the individuals involved in the protest said, "We are here in solidarity with water protectors from Standing Rock to urge U.S. Bank to divest from the Dakota Access Pipeline" (Murphy, 2017, para. 26).

Indigenous communities across the United States have also joined in on the naming rights trend, highlighting the power of Tribal sovereignty to weaponize capitalism against settler-colonial power imbalances and reclaim the narrative to combat the erasure of Indigenous Peoples in sport. In 2014, Gila River Casinos signed a nine-year naming rights agreement for the arena of the Arizona Coyotes, the state's professional hockey team (Schwarz, 2014). This was the first time a business owned by a federally recognized tribe signed such an agreement for one of the big four men's sports leagues (i.e., MLB, NBA, NFL, NHL). In 2022, the team and arena made headlines over the controversy. The Arizona Coyotes failed to find much success on the ice and failed financially, resulting in a declaration of bankruptcy in 2009 (Shoalts, 2021). In late 2021, Glendale city leaders threatened to lock the team out of the building after the Coyotes failed to pay the city and state $1.3 million in taxes (Paredes, 2022). The Coyotes eventually resolved the debt but would end up moving to the multipurpose arena at Arizona State University and come under criticism for downgrading to a facility with a mere 5,000 seat capacity (Bentley, 2022). It's hard to measure the public relations hit on the Gila River community for the attachment to this controversy. Still, if the perceived value garnered from naming rights deals is any indication, the negative connotations may persist. In addition to Gila River, several other Native communities have obtained naming rights for sports and entertainment venues as a means to promote their Tribal casinos.

Canada

There have been no professional stadium naming rights deals with First Nations in Canada to date. Notably, a minor league hockey arena home of the Fort McMurray Oil Barons was acquired by Centerfire Energy Group, headquartered on the Fort McMurray 468 First Nation reserve, in the fall of 2020 (McDermott, 2020).

Centerfire Arena highlights the complex relationship between Indigenous Nations, sport, and the fossil fuel industry. The capital from the oil industry provided the community with the necessary resources to purchase naming rights to the local arena. However, Fort McMurray 468 First Nation is also known globally as the epicenter for Indigenous environmental injustice and environmental racism vis-à-vis oil sands extractivism and settler colonialism (Agyeman, 2009; Estes, 2019; Heydon, 2018). Despite environmental justice challenges posed by connections to the fossil fuel industry and associated disproportionate environmental burdens experienced by Indigenous Peoples, Indigenous Nations are finding creative ways to carve out new partnerships with professional sport franchises and stadiums.

In 2018, the Musqueam, Squamish, and Tsleil-Waututh Nations were consulted by Canucks Sports and Entertainment to rebrand Vancouver's NLL franchise. Ultimately, the name "Warriors" was adopted, but partnership advancements within the NLL did not stop with branding (Vancouver Warriors, 2018). In December 2021, the NLL signed a partnership agreement with a subsidiary of Mohawk Online, Sports Interaction, for sports betting owned by the Mohawk Council of Kahnawake (Schwab, 2021). The deal also included rights to signage and other forms of advertising in the arenas. However, partnership pathways are limited in their ability to redistribute all sport benefits to Indigenous communities impacted by stadium-associated environmental injustice. Ultimately, remedies for Indigenous environmental injustice must be grounded in Indigenous ownership and the Land Back movement.

Ownership: Indigenizing the Stadium: Reclaiming Water, Land, and Space

As Indigenous Nations are present in the fight to reclaim spaces and natural resources that have sustained their people for centuries, the movement to "Indigenize the Stadium" is important. One pathway toward IEJ and Indigenizing the stadium is through *ownership*, whereby Indigenous Nations or communities reclaim land, power, visibility, and community well-being through ownership of professional team franchises or stadiums.

The preeminent example of Indigenizing the stadium and reclaiming Indigenous autonomy through sport is shown through the leadership of the Iroquois Nationals lacrosse team. We have not classified them as either a U.S. or Canadian case study intentionally, as the Iroquois Nationals have been an independent franchise of the Haudenosaunee Confederacy within the PLL since 1983 (Downey, 2013; Iroquois Nationals, n.d.). The Iroquois Nationals were not only a leader among Indigenous Nation team ownership but also in reclaiming the narrative of Indigenous sport. Ownership by Indigenous Nations is more than monetary benefits associated with sport capitalism. Ownership means the return of land. Ownership means the return of power. Ownership means the return of future generations of Indigenous youth's cultural connections to sport.

The following section details Indigenous-led ownership in both its current form and its promising future.

United States

In the WNBA, the Connecticut Sun are owned by the Mohegan Tribe and play their games at the Mohegan Sun Arena located on tribal lands (Hawley, 2020). As a part of the WNBA's 25th-anniversary celebration, teams created special jerseys designed to reflect stories of "female archetypes" in each of their communities. The Sun created three new jerseys with symbology and language inspired by the Mohegan tribe. It was important to the tribe to be the ones who determined what images would be associated with the tribe and the team. Chief Many Hearts Lynn Malerba said, "The jerseys are important because there has been so much cultural appropriation and also just a lack of understanding of truly what it means to be native in this country" (Eaton-Robb, 2021, para. 5). Beth "Morning Deer" Regan, Vice Chairwoman and Justice for the Mohegan Tribal Council of Elders, described the initiative as "a real collaborative effort with the tribal council, our elders, the chief and our medicine woman, who all had some voice in this" (Eaton-Robb, 2021, para. 11).

Canada

The CFL is exploring a new franchise in Nova Scotia. However, the proposed location of the new stadium is on the traditional lands of Millbrook First Nation (Palmeter, 2018). However, Millbrook First Nation was not consulted as a potential owner for the new franchise. Indigenous Nations are leading innovative development projects that would be excellently aligned with the future of professional sport if their acumen and talent were valued in the "owner's ring." There are currently no Indigenous Nation-owned teams in Canada, and the expansion of a professional team to the Atlantic provinces would be an optimal opportunity to build reconciliation into the future of professional sport development.

However, a group of First Nations in Saskatchewan did get close to owning the first stadium complex in Canada in 2010, when the city of Regina began accepting proposals for a new stadium complex. In response, a group of 10 First Nations known as the Independent First Nations of Saskatchewan put forward a proposal ("Casino Stadium Complex," 2010; Kruchak, 2010). More notably, this proposal also featured a stadium designed by an Indigenous architect, the world-renowned architect Douglas Cardinal (Kruchak, 2010). Ultimately, the proposal was not accepted, and in its place, the CFL selected HKS, Inc., an architectural firm headquartered in Dallas, Texas, to construct a new Mosaic Stadium. Cardinal had designed a world-class facility that would have featured Indigenous design for millions of sport enthusiasts (Douglas Cardinal Architect, 2010). Moreover, as a praxis of distributive justice, the monetary resources given to foreign architects rather than Indigenous Nations and Indigenous architects in their homelands directly manifested environmental injustice across sport colonialism.

Conclusion

Tracing the pattern of IEJ across professional sport stadiums in the United States and Canada, the chapter identified pathways to justice inclusive of acknowledgment, partnership, community engagement, and ownership. We have discussed the importance of land acknowledgments and recognizing the traditional homelands of Indigenous Peoples that sports stadiums reside on. While this is an important first step, it lacks accountability to Indigenous communities and fails to support Native Nations in their inherent right to exercise sovereignty and institute self-determination. The need for action steps to support Indigenous communities beyond the land acknowledgment is imperative.

So, what are some recommendations for working in solidarity with Indigenous communities and ensuring culturally responsive imagery, representation, programming, and partnerships? For this, we turn to the Agua Caliente Clippers as an example of a mutually beneficial partnership between a sports organization and a federally recognized tribe. In the spring of 2017, the Agua Caliente band of Cahuilla Indians and the Los Angeles Clippers announced that the tribe would be sponsoring a G League affiliate team, the Agua Caliente Clippers of Ontario (Goolsby, 2015). As part of this partnership and acknowledging that the team will be playing on Indigenous land, the tribe is not only sponsoring the team but naming them as well. The Agua Caliente Clippers represents a groundbreaking partnership, in that the tribe is not the mascot but rather is reclaiming space through sport, contemporary representation, and economic opportunities by being the team's official and exclusive casino partner. This exemplifies that partnerships with Indigenous Nations should be grounded in contemporary representation of local communities. This thereby supports reciprocal, Indigenous-driven collaboration, community engagement, and service that contribute to the success of Indigenous Peoples and communities.

The historical practice of Indigenous community representation in sport as being limited to mascot imagery is becoming antiquated. Indigenous communities are becoming decision-makers in representation, economic ventures, and the future of the sport industry. The necessity to acknowledge the Indigenous land on which sports teams participate translates across the sports world. Yet, such acknowledgment becomes obsolete if action is not taken as well. Sports team land acknowledgments must translate to a commitment to Indigenous Peoples through culturally-responsive education and programming, support of Indigenous Peoples through hiring practices, and mutually beneficial partnerships that promote sovereignty, self-determination, and economic opportunities for Indigenous Peoples and communities.

The greatest form of reclamation is for Indigenous Nations and communities to be owners of professional teams and the affiliated land and spaces that encapsulate contemporary stadia. As noted with the Mohegan Tribe acquisition of the WNBA Connecticut Sun, when an Indigenous Nation has full autonomy over the franchise and stadia, the authenticity of cultural integration and representation is palpable from the athletes' apparel all the way to the design of building areas and infrastructure.

References

3Down Staff. (2021, December 18). *Mississaugas of the Credit First Nation speaking out after Grey Cup land acknowledgement omission.* 3DownNation. https://3downnation.com/2021/12/18/missassaugas-of-the-credit-first-nation-speaking-out-after-grey-cup-land-acknowledgement-omission/

Agyeman, J. (Ed.). (2009). *Speaking for ourselves: Environmental justice in Canada.* UBC Press.

Appel, J. (2021, June 5). *Indigenous leaders say that new name—Edmonton Elks—is a step forward.* CTV News. https://edmonton.ctvnews.ca/indigenous-leaders-say-that-new-name-edmonton-elks-is-a-step-forward-1.5457856

Bentley, C. (2022, February 15). "It's going to be packed!" says Arizona Coyotes owner Xavier Gutierrez on new 5,000-seat arena. *Golf Digest.* https://www.golfdigest.com/story/arizona-coyotes-owner-xavier-gutierrez-new-arena-capacity-arizona-state-nhl-hockey

Blenkinsop, S. & Fettes, M. (2020). Land, language and listening: The transformations that can flow from acknowledging Indigenous land. *Journal of Philosophy of Education, 54*(4), 1033–1046. 10.1111/1467-9752.12470

Blu Barnd, N. (2017). *Native space: Geographic strategies to unsettle settler colonialism.* Oregon State University Press.

Bordson, B. (1997). Public sports stadium funding: Communities being held hostage by professional sports team owners case note and comment. *Hamline Law Review, 21*(3), 505–536.

Campbell, M., Cowser, J., Lucio, R., & Irvine, K. (2021). The Creators' Game: A conduit for youth development, community engagement, and American Indian cultural connections. *Social Work in Public Health, 36*(7–8), 832–846. 10.1080/19371918.2021.1965935

Caputo, P. (2020, July 19). *Authenticity, collaboration, respect: The story behind the Spokane Indians.* SportsLogos.net News. https://news.sportslogos.net/2020/07/19/authenticity-collaboration-respect-the-story-behind-the-spokane-indians/

Casino stadium complex proposed for Regina. (2010, March 4). CBC News. https://www.cbc.ca/news/canada/saskatchewan/casino-stadium-complex-proposed-for-regina-1.922371

Chiari, M. (2017, January 2). *Protesters hang from US Bank Stadium rafters to protest Dakota Access Pipeline.* Bleacher Report. https://bleacherreport.com/articles/2684655-protesters-hang-from-us-bank-stadium-rafters-to-protest-dakota-access-pipeline

Chicago Blackhawks. (n.d). *Native American initiatives.* https://www.nhl.com/blackhawks/team/native-american-initiatives#land

Condor, B. (2021, August 18). *Supporting "Land and Peoples".* Climate Pledge Arena. https://climatepledgearena.com/2021/08/18/supporting-land-and-peoples/

Delia, E. B. (2014). Subconscious (un)attachment to a sponsor: An irrational effect of facility naming rights. *Journal of Sport Management, 28*(5), 551–564. 10.1123/jsm.2013-0167

Downey, A. (2013). Engendering nationality: Haudenosaunee tradition, sport, and the lines of Gender. *Journal of the Canadian Historical Association, 23*(1), 319–354. 10.7202/1015736ar

Douglas Cardinal Architect. (2010). *Regina Stadium Entertainment Facility.* https://www.djcarchitect.com/work/civic/regina-stadium

Eaton-Robb, P. (2021, April 8). *Sun, tribal owners add Native American images to jerseys.* Associated Press. https://apnews.com/article/connecticut-native-americans-c8cf72f68-cede6fdde51993d3d6ff610

Estes, N. (2019). *Our history is the future: Standing Rock versus the Dakota Access Pipeline, and the long tradition of Indigenous resistance.* Verso Books.

Fitzgerald, J. (2022). Transitioning from urban climate action to climate equity. *Journal of the American Planning Association.* Advance online publication. 10.1080/01944363.2021.2013301

Forsyth, J. (2016). The illusion of inclusion: Agenda 21 and the commodification of Aboriginal culture in the Vancouver 2010 Olympic Games. *Public, 27*(53), 22–34. 10.1386/public.27.53.22_1

Fortier, C. & Hastings, C. (2019). A Field of Dreamers on stolen land: Practices of un-settling on the recreational softball diamonds of Tkaronto. *Journal of Sport History, 46*(2), 302–317. 10.5406/jsporthistory.46.2.0302

Fraser, C. & Komarnisky, S. (2017). 150 Acts of Reconciliation for Canada's 150. *Making Treaty 7 Cultural Society, 6.*

Fryberg, S. A., Markus, H. R., Oyserman, D., & Stone, J. M. (2008). Of warrior chiefs and Indian princesses: The psychological consequences of American Indian mascots. *Basic and Applied Social Psychology, 30*(3), 208–218. 10.1080/01973530802375003

Goolsby, D. (2015, November 19). Agua Calientes to sponsor Clippers for 3 seasons. *The Desert Sun.* https://www.desertsun.com/story/sports/basketball/2015/11/19/agua-calientes-sponsor-l-clippers-2015-16-season/76063442/

Government of Canada. (2021). *First Nations profiles interactive map.* https://geo.aadnc-aandc.gc.ca/cippn-fnpim/index-eng.html

Hawley, L. (2020). Building a basketball arena on tribal land: A collaborative approach for the National Basketball Association and American Indian tribes. *Arizona State University Sports and Entertainment Law Journal, 10*(2), 57–105.

Heydon, J. (2018). Sensitising green criminology to procedural environmental justice: A case study of First Nation consultation in the Canadian oil sands. *International Journal for Crime, Justice and Social Democracy, 7*(4), 67–82. 10.5204/ijcjsd.v7i4.936

Hristova, B. (2021, December 17). *Mississaugas of the Credit First Nation forgotten in Grey Cup land acknowledgment.* CBC News. https://www.cbc.ca/news/canada/hamilton/grey-cup-land-acknowledgement-1.6289165

Iroquois Nationals. (n.d.). https://iroquoisnationalslacrosse.com/

Jarratt-Snider, K. & Nielsen, M. O. (2020). *Indigenous Environmental Justice.* University of Arizona Press.

Jays Care Foundation. (2022). *Our approach.* https://www.mlb.com/bluejays/community/jays-care/our-approach

Kruchak, M. (2010, March 2). Renowned Canadian architect Douglas Cardinal designs spectacular domed stadium for Regina. *Regina Leader-Post.* https://leaderpost.com/news/renowned-canadian-architect-douglas-cardinal-designs-spectacular-domed-stadium-for-regina

McCormick, B (2021, November 8). Climate Pledge Arena: Sustainable stewardship. *Sports Business Journal.* https://www.sportsbusinessjournal.com/Journal/Issues/2021/11/08/In-Depth/Climate-Pledge-Arena.aspx

McDermott, V. (2020, November 27). Casman Centre is no more as Centerfire acquires naming rights to arena. *The Intelligencer.* https://fortmcmurraytoday.com/news/local-news/casman-centre-is-no-more-as-centerfire-acquires-naming-rights-to-arena

McGregor, D. (2018). Governing for Indigenous environmental Justice in Canada. In N. Gombay & M. Palomino-Schalscha (Eds.), *Indigenous places and colonial spaces: The politics of intertwined relations* (pp. 226–243). Routledge.

McGregor, D. & Nelson, E. (2022). Reconciling relationships with the Land through Land Acknowledgements. In J. Engle, J. Agyeman, & T. Chung-Tiam-Fook (Eds.), *Sacred civics* (pp. 122–132). Routledge.

McGregor, D., Whitaker, S., & Sritharan, M. (2020). Indigenous environmental justice and sustainability. *Current Opinion in Environmental Sustainability, 43*, 35–40. 10.1016/j.cosust.2020.01.007

Miller, W. S. & LaBlanc, C. (2009). Bingo?: An overview of the potential legal issues arising from the use of Indian gaming revenues to fund professional sports facilities. *Journal of Legal Aspects of Sport, 19*(2), 121–152.

MLSE Foundation. (2022). *Land acknowledgement*. https://www.mlsefoundation.org/land-acknowledgement

Murphy, B. (2017, January 3). Protesters arrested after unfurling banner during Vikings game at U.S. Bank Stadium. *Twin Cities Pioneer Press*. https://www.twincities.com/2017/01/01/protest-banner-disrupts-vikings-game/

Native Governance Center. (2019, October 22). *A guide to Indigenous land acknowledgment*. https://nativegov.org/news/a-guide-to-indigenous-land-acknowledgment/

Native Land Digital. (2021). https://native-land.ca

Nichols, D. (2020, September 24). Baseball and culture: A discussion about Native American imagery in sports. *The Spokesman Review*. https://www.spokesman.com/stories/2020/sep/24/baseball-and-culture-a-discussion-about-native-ame/#_=_

NLL teams will wear "every child matters" decal this season. (2021, September 30). Toronto Rock. https://torontorock.com/news/nll-teams-will-wear-every-child-matters-decal-this-season/

O'Bonsawin, C. M. (2010). "No Olympics on stolen native land": Contesting Olympic narratives and asserting indigenous rights within the discourse of the 2010 Vancouver Games. *Sport in Society, 13*(1), 143–156. 10.1080/17430430903377987

Olson, G. (2021, July 8). *Premier Lacrosse League to feature Anishinaabe tribe during Minnesota tour stop*. Fox 9 KMSP. https://www.fox9.com/news/premier-lacrosse-league-to-feature-anishinabe-tribe-during-minnesota-tour-stop

Orange Shirt Day. (n.d.). https://www.orangeshirtday.org/

Ottawa Senators. (2021, September 29). *Senators to recognize National Day for Truth and Reconciliation*. https://www.nhl.com/senators/news/senators-to-recognize-national-day-for-truth-and-reconciliation/c-326438050

Palmeter, P. (2018, October 30). *Millbrook not opposed to Shannon Park stadium proposal for potential CFL team*. CBC News. https://www.cbc.ca/news/canada/nova-scotia/millbrook-not-opposed-to-shannon-park-stadium-proposal-1.4882507

Paredes, J. (2022, April 25). *Glendale city leaders threatened to lock the team out of the building after the Coyotes failed to pay the city and state $1.3 million in taxes*. 12 News. https://www.12news.com/article/sports/nhl/coyotes/this-is-how-the-arizona-coyotes-time-in-glendale-ends/75-52818806-47a4-4d47-821b-45b3c3fc643b

Paraschak, V. (2019). #87: Reconciliation, sport history, and Indigenous Peoples in Canada. *Journal of Sport History, 46*(2), 208–223. 10.5406/jsporthistory.46.2.0208

Porter, R. (2005). *Sovereignty, colonialism and the Indigenous Nations: A reader*. Carolina Academic Press.

Premier Lacrosse League [@PremierLacrosse]. (2021a, April 12). *We're honored to share this Land Acknowledgment* [Image attached] [Tweet]. Twitter. https://twitter.com/PremierLacrosse/status/1382313306338185218/photo/1

Premier Lacrosse League. (2021b, July 9). Premier Lacrosse League players to wear orange helmet straps in support of the Indigenous communities. https://premierlacrosseleague.com/articles/premier-lacrosse-league-players-to-wear-orange-helmet-straps-in-support-of-the-indigenous-communities

Raptors, Maple Leafs add land acknowledgement. (2021, October 7). *Toronto Sun*. https://torontosun.com/sports/raptors-maple-leafs-add-land-acknowledgement

Schwab, D. (2021, December 23). *Canada's Sports Interaction signs partnership deal the National Lacrosse League*. Vegas Insider. https://www.vegasinsider.com/sportsbooks/sports-betting-news/canada-sports-interaction-signs-partnership-deal-national-lacrosse-league/

Schwarz, H. (2014, August 14). An Arizona tribe is going to be the first to have naming rights to a professional sports arena. *Washington Post*. https://www.washingtonpost.com/blogs/govbeat/wp/2014/08/14/an-arizona-tribe-is-going-to-be-the-first-to-have-naming-rights-to-a-professional-sports-arena/

Shoalts, D. (2021, December 17). Coyotes' long journey to nowhere takes another turn. *The New York Times*, B9.

Staples Center to become Crypto.com Arena in reported $700 million naming rights deal. (2021, November 16). ESPN. https://www.espn.com/nba/story/_/id/32650662/staples-center-become-cryptocom-arena-rich-naming-rights-deal

Toronto Raptors. (n.d.). https://culture.raptors.com/team-videos/northern-reflections-michael-linklater-takes-pride-in-his-indigenous-roots

Truth and Reconciliation Commission of Canada. (2015). *Calls to action*. Winnipeg.

Vancouver Warriors. (2018, September 21). *Vancouver's NLL team named Vancouver Warriors*. https://vancouverwarriors.com/news/team-brand-announced/

Whyte, K. (2017). Indigenous climate change studies: Indigenizing futures, decolonizing the Anthropocene. *English Language Notes*, *55*(1), 153–162.

Yates, C. (2021, October 28). *Manfred misses the mark with Braves*. Andscape. https://andscape.com/features/manfred-misses-the-mark-with-braves/

4
ENVIRONMENTAL IMPACTS OF SHADOW STADIA

Taryn Barry, Daniel S. Mason, and Lisi Heise

Stadium- and arena-anchored development projects remain an important part of urban redevelopment planning worldwide (Crompton, 2004; Johnson & Whitehead, 2000; Rosentraub, 2006). It has been argued that urban redevelopment through sport stadium projects results in both positive and negative outcomes for cities and their residents (Long, 2013; Rosentraub, 2009, 2014). However, while most attention is placed on the planning, scope, and construction of the new sports facility, less emphasis is on the facility left behind: the shadow stadium. *Shadow stadia* are vacated sites once occupied by major professional or amateur sports venues, where redevelopment of new stadia on that site has been deemed untenable. Shadow stadia sites offer both challenges and opportunities to local governments, developers, and communities once sports venues are vacated. Options to renovate or build a new stadium on a new site are often debated among owners of sport franchises that are housed in aging facilities. Some shadow stadia sites are repurposed for mixed-use development, while others are demolished or remain abandoned for years after facility use ceases.

Although the merits of urban redevelopment through sport stadia have been the subject of study and debate among local governments, the development industry, policymakers, community advocates, and academics alike, their focus is typically placed on the impacts of a new stadium development on its associated community. Thus, there is scant empirical research examining the impact of shadow stadia on their respective communities. In addition, the outgoing site is not typically incorporated into the broader analysis meant to provide a comprehensive outlook of the economic, social, or environmental impacts to local governments and voters—resulting in a lack of insight and empirical data that would ultimately aid in addressing this issue comprehensively.

Meanwhile, there is an emerging trend in stadium design and construction to capitalize on environmental sustainability initiatives and gain Leadership in Energy

DOI: 10.4324/9781003262633-5

56 Taryn Barry, Daniel S. Mason, Lisi Heise

and Environmental Design (LEED) certification from the U.S. Green Building Council, in addition to an increase in academic research focused on new stadia and urban development (Kellison et al., 2015; Sze, 2009; Triantafyllidis et al., 2018). For instance, Kellison and Hong (2015) identified growing pressure faced by architects and sport franchise owners to incorporate environmentally sustainable features into new stadia design, and subsequently concluded that demonstrated economic savings over the lifespan of the facility are a key driver in the adoption of pro-environmental architecture and design. We are not aware of related published research on the potential environmental impacts of shadow stadia.

This chapter explores the environmental impacts of shadow stadia through an environmental justice framework. It is critical for local governments, the development industry, policymakers, and community advocates to understand the implications of shadow stadia on the entirety of a project, and not continue to be excluded from assessments of new stadium development. As such, this exploratory chapter acts as a starting point for academics by providing an overview of redevelopment trends that have emerged from cities that have been challenged to solve planning blights created by vacant shadow stadia sites.

The chapter is organized as follows: It begins with a review of the literature on environmental justice and its potential relationship to the sports industry followed by a categorization of shadow stadia based on an overview of redevelopment projects worldwide, including a case study of each category. From there, future recommendations developed within an environmental justice framework will be presented.

An Environmental Justice Approach to Shadow Stadia

In defining shadow stadia and providing additional clarity regarding the complex environmental challenges posed by shadow stadia globally, this chapter has identified a subsequent requirement for action to be facilitated by urban redevelopment stakeholders both internal and external to the sport industry. In support of this action, we further propose an environmental justice approach to urban redevelopment projects that are anchored by sport facilities and their professional franchises. An environmental justice approach is relevant to investigating environmental impacts to communities in proximity of shadow stadia through the examination of residents who may already be subjected to other forms of disadvantage while being exposed to environmental risks (Schlosberg & Collins, 2014).

An environmental justice lens intersects issues of class, culture, race, and gender into the fold of environmentalism (Holifield, 2001). Environmental justice also emphasizes the environmental hazards such as noise and air pollution, waste, and greenspace degradation that impact where people work, live, and play (Novotny, 2000). Cox (2020) highlighted that environmental justice discourse is considered to have begun in the late 1970s in the United States, with a focus on the presence of negative urban environmental problems largely due to vacant facilities and sites (e.g., landfills, hazardous waste treatments, intensive agricultural and resource extraction sites) in poor areas where non-Whites generally tended to live (Agyeman, 2002; Myers, 2008). Environmental justice has been extended to encompass not only environmental risks to disadvantaged people but also their ability or inability to access environmental amenities provided through urban spaces, parks, and clean water—in major cities around the world (Agyeman et al., 2002).

Central to environmental justice scholarship is environmental racism, which should be analyzed via class, nation-state formation, and gender in a broader global framework (Pellow, 2002). Agyeman and Evans (2004) explained that environmental justice is based on the human right to be protected from environmental pollution and to live in a healthy environment. Furthermore, environmental justice can only be achieved when the source of emission from pollution validates the additional environmental risks upon a community and then resolves the disparities that were produced (Cotton, 2018; Shrader-Frechette, 2002). As such, community members must have access to the decision-making processes of local politicians and urban planners through open dialogue and the opportunity for consent (Schlosberg, 2007).

An example of research using an environmental justice lens in sport stadia is Sze's (2009) research on the Atlantic Yards project, a $4-billion mixed-use development project for a new arena for the Brooklyn Nets NBA team as well as retail, housing, and open greenspace. Sze used the proposal put forth by the Brooklyn Nets owner to illustrate how large-scale development planning for recreational facilities, stadiums, and arenas, combined with open greenspace, embody racial tension within urban development. Sze found that through narrative building, the master developer mobilized the environmental justice movement, raising attention on how corporate actors co-opt race, class, and the environment relative to sport. Since Sze's (2009) research, however, little to no research has been published on sport stadia and environmental justice.

Classifying Shadow Stadia

Many factors contribute to the obsolescence and vacancy of a sport arena or stadium. Capacity and safety regulations set by city governments, revenue and quality-based venue regulations set by league commissioners and boards of directors, the structure of franchise ownership, the needs of the surrounding community and neighborhoods, and national standards on site accessibility represent only some of these factors. There are also unique cultural, political, and economic circumstances that may influence the way cities proceed with shadow stadia site redevelopment. Despite these unique conditions, some consistencies appear in how shadow stadium sites are redeveloped.

To focus on how cities have previously coped with the vacancy of a significant sports franchise as an anchor tenant to a major stadium or arena and resulting shadow stadia site, stadiums, and arenas that were home to professional hockey, basketball, football, soccer, rugby, or cricket teams around the world were collected and analyzed. Olympic venues, motor-specific tracks, war-purpose venues, or renovated structures were excluded. In sum, 286 shadow stadium sites distributed across 22 countries were found and collated. The redevelopment plans for shadow sites were categorized in seven ways, including (a) mixed-use development, (b) grocery/retail, (c) residential, (d) replacement stadiums and infrastructure on the existing site, (e) community facilities, and (f) site vacancies.

While not all sites compiled fit absolutely into one of the categories summarized above, 27 other types of site redevelopment projects that were not as common emerged. These former venue sites included commercial buildings, corporate headquarters, industrial yards, government buildings, public or private hospitals, major roadways, military barracks, hospitals, parking lots, and storage facilities.

Several challenges arose during the research process to categorize shadow stadium site reuse. A lack of singular coordinated information source at the project level or municipal level meant that data points had to be collected from multiple sources. A secondary complicating factor was that proposed development plans and information varied depending on the source—with data often being presented differently between municipalities, development firms, sponsoring corporations, community organizations, and sport franchise ownership groups. Additionally, modifications to previously-approved development plans were not always captured by primary or secondary research sources. Additionally, information was often only available in the form of anecdotes from blogs or opinion pieces providing reviews or retrospectives of a development site several years post development.

Diverse philosophical positions often presented by source authors, coupled with a variety of available sources for many of the same shadow sites researched, meant that the eventual categorization of the shadow site was based on the cross-referencing of information presented by developers, municipalities, community organizations, or sports franchises. Primary sources included press releases, council reports, firsthand accounts, legal documents, sport franchise bylaws and constitutions, magazines, newsletters, blogs, and data collected from Google Maps regarding the shadow site's current physical state. In the case of primary sources being unavailable, and to gain the fullest scope of a development scenario as possible, academic studies and other periodicals were used to gather secondary information on development trends and additional details regarding the categorized examples presented in this chapter.

For this chapter, six case studies are highlighted across the redevelopment categories. Shadow stadia sites presented as cases were chosen based on an initial deductive coding analysis of environmental justice and environmental sustainability conceptualizations. In addition, the list of nearly 300 shadow stadia was refined to North American sites affiliated with the continent's four major men's professional sport leagues: MLB, the NBA, the NFL, and the NHL. These refinements were made to narrow down the dataset, effectively underscoring the environmental impacts of shadow stadia while providing practical recommendations for the future redevelopment of shadow sites in the North American context. Further, North American professional sports are closed leagues, meaning that the number of available franchises is purposefully limited, which can further exacerbate the issue of shadow stadia.

Mixed-use Redevelopment Strategies

Redevelopment plans comprise a combination of residential, retail, and community recreation/greenspace have become increasingly favorable options for cities. Of the 286 shadow sites examined worldwide, 35 of those sites' repurposing plans included some application of mixed-use development strategy. While the mixed-use redevelopment of a shadow site has occurred less frequently than other categories noted in these results, 12 countries spanning four continents are represented, dating back to the early 1900s. Although it does not appear that mixed-use redevelopment strategies have been constrained to geographic locations, this type of redevelopment appeared early in the 20th century and witnessed a resurgence in popularity in the 1990s and early 2000s.

Candlestick Park, San Francisco

Candlestick Park in San Francisco was the home of MLB's San Francisco Giants from 1960 to 2000, with the NFL's 49ers also calling the stadium home from 1971 to 2013. The owners of the 49ers—citing the strong winds on this waterfront property as negatively impacting playing conditions—relocated the team to Santa Clara in 2013, where Levi's Stadium was constructed for the start of their 2014 season (Munsey & Suppes, 2022). Levi's Stadium received LEED Gold certification from the U.S. Green Building Council for its construction, maintenance, and operation of the building (Levi's Stadium, 2016). Narratives of environmental sustainability are highlighted in promotional materials for the stadium, with the stadium's website sharing its commitment to recycling and reclaiming building products, its 27,000 square foot "green roof," solar panels used for PV electricity, the purchase of local supplies for farm-to-table concession stands, and the use of reclaimed water for field irrigation.

Meanwhile, without permanent tenants of the shadow site at Candlestick Park, and with no plans to repurpose the original stadium, the City of San Francisco chose to proceed in 2015 with mechanized structural demolition rather than implosion due to environmental pollution concerns by residents (Fernandez, 2015). The shadow stadium site at Candlestick Park has primarily remained an empty lot. Several attempts to revitalize and redevelop the area by local politicians, community leaders, and developers have been delayed or otherwise failed. A redevelopment plan initially scheduled for construction in 2019–2020 includes residential, retail, office, parks, and arts and entertainment space, and is currently delayed (Fivepoint, 2022).

The surrounding neighborhood of Bayview, home to the Candlestick Park site, is located near the notoriously contaminated Bayview-Hunters Point Shipyard (Brinklow, 2018). This site has generated complex debate on issues such as environmental racism. Bayview-Hunters Point comprises two-thirds of San Francisco's sources of pollution and approximately one-third of the city's hazardous waste sites (Candlestick Park Eco-Stewards, 2022).

The juxtaposition of Candlestick Park (and its many failed redevelopment attempts and its experiences of environmental injustice) with Levi's Stadium in Santa Clara, which touts its LEED certification, and pro-environmental practices, indicates an opportunity for cities to be more diligent in the stadia- and arena-anchored redevelopment process, to avoid resulting contrasting environmental conditions between new stadia and shadow stadia sites.

Grocery or Retail

Fourteen stadium or arena development deals from the nearly 300 sites reviewed were found to have involved a partnership with or received funding from a major grocery chain as a part of the redevelopment of the resulting shadow site. This funding supported the team's relocation, the construction of the new site, or both. Most redevelopment plans anchored by grocery chains have been concentrated primarily in the United Kingdom and have occurred between the 1960s and the late 2000s.

Maple Leaf Gardens, Toronto

Toronto's Maple Leaf Gardens is a unique example of a shadow stadia site that was challenged in its repurposing by an historic designation preventing the building's demolition. Maple Leaf Gardens, built in 1931 and considered a cathedral of hockey, was most famously known for being the home to the Maple Leafs NHL team until 1999. It is also considered a valued piece of Canadian hockey history where the Leafs won 11 Stanley Cup championships from 1932 to 1967 (CBC Digital Archives, 1990). The Toronto Raptors of the NBA also played home games in Maple Leaf Gardens from 1997 to 1999. When the Maple Leaf Sports & Entertainment (MLSE) group acquired both franchises, they built a new multi-purpose arena in downtown Toronto that could serve both sport and entertainment events and accommodate more luxury suites for corporate sponsors. MLSE opened the new arena, the Air Canada Centre (now Scotiabank Arena), in 1999.

Maple Leaf Gardens was designated a National Historic Site of Canada in 2007; Maple Leafs owners stipulated that the use of the facility in the future could not be used for hockey so that it would not compete with the revenue of the professional NBA and NHL teams in the new arena. As such, MLSE refused to sell Maple Leaf Gardens to anyone who proposed to use it as an arena in competition with the Air Canada Centre. As a result, the arena sat empty for nearly 10 years while several potential buyers struggled to conceptualize a financial or physical plan for the

FIGURE 4.1 Maple Leaf Gardens in Toronto, pictured in 2016. ("Maple Leaf Gardens" by Jeff Hitchcock is licensed under CC BY 2.0.)

building (Boccia, 2013). A deal was finalized with grocer Loblaws and Ryerson University in 2009, and the facility was renovated and repurposed as a multiuse facility (Mattamy Athletic Centre, 2022). A Loblaws grocery store was put in on the lower floor for residents. At the same time, the arena ice surfaces, later named Mattamy Athletic Centre, was taken over by Ryerson's men's hockey program for games and practices. Community and youth hockey also have access to the facility (Mattamy Athletic Centre, 2022). Ryerson's new athletic facilities provided a boost for local university students and community athletic venues, while residents have identified the addition of a major grocer to the densely populated urban area as a long-anticipated addition (Gee, 2010).

The repurposing of Maple Leaf Gardens into community retail and grocery space, as well as a university and youth-centered facility, is rare among shadow sites. In fact, most open, outdoor, single-spaced stadiums that serve football, baseball, soccer, lacrosse, or cricket rarely, if ever, are repurposed from the original structure, except for some cases in the United Kingdom. Typically, those repurposed are closed-roof, multiuse arenas that appear to have a longer lifespan and can be more easily and inexpensively repurposed.

From a sustainability perspective, Maple Leaf Gardens was successful since it represents an urban redevelopment project that repurposed a facility that serves a diverse, student-centric community in Old Toronto. From heritage preservation, community development, and post-secondary education perspectives, the adaptive reuse of Maple Leaf Gardens could be considered a standard in multiuse shadow stadium site development.

Residential Redevelopment

A larger proportion of sites surveyed are categorized as residential developments. From the data reviewed, there were 80 sites repurposed for different types of residential housing, whether for apartment-style condominium towers, row housing, or community housing for low-income residents or senior citizens. Residential redevelopment of shadow sites has provided an opportunity for municipalities to boost urban density or provide services in communities needing adequate social housing (Santee, 2012).

Amway Arena, Orlando

Amway Arena, an indoor arena that opened in 1989 and served as home to the NBA's Orlando Magic until 2010, was demolished in 2012 and is presently being replaced by a residential development called Creative Village (City of Orlando, 2022). In the years leading up to the decision for the Magic to move to a new site in downtown Orlando, the arena had no structural issues (Munsey & Suppes, 2022). However, with the emergence of luxury suites in other renovated and new arenas, Magic owners were determined to partner with the City of Orlando to build a new stadium downtown that could generate more revenue for the franchise, rather than adding to or renovating the current stadium.

In its place, the City of Orlando has developed Creative Village, a community with greenspace, housing at varying price points, as well as educational and commercial structures to grow the area's tech industry (City of Orlando, 2022). One way they have approached sustainability in this project was to recycle the materials of the demolished arena and use the concrete as the foundation for Creative Village (City of Orlando, 2022). In addition, the Parramore community, the historic and diverse neighborhood that situates Creative Village, has been vocal about creating opportunities for residents in new educational and job training, providing housing options across a wide range of income levels, and supporting business growth (City of Orlando, 2022).

While the City of Orlando employed narratives of intersectionality, environmental justice, and environmental sustainability in their marketing and promotion of this project, more empirical research is recommended once Creative Village is completed to examine potential concerns such as rising real estate prices, taxes, and gentrification in the surrounding neighborhood.

Replacement Stadium or Infrastructure on Existing Site

Many municipalities and franchise owners choose to build an expanded, modern stadium or arena on the preexisting site or an adjacent piece of land. This preference is often attributed to a lack of space large or central enough to accommodate a new stadium in an already dense urban area, a lack of municipal infrastructure that could support the venue in a more suburban location, or that the shadow site exists in a favorable area supported by infrastructure, business, and entertainment options. In our analysis, 20 stadiums were (a) developed on an adjacent piece of land while the existing site was converted into parking or related infrastructure facilities or (b) built on the same site after its predecessor was demolished; in the latter case, the affected team used a temporary home during the construction.

Yankee Stadium, New York City

Yankee Stadium, home to the New York Yankees MLB team, is one of the most recent examples within this category of redevelopment. Located across the street from the original Yankee Stadium, Macombs Dam Park provided the Yankees with an opportunity to expropriate the public park for its new ballpark while games continued at the original stadium until construction was completed in 2009 (New York City Department of Parks and Recreation, n.d.). The new Yankee Stadium incorporated design elements from the original stadium and linked existing forms of public transportation with a new metro stop in 2009. A larger portion of the original site is now occupied by Heritage Field, a large community park to replace the recreation space lost to the new Yankee Stadium build (New York City Department of Parks and Recreation, n.d.).

This strategy was not devoid of controversy, as community groups launched political and legal battles against the development group for what they perceived to be the destruction of parkland alongside a failed commitment to have replacement community recreation facilities open for use before the new Yankee Stadium's opening (Jaccarino, 2010; see also Chapter 9). The local community board voted against the new stadium plan and cited health concerns associated with increased traffic, lack of community input into the plan, and the risky precedent of turning over public parkland for private consumption in the core of a residential community (Damiani et al., 2007). Today, the new stadium construction has displaced children from more than 20 local schools and countless residents that used the parks where the new facility is located. When the community group Save Our Parks challenged the taking of the parkland in court, a state judge dismissed the case partially based on the city's promise to build interim parks during the construction phase of the project. However, the temporary parks did not open until months after the initial date promise. Furthermore, the new Yankee Stadium project violated the city administration's vision for a sustainable city by cutting down trees during construction. Trees were then replaced with synthetic turf made of recycled rubber and potentially carcinogenic materials. Finally, the long-term maintenance of replacement parks was also a concern, as advocacy reports documented inadequate park maintenance in low-income neighborhoods (e.g., South Bronx) in comparison to wealthier neighborhoods (Citizens Budget Commission, 2007).

Yet despite the controversy, in 2019, the Yankees became the first major North American professional sports team to sign on to the United Nations Sports for

64 Taryn Barry, Daniel S. Mason, Lisi Heise

Climate Action Framework, which strives to bring greenhouse gas emissions in line with the Paris Climate Change Agreement (Hoch, 2021). With that, the new Yankee Stadium focuses on procurement, operational practices, and community collaboration with local agencies and businesses that align with ecological intent (United Nations Climate Change, 2019). More current empirical research should be conducted in the neighboring communities around Yankee Stadium to understand if the environmental goals of the organization and the needs of the residents are being met.

Community Facilities

Not all shadow site redevelopment projects are developed for or by private, for-profit corporations. Non-profit and charitable organizations have also benefitted from shadow site redevelopment opportunities. Though the donation of land from former franchise owners to these organizations has occurred less frequently, the Red Cross, YMCA, and Boys and Girls Clubs have been recipients of former stadium and arena lands across North American cities.

Crossing 12 countries represented in this study and of 286 sites reviewed, 48 are categorized as having been transformed into public parks, community recreation areas, or high school or post-secondary facilities, or donated to non-profit or charitable organizations. Although some venues have been torn down and replaced by outdoor public park and recreation spaces, others remain permanent and serve as rehabilitated multipurpose sport, recreation, and entertainment facilities.

Kezar Stadium

Kezar Stadium was constructed between 1922 and 1925 in the southeast corner of Golden Gate Park in San Francisco, California. It was originally built to house baseball and football with a capacity of over 59,000 spectators (Turbow, 2012). Kezar Stadium is owned by the City and County of San Francisco and operated by San Francisco Recreation & Parks Department. After the San Francisco 49ers moved to Candlestick Park in 1971, Kezar became a popular concert venue until it was demolished in 1989 and rebuilt with a smaller footprint of 10,000 seats, leading to the moniker, "Little Kezar." This smaller capacity allowed the venue to become financially feasible for many amateur, semi-professional and community sport clubs and events, including Major League Lacrosse, the United Soccer League, Major League Soccer, Pro Cricket League, and several high school leagues (Turbow, 2012).

In 2014, Kezar Stadium closed for renovations carried out by the city that included a replacement running track, new walkways and curbs, an upgraded sound system, and 1,000 historic Candlestick Park seats for public use. The multisport stadium includes an eight-lane, all-weather track and large grass athletic field and provides access for local lacrosse, soccer, football, and track and field teams and events year-round. It also provides community use for joggers, runners, and adult soccer leagues (Golden Gate Park, n.d.).

While Kezar Stadium, the shadow site of Candlestick Park, was demolished and rebuilt into an operational facility for residents, community members, and amateur sport leagues and tournaments, Candlestick Park, the shadow site of Levi's Stadium, remains undeveloped and controversial. Kezar Stadium is a positive exemplar of shadow site development. One major advantage is its location in Golden Gate Park, a large urban park that consists of over 1,000 acres of public grounds, welcomes millions of visitors annually, and is the third most-visited city park in the United States (Brinklow, 2018). Since 2019, the park has used 100% renewable electricity to offset its carbon footprint (O'Gallagher, 2022).

Long-Term Site Vacancies

Long-term site vacancies existed in 30 of the sites reviewed. It was found that many redevelopment projects within the categories had experienced periods of vacancy that resulted in underutilized and blighted spaces, often in dense urban areas, and taxing on municipal infrastructure. Vacant shadow sites represent overlooked opportunities for tax revenue generation and often require the support of social and emergency response services to deal with the human- and infrastructure-related encounters resulting shadow stadia.

Often, vacant shadow sites are temporary; however, many stadiums have experienced longer durations of uncertainty while negotiations took place between municipal government, lawyers, and community groups, or while potential stakeholders assessed the market conditions or development partnership prospects (Balkissoon, 2009).

Astrodome, Houston

The Astrodome, billed as the "8th Wonder of the World," is a multipurpose stadium in Houston, Texas (National Trust for Historic Preservation, 2015). The stadium still stands today, but it has been largely abandoned since the Oilers (NFL) moved to Nashville in 1996, and the Astros (MLB) moved to a downtown location in 1999 due to the dilapidated state of the building and turf (Munsey & Suppes, 2022). When Houston attracted a new NFL franchise in 2002, a new retractable-roof stadium was built next door to the Astrodome (National Trust for Historic Preservation, 2015).

Nonetheless, there have been multiple failed plans and proposals to repurpose the Astrodome (Munsey & Suppes, 2022). In 2008, the facility was cited for numerous building code violations; thus, maintenance workers and security guards are the only people allowed to enter the Astrodome. Plans for repurposing the Astrodome have included a luxury hotel, convention center, and community park. More recently, in 2018, Harris County officials approved a $105-million

FIGURE 4.2 The Houston Astrodome, pictured in 2004. ("North Elevation, Looking South—Houston Astrodome" by Jet Lowe, Historic American Engineering Record, Library of Congress.)

plan to elevate the floor and repurpose it into below-ground parking for games and events in the adjacent Houston Texans stadium, but a year later, the city canceled the plans due to unforeseen costs (Spedden, 2019).

Several reasons explain why the Astrodome was not torn down. First, the City of Houston rejected demolition plans because of the environmental hazards from asbestos and its potential effects on the dense neighboring community (Richard, 2014). Second, in addition to the costs of demolition being high, the Astrodome also holds historic significance in Houston as a sport venue and its use as an emergency shelter after Hurricane Katrina in 2005 (National Trust for Historic Preservation, 2015). Therefore, in 2017, the Texas Historical Commission endorsed the Astrodome as an historic structure, which means it could only be demolished after authorization from the commission.

The Astrodome may have historical and cultural significance in Houston, yet two professional teams leaving the facility over 20 years ago have cast a shadow on the neighborhood and community to this day. The boarded-up stadium is not only a city blight, but it also illustrates the lack of planning from city officials and the influence that major league sports teams owners have in deciding how urban landscapes develop.

Recommendations

Rosentraub (2009) recommended that "uber-planning," as opposed to an evolutionary approach to urban development, be required for successful arena- and stadium-anchored urban development to occur. This means that planning must be much larger in scale and purposeful, with a substantial combination of public and private funding and input, instead of an expectation that an urban area requiring revitalization will occur over time organically. In addition to Rosentraub's (2009) still timely recommendation, this chapter provides guidance for local governments, the development industry, policymakers, community advocates, and academics alike, established on an environmental justice approach to arena-anchored urban development and their shadow stadia, whereby race, class, culture, and gender intersect with the ecological impacts of where people live, work, and play. These recommendations are as follows:

1. Make plans for the repurposing of old arenas and stadiums prior to a professional sport franchise moving locations. The city must facilitate and drive this dialogue and planning.
2. Cities and sport franchises should integrate sustainability elements into both the planning of the new stadium *and* the repurposing of the shadow site.
3. Sport franchises, their owners, and master developers must be held financially accountable for any failed shadow site redevelopment plans and potential environmental risks.
4. Wherever possible, arena-anchored urban redevelopment projects should reuse building materials from demolition for the construction of the new shadow site.
5. Enclosed arenas, rather than open-air, single-use stadiums, may offer future repurposing optimization, as found within the retail and grocery category. Therefore, cities should look to secure or seek out sport franchises that can play in multiuse, closed facilities.
6. A resident-led, community-based environmental justice organization should be formed and integrated with all urban stadium districts. This organization should be committed to collaborating with city planners and master developers. This entity would serve a purpose similar to a stadium authority, but instead of economic development goals, it would focus on environmental justice outcomes.
7. A participatory research methodology approach that gathers and articulates lived experience in affected communities must be a fundamental driver of public decision-making related to stadium development, especially prior to construction.
8. Future research is required on the outcomes of shadow stadia (e.g., demolished stadiums and delayed plans, demolished stadiums and completed projects, repurposed stadiums, abandoned stadiums).

68 Taryn Barry, Daniel S. Mason, Lisi Heise

Conclusion

This chapter aimed to fill a gap in the literature by examining shadow stadia; in doing so, issues of environmental justice should be considered and planned for when major league sports teams and city leaders move their teams and build new facilities. The classification discussed in this chapter is an essential first step in understanding, defining, and explaining the types of shadow stadia that exist worldwide. In particular, environmental impacts should be explored in future empirical research to investigate a given urban landscape's cultural, economic, political, geographical, climatic, and environmental influences.

References

Agyeman J. (2002). Constructing environmental (in)justice: Transatlantic tales. *Environmental Politics, 11*(3), 31–53. 10.1080/714000627

Agyeman, J., Bullard, R. D., & Evans, B. (2002). Exploring the nexus: Bringing together sustainability, environmental justice and equity. *Space & Polity, 6*(1), 77–90. 10.1 080/13562570220137907

Agyeman, J. & Evans, B. (2004). "Just sustainability": The emerging discourse of environmental justice in Britain? *The Geographical Journal, 170*(2), 155–164. 10.1111/j.001 6-7398.2004.00117.x

Balkissoon, D. (2009, November 30). Ryerson and Loblaws make a deal for Maple Leaf Gardens. *The Toronto Star.* https://www.thestar.com/news/gta/2009/11/30/ryerson_and_loblaws_make_a_deal_for_maple_leaf_gardens.html

Boccia, E. (2013). Maple Leaf Gardens: More than a hockey arena. *Heritage Toronto.* http://heritagetoronto.org/maple-leaf-gardens/

Brinklow, A. (2018, August 22). *Golden Gate Park ranked third most popular park in US. Curbed.* https://sf.curbed.com/2018/8/22/17769694/golden-gate-park-trust-public-land-parkscore-2018

Candlestick Park Eco-Stewards. (2022). *The Point.* http://www.candlestickconnect.org/#the-point

CBC Digital Archives. (1990, September 19). *Inside the palace: A history of Maple Leaf Gardens.* CBC. https://www.cbc.ca/archives/entry/inside-the-palace-a-history-of-maple-leaf-gardens

Citizens Budget Commission. (2007). *Making the most of our parks.* CBCNY. https://cbcny.org/sites/default/files/reportsummary_parks_09012007.pdf

City of Orlando. (2022). *Creative Village: Vision.* https://creativevillageorlando.com/vision/

Cotton, M. (2018). Environmental justice as scalar parity: Lessons from nuclear waste management. *Social Justice Research, 31*(3), 238–259. 10.1007/s11211-018-0311-z

Cox, P. (2020). Environmental justice, waste management, and the circular economy. In T. Tudor & C. J. Dutra (Eds.), *The Routledge handbook of waste, resources and the circular economy.* Routledge.

Crompton, J. (2004). Beyond economic impact: An alternative rationale for the public subsidy of major league sports facilities. *Journal of Sport Management, 18*(1), 40–58. 10.1123/jsm.18.1.40

Damiani, B., Markey, E., & Steinberg, D. (2007). *Insider baseball: How current and former public officials pitched a community shutout for the New York Yankees.* Good Jobs New York. https://www.goodjobsfirst.org/sites/default/files/docs/pdf/insider_baseball_report.pdf

Etzion, D. (2007). Research on organizations and the natural environment, 1992–present: A review. *Journal of Management, 33*(4), 637–664. 10.1177/0149206307302553

Fernandez, L. (2015, February 4). *Demolition of Candlestick Park underway; new development to replace old stadium.* NBC Bay Area. https://www.nbcbayarea.com/news/sports/demolition-of-candlestick-park-underway-new-development-replacing-stadium/114347/

Fivepoint. (2022). *Candlestick San Francisco.* https://www.candlesticksf.com/

Gee, M. (2010). *The Ryerson revolution: How the once dumpy polytechnic is redrawing downtown.* Toronto Life. https://torontolife.com/city/the-ryerson-revolution-how-the-once-dumpy-polytechnic-is-redrawing-downtown/

Golden Gate Park. (n.d.). *Kezar Stadium.* https://goldengatepark.com/kezar-stadium.html

Hoch, B. (2021, April 22). *Yankees making stadium greener than ever.* MLB. https://www.mlb.com/news/yankee-stadium-among-greenest-parks-in-sports

Holifield, R. (2001). Defining environmental justice and environmental racism. *Urban Geography, 22*(1), 78–90. 10.2747/0272-3638.22.1.78

Jaccarino, M. (2010, June 21). Parks near Yankee Stadium set to open, but critics say city is still shortchanging residents. *The New York Daily News.* https://www.nydailynews.com/new-york/bronx/parks-yankee-stadium-set-open-critics-city-shortchanging-residents-article-1.181483

Johnson, B. K. & Whitehead, J. C. (2000). Value of public goods from sports stadiums: The CVM approach. *Contemporary Economic Policy, 18*(1), 48–58. 10.1111/j.1465-7287.2000.tb00005.x

Kellison, T. B. & Hong, S. (2015). The adoption and diffusion of pro-environmental stadium design. *European Sport Management Quarterly, 15*(2), 249–269. 10.1080/16184742.2014.995690

Kellison, T. B., Trendafilova, S., & McCullough, B. P. (2015). Considering the social impact of sustainable stadium design. *International Journal of Event Management Research, 10*(1), 63–83.

Levi's Stadium. (2016, October 6). *Levi's Stadium achieves LEED gold certification for operations and maintenance of an existing building.* https://www.levisstadium.com/2016/10/levis-stadium-achieves-leed-gold-certification-for-operations-and-maintenance-of-an-existing-building/

Long, J. G. (2013). *Rethinking Olympic infrastructure.* LSE City Transformations. https://urbanage.lsecities.net/essays/rethinking-olympic-infrastructure

Mattamy Athletic Centre. (2022). *Arena highlights history.* https://www.mattamyathleticcentre.ca/venue-info/arena-highlights-history

Munsey & Suppes. (2022). *Ballparks.* https://ballparks.com/

Myers, G. A. (2008). Sustainable development and environmental justice in African cities. *Geography Compass, 2*(3), 695–708. 10.1111/j.1749-8198.2008.00111.x

National Trust for Historic Preservation. (2015, October 22). *The history of the Astrodome in 8 cool items.* https://savingplaces.org/stories/history-of-astrodome-in-8-cool-items#.YZOGky0RpmA

New York City Department of Parks & Recreation. (n.d.). *The Yankee Stadium park redevelopment project.* http://www.nycgovparks.org/park-features/future-parks/yankee-stadium-redevelopment

Novotny P. (2000). *Where we live, work and play: The environmental justice movement and the struggle for a new environmentalism.* Greenwood Publishing Group.

O'Gallagher, M. (2022). *Golden Gate National Recreation Area is now carbon neutral. Here's what that means.* Golden Gate National Parks Conservancy. https://www.parksconservancy.org/park-e-ventures-article/golden-gate-national-recreation-area-now-carbon-neutral-heres-what-means

Pellow, D. N. (2002). *Garbage wars: The struggle for environmental justice in Chicago.* MIT Press.

Richard, K. (2014, August 14). *More Astrodome seats may be sold by Harris County.* Ballpark Digest. https://ballparkdigest.com/201408197571/at-the-ballpark/the-front-office/more-astrodome-seats-may-be-sold-by-harris-county

Rosentraub, M. S. (2006). Sports facilities and urban redevelopment: Private and public benefits and a prescription for a healthier future. *International Journal of Sport Finance, 1*(4), 212–226.

Rosentraub, M. S. (2009). *Major league winners: Using sports and cultural centers as tools for economic development.* CRC Press.

Rosentraub, M. S. (2014). *Reversing urban decline: Why and how sports, entertainment, and culture turn cities into major league winners.* CRC Press.

Santee, E. (2012, November 28). *Stadiums that shape downtowns: The impact of stadiums on urban redevelopment.* Populous. https://populous.com/stadiums-that-shape-downtowns-the-impact-of-stadiums-on-urban-redevelopment

Schlosberg, D. (2007). *Defining environmental justice: Theories, movements, and nature.* Oxford University Press.

Schlosberg, D. & Collins, L. B. (2014). From environmental to climate justice: Climate change and the discourse of environmental justice. *WIREs Climate Change, 5*(3), 359–374. 10.1002/wcc.275

Shrader-Frechette, K. S. (2002). *Environmental justice: Creating equality, reclaiming democracy.* Oxford University Press.

Spedden, Z. (2019, September 10). *Astrodome renovation plan has stalled.* Ballpark Digest. https://ballparkdigest.com/2019/09/10/astrodome-renovation-plan-has-stalled/

Sze, J. (2009). Sports and environmental justice: "Games" of race, place, nostalgia, and power in neoliberal New York City. *Journal of Sport and Social Issues, 33*(2), 111–129. 10.1177/0193723509332581

The Canadian Press. (2011, December 9). *Rogers, Bell buy control of MLSE: Deal includes NHL's Maple Leafs, NBA's Raptors.* CBC. https://www.cbc.ca/sports/hockey/nhl/rogers-bell-buy-control-of-mlse-1.997655

Triantafyllidis, S., Ries, R. J., & Kaplanidou, K. (2018). Carbon dioxide emissions of spectators' transportation in collegiate sporting events: Comparing on-campus and off campus stadium locations. *Sustainability, 10*(1), 1–18. 10.3390/su10010241

Turbow, J. (2012, January 21). West coast brew gave Kezar Stadium its color. *The New York Times.* http://www.nytimes.com/2012/01/21/sports/football/colorful-history-of-kezar-stadium-49ers-former-home.html?_r=0

United Nations Climate Change. (2019, April 3). *New York Yankees first major North American team to join UN Sports for Climate Action.* https://unfccc.int/news/new-york-yankees-first-major-north-american-team-to-join-un-sports-for-climate-action

5
STADIUMS AND STATE ENVIRONMENTAL POLICY ACTS

Kellen Zale

The development of new sports stadiums is often promoted by lawmakers and supported by community members as a source of increased economic activity and revitalization of disinvested areas. At the same time, the construction and ongoing operations of new stadiums can cause a range of negative environmental impacts. While the overall emissions and pollution impacts associated with sports stadiums are relatively low compared to other realms of human activity (such as transportation), the negative environmental impacts of individual stadiums are not insignificant.

Some of the negative environmental impacts associated with stadium developments are diffuse, such as increased greenhouse gas emissions and fossil fuel usage associated with construction activities, affecting even those who do not live or work near the stadium (Gosalvez, 2020; "Reducing Sports' Impact," 2013). Other impacts are highly concentrated and localized in the neighborhoods where the stadium is built. For example, stadium development typically results in the loss of permeable surfaces—and potential for increased flooding and runoff pollution—when vacant or less developed land is replaced by asphalt parking lots and AstroTurf (Grant, 2014). Biodiversity losses are often associated with new stadiums both indirectly (loss of habitat) and directly (such as bird strikes from glass facades; International Union for Conservation of Nature, 2019; Moylan, 2019). The ongoing operations of stadiums also impose additional localized impacts, such as spikes in air pollution from increased vehicular traffic associated with stadium events (Gosalvez, 2020; "Reducing Sports' Impact," 2013). Furthermore, stadium development often results in changes to the built environment (such as the demolition of existing homes and businesses) that can cause community displacement, which itself may have associated negative environmental impacts (Abdul-Kahbir, 2018).

As discussions in other chapters of this book have illustrated, these and other types of negative environmental impacts associated with stadiums are often felt

DOI: 10.4324/9781003262633-6

most acutely by environmental justice communities: stadiums are often built in low-income communities and communities of color, where land acquisition costs are often lower and where structural inequities have resulted in residents having less power to oppose such projects than residents of wealthier, whiter communities (Abdul-Kahbir, 2018). These same communities have often been disproportionately burdened with environmental disamenities (such as polluting facilities and freeways) as well as disenfranchised from the decision-making processes that have produced these development patterns. While stadiums may be supported by many community members—including members of economic justice communities—because of their anticipated economic benefits (as well as the more amorphous civic and reputational attachments associated with professional sports teams that play in stadiums), stadium projects nonetheless pose the risk of a variety of negative environmental impacts disproportionately affecting environmental justice communities.

The question then becomes, what tools are available to address this issue? Non-legal, voluntary responses are one possibility. Developers of stadiums may be motivated by reputational interests as well as potential cost savings and consumer expectations to undertake voluntary actions to address some of the negative environmental impacts associated with the construction and ongoing operations of stadiums. And in fact, several stadiums constructed in recent years have included a variety of features designed to address some of their environmental impacts (Grant, 2014; "Reducing Sports' Impact," 2013).

Stadium developments also must comply with all applicable laws, whether local, state, or federal.[1] Stadium developments typically require local land use approvals (such as zoning and planning approvals) to construct a stadium. While not traditionally focused on environmental considerations (Nolon 2003), many local land use regulations do take environmental considerations into account and thus may serve as a legal tool to address some of the environmental impacts of stadiums. In addition, under some circumstances, federal environmental laws may be applicable to particular stadium developments.[2] For example, federal environmental laws, such as the Clean Water Act (CWA) or Endangered Species Act (ESA), may be applicable to stadium developments if particularized circumstances associated with a stadium trigger the provisions of those laws.[3] And in 16 states, as well as Washington, D.C., and Puerto Rico, state environmental policy acts (SEPAs), which establish a legal framework for identifying (and in some states, requiring mitigation of) the environmental impacts of statutorily-defined activities, may be applicable to proposed stadium developments.

SEPAs offer an important source of existing legal authority to address negative environmental impacts from land use activities disproportionately affecting environmental justice communities. However, in practice, SEPAs may fail to adequately address environmental justice concerns in the context of stadium developments. This chapter unpacks both the potential utility and shortcomings of SEPAs in this context. It begins with an overview of the legal framework for SEPAs, including an analysis of the interplay between environmental review under

SEPAs and environmental justice, before turning to a discussion of how stadium developments in California have been able to legally avoid environmental review under that state's SEPA.

SEPA Overview

SEPAs are one of the primary legal mechanisms used in a number of states to identify and address the potential environmental impacts of land use activities in the built environment. Sixteen states, as well as Washington, D.C., and Puerto Rico, have enacted SEPAs (Council on Environmental Quality, n.d.). SEPAs are often referred to as "little NEPAs," since they are modeled on NEPA, the federal National Environmental Policy Act. Like NEPA, SEPAs are intended to require state and local governments to identify (and, in some states, mitigate when feasible) the potential adverse environmental impact actions that fall within the scope of the state's SEPA (Council on Environmental Quality, n.d.).

As with NEPA, SEPAs have been the subject of both praise and criticism.[4] Supporters of these laws emphasize their crucial role in protecting environmental resources, reducing pollution and other adverse environmental impacts, and providing transparency and accountability to the public. However, the laws have also been criticized for the delay and expense they can add to projects and for how opponents can use SEPAs to delay or derail projects, even those that would actually be beneficial for the environment such as affordable housing or mass transit or green infrastructure. Various reforms have been enacted in the decades since the laws' enactments to address some of these concerns, and other more far-reaching reforms have been proposed to SEPAs in various states. At the same time, supporters of SEPAs emphasize that the laws' goal of ensuring environmental considerations is incorporated into governmental decision-making necessarily entails additional time and complexity in decision-making and that some reforms proposed by critics would undercut the core purposes of the laws: "NEPA and state environmental protection acts, such as [the California Environmental Quality Act; CEQA], were enacted precisely because lawmakers were failing to consider the environmental impacts of their decisions in the absence of a legal mechanism to force them to do so" (Zale, 2013, p. 863).

Before turning to an analysis of the legal framework of SEPAs, a few preliminary comments are warranted with respect to the interplay between environmental justice and SEPAs. First, it is important to recognize that SEPAs are not environmental justice laws per se: Like much of environmental law, SEPAs are focused on "improving overall ambient environmental conditions [and not] the distributional consequences of where pollution is occurring" (Rechtschaffen et al., 2009, p. 22). Although there are certain features in the statutory frameworks of some SEPAs that do offer a mechanism for considering distributional consequences as part of the environmental review (discussed below), SEPAs were not drafted to explicitly address the disproportionality in how environmental harms are experienced by different communities, and the phrase "environmental justice" does not appear in the statutory language of any SEPA (Freij, 2022).

Even SEPAs considered to be the most robust (or, to critics, the most burdensome) in terms of scope, such as California's CEQA, have been recognized as not mapping neatly onto environmental justice: "Precisely because [environmental] regulatory standards are intended to achieve the greatest good for the greatest number of people, such standards fail to take into account the special characteristics and vulnerabilities of minority populations and the poor" (Yang, 2002, p. 15). For example, economic and social harms, such as the loss of lower-income housing and community displacement that are often associated with major developments like stadiums, are not considered to fall within the scope of most SEPAs (with the notable exception of New York's SEPA, the State Environmental Quality Review Act [SERQA]). Furthermore, the calculus of environmental benefits and burdens can be challenging to reconcile when attempting to incorporate environmental justice principles into the environmental review model of SEPAs:

> [The] blending of EJ principles into CEQA territory ... [can] create additional obstacles to achieving state-level environmental and climate progress, such as the establishment of national transmission corridors for electricity, the approval of projects to create renewable energy supplies, and the authorization of programs designed to reduce greenhouse gas emissions, among others.
>
> *(Hsiao & Jeffers, 2012)*

Nonetheless, the fact that SEPAs are not perfectly aligned to the environmental justice model is not itself determinative of whether the statutes can be used to address environmental justice concerns. As will be discussed in more detail herein, the statutory scope of some SEPAs has been recognized by lawmakers and courts in several states as encompassing environmental justice concerns, both through specific statutory provisions (such as cumulative impact analysis) and through public participation requirements (Fleming, 2002; Gerrard & Foster, 2008; Johnson, 1997; Ramo, 2013). Furthermore, because there are few other applicable sources of law in most states to address environmental justice concerns in the context of stadiums (Bonorris & Targ, 2010), SEPAs remain an important, if imperfect, tool for addressing environmental justice concerns in this context. At the same time, it is worth recognizing that even if all stadium developments were subject to full environmental review under a particular state's SEPA, such laws do not necessarily offer the type of legal framework needed to completely address the types of environmental justice concerns associated with stadium developments.

Returning to the overview of SEPAs' legal frameworks, SEPAs vary by state as to what types of actions they apply to and as to what types of requirements they impose with regard to covered actions. With regard to what types of actions they apply to, SEPAs generally take one of two approaches. In some states, SEPAs mirror the NEPA model and are only applicable to government-sponsored projects and actions such as constructing a new state highway or adopting or amending a state agency regulation. In other states, including New York and California, SEPAs are more far-reaching than the federal law they are modeled on (i.e., NEPA) and apply to both government-sponsored projects and private developments if those private developments require one or more permits or other discretionary governmental approvals. In states with the latter type of SEPAs, a stadium developer needing land use approvals from local government regulators (which major developments such as stadiums invariably require) will be subject to SEPA, and the land use regulatory process will incorporate the requirements of the state's SEPA.[5]

However, not all actions that would seem to fall within the definition of "project" under a state SEPA will necessarily be subject to environmental review. Many SEPAs contain statutory exceptions exempting certain activities from environmental review. For example, California's CEQA contains several types of exemptions (CEQA Portal, 2020a), including ministerial action exemptions, categorical action exemptions, and a variety of other statutory exemptions encompassing a range of activities where a legislative determination has been made that "the requirement of CEQA compliance is considered to be outweighed by other considerations, even though the activity may pose a significant threat to the environment" (Zale, 2013, p. 843).

If an action does fall within the SEPA's definition of "project," the specific SEPA's statutory provisions (as well as implementing regulations promulgated by state agencies) determine the steps in the environmental review process. Details of the process vary by state, but broadly speaking, the framework described below reflects the environmental review process under most SEPAs.

First, assuming the action is not exempt, SEPAs require that an initial assessment be prepared and submitted by the project proponent to the government entity reviewing its application.[6] This governmental entity is typically referred to as the "lead agency" and it will be the coordinating decision-making entity moving forward.[7] Upon receipt of the initial assessment, the lead agency must make a determination using standards set out in the applicable SEPA as to whether a full environmental assessment must be prepared (mirroring the language in NEPA, many state SEPAs refer to this document as an "environmental impact statement" [EIS] or "environmental impact report" [EIR]).

The standard used to determine whether an EIS will be required varies somewhat by state. In general, most SEPAs set a fairly low threshold, reflecting the laws' goal of ensuring that environmental considerations be taken into account in government decision-making. For example, in California, a lead agency must decide whether the proposal could have a "significant effect on the environment," with "environment" defined broadly as "the physical conditions which exist within the area which will be affected by a proposed project, including [but not limited to] land, air, water, minerals, flora, fauna, noise, objects of historic or aesthetic significance."[8] If the lead agency determines that the project could significantly affect one or more of these areas of concern, an EIS will be required.

Alternately, if it appears that there is no potential for adverse environmental impacts from the proposed project based on the initial assessment, the lead agency issues a negative declaration ("ND"), which allows the developer to move forward on their proposal with no further actions required under SEPA. A lead agency may also be authorized under its state's SEPA to issue a conditional ND, which provides that a developer may move forward with no further environmental review if they agree to undertake the specified conditions. Under some state SEPAs, there may be statutory requirements for public comment or hearings before the issuance of an ND or conditional ND.

If an EIS is required, state-specific statutory language in each SEPA sets out the standards that must be included and analyzed. A process called scoping, which is used to identify what will be the focus and content of the draft EIS, is usually the first step before preparation of an EIS is undertaken. Typically, SEPAs require that the draft EIS identify the impacts of the proposed project across numerous areas of environmental concern (such as air quality, noise, habitat, or traffic) and compare the impacts the project would have on those issues to the status quo (i.e., to the "no development" alternative; as well as possibly to other alternatives to the proposed development).

SEPAs in a number of states require that the EIS take into account the cumulative impacts the project will have on areas of environmental concern. Cumulative impact analysis is intended to ensure that the larger context in which the project is being proposed is considered by requiring that its impacts be analyzed in connection with the effects of past, current, and foreseeable future projects, even if the incremental impacts from individual project proposal might be relatively modest (CEQA Portal, 2020b). In the context of stadium projects, to the extent that stadium developments pose the risk of cumulative negative environmental impacts in environmental justice communities, those impacts must be identified in environmental review under SEPAs with cumulative impact analysis requirements.

As to whether an EIS must consider other types of impacts on environmental justice communities, states take varying approaches, depending on the SEPA's specific statutory language as well as how that state's courts have interpreted their state's SEPA. Courts in a few states, notably New York, have explicitly recognized that environmental review under their SEPA requires analysis in an EIS of socioeconomic impacts, while courts in other states (including California, otherwise considered to have one of the most robust SEPAs) have concluded that such impacts are outside the scope of environmental review under their SEPA.

Preparation of a draft EIS is the responsibility of the project applicant; for a major development project such as a stadium, the preparation of the draft EIS can take months, and costs can be significant, with the reports for such projects often spanning hundreds or thousands of pages. Once the project applicant (usually with the assistance of an environmental consulting firm) has prepared the draft EIS, it is submitted to the lead agency. The lead agency then must make the draft EIS available for public comment for a designated period of time as well as hold public hearings as statutorily required. SEPAs typically do not require that the lead agency take any specific action with regard to public comments received or raised at public hearings, but the lead agency is normally required to respond to public comments as well as authorized to recommend that the developer amend the draft EIS to address concerns raised by public comments.

The public participation requirements of SEPAs have been recognized as another way in which SEPAs can promote environmental justice, since these statutory requirements can facilitate the "participation of low-income and minority people in governmental decisions and by attacks on the environmental decision making process" (Arnold, 1998, p. 60). While the functionality of SEPAs is often viewed through a purely legal lens,

> For an EJ lawyer, NEPA/CEQA is more of a legal tool used for political solutions. The goal is to involve communities in this process to ensure that the assessment creates informed and therefore accountable decision making because decision makers are required to respond to submitted comments.
>
> *(Youngblood, 2019, pp. 473–474)*

After the expiration of the public comment and hearing period, the lead agency is responsible for issuing a final EIS within a statutorily designated time. The final EIS prepared by the lead agency will typically be based on the draft EIS prepared by the developer but will often include changes, including rejections or modifications of assumptions or conclusions set out in the draft EIS.

Once the final EIS is completed, the findings identified in the final EIS must be considered by the lead agency before its ultimate decision on the developer's underlying application (which, in the context of stadium developments, is typically underlying land use approvals such as rezoning). At this final stage of the lead agency deciding whether to approve, conditionally approve, or deny the applicant's project, SEPAs take one of two approaches with regard to whether any substantive mandates are required of the lead agency.

Most SEPAs mirror the federal NEPA model, which is considered a procedural model that does not impose any substantive requirements. By requiring that environmental review be conducted, NEPA (and state SEPAs that mirror its approach) is intended to ensure that the government is informed as to the environmental consequences of its decisions. Although there is an implicit expectation that this awareness will influence the substantive decisions made, NEPA (and state SEPAs that mirror its approach) does not require any particular substantive action in response to the findings of the environmental review process: "Thus, even if the EIS reveals drastic environmental impacts that would occur as a result of the proposed project, under NEPA and most state environmental protection laws, the project can go forward" (Zale, 2013, p. 844).

Some SEPAs, however, impose not only procedural requirements but also substantive mandates. For example, under CEQA in California, a project with significant environmental impacts (as determined by the EIS [referred to as an EIR under CEQA]) may not be approved as proposed "if there are feasible alternatives or feasible mitigation measures available which would substantially lessen the significant environmental effects of such projects."[9] Similarly, in New York, SERQA requires that in making their decision on whether to approve a project, agencies "act and choose alternatives which, consistent with social, economic and other essential considerations, to the maximum extent practicable, minimize or avoid adverse environmental effects."[10] Such substantive mandates are a key reason that these states' SEPAs are considered more protective of the environment (and, to critics, more burdensome) than SEPAs in states that follow the purely procedural NEPA approach.

In accordance with the public interest goals of protecting the environment from harm and ensuring environmental considerations are incorporated into governmental decision-making, state SEPAs tend to have liberal standing requirements, which allow any member of the public (whether an individual neighbor, an interest group, or a business competitor) to file legal challenges to projects going through environmental review under SEPA. Legal challenges can be filed at various stages in the process; thus, legal challenges can be made to the initial determination that the project is not subject to CEQA, or to the intermediate decision as to whether an EIS is required, or to specific aspects about the adequacy of an EIS. While the vast majority of projects that go through environmental review under SEPAs are not subject to legal challenge (Smith-Heimer et al., 2016),[11] major development projects such as stadiums are more likely to face legal challenge both because of their high-profile (and often controversial) nature and because, as major developments, they are more likely to have major impacts.

The potential for legal challenges to projects under SEPAs is both an integral feature of the laws and a significant source of criticism. To avoid the possibility of delay and expense associated with legal challenges under SEPAs, some stadium projects—particularly in California—have taken the approach of utilizing exemptions from environmental review under that state's SEPA. The next section turns to a closer analysis of the approaches used by stadium developments in California to legally avoid environmental review under CEQA.

Stadiums' Legal Avoidance of Environmental Review under CEQA

While there are tensions in incorporating environmental justice into the environmental review model of SEPAs as discussed above, SEPAs—particularly those with substantive mitigation provisions such as California's CEQA—offer one of the few available existing legal tools that can be leveraged to respond to environmental impacts of stadiums on environmental justice communities. However, SEPAs can only perform their information-forcing and mitigation functions if stadium developments are actually subject to the requirements of a state's SEPA.

At first glance, a major development such as the construction of a new stadium would seem to fit squarely within the statutory scope of a law like California's CEQA since, as noted above, CEQA is one of the few SEPAs that applies broadly to both governmental activities and private developments that require discretionary approvals from a governmental entity, which a major development like a stadium will invariably require. However, over the past two decades, there has been a repeated pattern of stadium projects in California legally avoiding, either in whole or in part, environmental review under CEQA. While the specific circumstances for different stadiums vary somewhat as discussed below, stadium projects in California have legally avoided environmental review through one of two approaches: (1) qualifying for legislative exemptions from full environmental review under CEQA; or (2) utilizing CEQA's ballot box loophole, which entirely exempts the voter ballot initiative process (whether an actual election is held) from environmental review under CEQA.

This section focuses on environmental review of stadiums in California under CEQA specifically because it is where the pattern of legal avoidance of environmental review is most clearly evident and because it starkly illustrates how one of the most robust (or, to critics, burdensome) SEPAs can nonetheless fail to be an effective mechanism for addressing the adverse environmental impacts to environmental justice communities posed by stadium developments.

Stadium-Specific Legislative Exemptions from CEQA

The first method by which several stadium developments in California have legally avoiding environmental review under CEQA is by qualifying for legislative exemptions which exempt their projects in whole or in part from otherwise applicable provisions of environmental review under CEQA. One such legislative exemption identified in Table 5.1 below (for the proposed City of Industry stadium) provided a complete exemption from CEQA; the other legislative exemptions identified in Table 5.1 do not entirely exempt stadium projects from CEQA but rather partially exempt stadium projects from full compliance with the normally applicable environmental review process under CEQA. The specific details of the legislative exemptions vary by individual exemption, but several of the legislative exemptions provide for expedited judicial review and limitations regarding venue for any lawsuits challenging the projects. Some of the legislative exemptions identified in Table 5.1 were enacted to apply specifically to a single stadium development, while others were enacted to apply more broadly to certain types of statutorily defined land use activities that include stadiums as well as a certain other types of major developments that fall within the scope of the legislative exemption.

The California state legislature's justifications for enacting both stadium-specific CEQA exemptions and the broader major development CEQA exemptions are

TABLE 5.1 Stadium Projects Receiving Legislative Exemptions from the California Environmental Quality Act

Location	League and Team	Status	Year of Exemption	Summary of Legislative Exemption
City of Industry	NFL (numerous teams considered for relocation)	Proposed, never built	2009	AB 81 was enacted in 2009 and provided a complete exemption from CEQA for a proposed stadium development in the City of Industry.[a]
Los Angeles	NFL (numerous teams considered for relocation)	Proposed, never built	2011	AB 900 was enacted in 2011 and provided for an expedited CEQA process for "environmental leadership projects," which are defined as certain types of large-scale projects meeting specified heightened environmental standards and providing significant economic benefits.[b]
San Francisco	NBA Golden State Warriors	Constructed (Chase Center)	2011	This stadium utilized the partial exemption provided by AB 900 discussed above.
Sacramento	NBA Sacramento Kings	Constructed (Golden 1 Center)	2013	SB 743 was enacted in 2013 and provided for an expedited CEQA process for certain types of transit-served infill development projects.[c]
Inglewood[d]	NBA Los Angeles Clippers	Currently in construction (Intuit Dome)	2018	AB 987 was enacted in 2018 and provided for an expedited CEQA process specifically for the City of Inglewood sports and entertainment development based on the AB 900 procedures.[e]
Oakland	MLB Oakland A's	In litigation, construction not yet begun	2018	AB 734 was enacted in to was enacted in 2018 and for an expedited CEQA process specifically for the City of Oakland sports and mixed-use development based on the AB 900 procedures.[f]

Notes

a Cal. Gov't Code § 65701 (2010).

b Cal. Pub. Res. Code § 21178 (2011).

c Cal. Pub. Res. Code § 21168.6.6 (2014).

d Note that this Inglewood stadium is different from another stadium in Inglewood discussed below, the Rams stadium, which also avoided CEQA review, but through a different legal approach (using the ballot initiative process exemption).

e Cal. Pub. Res. Code § 21168.6.8 (2018).

f Cal. Pub. Res. Code § 21168.6.7 (2019).

essentially the same: Because the economic benefits of the projects allegedly outweigh potential environmental concerns and because legal challenges to the project could lead to years of delay (or entirely derail) the stadium, a lesser degree of environmental review under CEQA is warranted.[12] However, as numerous critics of stadium exemptions and other project-specific exemptions enacted by the state legislature have pointed out, this argument proves both too much and too little. As a former elected official in California noted: "[If] hospitals, police stations, freeways and all sorts of valuable projects manage to be built without the necessity of CEQA exemptions," why are stadiums exempted from complying "with the same environmental regulations that govern virtually all projects in California?" (as cited in Pettit, 2009, para. 12). Furthermore, if an exemption or streamlined environmental review for a major league stadium is justified because the stadium results in economic benefits that outweigh potential environmental impacts, why aren't exemptions or streamlined reviews justified for other projects for which the same argument can be made (Biber, 2011)? The result of project-specific exemptions like those granted for stadium developments is an uneven playing field; as a *Los Angeles Times* columnist observed, the exemptions represent "another step toward two-tier government: One tier for the wealthy and well-connected, one for the rest of us" (Hiltzik, 2011, para. 22).

One possible response to such concerns might be that the relief from full compliance with CEQA provided by the legislative exemptions for stadiums is relatively modest and does not eliminate any of the major steps in the environmental review process under CEQA. For example, some of the legislative exemptions identified in Table 5.1 below require that any lawsuits challenging the stadium project under CEQA be filed in the state Court of Appeal, rather than in Superior Court, as well as fast-track judicial review of those challenges by imposing a time limit (varying by specific legislative exemption, but generally from approximately six to nine months) for courts to issue a decision. While less far-reaching than the full CEQA exemption granted to the City of Industry stadium proposal, such partial exemptions nonetheless have the potential to undercut CEQA's goals of public participation and ensuring environmental considerations are incorporated into governmental decision-making: Appellate court litigation is typically more complex and expensive than trial court litigation, and requiring courts to fast-track decisions regarding the adequacy of EIS documents that often span thousands of pages may lead to rushed decisions on complex scientific issues.

This is not to say that CEQA reform is not needed: as noted above, there have been calls for streamlining CEQA not only from critics but also from supporters of the law. But piecemeal, project-specific exemptions like those granted to stadiums not only fail to provide needed comprehensive reform, but also fail to reflect the actual environmental impacts projects may have. As Berkeley Law Professor Eric Biber has explained:

> Once you start exempting specific projects, you create a political dynamic where other project proponents want those exemptions—and eventually the only projects that are covered by CEQA are politically unpopular ones (or

82 Kellen Zale

more accurately, projects that don't have politically powerful sponsors). But of course, there's no reason to assume that the projects that are exempted from CEQA really are more environmentally beneficial than the ones that aren't.

(Biber, 2017, para. 1)

A summary of the stadium projects in California that have received legislative exemptions from CEQA is provided in Table 5.1. The projects are listed chronologically, from oldest to most recent. At the time of publication, several of these stadium projects have been completed or are currently in construction; one is currently being litigated and construction has not yet begun; and one was never built due to a competing stadium being built instead.

CEQA's Ballot Box Loophole

A second approach utilized by stadium developments in California to avoid environmental review under CEQA has been through a statutory exemption in CEQA for the voter-sponsored ballot initiative process (the "ballot box loophole"). Under CEQA, any type of voter-sponsored ballot initiative is not considered a "project"; and since by definition, CEQA only applies to "projects," voter-sponsored ballot initiatives are thus completely exempt from environmental review under CEQA. This is the case whether the ballot measure is adopted by voters through an election or if it is adopted by a local legislative body without holding an election (which California election law authorizes).[13] Thus, if a stadium project is approved through the voter-sponsored ballot initiative process—either as a result of an election or as a result of the local legislative body adopting the measure without an election—CEQA is completely inapplicable, even though the exact same project would be subject to full environmental review under CEQA if it went through the normal land use approval process (Zale, 2013, p. 851).

The underlying legal reasoning as to why the ballot box loophole exists is complicated and has been addressed in more detail elsewhere by this author, but essentially, the ballot box loophole stems from certain statutory provisions in CEQA exempting ministerial actions from environmental review and the interpretation the California courts have given to those statutory provisions, as well as the courts' expansive interpretation of the initiative power[14] and conclusions regarding the incompatibility of environmental review under CEQA with certain provisions of state election law.[15]

The use of the ballot box loophole to circumvent the environmental review that would otherwise be required under CEQA has been criticized by this author and others (Addison, 2019; Biber, 2017; Hiltzik, 2011; Rainwater & Stephenson, 1998; Zale, 2013, 2016). With regard to exempting ballot measures adopted by voters in an election, while there are statutory language and policy considerations that provide the legal basis for the exemption, there are competing arguments that the exemption is not justified (Zale, 2013).[16] Particularly because the initiative process is supposed to put voters in the position of legislators, the fact that the ballot box loophole results in voters being deprived of information about the environmental impacts of a proposal that legislators would have thanks to CEQA, undercuts the goals of both CEQA and the initiative process:

> [T]o truly achieve the initiative's goals of empowering citizen lawmakers, voters should have access to the same information about environmental impacts that legislators have … [particularly since] NEPA and state environmental protection acts, such as CEQA, were enacted precisely because lawmakers were failing to consider the environmental impacts of their decisions in the absence of a legal mechanism to force them to do.
>
> *(Zale, 2013, pp. 863, 869)*

The exemption for legislative adoption of proposed ballot initiative proposals without any election even being held is even more normatively problematic, since it raises concerns about minority rule being used to evade environmental review. This is because all that is required for a voter-sponsored ballot measure to be certified for the ballot is signatures from a mere 15% of the jurisdiction's eligible voters. Once certified, the local legislative body can adopt the ballot measure without actually ever holding an election, and thereby completely avoid CEQA (despite the fact this is the very same legislative body whose decisions would be subject to CEQA if it had approved the project through the normal legislative or administrative process).

Three stadium projects in California (summarized in Table 5.2) have utilized the ballot box loophole to legally avoid CEQA; two of these stadiums have been constructed, while one was never built due to a competing stadium being

TABLE 5.2 Stadium Projects Using Ballot Box Loophole

Location	League and Team	Status	Citizen-sponsored Ballot Initiative	
			Year Adopted	*Method of Adoption (Election or Council Action)*
Santa Clara	NFL San Francisco 49ers	Constructed (Levi's Stadium)	2010	Council action
Carson	NFL (numerous teams considered for relocation)	Proposed, never built	2015	Council action
Inglewood	NFL Los Angeles Rams	Constructed (SoFi Stadium)	2015	Council action

84 Kellen Zale

constructed instead. Notably, all of these stadium proposals utilized the ballot box loophole without an actual election by voters; in all three cases, the local legislative body adopted the proposed ballot initiative without an election.

Conclusion

This chapter has aimed to provide an overview of SEPAs and examine what these types of laws can—and cannot—do to respond to environmental justice concerns in the context of stadium developments. While the analysis has highlighted limitations of SEPAs—both in terms of the tensions in using laws designed to address overall adverse environmental impacts to also try to address distributional consequences and in terms of stadiums' legal avoidance of environmental review under California's CEQA through legislative exemptions and the ballot box loophole—SEPAs nonetheless remain one of the more robust sources of existing legal authority to address negative environmental impacts of major developments in the built environment such as stadiums. As such, they are an important legal (and political) lever for advancing environmental justice goals related to stadium projects in states with these laws.

Notes

1 Another legal tool that can provide a lever for addressing environmental justice concerns associated with stadium developments are community benefits agreements (CBAs). These are contracts between a developer and local organizations representing residents which can be used to address a variety of issues, including environmental concerns. However, unlike state SEPAs—which a stadium development will be mandatorily subject to if they fall under the applicable jurisdictional parameters—entering into a CBA is typically optional for a developer and whether a developer decides to enter into a CBA often turns on reputational concerns and the extent of political leverage opponents have (Been, 2010).

2 Environmental justice litigation is also possible under federal civil rights laws, such as Title VI of the Civil Rights Act (which prohibits recipients of federal funds from discriminating on the basis of race and other protected categories), but the Supreme Court has limited the circumstances under which such lawsuits would likely be successful (Gerrard & Foster, 2008).

3 For example, if a stadium were to require infill of wetlands designated under the CWA, or affect habitat deemed critical to a listed species under the ESA.

4 Citations are not provided here since there is a vast amount of legal literature, as well as media commentary, on this issue, particularly with respect to California's CEQA. For example, a Google search for "CEQA reform" brings up nearly 100,000 results, while a Lexis Nexis search for "CEQA or SEPA or NEPA and reform" brings up nearly 7,000 secondary sources in that database.

5 Even in states without this type of SEPA, traditional local land use regulation, such as zoning and site plan review, may serve as a legal mechanism for addressing certain types of environmental impacts (Nolon, 2003).

6 In the case of most major stadium developments, since the applicant is typically applying for land use approvals (such as rezoning or variances or site plan review, or all of the above), the initial assessment is submitted to and reviewed by the respective government entity tasked with approval decision (which will typically be a local legislative

Stadiums and State Environmental Policy Acts 85

body such as the city council or county commission, or a local administration agency, such as the zoning board of appeals or planning and zoning commission).

7 If multiple approvals are required for the developer's project from different governmental entities, SEPAs typically contain provisions for designating one of them as the lead agency.

8 Cal. Public Resources Code § 21068.

9 Cal. Pub. Res. Code § 21002.

10 N.Y. Envtl. Conserv. Law § 8–0109(8).

11 From 2013 to 2016, "the estimated rate of litigation for all CEQA projects undergoing environmental review (excluding exemptions) was 0.7%" (1 out of every 100 projects; Smith-Heimer et al., 2016, p. ii).

12 In addition, some of the legislative exemptions include requirements that the developer takes specified actions intended to be environmentally beneficial (such as installing electric charging stations in the stadium parking lot) in order to qualify under the exemption. See AB 987: Cal. Pub. Res. Code § 21168.6.8.

13 Tuolumne Jobs & Small Business Alliance v. Superior Court, 330 P.3d 912, 921 (Cal. 2014; "CEQA review is not required before direct adoption of an initiative, just as it is not required before voters adopt an initiative at an election").

14 While some states with SEPAs (such as Washington state) do not allow land use decisions to be made via voter initiative process, in California, voters have the power to enact land use decisions via ballot initiative (such as planning and zoning approvals of a stadium project requires). DeVita v. Cnty of Napa, 889 P.2d 1019, 1027 (Cal. 1995; "If doubts can [be] reasonably resolved in favor of the use of [the] reserve initiative power, courts will preserve it").

15 CEQA only applies to "projects," which the California courts defined as (i) discretionary actions (ii) undertaken or approved by a government entity (iii) that may result in physical change to the environment. Stein v. City of Santa Monica, 168 Cal. Rptr. 39, 39 (Ct. App. 1980). Adoption of a voter-sponsored ballot initiative is not considered a "project," regardless of whether it is adopted by voters through an election or by a local legislative body without holding an election; the former approach does not involve any discretionary action by a governmental entity (only voters), while the latter approach, despite involving a governmental entity, does not involve discretionary action, since the decision to adopt the ballot measure directly without holding an election is considered "the functional equivalent of the city's only other option—certifying it for the ballot and submitting it to a vote of the people" (Zale, 2013, p. 863)—and thus a ministerial one.

16 Statutory language in CEQA defines projects as discretionary governmental actions, which if literally interpreted, can be understood to not include voter-sponsored ballot initiatives (which is how the California courts have interpreted it). Stein v. City of Santa Monica, 168 Cal. Rptr. 39 (Ct. App. 1980); DeVita v. Cnty of Napa, 889 P.2d 1019 (Cal. 1995). However, as this author has argued elsewhere, if this statutory language is understood in the context of CEQA's goals, it does not necessarily foreclose such measures from being considered within the scope of CEQA: "CEQA's focus is on the underlying activity that may adversely impact the environment: the end result permitted by that piece of paper. Regardless of whether that end result is brought about by the 'granting … of a piece of paper' or the outcome of a citizen vote, … it should be considered a project to which CEQA applies … Using the discretionary action of a public agency as a trigger for CEQA applicability simply provides a practical way to get at the underlying activities. If the same underlying activities would result from something other than the discretionary action of a public agency (i.e., from an initiative election), then that action should also be considered within CEQA's scope, and the definition of 'project' should be adjusted accordingly" (Zale, 2013, pp. 855, 859).

86 Kellen Zale

References

Abdul-Kahbir, L. (2018, September 25). *From Chavez Ravine to Inglewood: How stadiums facilitate displacement in Los Angeles.* Law Meets World, UCLA Law Review. https://www.uclalawreview.org/from-chavez-ravine-to-inglewood-how-stadiums-facilitate-displacement-in-los-angeles/

Addison, B. (2019, March 17). *How sports stadiums circumvent environmental laws to streamline their way to reality.* Longbeachize. https://lbpost.com/longbeachize/addison-stadiums-gentrification-environmental-laws-ceqa/

Arnold, C. (1998). Planning Milagros: Environmental justice and land use regulation. *Denver University Law Review, 76*(1), 1–153.

Been, V. (2010). Community benefits agreements: A new local government tool or another variation on the exactions theme? *University of Chicago Law Review, 77*(1), 5–35.

Biber, E. (2011, September 11). *A dangerous bill.* Legal Planet. https://legal-planet.org/2011/09/11/a-dangerous-bill/

Biber, E. (2017, September 7). *The CEQA exemption that ate LA.* Legal Planet. https://legal-planet.org/2017/09/07/the-ceqa-exemption-that-ate-la/

Bonorris, S. & Targ, N. (2010). Environmental justice in the laboratories of democracy. *Natural Resources & Environment, 25*(2), 44–49. https://www.jstor.org/stable/40925257

CEQA Portal. (2020a, February 2). *CEQA exemptions.* https://ceqaportal.org/tp/CEQA%20Exemptions%20Paper%202020%20Update.pdf

CEQA Portal. (2020b, December 18). *Cumulative impacts.* https://ceqaportal.org/tp/CEQA%20Exemptions%20Paper%202020%20Update.pdf

Council on Environmental Quality. (n.d.). *State and local jurisdictions with NEPA-like planning requirements.* https://ceq.doe.gov/laws-regulations/states.html

Fleming, J. R. (2002). Justifying the incorporation of environmental justice into the SEQRA and permitting processes. *Albany Law Environmental Outlook Journal, 6*(2), 55–88.

Freij, L. (2022). Centering environmental justice in California: Attempts and opportunities in CEQA. *Hastings West Northwest Journal of Environmental Law and Policy, 28*(1), 75–110.

Gerrard, M. B. & Foster, S. R. (Eds.). (2008). *The law of environmental justice: Theories and procedures to address disproportionate risks* (2nd ed.). American Bar Association.

Grant, Jr., T. J. (2014). Green monsters: Examining the environmental impact of sports stadiums. *Villanova Environmental Law Journal, 25*(1), 149–176.

Gosalvez, E. (2020, November 6). *Sport and the environment: What is the connection?* NC State University. https://cnr.ncsu.edu/news/2020/11/sport-and-the-environment-what-is-the-connection/

Hiltzik, M. (2011, September 13). California special exemption for NFL stadium plan not so special. *Los Angeles Times.* https://www.latimes.com/business/la-xpm-2011-sep-13-la-fi-hiltzik-20110914-story.html

Hsiao, P. & Jeffers, J. (2012). *Environmental justice and environmental impact analysis—A California case study.* American Law Institute Course of Study – Environmental Law, ST038 ALI-ABA 673.

International Union for Conservation of Nature. (2019). *Mitigating biodiversity impacts of new sports venues.* https://portals.iucn.org/library/sites/library/files/documents/2019-004-En.pdf

Johnson, S. M. (1997). NEPA and SEPA's in the quest for environmental justice. *Loyola of Los Angeles Law Review, 30*(2), 565–606.

Moylan, M. (2019, November 19). U.S. *Bank stadium officials weigh options to reduce bird deaths.* Minnesota Public Radio News. https://www.mprnews.org/story/2019/11/15/us-bank-stadium-officials-weigh-options-to-reduce-bird-deaths

Nolon, J. (2003). In praise of parochialism: The advent of local environmental law. *Harvard Environmental Law Review, 26,* 365–416.

Pettit, D. (2009, September 9). *A stadium full of excuses.* National Resources Defense Council. https://www.nrdc.org/experts/david-pettit/stadium-full-excuses

Rainwater, J. & Stephenson, S. (1998). Too late in the game: How ballot measures undercut CEQA. *Golden Gate University Law Review, 28*(3), 399–428.

Ramo, A. (2013). Environmental justice as an essential tool in environmental review statutes: A new look at federal policies and civil rights protections and California's recent initiatives. *Hastings West-Northwest Journal of Environmental Law and Policy, 19*(1), 41–82.

Rechtschaffen, C., Gauna, E., & O'Neill, C. (2009). *Environmental justice: Law, policy & regulation* (2nd ed.). Carolina Academic Press.

Reducing sports' impact on the environment. (2013, December 13). *Knowledge at Wharton.* https://knowledge.wharton.upenn.edu/article/reducing-sports-impact-environment/

Smith-Heimer, J., Hitchcock, J., Roosa, P., & Guerrero, C. (2016). *CEQA in the 21st century: Environmental quality, economic prosperity, and sustainable development in California.* Rose Foundation for Communities and the Environment.

Yang, T. (2002). Melding civil rights and environmentalism: Finding environmental justice's place in environmental regulation. *Harvard Environmental Law Review, 26,* 1–32.

Youngblood, C. (2019). Put your money where their mouth is: Actualizing environmental justice by amplifying community voices. *Ecology Law Quarterly, 46*(2), 455–484. 10.15779/Z383J3919J

Zale, K. (2013). Changing the plan: The challenge of applying environmental review to land use initiatives. *Ecology Law Quarterly, 40*(4), 833–878. 10.15779/Z381R9F

Zale, K. (2016, January 19). *How the NFL ducked CEQA.* Law Professor Blogs Network. http://lawprofessors.typepad.com/environmental_law/2016/01/how-the-nfl-ducked-ceqa.html

PART II

Case Studies

6

STADIUMS, RACE, AND WATER INFRASTRUCTURE: FLOODING ON ATLANTA'S SOUTHSIDE

Marni Davis, Richard Milligan, and Andy Walter

Residents of Atlanta's Peoplestown and Summerhill neighborhoods, just south of the city's downtown, have suffered from regular localized floods for generations. Poor drainage, coupled with inadequate stormwater and sewer infrastructure, has exposed properties and people to untreated sewage. In 1908, W.E.B. Du Bois described the conditions of Black housing in this area, observing "much stagnant water, pools and the like, and an unfinished sewer system that masses of filthy sediment near these houses" (Du Bois, 1908, p. 59). In more recent times, residents in these neighborhoods complain that such problems have increasingly plagued the neighborhoods since the 1960s as a result of the construction of two massive sports stadiums in the area: first, the Atlanta-Fulton County Stadium, which was used by multiple professional teams from 1966 until it was razed by the city in 1997; followed by the Centennial Olympic Stadium, which was built for the 1996 Olympics, became a major league baseball stadium in 1997, and has most recently been retrofitted as a college football venue.

The effects of sport stadium construction were made exceedingly clear in July 2012, when heavy rains overwhelmed the local sewer system, and the streets directly east of the stadium experienced ponding and sewage overflow. The damage to neighborhood residents' homes led several to file complaints and lawsuits against the city (Leslie, 2014). These floods were an unpleasant repeat of a similar occurrence in 2009 when a devastating 500-year flood event devastated much of the Atlanta metro region. Investigative journalists from the *Atlanta Journal-Constitution* had pointed to "explosive development, poor planning, and neglected infrastructure," as well as a 20% increase in impervious surface over the previous decade, all of which "helped turn even unremarkable rainstorms into costly, property-wrecking events in metro Atlanta" (Vogell, 2010, para. 1).

The level of flooding experienced in the "stadium neighborhoods" on Atlanta's southside stem from inadequate planning and aging infrastructure. The majority of

DOI: 10.4324/9781003262633-8

residents in these neighborhoods are Black and working class; the flooding of city streets, and the attendant damage to homes, have thus disproportionately impacted populations that are most vulnerable to such events. According to one study, Black and Hispanic residents across the region of southeastern metro areas stretching from Charlotte to Atlanta are more disparately exposed to flood risk than low-income communities in general. The study points to Summerhill and Peoplestown as among the two most racially disproportionate areas of flood risk across this megaregion; both areas are in the headwaters of the South River, and both are adjacent to highways as well as downstream of stadium infrastructure. The study's author highlights the stadium neighborhoods of Summerhill and Peoplestown as a "noteworthy example of racial inequities in urban flood risk" (Debbage, 2019, p. 11).

These stadiums transformed their local environment, contributing to the instability of the surrounding neighborhoods in many ways. The presence of stadiums in a flood-prone section of the city—in neighborhoods that are also, in the majority, Black and poor—maps neatly onto our understanding of the history of race, class, and urban development. One might say that both sewer outflow *and* stadiums have frequently been dumped into urban areas also known for racialized poverty.

But a closer look at the history of Atlanta's southside stadium neighborhoods shows that the problem of flooding and sewage infrastructure predates the construction of the stadiums by many decades. In fact, this section of Atlanta was a site of contestation over race, infrastructure, and segregation dating back to its early development, more than a century ago. Originally a mixed-race and economically varied area, these streets were granted attention and resources by the city's power structure. But the area only accessed these resources when the residents demanding them were themselves part of the power structure. As the 20th century progressed, Atlanta's white elite moved away from the area, in part because of the sewer and other aging infrastructural elements; at the same time, the proportion of Black and economically disadvantaged residents grew.

While stadiums have exacerbated the flooding problem in southside neighborhoods, and they have inhibited fixes, it is their very siting that points to root causes. As this section of the southside came to be neglected by Atlanta's municipal officials, it became a locus of increased Black settlement and infrastructural deterioration, in a city increasingly segregated by both race and class. This created an urban space that city leaders and planners could identify as an appealing location for a stadium surrounded by massive paved parking lots. Therefore, if we are to understand the environmental damage Atlanta's southside stadiums have done to nearby Black communities, we must consider the central role that race and inequity have played in the historical process of Atlanta's urban development.

Part One: The Most Dangerous Sewer in Town

In 1895, when Ralph A. Sonn submitted his annual report as superintendent of Atlanta's orphanage for Jewish children, he pointed to several structural issues requiring immediate attention. Of particular concern to Sonn was the 400 feet of

FIGURE 6.1 Detailed view of Atlanta's southside neighborhoods in 1892. Hebrew Orphans' Home, identified by its large tower, can be seen just below Love St. The ravine and sewage tunnel are visible nearby. ("Bird's eye view of Atlanta, Fulton Co., State capital, Georgia" by Augustus Koch, Hughes Litho. Co., and Saunders and Kline, Library of Congress)

ravine that cut across the entire eastern half of the building's grounds (see Figure 6.1). It ran alongside the playground, he warned, and thus was not only an "eyesore" but also "constitute[d] a menace to life and limbs" for adventurous youngsters who ventured down the vertiginous slope and into the rocky stream. For Sonn, the ravine was a shameful presence on the Hebrew Orphans' Home property, "reproachingly staring at us" and demanding action (Sonn, 1895).

Superintendent Sonn had reason to be concerned, and not only because the ravine was unsightly, or the children in his care might clamber down and hurt themselves. The ravine in question was downstream from the Loyd Street sewer. In a city known for its inadequate wastewater system, this sewer had a particularly terrible reputation. The *Atlanta Constitution* called it "the most dangerous sewer" in town, and condemned city leaders for creating a network of open sewage ditches that ran through crowded neighborhoods, exposed residents to "the most dread diseases known to medical science," and undermined property values ("Foul Sewers," 1901, p. 9).

The Loyd Street sewer was initially constructed in the 1870s to move wastewater out of Atlanta's central business district. The sewer lines that ran through downtown originally ended at the district's southern border, dumping into a spring formed by the headwaters of Intrenchment Creek, a tributary of the South River watershed. The municipal sanitary commission had the spring bed widened and lined with rocks, in hopes that fecal matter, garbage, chemicals, and rotting animal carcasses would move quickly southward and not seep into the ground below. But the lining failed to prevent seepage, and when trash and waste caught on the rocks, the flow of sewage was blocked. On such occasions, as well as during heavy rains that caused the stream to overflow, the sewer's vile contents spilled out onto the street (Borden, 2014; Elmore, 2010).

Over the decades that followed, the area directly south of downtown Atlanta developed into a densely populated neighborhood. This section of the city's second ward was a mix of races and classes, owners and renters, native- and foreign-born—an unsegregated residential area typical of the turn-of-the-century urban South (Hanchett, 1998). Along some blocks it was quite fashionable: members of the city's white business and political elite bought properties on Pryor and Washington Streets, which ran parallel to the sewage culvert, and even on Loyd Street itself. (The city redesignated it Central Avenue in 1900, in recognition that the sewer's "unpleasant notoriety" had tarnished the street's name; "Street Matters," 1900.) Black residents in this part of the second ward were generally relegated to the back alleys of white residential streets, where they lived in squalid rental properties.

Proximity to the sewer was not without its advantages. Homeowners who could afford to install flush toilets might otherwise simply drain their household waste onto a nearby vacant property. Or they would terminate the drainage pipe in the alley behind their abode, wreaking havoc on the homes and health of Black residents. With an open sewer close by, flush toilets could be piped directly into the ditch. Some homeowners and neighborhood committees even widened or extended the sewage ditch at their own expense, without city oversight or regulation (Borden, 2014; Galishoff, 1985).

Though the Loyd Street sewer provided this minimal convenience, it was generally regarded as a smelly scourge and a health hazard. Jacob Haas, the real estate developer and banker turned city alderman who chaired the sewer committee, was acutely aware of the dangers it posed. Not only did he live a block away on Washington Street, but he had facilitated the purchase of the land lots on which the Hebrew Orphans' Home stood. Under his leadership, the city council regularly committed funds to the block-by-block improvement of its trunk sewers, even commissioning a nationally renowned civil engineer to redesign and modernize Atlanta's sewer plan (Elmore, 2010).

But these efforts always proved insufficient, as real estate development and population growth continually outpaced municipal response. In 1890, the city spent more than $12,000 extending and covering the Loyd Street sewer from downtown to Georgia Avenue, three-quarters of a mile south. Within a year, a dozen residents of the recently developed blocks surrounding the sewer's new mouth threatened to sue the city for damages, on the grounds that the fumes "brewed bad atmosphere" and the bacteria borne of the sewer's contents caused "sickness of a serious nature in our community" ("The Deadly Sewer," 1891, p. 2).

Both white and Black neighborhood leaders demanded better sewer infrastructure on the southside. In addition to the main Loyd Street sewer trunk that ran through the second ward, a parallel branch coursed southward in the third ward, several blocks to the east. Known as the Connally Street sewer, it dumped its contents into Summerhill, a mixed-class neighborhood that was one of the city's oldest Black residential settlements. In 1895, the sewer committee noted the many lawsuits for damages "caused by the foul condition of the open branch," and recommended that it be extended out of the crowded neighborhoods ("Work on Trunk Sewers," 1895, p. 5). By 1910, the Connally Street sewer had been expanded south and connected to the Loyd Street sewer at Atlanta Avenue, where that branch bent eastward. This put the new mouth of the sewer in an area just south of Summerhill that was mostly white, but where the number of Black residents was growing.

Despite the newly combined sewer's importance to neighborhood advocates of both races, their context prevented them from joining their efforts. White Atlantans increasingly sought to delineate and enforce racial boundaries in residential neighborhoods. After watching other southern cities undertake similar efforts, in 1913, Atlanta's city council approved a zoning ordinance legislating residential segregation by race. That law was soon declared unconstitutional; nevertheless, white city officials, urban planners, and real estate developers spent the next half century attempting to limit Black "encroachment" into neighborhoods that had been designated white (Lands, 2009; Silver & Moeser, 1995). As a result, debates about allocating funds to improve infrastructure and civic amenities would be inextricably intertwined with conflicts over race and neighborhood.

The problem of the Loyd Street sewer reemerged in the city's infrastructure debates in the early 1920s, after passage of a massive bond issue to finance improvements to waterworks, sewers, and public schools. During this same era, Atlanta's municipal leadership sought to impose yet another zoning plan on the city, with the explicit intent of keeping Black residents from moving into neighborhoods that had been designated white. Such race-based planning would be difficult to implement in older, mixed-race sections. Debates over a city block's past, present, and future racial makeup shaped discussions of infrastructure spending on the southside—especially those classified by the new zoning plan as racially "undetermined," as was the section south of Summerhill where the Loyd Street sewer terminated.

Among the new school facilities, the city proposed was an all-white girls' high school. In April 1922, the Board of Education voted 4–3 to purchase the Hebrew Orphans' Home property, as it was located centrally to white neighborhoods on the city's southside and accessible by multiple streetcar lines ("Board Approves," 1922). But within days of the announcement, the board members who had voted against the plan mustered their allies—including the principal of Girls' High, and several white southside neighborhood organizations—to publicize their collective concerns. In addition to being too small for the school's needs, they pointed out that this property was beset by a problematic sewer.

"Everybody knows," insisted one southside civic group, that the orphanage was a "catch basin" in an already "low and unhealthy section of Atlanta." Rainwater from the streets to the west drained onto the orphanage property, which flooded in wet weather "on account of the main sewer that passes entirely through the playgrounds" ("Orphanage Site," 1922, p. 6). A Board of Education member who had opposed the purchase of the orphanage concurred: "affidavits can be obtained from adjoining property owners," he declared, "that half of the property is completely inundated by water, sometimes two feet or more, the sewer system being inadequate during excessive rains" ("Bond Commissioners," 1922, p. 23).

In the end, Girls' High would be built two miles east, in a different southside neighborhood. Meanwhile, white residents of the second and third wards demanded that the bond funds be directed toward extending the Loyd Street sewer from its current terminus at Connolly and Atlanta to the city limits. They also asked the city to amend the proposed zoning plan, so that Black residential "encroachment" in the third ward would be prevented east of Connally Street—thereby increasing the probability that the area along these sewer lines would become majority Black ("Vote for Extension," 1922).

In the decades that followed, white Atlantans of economic means left the southside for the suburbs springing up in the north of the city, while growing numbers of middle-class Black Atlantans moved to the "Negro suburbs" being built on the west side. Though the southside neighborhoods they left behind remained racially mixed, the area fell into disrepair, a process that was hastened by its categorization as high risk for loans and investment. These streets continued to flood: in 1929, runoff from a springtime downpour knocked the Washington Street streetcar off its rails ("Inch of Precipitation," 1929); and in 1942, heavy rains flooded the same blocks that had concerned superintendent Sonn of the Hebrew Orphans' Home 50 years before ("Violent Hail," 1942). By 1950, the majority of dwellings in the census tracts through which the Loyd and Connolly sewers had flowed were decades old, renter-occupied, and lacking in modern plumbing facilities—all qualities that would lead to its being designated a "slum."

Part Two: The Greatest Site for a Sports Stadium

Atlanta Stadium opened on April 9, 1965, the first of two large stadiums constructed on a site between the historic Loyd and Connally sewers. Completed in a single year, the stadium's completion marked a milestone in a sweeping transformation of the neighborhoods immediately south of Atlanta's downtown. Two massive projects coalesced to dramatically alter the built environment and the social make-up of these neighborhoods. First, a limited-access highway corridor through the neighborhoods that had been conceived in the mid-1940s was mostly completed by the late 1950s. Multiple lanes of impervious road surface now formed the western borders of the Summerhill and Peoplestown neighborhoods, and a massive clover leaf interchange separated them from the downtown. Second, the city undertook "urban renewal" on a large tract that included land in these two neighborhoods and another adjacent to them called Mechanicsville. Authorized by the Housing Act of 1949, urban renewal involved the use of federal money for "slum clearance" to clear land for new and better housing. On this southside land, formally designated the Rawson-Washington Urban Redevelopment Area, the city accomplished the former and never the latter. Instead, Atlanta Stadium was constructed on the very portion of the redevelopment area that had been set aside for new housing since 1958 (see Figure 6.2) but remained un-rebuilt by 1962, when Atlanta Mayor Ivan Allen began

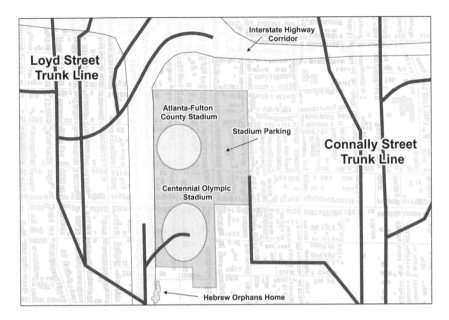

FIGURE 6.2 Present-day sewer lines, stadium footprints, and interstate highway corridor overlaid on 1930 Atlanta map of roads and buildings

to sell it to owners of Major League Baseball teams as "the greatest site for a sports stadium in America" (Bisher, 1966, p. 16).

Estimates of displacement resulting from interstate highway construction and urban renewal indicate that thousands of people were forced to relocate from the stadium neighborhoods between 1950 and 1970 (Keating, 2001). The impact in Summerhill was particularly dramatic, as 10,000 of 12,500 people were displaced by one estimate (Trutor, 2021). This displacement was, in fact, a primary goal of urban renewal, as city leaders sought to "protect" downtown from these neighborhoods where an increasing share of residents were Black, due both to white flight and Black in-migration (Keating, 2001). City planners maintained an ongoing series of maps that carefully charted changing "negro residential areas." A succession of these maps from the early 1950s to the late 1960s showed Black residential space steadily expanding in neighborhoods surrounding the downtown area on the east, west, and south sides. According to these maps, "negro expansion" was occurring in Rawson-Washington area and, specifically, across the site of the future stadium. Highway construction and urban renewal offered city leaders a means to dramatically alter this pattern. Thus, the plan for the Rawson-Washington area envisioned a low-density commercial and residential district, featuring new parks and housing for whites, forming a structural barrier between downtown and Black neighborhoods to the south. But lack of interest from developers and political resistance put this plan on hold. Thus, while the urban renewal plan never called for a stadium to serve as a buffer, Atlanta Stadium (soon to be renamed Atlanta-Fulton County Stadium) and its enormous parking lots served the intended purpose.

98 Marni Davis, Richard Milligan, and Andy Walter

Surrounded by large parking lots on three sides and an interstate highway on the fourth, Atlanta Stadium added thousands of square feet of impervious land cover in the stadium neighborhoods, especially Summerhill. The stadium exemplified the wave of modern-era stadiums built during the 1960s and early 1970s by which "sports space was untangled from dense urban neighborhoods and plopped into enormous parking fields" (Lisle, 2017, p. 100). Previously, stadiums of any size had been nestled, if not shoehorned, into the urban fabric, which typically resulted in unique and often peculiar shapes and sizes, new stadiums "dismissed the social and natural environments beyond [their] walls as if they weren't even there" (p. 58). Emancipated from the built environment, modern stadiums eschewed idiosyncrasy in their design in favor of symmetry. The moniker "concrete doughnuts" captured their distinguishing form and building material.

Arguably, however, the most important feature of modern stadiums was not their design but their promise to accommodate suburban fans with easy and plentiful automobile access and storage. Atlanta was suburbanizing rapidly during the 1960s as tens of thousands of people, mostly white, relocated themselves to new housing developments beyond city boundaries and increasingly distant from the urban core. In 1966, when the Braves made Atlanta Stadium the team's new home ground, the dominance of the automobile in linking fans to the stadium was immediately evident. An economic impact study completed by the Georgia Institute of Technology found that 81% of attendees arrived at the stadium by automobile during the stadium's first full year of use in 1966. Nearly half (46%) of those who attended a game traveled more than 10 miles to get to the stadium (Schaefer et al., 1967).

In 1990, the City of Atlanta was selected to host the 1996 Olympic Games. The city's bid included a plan to construct an 80,000-person stadium on the site of Atlanta-Fulton County Stadium's enormous south lot. Centennial Olympic Stadium would serve as the venue for the Games' opening and closing ceremonies and the track-and-field events, while Atlanta-Fulton County Stadium would host the baseball tournament. As planned, at the close of the Paralympic Games, which immediately followed the Olympic Games, Centennial Olympic Stadium was converted to a baseball stadium for the Braves, while Atlanta-Fulton County Stadium was demolished and replaced by a parking lot. Thus, the new stadium did not significantly expand the overall stadium-and-parking-lot footprint. During the stadium swap, city and Olympic planners failed to substantively address stadium-related nuisances experienced by neighborhood residences, and the environmental (among other) issues endured (Burns, 2013).

Part Three: Detaining Stormwater, Displacing Residents

At the close of the 20th century, the City of Atlanta was forced to confront sewage problems. In 1996, the Upper Chattahoochee Riverkeeper sued the City of Atlanta for violations of the Clean Water Act. The city's sewer system regularly spilled insufficiently treated sewage into neighborhood streams and creeks. These sewage overflows disparately impacted the predominantly Black neighborhoods on the west

FIGURE 6.3 Staging of the 1996 Paralympic Games at Centennial Olympic Stadium. Atlanta-Fulton County Stadium is visible beyond the outfield. (Photo by John Sherwell, Australian Paralympic Committee, http://paralympic.org/au/, is licensed under CC BY-SA 3.0)

side, downstream of the football and basketball stadiums, and those on the southside, downstream of soon to be demolished Atlanta-Fulton County Stadium and the newly constructed Centennial Olympic Stadium (Habersham, 2019; see Figure 6.3). The lawsuit resulted in a consent decree that required as much as $4 billion of infrastructure investments over the first 20 years of the 21st century to limit releases and spills of sewage (ICOWMTF, 2020; Klepal, 2016; Vogell, 2010).

Advocates for disproportionately impacted neighborhoods like Peoplestown and Summerhill pushed for this consent decree to require separation of the city's combined stormwater and sewage infrastructure. Despite this advocacy, the parties to the lawsuit—including the City of Atlanta, the Environmental Protection Agency, and the Riverkeeper—elected for a remedy with limited separation, leaving the combined sewage infrastructure largely intact and instead expanding storage capacities. Today, Summerhill and Peoplestown residents continue to live in a combined sewershed, where stormwater and sanitary sewage flow together underneath homes and roadways, frequently overwhelming the infrastructure and flooding houses (Rhone, 2020).

The interstate infrastructure and the stadium site, including the extensive parking lots, have greatly increased the volume and intensity of stormflows entering this combined sewer infrastructure (ICOWMTF, 2020). Whenever it rains, stormwater flows quickly from impervious surfaces into detention basins, storage tanks, and sewage lines. Today, the stadium, which has been purchased and redeveloped by Georgia State University (GSU), contributes a tremendous volume of stormwater flows into this combined system. When the combined flows exceed capacity, Peoplestown and Summerhill experience flooding that includes untreated sewage.

The combined sewage infrastructure and continuing overflows of insufficiently treated sewage also affect the communities farther downstream. When this infrastructure is not over capacity, the combined flows reach the Custer Avenue Combined Sewer Overflow (CSO) facility, just downstream of these neighborhoods. When combined flows are too much for this facility, however, minimally treated sewage is released into Intrenchment Creek, the tributary to the highly segregated upper South River watershed that the national American Rivers organization has highlighted as a prominent site of environmental injustice (American Rivers, 2021). The stormwater impact of stadium development greatly exacerbates sewer overflows in the headwaters of South River, and directly contributes to the environmental injustice of sewage flowing through a highly segregated, majority Black landscape.

In 2012, in response to several floods, the city took action to repair damaged homes. It also developed a plan to reduce area flooding and combined sewer spills. These efforts were codified in the Southeast Atlanta Green Infrastructure Initiative (SAGII). To contain some of the runoff, the city spent $20 million to install a 5.9-million gallon stormwater detention vault under the media lot of the stadium, the site of the ravine on the former Hebrew Orphans' Home property. In addition, the city spent another $15 million to install permeable pavers and bioswales for infiltrating stormwater before it enters the combined sewers (Habersham, 2019; Rhone, 2020). In 2014, under the SAGII, the city approved $66 million to purchase and raze 26 homes in a flood mitigation plan, and to install a park and a pond to control excess flooding (Wickert, 2016).

While the flood control and green infrastructure initiative was underway, and the city was trying to purchase two dozen homes just downstream of the stadium, the Atlanta Braves announced plans to relocate to a new stadium in Cobb County, 12 miles north. In 2014, GSU, in collaboration with Carter USA, a private developer, unveiled a $300-million proposal to purchase and revamp Turner Field into a football facility and mixed-use development that would expand the university's campus (Leslie, 2015a). Residents who had already suffered from the displacements and flooding impacts of previous stadium projects feared the new development plans would lead to further rounds of displacement. Their fear proved justified when the city passed an ordinance authorizing the use of eminent domain to acquire the properties of residents who refused to sell (Ashly, 2020). According to an analysis of Georgia's eminent domain law, "Atlanta's history of eminent domain is filled with instances of condemnation being used as a cover to displace entire neighborhoods" (Bowcott & Schwahn, 2018, p. 205).

With stark remembrance of previous rounds of displacement ushered in by the original stadium project and the Olympics, residents pushed back at the proposed GSU redevelopment and the SAGII projects requiring the demolition of two dozen homes. Nevertheless, by 2015, about 20 homeowners had agreed to sell. But several refused, including revered community leader, Mattie Jackson, who was then aged 93 and had lived on the boundary between Peoplestown and Summerhill all of her life (Bowcott & Schwahn, 2018; Leslie, 2015b). Three weeks after negotiations and bidding for the stadium purchase ended, in February 2015, the Atlanta Regional Commission provided a $212,000 grant to Atlanta for a Livable Centers Initiative study intended to include residents in a planning process to address the sewage and flooding problems (Blau, 2015). But many residents suspected that the LCI process was too little, too late. Refusing to be displaced, in October 2015, organizers delivered a petition with more than 5,000 signatures to City Hall and demanded a meeting with Mayor Kasim Reed (Leslie, 2015b). Pressure on the city, GSU, and Carter USA to negotiate a community benefits agreement mounted, and residents fought pressure to leave their homes for the stormwater detention park and pond.

Stadium neighborhoods continue to deal with the environmental injustices of flooding and sewage even as they fight to remain in their homes. As in the '60s and '90s, stadium redevelopment is again displacing Black communities despite organized resistance. In 2016, as several residents continued to fight for their homes, the city sued the residents who refused to leave and condemned three homes, and residents reported various intimidation tactics including parking police vehicles in front of their homes and trying to shut off utilities (Ashly, 2020). Lawsuits have been brought by four homeowners who argue that their homes have not been impacted by the flooding, and that their displacement is not required for the flood control projects, but they are still facing eminent domain, and while continuing to reside in their homes, they have lost property rights. In the spring of 2017, GSU and Carter evaded the demands for a binding community benefits agreement by splintering community organizations making collective demands, and instead negotiating with a subset of residents, resulting in an agreement to which many of the residents and organizations refused (Godwin, 2017a). Protest against the redevelopment swelled and protestors, including members of the Housing Justice League, set up an encampment, known as "tent city," at the stadium. After more than two months, with then-GSU President Mark Becker denigrating the backlash as merely a "publicity stunt," GSU police raided the encampment early in the morning, destroying and confiscating property, and dispersing the protestors (Godwin, 2017b). At another student-led sit-in in April that year, GSU police arrested five people, including four students, for protesting the university and developer's refusal to negotiate in good faith for a community benefits agreement (Tatum, 2017). Despite promises from current mayor Andre Dickens, several residents continue to face eviction through the city's claim to eminent domain. While the stormwater park and pond has been delayed, the stadium redevelopment has proceeded without a community benefits agreement, and intense gentrification has ensued.

Much as the highway and stadium infrastructure during mid-20th-century urban renewal displaced thousands of Black residents and stymied advocates for increased public housing, 21st-century stormwater and sewage projects are again displacing Black residents in the shadow of the redeveloped stadium. The investments in stormwater infrastructure are not only using eminent domain to push out historic residents but they are also coincident with extreme gentrification and insufficient efforts to guarantee

102 Marni Davis, Richard Milligan, and Andy Walter

affordable housing that is pushing out even more Black residents from these historic communities. Historic communities who have had to live with flooding and sewage problems greatly exacerbated by the early installments of the stadium site are now being displaced by the redevelopment of the stadium and the environmental gentrification that is spurned by the flood and sewage control projects, a pattern that has repeated in Black communities of Atlanta throughout the 21st century.

Conclusion

Today, the streams that once served as the Loyd and Connally Street sewers run underground through Summerhill and Peoplestown, and are obscured at street level. But the blocks surrounding the land where these historical trunk sewers once stood still feel their presence—especially when it rains, and stormwater runoff overwhelms the local drainage system, causing flooding and sewage overflow. Efforts are currently underway to mitigate flooding with retention ponds, increased greenspace, and permeable pavers; but these endeavors have coincided with the area's astonishingly rapid gentrification. The initial construction of the stadiums had crushed the surrounding neighborhoods; now, stadium redevelopment, among other factors, has resulted in skyrocketing property values, increased rent and property taxes, and, yet again, the possibility of displacement for low-income Black residents.

As is the case in many American cities, Atlanta's sports stadiums have exacerbated racial segregation and inequality. The history of Atlanta's southside stadium development, however, suggests that the infrastructural deficiencies in these neighborhoods, and the flooding they caused, were at first regarded as problems worth solving for the sake of the white property owners who lived there. Once those property owners had left, the city chose to pave over the problematic sewers, rather than replace them, building one stadium and then another atop it all. This account of Atlanta's southside stadiums, and the decisions that led to their construction despite the problems they would cause nearby residents, offers a window onto the historical processes that have culminated in racial inequity and environmental injustice.

References

American Rivers. (2021). *America's most endangered rivers.* https://www.americanrivers.org/wp-content/uploads/2021/04/MER2021_FINAL_Report_ReducedSize-1-1.pdf

Anguelovski, I., Cole, H. V. S., O'Neill, E., Baró, F., Kotsila, P., Sekulova, F., Pérez del Pulgar, C., Shokry, G., García-Lamarca, M., Argüelles, L., Connolly, J. J. T., Honey-Rosés, J., López-Gay, A., Fontán-Vela, M., Matheney, A., Oscilowicz, E., Binet, A., & Triguero-Mas, M. (2021). Gentrification pathways and their health impacts on historically marginalized residents in Europe and North America: Global qualitative evidence from 14 cities. *Health & Place, 72,* 102698. 10.1016/j.healthplace.2021.102698

Ashly, J. (2020, November 30). The Black residents fighting Atlanta to stay in their homes. *Al Jazeera.* https://www.aljazeera.com/features/2020/11/30/atlanta-gentrification

Bisher, F. (1966). *Miracle in Atlanta: The Atlanta Braves story.* The World Publishing Company.

Blau, M. (2015, December 11). Will residents actually have a say in the future of Turner Field? A mix of cautious optimism and hard-earned skepticism surrounds the planning process for the Ted. *Atlanta Magazine.* https://www.atlantamagazine.com/news-culture-articles/will-residents-actually-have-a-say-in-the-future-of-turner-field/

Board approves orphanage site for Girls High. (1922, April 26). *Atlanta Constitution,* 1.

Bond commissioners to inspect proposed sites. (1922, April 28). *Atlanta Journal,* 23.

Borden, S. (2014). *Thirsty city: Politics, greed, and the making of Atlanta's water crisis.* State University of New York Press.

Bowcott, A. M. & Schwahn, D. M. (2018). HB 434-Eminent Domain. *Georgia State University Law Review, 34*(1), 1–18. https://readingroom.law.gsu.edu/gsulr/vol34/iss1/9

Burns, R. (2013, June 21). The other 284 days. *Atlanta Magazine.* https://www.atlantamagazine.com/great-reads/turner-field-development/

City of Atlanta. (2014, October 6). Ordinance 14-O-1471. https://atlantacityga.iqm2.com/Citizens/Detail_LegiFile.aspx?ID=5327&highlightTerms=14-O-1471

The deadly sewer. (1891, September 23). *Atlanta Constitution,* 2.

Debbage, N. (2019). Multiscalar spatial analysis of urban flood risk and environmental justice in the Charlanta megaregion, USA. *Anthropocene, 28,* 100226. 10.1016/j.ancene.2019.100226

Department of Watershed Management. (2017, November). *Intrenchment and Sugar watershed improvement plan.* City of Atlanta. https://drive.google.com/file/d/1tillYR6seVSAAxBM5st_2YHiskuwykGQ/view

Department of Watershed Management. (2019, May). *South River watershed improvement plan.* City of Atlanta. https://drive.google.com/open?id=1V2K4NxI7HVrTLCIEsegKlYmcKBdFazKi

Du Bois, W. E. B. (1908). *The Negro American family.* The Atlanta University Press.

Elmore, B. (2010). Hydrology and residential segregation in the postwar South: An environmental history of Atlanta, 1865-1895. *The Georgia Historical Quarterly, 94*(1), 30–61.

Foul sewers menace life. (1901, November 17). *Atlanta Constitution,* 9.

Galishoff, S. (1985). Germs know no color line: Black health and public policy in Atlanta, 1900–1918. *Journal of the History of Medicine and Allied Sciences, 40*(1), 22–41. 10.1093/jhmas/40.1.22

Godwin, B. J. (2017a, April 26). Neighbors at odds over GSU-Turner Field agreement. *Atlanta Journal-Constitution.* https://www.ajc.com/news/local/neighbors-odds-over-gsu-turner-field-agreement/qVD5XK86kv3Z4rWUjMjjhK/

Godwin, B. J. (2017b, June 2). GSU police remove 'Tent City' from Turner Field. *Atlanta Journal-Constitution.* https://www.ajc.com/news/local/gsu-police-remove-tent-city-from-turner-field/1jiX0S2KNSzA3i9K36HRyO/

Habersham, R. (2019, October 15). Peoplestown residents to city: Fix our flooding problems. *Atlanta Journal-Constitution.* https://www.ajc.com/news/local/peoplestown-residents-city-fix-our-flooding-problems/vsejkIfuUuIVLfqQejn0VK/

Hagen, L. (2017, June 2). *GSU police clear activist tent city outside Turner Field.* WABE. https://www.wabe.org/gsu-police-clear-activist-tent-city-outside-turner-field/

Hanchett, T. W. (1998). *Sorting out the New South city: Race, class, and urban development in Charlotte, 1875–1975.* University of North Carolina Press.

Inch of precipitation adds to heavy total for month. (1929, May 28). *Atlanta Constitution,* 8.

The Intrenchment Creek One Water Management Task Force (ICOWMTF). (2020). *Intrenchment Creek one water management plan: Advancing equity and addressing flooding and combined sewer spills in the heart of Atlanta.* https://www.americanrivers.org/wp-content/uploads/2020/12/20201015_IC_OneWater_TaskForce_Report.pdf

Keating, L. (2001). *Atlanta: Race, class and urban expansion.* Temple University Press.

Klepal, D. (2016, May 10). Atlanta sewage spill fines get initial approval. *Atlanta Journal-Constitution*. https://www.ajc.com/news/local-govt--politics/atlanta-sewage-spill-fines-get-initial-approval/TewBi9p6XfdGLEImooBSdN/

Koch, A., Hughes Litho. Co., & Saunders and Kline. (1892). *Bird's eye view of Atlanta, Fulton Co., State capital, Georgia*. Library of Congress. https://www.loc.gov/item/75693189/

Lands, L. (2009). *The culture of property: Race, class, and housing landscapes in Atlanta, 1880-1950*. University of Georgia Press.

Leslie, K. (2014, May 23). For Turner Field neighbors, a time of cautious hope. *Atlanta Journal-Constitution*. https://www.ajc.com/news/local/for-turner-field-neighbors-time-cautious-hope/FCrFJoJd2P3ZgzjUFBKpyK/

Leslie, K. (2015a, August 13). Braves will exit Turner Field by Dec. 31, 2016. *Atlanta Journal-Constitution*. https://www.ajc.com/news/local-govt--politics/braves-will-exit-turner-field/icvsZ7ydLCuvjMqxtqMVmM/

Leslie, K. (2015b, October 6). Hold-outs in Peoplestown flooding plan to meet with Reed. *Atlanta Journal-Constitution*. https://www.ajc.com/news/local-govt--politics/hold-outs-peoplestown-flooding-plan-meet-with-reed/dldvwfdtuCXsIc4vC4iYzJ/

Lisle, B. (2017.) *Modern coliseum: Stadiums and American culture*. University of Pennsylvania Press.

Orphanage site opposed by civil organizations. (1922, April 30). *Atlanta Constitution*, 6.

Rhone, N. (2020, July 11). No simple solutions to stormwater challenges. *Atlanta Journal-Constitution*. https://www.ajc.com/news/local/simple-solutions-stormwater-challenges/lYZp17wxl67gV3DKYIW6LJ/

Schaefer, W. A., Houser, G. D., & Weinberg, R. A. (1967). *The economic impact of the Braves on Atlanta: 1966*. Industrial Management Center, Georgia Institute of Technology. http://allenarchive.iac.gatech.edu/items/show/10070

Silver, C. & Moeser, J. V. (1995). *Separate city: Black communities in the urban South, 1940–1968*. University Press of Kentucky.

Sonn, R. (1895). Superintendent's Report. *Hebrew Orphans Asylum Sixth Annual Report*, 73. Jewish Educational Loan Fund (Box 2, Folder 1), Cuba Family Archives at the Breman Jewish Museum, Atlanta, GA.

Street matters occupied council. (1900, August 21). *Atlanta Constitution*, 6.

Tatum, G. (2017, April 11). *Five arrested by GSU during sit-in protest for Turner Field CBA*. Atlanta Progressive News. https://atlantaprogressivenews.com/2017/04/11/five-arrested-by-gsu-during-sit-in-protest-for-turner-field-cba/

Trutor, C. (2021). *Loserville: How professional sports remade Atlanta—and how Atlanta remade professional sports*. University of Nebraska Press.

Violent hail and thunderstorm floods streets, disrupts traffic. (1942, March 16). *Atlanta Constitution*, 1.

Vogell, H. (2010). Failure to control storm water makes floods more likely. *Atlanta Journal-Constitution*. https://www.ajc.com/news/local/failure-control-storm-water-makes-floods-more-likely/MwghAnvbttZOiXuSfAxSjM/

Vote for extension of Lloyd St. Sewer. (1922, June 18). *Atlanta Constitution*, 5.

Wickert, D. (2016, May 25). Local governments struggle to prevent floods. *Atlanta Journal-Constitution*. https://www.ajc.com/news/local-govt--politics/local-governments-struggle-prevent-floods/2Cp0icFSzx7Fzg66Jybu8N/

Work on trunk sewers. (1895, January 7). *Atlanta Journal*, 5.

7

INTRACITY TEAM RELOCATION AND ENVIRONMENTAL JUSTICE IN BALTIMORE

Jessica R. Murfree and Walker J. Ross

Both the playing of sports as well as the business of sports have pronounced impacts on the natural environment (McCullough et al., 2020). Some of the ways in which sport changes the natural environment around it include altering landscapes to accommodate playing fields, constructing venues to host events, increasing transportation to competitions, requiring the consumption of resources, and creating harmful byproducts (e.g., waste, pollution, and other emissions). These effects burden the communities that host sport teams and events, but these impacts are not necessarily distributed equally. Some people and some communities have historically experienced more hardship than others as a result of the environmental impact of sport and will continue to do so as long as injustices exist. Baltimore, Maryland, offers a case of this unequal distribution of environmental impacts as a result of professional sport teams—particularly due to the relocation of the Baltimore Orioles and Ravens from predominantly White, suburban Baltimore to the city center, where the revitalization efforts will largely benefit White residents over the non-White residents in nearby neighborhoods. In this chapter, we explore the history of sport team intracity relocation and environmental discrimination in Baltimore. Additionally, we provide a discussion on what can be learned from examining this community.

Stadium Relocation in Baltimore

The history of sport in Baltimore spans multiple sports and events, from the glamour of the Preakness Stakes to the physicality of lacrosse. Still, perhaps no two sports represent the history of professional sport in Baltimore better than baseball and football. As home to the Baltimore Orioles of MLB and the Baltimore Ravens of the NFL, Baltimore has carved out its place in American sport history through the multiple World Series and Super Bowl championships that each club has won.

DOI: 10.4324/9781003262633-9

While the Orioles have maintained a presence in Baltimore since 1954, football has taken several forms in Baltimore. Before the Ravens moved from Cleveland to Baltimore in 1996, the Colts resided in Baltimore from 1953 (there were previous iterations of the Colts prior to this) through 1984, when the team infamously moved to Indianapolis overnight (Wilson, 2014). All three teams (Orioles, Colts, and Ravens) at one time or another played in and shared a home field, Memorial Stadium, which is one of the subjects of this chapter.

Opened in its final form in 1949, Memorial Stadium was a multipurpose venue built for hosting both football and baseball in the Ednor Gardens-Lakeside neighborhood of northeast Baltimore. This residential neighborhood is just outside of the city center of Baltimore, which was on trend for a time when many cities were building stadiums in suburban areas. It was a suitable host for both teams until then-Colts owner Robert Irsay began negotiations with the City of Baltimore improve to the venue or construct a new one. When those negotiations failed, Irsay moved the Colts overnight to Indianapolis in 1984, which rattled local politicians and citizens alike. Suffering from this loss of the Colts, local politicians immediately planned a new stadium in a former warehouse district and railyards in downtown Baltimore for the Orioles. This ballpark, Oriole Park at Camden Yards, opened in 1992 (Smith, 2001).

FIGURE 7.1 Baltimore Memorial Stadium. (Photo by James W. Rosenthal, Historic American Buildings Survey, Library of Congress)

FIGURE 7.2 Oriole Park at Camden Yards. (Photo by Chris6d is licensed under CC BY-SA 4.0)

The NFL returned to Memorial Stadium in 1996, when Cleveland Browns owner Art Modell relocated the franchise to Baltimore as the Ravens. After two seasons, the Ravens opened a new downtown stadium next to Oriole Park at Camden Yards. The Orioles and Ravens still occupy these stadiums today, while Memorial Stadium was finally demolished in 2002 after several years of abandonment.

The Orioles and Ravens moved approximately 3.5 miles from the Ednor Gardens-Lakeside neighborhood to downtown Baltimore. Their moves followed a trend of professional sports teams relocating from the suburban outskirts to new facilities in the hearts of cities (Schneider, 2018). The moves in Baltimore were largely touted as being the result of the declining status of Memorial Stadium as well as a desire to keep Baltimore as a major sport city (Smith, 2001). Many teams might suggest that their intracity stadium moves are due to accessible land, desired economic opportunities, or locations closer to fanbases, but it is possible that these stadium moves are also partially the result of environmental discrimination (Banzhaf et al., 2019). The remainder of this chapter explores this concept in the case of the Orioles, Ravens, and the city of Baltimore.

Civil Rights and Baltimore

From the 1830s, when both enslaved and free people of color shared the community, to 2015 protests outside of Oriole Park after the murder of Freddie Gray

(Johnson, 2015), Baltimore has been influenced by movements for civil rights throughout its history. The city saw decades of segregation and social injustice, both *de jure* and *de facto*, via Jim Crow laws, redlining of Black residents, and gentrification (Olson, 1997). In the 1960s and 1970s, White residents fled the city, resulting in Black residents comprising the majority of the population. Yet, during this period, Black residents represented less than 30% of city council membership (Pietila, 1979). Black residents constantly fought discriminatory policies and practices. Over time, Black residents in Baltimore did have victories in their long fight for civil rights through national-level policy changes in the form of the *Brown v. Board of Education* Supreme Court decision and the passage of the Civil Rights Act of 1964, but this fight was never completely over. Unfortunately, many Black households still experience deep economic and social inequity today.

There are numerous specific examples of discrimination in public life over the course of Baltimore's history in schools, housing, policing, and employment. These elements of racial discrimination actively contribute to the environmental injustices in Baltimore. A few examples related to environmental injustice are worth highlighting for this chapter. Highway projects touted to bring urban renewal and economic activity to Baltimore disproportionately displaced and segregated Black neighborhoods, as did other highway projects across the United States (Archer, 2021). This not only destroyed these neighborhoods, but it also placed a pollution burden upon these neighborhoods located so close to busy highways. Proximity to traffic is considered an indicator of environmental justice from the U.S. Environmental Protection Agency (EPA).

Discrimination also existed in many areas of sport and recreation, including access to parks, playgrounds, basketball courts, tennis courts, pools, and beaches. For example, Black golfers were limited in their access to courses or even barred completely (Wells et al., 2008). Citywide protests and lawsuits in the 1940s and 1950s led to courts overturning Baltimore policies on racial segregation in parks and pools (Wiltse, 2009). Indeed, the history of Baltimore is very much a history of discrimination and the fight against this discrimination. With this history in mind, we can begin to take a deep dive into the concept of environmental discrimination within this community.

Environmental Discrimination and Injustice in Baltimore

Ultimately, societal factors that altered the landscape of the city of Baltimore, including their major teams' movement within the city, have resulted in further racial discrimination. As seen through the Civil Rights Movement, where there is racial discrimination of any kind, there are social and environmental injustices. White flight (and perhaps White return, as defined below), the gentrification of the city's neighborhoods, and environmental racism all have ties to the Orioles' and Ravens' short-distance relocation and contribute to such injustice. As detailed in the sections below, these byproducts of historical racial segregation have resulted in increased environmental discrimination.

The Round Trip of White Flight

White flight refers to the large-scale migration of White people from urban to suburban areas in the 1950s–70s, coinciding with the American Civil Rights movement. The term "flight" denotes how suddenly and swiftly the movement to the suburbs took place, as more and more Black and Brown people came to reside and work in city centers. By the 1970s, the White majority in the heart of Baltimore had dissipated (Short, 2006). Across the United States, Black populations' "Great Migration" inward to the heart of metropolitan cities from more rural areas was simply a byproduct of opportunity. Elements of the perfect storm that produced the explosion in Baltimore's Black population included White affluence and residential mobility, a decline in European immigration due to the World Wars, and plenty of available manufacturing and transit jobs that brought more appeal than agricultural labor (Cassie, n.d.; Depro et al., 2015; Frey, 1980).

The end of World War II saw industrial epicenters like Baltimore surge in economic productivity, a time when business and political leaders in the area hunted for major-league sport franchises to echo such growth. However, Miller (1992) wrote, "After the war, middle-class whites had accelerated their flight to the suburbs. With them went industry, jobs, and a large proportion of the city's tax revenues" (p. 188). As a simultaneous consequence, Baltimore's opportunities for employment siphoned more Black people into the city while also experiencing more poverty, crime, and racial tension. The search for major-league teams to compete in Baltimore was viewed explicitly as a way to invest in, revitalize, and improve the city's appearance, or in more certain terms, bring wealthy White people back—and it did.

More recently, the selective nature, or freedom, of White mobility in the United States has seen a return to city centers, which is mirrored in today's urban gentrification and discussed in the next section (Zapatka & Beck, 2021). In fact, we suggest that like White flight, there is a more recent phenomenon we will call *White return*: as the heart of Baltimore's Black population declines, the affluent White millennial population rises (Yeip, 2015). By 2010, and as Baltimore's entire population diminished, White Americans made up less than 30% of Baltimore's population (U.S. Census Bureau, 2010). However, the ones returning, perhaps inpouring, are White millennials. Specifically, Baltimore is seeing a resurgence in young (mid-20s and 30s), educated, White people who move for work and can afford the luxury apartments in places where industries once stood (Zhang, 2019). Referred to as a "disappearing act" by David McFadden (2018) for the Associated Press, Baltimore's Black roots are steadily deteriorating. Likewise, Michael Snidal (2017) of Baltimore's Citizens Planning and Housing Association, Inc. (CPHA) penned an op-ed to the *Baltimore Sun* calling for the city to enforce and uphold equitable policies to combat "reverse migration" (para. 3) and "Black flight" (para. 1).

Gentrifying Baltimore and Losing Baltimoreans

Typically, the gentrification process leads to communities, neighborhoods, or entire cities displacing groups of people. More often than not, that exchange has been lower socioeconomic communities for wealthier communities. Given the overlap of socioeconomic status and race in America, that exchange is also traditionally poorer, marginalized, communities of color for more affluent White communities. This mirrors Baltimore's desire to *revitalize* the city with the attraction of major-league sports. However, the actions to gentrify Baltimore's neighborhoods are characterized as upgrading and rejuvenation (McFadden, 2018). Yet, compared to other gentrified cities in the United States, Baltimore is fairly unique. Where most cities gentrify and displace communities of color, mostly White neighborhoods in Baltimore are the ones being gentrified—a commitment to continuously invest in White communities, people, schools, and businesses (Meehan, 2019). Not only does this uphold segregated norms of decades past but it also attracts wealthier White people to already predominantly White neighborhoods.

In some regards, gentrification is seen as a good, necessary thing. Often, gentrification leads to increased home values, education rates, and income levels, all considered positive community factors (Mullenbach & Baker, 2020). For example, the Abell Foundation, a Baltimore organization dedicated to social, economic, and environmental preservation, contrasted gentrification with neighborhood decline despite acknowledging Baltimore's racial, political, and economic polarization (Mallach, 2020). Yet, the close association of gentrification with race, and frankly the optics of that association, are largely why it is such a contested issue. Since the acquisition of major-league football and baseball teams, Baltimore's city leadership has given numerous indications that the goal of investment has been in White communities and for White people. As opposed to actively displacing families belonging to minoritized racial groups and marginalized socioeconomic groups, Baltimore's gentrification deliberately attracts younger White professionals who are flocking into the city (Zhang, 2019).

As discussed, (un)intentional racial segregation practices are maintained so long as the same patterns of gentrification persist. This also helps us explain why more and more Black and Brown families are leaving the Baltimore area altogether (Zhang, 2019). It is no surprise that Baltimore's census data is seeing a decline in poorer White families, Black individuals and families, and Latinx individuals and families (Mallach, 2020). Even in an era post legal racial segregation, urban planning decisions still contribute to racially divided trends, team relocations included. City decision-making around where to build major-league stadiums—which includes decisions on where to develop and invest money in supporting the teams—illustrates these practices. Additionally, race-based decision-making disguised as renewing or upgrading neighborhoods propagates environmental justice issues where a city's major sport teams and venues attract and follow the movement of its affluent residents and employers. That is why Camden Yards, formerly industrial warehouses and railyards, and today's home of the Orioles and Ravens, is credited as being the site of Baltimore's urban *revival*, a "strategic hamlet of gentrification and displacement … a [cathedral] to economic and racial apartheid" (Zirin, 2015, para. 4).

Yesterday's Discrimination Leading to Today's Injustices

Through the Great Depression and both World Wars, American sports grew as a refuge for participators and spectators alike. These are some reasons why sport in the United States remains so revered and essential to American culture. The once-booming Black urban population of 1940s Baltimore saw the cultural amplification of Negro Leagues baseball and the murmurings of a soon-to-be integrated Major League as a hopeful forecast of upward mobility and equality (Leffler, 1992). Memorial Stadium brought such hopeful excitement to the city: a new, multiuse football and baseball park to rival other large sport markets like New York City and Philadelphia. However, Black baseball teams and fans were often priced out of competing at Memorial Stadium, and still had to find other opportunities for equitable play. The alternative for Black baseball enthusiasts and the Negro Leagues' Black Sox was an additional stadium, Maryland Baseball Park, located in a rocky, unlit area that was either expensive to commute to or unsafe to walk to (Leffler, 1992). The former Maryland Baseball Park site is just a few blocks away from M&T Bank Stadium, the current home of the Baltimore Ravens.

When the Orioles and Ravens relocated to their respective parks at Camden Yards in the mid-1990s, after the Ravens spent just two seasons at Memorial Stadium, the plot that remained sat empty for four years. This abandonment coincided with the demographic shift in the neighborhoods surrounding Memorial Stadium, that is, *White return*. Eventually, the stadium was demolished, and the area was transformed into many things, including senior-living apartment complexes, a YMCA, a predominantly Black all-girls high school with a history of police brutality ("Eastern High School," 1970), and portions of Johns Hopkins University and medical centers (Kelly, 2021). Additionally, the area had places for dining, shopping, and business, among others.

Today, the area where Black Baltimoreans were discouraged from occupying space and playing baseball is now almost fully a retirement community with plans for a new $15.3-million hospice care center (Kelly, 2021). How a city landscape changes over time helps explain the environmental injustices that remain. For example, Memorial Stadium-area neighborhoods fall in the 80–90th percentiles on the EPA's People of Color Population Index. Likewise, the Memorial Stadium site falls in the 95–100th percentiles on their Environmental Justice Demographic Index, which accounts for a cumulative score for areas' low-income and minority percentages. On the contrary, the Camden Yards site, where the Orioles and Ravens currently compete, sits at the 60th-and-below percentiles on the People of Color Index and between the 60–90th percentiles on the Demographic Index (U.S. Environmental Protection Agency, 2021).

Areas experiencing urban and economic blight are the spaces that historically need more safe, well-lit, affordable, and accessible greenspaces for sports, recreation, and leisure activities (Floyd & Johnson, 2002; Mullenbach & Baker, 2020). An opportunity to build and invest in such space existed as Memorial Stadium began to deteriorate structurally. When Memorial Stadium was thriving, Black Baltimoreans could neither live in the area nor play baseball there. Due to the teams' relocation and the area shifting to a predominantly Black neighborhood, the opportunity for accessible sport and recreation was short-lived as the area became used for other purposes (Noor et al., 2021). For example, access to the YMCA sport and recreation services requires a paid membership.

In the case of Baltimore, it becomes easy to see how communities bearing disproportionate burdens of harmful environmental effects are affected by teams' intracity relocation. Essentially, a wake of injustice can be left by this movement. Ultimately, centuries of racially discriminatory practices contributed to the environmental injustices accentuated by the Orioles and Ravens moving to Camden Yards. As mentioned, there is a myriad of reasons why professional sport teams relocate. Regardless of their intentions, there are greater, observable socioenvironmental symptoms of team and venue relocation that mirror and accentuate historical discrimination practices in the United States still to this day. For example, the lasting effects of racial segregation ordinances still led to minimal neighborhood integration in Baltimore (Yeip, 2015). Likewise, Boone and colleagues (2007) explored environmental injustices related to the distribution of parks and greenspaces in Baltimore and found the neglected and developed areas remain split along historical, racial boundaries. These boundaries are well-defined in Baltimore and are referred to as the "Black butterfly and the White 'L'"—indicative of the two shapes made on the map of Baltimore by over a century of racism in the city's policies and government (Brown, 2016). To this day, despite some line-blurring, the butterfly and L shapes persevere (Yeip, 2015).

Remaining outcomes of a racially segregated Baltimore contribute to extensive environmental injustices beyond team relocation. For example, White neighborhoods in Baltimore benefit from concentrated tax increment financing (or TIF) that brings hundreds of millions of dollars to those areas, public schools with greater access to resources, areas protected from highways and major polluters, and access opportunities such as bikeshares and greenways (Brown, 2016). Likewise, Black neighborhoods are often under-resourced, redlined, food deserts plagued by police brutality.

Environmental Injustice via Urban Decay and Renewal

One of the observed impacts of the intracity relocation of the Orioles and Ravens is the notion of urban decay and gentrification around the stadium itself and subsequent environmental changes. Urban decay is considered to be when a functioning city or part of a city begins to lose functional ability (Grogan & Proscio, 2001). It is often marked by population decline, loss of jobs, instability, increased pollution, deterioration of buildings and infrastructure, and a general decrease in the quality of life. Additionally, it is associated with the previously mentioned White flight. Addressing urban decay requires urban renewal: investing in the construction of homes, businesses, and other projects through targeted investment to bring economic stability to an area (Caves, 2004). However, decision-making regarding such investment often highlights existing social and environmental inequities. Urban renewal often creates gentrification that has been shown to help White residents and harm non-White residents (Parks, 2016). Thus, White residents who have been afforded social mobility (i.e., through wealth and good health) may return to these renewed areas where newer, higher-value spaces are now available.

At the time of the Memorial Stadium construction, Ednor Gardens-Lakeside was an established, pristine, and stable community. The Waverly neighborhood on the western edge of the stadium was likewise experiencing planned residential and commercial growth as the city center declined. This area was a desirable location for the stadium as it would protect the value of the surrounding properties while providing a safe environment for mostly White spectators. However, as the teams left and Memorial Stadium deteriorated, so did the neighborhood around it. By leaving the Ednor Gardens-Lakeside neighborhood, both teams left behind a blighted stadium that only contributed to the environmental decline of the immediate blocks around the stadium. What were once bustling parks and playgrounds became unmanaged plots and high-density housing.

Ultimately, both teams moved only a couple of miles to the city center of Baltimore just west of the Inner Harbor, an area that was previously an industrial site, dockyards, and railyards. This was an area of urban decay with all of the previously mentioned markings (including pollution and environmental degradation), but it was already set on a path of renewal by creating greenspaces, recreational areas, and office developments. These stadium projects were set to be part of the efforts to renew one specific section of this area, but with these renewal efforts came the prospect of gentrification. These renewal efforts would not benefit Black and Brown residents in nearby neighborhoods. Instead, it was a reinvestment in an already predominantly White area within the city. The city's reinvestments created further opportunities for young, affluent, White individuals to move in. Thus, the environmental restoration efforts achieved as a result of the renewal were not for the previous residents as much as it was for new residents moving in.

Back in Ednor Gardens-Lakeside, Memorial Stadium sat empty for several years and turned into a nuisance that had to be demolished. The area that was once unwelcoming to Black residents and professional baseball players had since seen a shift in racial demographics. Black flight (away from the heart of Baltimore) and White return (to the city center) transitioned Ednor Gardens-Lakeside into a predominantly people of color neighborhood. In Memorial Stadium's place, the area was leveled and replaced with a YMCA, playground, youth baseball field, apartments, and businesses (Stetka, 2020). Stadium Place, as it is now called, is a renewal effort of the Memorial Stadium site that will hopefully benefit the residents of the neighborhood in an environmentally just way for generations to come, and not further encourage the cyclical process attracting and supporting solely newer, White residents.

Conclusion

The once brand-new Camden Yards area is now considered historical and revered, but not everyone was excited about the move. As Baltimore's teams began to look elsewhere in the city for stadiums, Memorial Stadium's neighbors began to worry about a changing neighborhood resulting from the economic impact lost—particularly the loss of stadium-supported businesses and workers moving out (Traum, 2007). The demolition of Memorial Stadium and the teams' relocations toward Baltimore's Inner Harbor struck mostly a nostalgic response from opposing residents and fans. Memories of a memorial for war veterans coupled with a familiar fondness toward America's favorite pastime sparked a longing for tradition through the Waverly and Ednor Gardens-Lakeside communities (Degraci, 1991). While some were excited for an opportunity for *upscale* retail and dining in their quintessential neighborhood, others were concerned about what those developments would do to their community (WBAL-TV 11 Baltimore, 2022). However, the motive for the Maryland Stadium Authority to build in the Camden Yards district was not based on memories or nostalgia, but an economic opportunity that fell on racial lines (Durington et al., 2009; Gearhart & Hunt, 2000). Opposition to the Ravens' later development in Camden Yards was muddled by the excitement for the NFL to return to Baltimore in a more permanent way, again highlighting the economic motivation above the community's financial and environmental burdens (Whiteside, 1996). It is hard to ignore that an increasingly diverse neighborhood was abandoned, leaving behind a deteriorating stadium in favor of a new development in a gentrifying area of Baltimore that is rapidly becoming less diverse.

Although various factors can explain why Baltimore's major men's professional sport teams relocated and why racial discrimination in Baltimore has led to demographic shifts within its neighborhoods, the environment may have played a role in these changes. Namely, that access to a clean environment for sport and recreational opportunities varies according to the racial composition of neighborhoods. Investment made in improving environmental resources in the benefit of sport prioritizes White residents, both current and future. Both the Orioles and Ravens have played a role in the environmental transformation of their communities via the original opening of Memorial Stadium, the decline of Memorial Stadium, and their relocation to Camden Yards. The new venues have led to new investments in the area that have improved environmental access and amenities to the benefit of White residents in both neighborhoods at different periods. However, in the decline and abandonment of the Memorial Stadium site, an environmental nuisance was left to a newly Black neighborhood. Regardless of intentionality, it is without a doubt that the burdens of environmental degradation are most harmfully felt in non-White communities. The history of the Orioles and Ravens in Baltimore is a striking example of this phenomenon.

References

Archer, D. N. (2021). Transportation policy and the underdevelopment of Black communities. *Iowa Law Review*, *106*(5), 2125–2151.

Banzhaf, S., Ma, L., & Timmins, C. (2019). Environmental justice: The economics of race, place, and pollution. *Journal of Economic Perspectives*, *33*(1), 185–208. 10.1257/jep.33.1.185

Boone, C. G., Buckley, G. L., Grove, J. M., & Sister, C. (2007). Parks and people: An environmental justice inquiry in Baltimore, Maryland. *Annals of the Association of American Geographers*, *99*(4), 767–787. 10.1080/00045600903102949

Brown, L. (2016, June 28). Two Baltimores: The White L vs. the Black butterfly. *The Baltimore Sun/Baltimore City Paper*. https://www.baltimoresun.com/citypaper/bcpnews-two-baltimores-the-white-l-vs-the-black-butterfly-20160628-htmlstory.html

Cassie, R. (n. d.). The Great Migration: How Black families came "up South," faced down Jim Crow, and built a groundbreaking Civil Rights movement. *Baltimore Magazine*. https://www.baltimoremagazine.com/section/historypolitics/the-great-migration/

Caves, R. W. (2004). *Encyclopedia of the city*. Routledge.

Degraci, J. (1991, October 5). Memorial Stadium memories live forever. *South Florida Sun-Sentinel*. https://www.sun-sentinel.com/news/fl-xpm-1991-10-06–9102090963-story.html

Depro, B., Timmins, C., & O'Neil, M. (2015). White flight and coming to the nuisance: Can residential mobility explain environmental injustice. *Journal of the Association of Environmental and Resource Economists*, *2*(3), 439–468. 10.1086/682716

Durington, M., Maddox, C., Ruhf, A., Gass, S., & Schwermer, J. (2009). Civic engagement and gentrification in metropolitan Baltimore. *Metropolitan Universities*, *20*(1), 101–114. https://journals.iupui.edu/index.php/muj/issue/view/1139

Eastern High School: A picture of turmoil. (1970, February 21). *The Afro-American*, 19.

Floyd, M. F. & Johnson, C. Y. (2002). Coming to terms with environmental justice in outdoor recreation: A conceptual discussion with research implications. *Leisure Sciences*, *24*(1), 59–77. 10.1080/01490400252772836

Frey, W. H. (1980). Black in-migration, White flight, and the changing economic base of the central city. *American Journal of Sociology*, *85*(6), 1396–1417. 10.1086/227170

Gearhart, T. & Hunt, J. (2000, November 8). Save Memorial Stadium. *The Baltimore Sun*. https://www.baltimoresun.com/news/bs-xpm-2000-11-09–0011090011-story.html

Grogan, P. S. & Proscio, T. (2001). *Comeback cities: A blueprint for urban neighborhood revival*. Basic Books.

Johnson, A. (2015, April 28). *Empty seats: Orioles close baseball game to the public after Baltimore riots*. NBC News. https://www.nbcnews.com/storyline/baltimore-unrest/orioles-close-baseball-games-public-after-baltimore-riots-n349856

Kelly, J. (2021 January 23). Building a place of ease at the old Memorial Stadium. *The Baltimore Sun*. https://www.baltimoresun.com/maryland/baltimore-city/bs-md-kelly-gilchrist-20210123-66qap5iccfga7j3fgpzp664mgy-story.html

Leffler, R. V. (1992). Boom and bust: The Elite Giants and Black baseball in Baltimore, 1936–1951. *Maryland Historical Magazine*, *87*(2), 171–186. https://www.mdhistory.org/publications/maryland-historical-magazine-online/

Mallach, A. (2020). *Drilling down in Baltimore's neighborhoods*. The Abell Foundation. https://abell.org/publications/drilling-down-baltimores-neighborhoods

McCullough, B. P., Orr, M., & Kellison, T. (2020). Sport ecology: Conceptualizing an emerging subdiscipline within sport management. *Journal of Sport Management*, *34*(6), 509–520. 10.1123/jsm.2019-0294

McFadden, D. (2018, December 29). *Baltimore trying to stem decades-long disappearing act*. AP News. https://apnews.com/article/us-news-race-and-ethnicity-baltimore-neighbor hoods-ap-top-news-c852e9751cd744b7a27fa9333c14d1a0

Meehan, S. (2019, March 20). Baltimore among nation's most gentrified cities, study shows. *The Baltimore Sun*. https://www.baltimoresun.com/maryland/baltimore-city/bs-md-ci-gentrification-study-20190319-story.html

Miller, J. E. (1992). The dowager of 33rd Street: Memorial Stadium and the politics of big-time sports in Maryland, 1954–1991. *Maryland Historical Magazine, 87*(2), 187–200. https://www.mdhistory.org/publications/maryland-historical-magazine-online/

Mullenbach, L. E. & Baker, B. L. (2020). Environmental justice, gentrification, and leisure: A systematic review and opportunities for the future. *Leisure Sciences, 42*(5–6), 430–447. 10.1080/01490400.2018.1458261

Noor, J., Shull, T., Leyder, E., Bishop, A., Leighton, K., Harris, K., Bukowski, I., Dunn, K., Bishop, C., Coffin, J., Patterson, D., Wang, S., Medhi, B., Anderson, V., Jones, D., Wallace, J., Hoard, A., Dildine, A., Dildine T., Ryan, D., Baker, S., Little, J., Flint, C., Chowdhuri, S., Clinton, R., Douglass, R., Bochnowski, A., & Logue, J. (2021, June 30). East Baltimore community's only green space fenced off by Weinberg Y, residents unite in protest. *The Baltimore Sun*. https://www.baltimoresun.com/opinion/readers-respond/bs-ed-rr-0703-stadium-place-fence-20210630-z6xgyjb245gfti72dakqrwae6u-story.html

Olson, S. H. (1997). *Baltimore: The building of an American city*. Johns Hopkins University Press.

Parks, C. (2016, November 5). Urban renewal hurt African Americans, officials say. Now Portland leaders want to make amends. *The Oregonian/OregonLive*. https://www.oregonlive.com/portland/2016/11/urban_renewal_african_american.html

Pietila, A. (1979, March 18). The Afro-Baltimoreans–I: Black community's power is on the rise, but some traditions are being challenged. *The Baltimore Sun*, 1.

Schneider, K. (2018, January 19). Welcome to the neighborhood: America's sports stadiums are moving downtown. *The New York Times*. https://www.nytimes.com/2018/01/19/business/sports-arena-development.html

Short, J. R. (2006). *Alabaster cities: Urban U.S. since 1950*. Syracuse University Press.

Smith, C. (2001). *Storied stadiums*. Carroll & Graf.

Snidal, M. (2017, March 30). City must fight Black flight. *The Baltimore Sun*. https://www.baltimoresun.com/opinion/readers-respond/bs-ed-shrinking-letter-20170330-story.html

Stetka, B. (2020, May 7). *Memorial Stadium is still here—just look around*. Major League Baseball. https://www.mlb.com/news/featured/memorial-stadium-is-still-here-just-look-around

Traum, A. (2007, October 11). Waverly residents try to regain neighborhood's glory days. *The Johns Hopkins News-Letter*. https://www.jhunewsletter.com/article/2007/10/waverly-residents-try-to-regain-neighborhoods-glory-days-40429/

U. S. Census Bureau. (2010). *Quick facts: Baltimore city, Maryland 2010*. https://www.census.gov/

U. S. Environmental Protection Agency. (2021). *EJScreen: Environmental justice screening and mapping tool*. www.epa.gov/ejscreen

WBAL-TV 11 Baltimore. (2022, April 7). *Residents react to redevelopment plan for Memorial Stadium (Archives)* [Video]. YouTube. https://www.youtube.com/watch?v=mmwidBDKoWo

Wells, J. E., Buckley, G. L., & Boone, C. G. (2008). Separate but equal? Desegregating Baltimore's golf courses. *Geographical Review, 98*(2), 151–170. 10.1111/j.1931-0846.2008.tb00294.x

Whiteside, K. (1996, August 12). Ravenous for football: To Baltimore Colts fans who had been singing the blues for 12 years, the Ravens' preseason opener was sweet music. *Sports Illustrated.* https://vault.si.com/vault/1996/08/12/baltimore-ravens-inaugural-season-1996

Wilson, P. B. (2014, March 29). Thirty years later, remembering how the Colts' move went down. *USA Today.* https://www.usatoday.com/story/sports/nfl/colts/2014/03/29/indianapolis-baltimore-move-30-year-anniversary-mayflower/7053553/

Wiltse, J. (2009). *Contested waters: A social history of swimming pools in America.* University of North Carolina Press.

Yeip, R. (2015, May 1). Baltimore's demographic divide. *The Wall Street Journal.* http://graphics.wsj.com/baltimore-demographics/

Zapatka, K. & Beck, B. (2021). Does demand lead supply? Gentrifiers and developers in the sequence of gentrification, New York City 2009-2016. *Urban Studies, 58*(11), 2348–2368. 10.1177/0042098020940596

Zhang, C. (2019, June 20). Baltimore's white population swells with millennials, resembling D.C., Brooklyn. *The Baltimore Sun.* https://www.baltimoresun.com/maryland/baltimore-city/bs-md-census-estimate-population-race-20190619-story.html

Zirin, D. (2015, April 28). *Apartheid games: Baltimore, urban America, and Camden Yards.* The Nation. https://www.thenation.com/article/archive/apartheid-games-baltimore-urban-america-and-camden-yards/

8
OLD AND NEW STADIUM DEVELOPMENT IN MIAMI

Laura Sivels

When it comes to professional sports teams, claims of their economic benefits have been largely refuted. While sports teams generate intangible benefits such as fan identification and civic pride, examining who bears the burden of their costs is vital. In addition to the increased traffic, waste, and other stressors, if public funds are invested in a professional team, those funds are no longer available for other community benefits like education, parks, or climate adaptation. This chapter will examine the redevelopment of an old stadium for the Miami Marlins in Little Havana and the search for a new stadium for Inter Miami CF in Miami, Florida. With a majority migrant, BIPOC, and non-English speaking population, a significant presence of income inequality, and the home to five major league teams, Miami provides a unique case study for environmental justice and sports stadiums.

A Multicultural Hub

Miami is well-known for its iconic beaches and a melting pot of cultures and ethnicities. Located in southeast Florida, Miami is closer to the Bahamas and Cuba than Georgia, the nearest neighboring state in the United States. With over 20 miles of beaches on the Atlantic coast and beautiful weather year-round, it is a world-renowned tourism destination and the full-time home to 30 of the world's billionaires (Viglucci, 2019). The Greater Miami area is home to five major league sports teams—the Miami Dolphins (NFL), the Miami Heat (NBA), the Miami Marlins (MLB), the Florida Panthers (NHL), and the newest team, Inter Miami CF (MLS).

Before 1960, Latinos comprised less than 5% of the current Miami-Dade County population. However, since the 1960s, Miami's Latino population has grown rapidly as Cuban migration to the United States increased. In 1960, the Latino population of Miami was estimated to be 50,000; 580,000 in 1980; 1.2 million in 2000, and, as of

DOI: 10.4324/9781003262633-10

the 2020 census, Miami-Dade County is estimated to be the home of 1.9 million Latino residents (Boswell, 1987; U.S. Census Bureau, 2020).

Though Miami is generally thought of as a new immigrant city regarding Cuban and Latino immigrants, its proximity to non-Hispanic countries in the Caribbean also attracts a sizeable Black population. Dunn (1997) outlined the evolution of Black Miamians throughout the 20th century, beginning with Black Bahamian immigrants in the 1890s, who played a substantial role in the early development and incorporation of Miami. During the incorporation of Miami in 1896, the White residents pleaded with Black men to acquire the necessary number of votes to reach the state law minimum number of registered voters to incorporate the city; 44% of the votes to incorporate the city were those of Black men. However, soon after incorporation, the Black community was disenfranchised and segregated into "Colored Town," later known as Overtown. In addition to the Cuban mass migration in the late 20th century, many Haitians migrated to Miami. During this time, the predominantly Black neighborhood of Lemon City transformed into the current neighborhood of Little Haiti as Haitians were detained and taken in government buses to the Black section of town. As of 2020, approximately 450,000 (16.5%) of the Miami-Dade population identified as Black (U.S. Census Bureau, 2020).

According to the U.S. Census Bureau's American Community Survey (2021), other intersections exist in Miami's melting pot, including a 54.6% foreign-born population, 70% with limited English, and one of the worst income inequality estimates in the United States. These are all demographic groups commonly affected by environmental inequity (Bullard, 2007; Huang & London, 2012).

Sea-Level Rise and Climate Gentrification

With Miami's adored beaches and miles of coastline, it is not surprising that home values are highest along the coast. For example, Miami Beach, one of many coastal cities in the Miami area, was estimated to have roughly 2,000 owner-occupied homes worth more than $2 million each in 2019 (U.S. Census Bureau, 2021). Unlike many parts of the United States, where low-income populations are most vulnerable to flooding, Miami has the opposite problem (U.S. Environmental Protection Agency, 2021). As climate change drives sea-level rise, the traditionally valuable property has an ill-fated outlook of chronic flooding. This outlook causes homeowners and developers to look for higher ground in Miami at a lower risk to the climate impacts Miami is already seeing.

Between 2005 and 2016, the Miami-Dade area lost $465 million in real-estate market value due to recurrent tidal flooding and projected increases (McAlpine & Porter, 2018). In a high-end sea-level rise scenario of 1.5–2 meters, it is projected that 2 million residents would need to move due to chronic inundation (McLeman, 2018).

Socially vulnerable and predominantly BIPOC neighborhoods such as Little Havana, Liberty Square, Overtown, and Little Haiti are located on high ground that FEMA considers minimal risk for flood hazards. With historically lower property values and increased demand for higher elevation property in Miami, these communities are at an increased risk of displacement due to climate gentrification. This movement is considered the "superior investment pathway," one of three pathways of climate gentrification outlined by Keenan et al. (2018) and defined as a "behavior of moving financial capital to a geography that offers superior risk-adjusted returns for accommodating real estate and infrastructure" (p. 2).

This climate gentrification has exacerbated the cost of living and disrupted cultural hubs across Miami. Historically, immigrants had little choice on where to settle in Miami. In 1934, President Roosevelt's administration passed the National Housing Act and created a pathway for middle- and low-income families to purchase a home. This process allowed the Home Owners Loan Corporation to develop residential security maps using racial hierarchies to appraise and score different neighborhoods (Aalbers, 2020). This practice, redlining, was used in Miami to explicitly exclude African Americans from the desirable areas of the city, like Miami Beach, and segregated Black Miamians into neighborhoods like Overtown and Liberty City. When the U.S. government established the Cuban Refugee Emergency Center in the early 1960s, Miami became the new home to many Cuban migrants. Little Havana, which had previously been a lower-middle-class Jewish neighborhood, quickly became the social, economic, political, and cultural center for Cuban exiles due to the availability of affordable housing and proximity to refugee centers (Bucuvalas, 2013). These communities are now established cultural hubs, but they risk losing their homes and communities to wealthier residents due to climate gentrification.

Climate gentrification cannot be overlooked when considering the environmental justice implications of sports stadium development in Miami. Team investors and owners have just as much benefit in moving their financial capital or future investments to the geography that offers superior risk-adjusted concerns.

Miami Orange Bowl in Little Havana

Built as a Depression-era revitalization project in 1936, the Miami Orange Bowl had long been a staple in the area now considered Little Havana. The outdoor stadium was developed for the University of Miami football games and became the home of the Orange Bowl college football game. The Miami Orange Bowl remained home to the Miami Hurricanes college football team until 2007. It also was the home stadium of the Miami Dolphins NFL team until 1987 (Miami Marlins, 2022b).

The Orange Bowl has long since been a landmark in the Little Havana neighborhood, with residents nostalgically admiring growing up in the shadows of the Orange Bowl stadium and using the Orange Bowl grounds as a sort of playground for kids in the community (D'Angelo, 2012). The Orange Bowl also provided value to the community by serving as a safe space and refuge. During

Hurricane Wilma in 2005, it was a FEMA relief center; before that, it served as a refugee camp to Cuban asylum seekers during the Mariel boatlift in 1980 (Associated Press, 2005; Larzelere, 1988).

Though a long-time landmark, the stadium had not been largely renovated since its 1930s development. Discussions of stadium renovations began in the early 2000s as the stadium was hard to navigate, the facade was rusting, and it was missing modern stadium amenities like suites and video-replay screens. Foreshadowing the projected increase in severe weather events in Miami, Hurricane Wilma caused structural damage to the stadium in 2005, which accelerated the discussion of tearing down the facility (Kelly, 2005). As renovations stalled, the Miami Hurricanes decided to leave their 70-year home at the Orange Bowl and move to Dolphin Stadium in 2007. This move opened up the potential for a new life at what was once the Orange Bowl stadium.

The Emergence of Marlins Park

Simultaneously, the Miami Marlins (then the Florida Marlins) became increasingly frustrated playing at Dolphin Stadium, designed for football and not baseball. While economical to share a stadium with a sport with opposing schedules, the seating was developed for football gameplay and was, thus, not ideal for baseball spectators. In addition, because of the open-air design, the Marlins were encountering environmental-related concerns like frequently encountered rain delays and sweltering conditions for fans and players alike (Associated Press, 2011).

The Marlins had considered relocating out of Florida, which provoked government officials like Florida Governor Charlie Crist to publicly support public funding for a new stadium to retain economic opportunities in the area (Klas & Caputo, 2007). In 2009, the Marlins, the City of Miami, and Miami-Dade County reached an agreement for a $551-million ballpark development on the former Orange Bowl site in Little Havana. The project came out to $654 million, with the team covering less than 20% of the cost (Burgess, 2009). In 2012, the new Marlins Park (now loanDepot park) opened in Little Havana.

Public Financing of Marlins Park

The Miami-Dade county commission agreed to pay $368 million, two-thirds of the development for stadium construction, roads, and utilities (Burgess, 2009). With a 9–4 vote, the county decided to forgo investments in other initiatives and fund the Marlins' ballpark project. The county did not hold a taxpayer vote to decide if public money should support the investment. A portion of the taxpayer funding used to fund Marlins Park, almost $300 million, was directly diverted from funds slated for other community redevelopment projects in Overtown (previously mentioned as a historically Black "Colored Town"; Marquez, 2009). In total, Miami-Dade County borrowed about $409 M for the project through bonds, a total the county is projected to pay back tenfold. The *Miami Herald* examined only one of the $91-million loans and found that the total debt for that loan will cost the county $1.18 billion by the time it is paid off in 2048 (Hanks, 2013). Researchers from the Brooking Institute's Metropolitan Program had a similar estimate of $2.4 billion over 40 years (Tomer & Kulkarni, 2012). With either projection, the outlook is poor.

With Miami facing severe sea-level rise and chronic inundation across the coast, issues of extreme heat as a danger to the community, and other climate public health drivers, the cost for Miami to pay for climate adaptation will grow exponentially over the coming decades. By utilizing taxpayer funding to pay for Marlins Park, the city is bypassing the opportunity to use more than $2 billion on climate mitigation, public health, and other economic justice funds. Every dollar Miami-Dade borrowed will be paid back $13—money that isn't being utilized to protect the most vulnerable in Miami.

FIGURE 8.1 loanDepot Park. ("Marlins Park Front Plaza" by Dan Lundberg is licensed under CC BY-SA 2.0)

A Refuge in an Uncertain Climate Future

A key driver of the Marlins' and County's investment in the stadium was the need for a weather-proof design. Kellison and Orr (2021) explored climate change as a vehicle for urban transformation and used Marlins Park as one of the case studies in their analysis. Using Orr and Inoue's (2019) Climate Vulnerability of Sport Organizations framework, they identified the Marlins as being in a fortified state.

However, the Marlins' have a high risk of potential climate impacts in Miami; the organization also now has a high level of adaptive capacity with the new stadium development.

The Marlins' successfully developed a stadium with a three-panel retractable roof to hold up to severe weather and protect that inside. It is also the first MLB ballpark to achieve LEED Gold certification. It takes extra effort to reduce water, energy, and resource use, and to adopt intentional waste management, all of which burden the local community less. To combat Miami's increasing extreme heat, they designed a white membrane roof to deflect heat from the roof and let in a natural breeze when the panels are open (Miami Marlins, 2022a).

A climate-resilient stadium provides an opportunity to be a haven in an era of climate change, similar to how the Orange Bowl stadium provided community value and safety for Cuban refugees in the 1980s. By developing a stadium that is resistant to climate impacts, especially hurricanes and coastal flooding in South Florida, the stadium has the opportunity to serve as a shelter following severe weather events for those vulnerable in the surrounding areas.

In fact, during the early discussions of the development and subsidization of Marlins Park, the mayor and city manager of Weston (a nearby suburb) proposed a public-private partnership to Miami elected officials and the Marlins team president that would justify public financing of the stadium project if it could be used as a hurricane shelter equipped with showers, food, water, and generators in the case of natural disaster (Kollin & Talalay, 2005). Though the idea didn't take off, it is crucial to consider the additional value stadiums could bring for equitable resilience. Because Marlins Park was designed with resilience in mind, it also has the potential to be of immense service to the community in times of need after disasters.

So far, however, that has not been the case. As expected, the stadium has withstood the elements, as evidenced by Hurricanes Irma and Dorian that had come through the area. However, the stadium did not serve as shelter even though over 75,000 South Florida residents sought refuge from the storm (Florida House of Representatives, 2018). To add insult to injury, as Little Havana residents scrambled to protect their belongings from Hurricane Irma, two of the publicly funded parking garages that could protect vehicles from high winds and flooding remained empty and closed to the public (Koh, 2017). Secure, high-ground parking for their vehicle could be an added layer of security and resilience for many residents in the area, providing access to transportation, and possibly shelter, in the aftermath of the storm. The City of Miami and the Miami Parking Authority, not the Marlins, have jurisdiction over the hurricane parking protocol to decide to let community members use the garage. However, the Marlins and the City should plan accordingly and push for residents to utilize the precious parking real-estate in the low-income, migrant community during natural disasters. Sports stadiums and Marlins Park could provide a safe space and refuge to the local community during a hurricane. Individuals seeking refuge should not have their property, transportation, or assets ruined in the face of disaster while multiple large parking garages in the neighborhood remain empty.

The Search for an Affordable, Dry Stadium Site

As the newcomer MLS team Inter Miami CF searched for a new stadium, the impacts of climate gentrification were in full force. As outlined previously, investors and developers prey on climate gentrification areas because they have relatively low costs and climate risks compared to the historically more desirable areas. Initially, David Beckham, president of Inter Miami CF, considered a site at Port Miami next to the Miami Heat's arena, an idea that was almost immediately dismissed due to space and cost concerns (Flechas, 2022). The first viable site for the future soccer stadium was in Little Havana, the Cuban cultural hub and predominantly low-to-moderate-income Latino neighborhood. The $200 million development would be adjacent to Marlins Park (Veiga & Smiley, 2015). However, the most significant difference is that Marlins Park was developed on existing stadium land. The Inter Miami CF stadium would displace residents in a highly gentrified area that has already experienced hikes in the cost of living.

In a statement to the *Miami Herald*, Beckham's lobbyist Neisen Kasdin said, "We have been communicating with the property owners in good faith, offering several millions of dollars above market value, but we will not agree to completely unreasonable prices" (para. 10). That may sound like a generous offer until one considers that 80% of Little Havana is renter-occupied. If the development had taken place, the residents would likely be displaced without seeing a dollar of the generous offer (Plusurbia & The National Trust for Historic Preservation, 2019).

Although discussions with the city and school board, who owned some of the lands, were going well, Beckham's team needed to negotiate with the property owners within the proposed stadium footprint. As reported in the *Miami Herald*, one retiree said, "I don't want to sell this house. I've lived here for 38 years. I am 85 years old. I don't want to leave. … Sometimes I sit on the stoop, and I sunbathe. That has no price" (Veiga & Smiley, 2015, para. 26).

After rejection at the Little Havana site, the Beckham team considered an area in Overtown, the predominantly Black neighborhood on higher ground that is also at risk of climate gentrification. In March 2016, Beckham's ownership group, Miami Beckham United, paid nearly $19 million for six acres in Overtown (Hanks, 2016). This purchase was two-thirds of what would be needed for the site, with the remaining three acres under negotiation with Miami-Dade County, which had been using the land as a truck depot. However, community organizations, including the Overtown Spring Garden Community Collective, didn't buy into the message of community revitalization and instead protested for the hundreds of families that lived in nearby public housing facing threats of displacement from the new investment (Hanks, 2018). Paradoxically, long-term residents, once segregated to this neighborhood because of its undesirability, were now confronting the possibility developers could buy their properties because of their (relatively) low costs and low-risk assessment from sea-level rise.

In March 2018, a new potential site emerged, Melreese Country Club, a city-owned golf course on Miami's most prominent parkland in Grapeland Heights next to Miami International Airport (Flechas, 2022). This proposed site, designed as a mall, park, and stadium complex called "Miami Freedom Park," quickly gained traction. In November 2018, 60% of Miami voters authorized city administrators to waive competitive bidding requirements so the government could soon negotiate a 99-year lease with the team's ownership to develop Miami Freedom Park (Flechas, 2019).

When it comes to sea-level rise, the proposed location is not considered high-risk for climate gentrification, as its elevation is lower than Overtown and Little Havana. According to the Union of Concerned Scientists' GIS projections, the land is likely to face chronic inundation within the timeline of the 99-year lease (Spanger-Siegfried, 2017). However, its proximity to the airport will likely permit continued collaboration with the local government on climate adaptation for the area.

While negotiations of the site in Grapeland Heights are underway, Beckham's team has kept the land in Overtown as a backup development. Many of the residents in Grapeland Heights favor the new site because, in addition to the stadium, the plans also include a 58-acre public park, the removal of contaminants at no cost, and a one-mile bicycle path around the project. Because the land is only used as a county-owned golf course, no residents would be displaced. However, the development is already facing some pushback by local officials on the burdens an increase in local traffic could have on the local community (Hanks, 2021).

As stadium development conversations continue, Inter Miami CF currently has a temporary arrangement in nearby Fort Lauderdale. The story of David Beckham's Inter Miami CF stadium development is far from over. However, much is to be learned about the role that community residents like those in Overtown and Little Havana played to protect these valuable, climate-resilient communities from commercial development. In addition, sports team developers need to have a more robust consideration of the disproportionate impacts on the local community and ensure equitable development with a focus on community investment rather than disrupting cultural neighborhoods and claiming high-value real estate for sports rather than livelihoods.

Conclusion

As climate mitigation conversations and negotiations take place across the globe, communities in Miami await their fate, which will largely be decided by the frequency and severity of flooding from sea-level rise. These stadium developments in Miami are just a case study for decisions in development that are going to be increasingly necessary in coastal cities around the world.

Miami is a justifiably desirable community for sports teams, with all five major men's leagues represented and widespread local support for the city's professional and collegiate teams. The sporting structure in Miami is just one thread of the community's culture. Another is its status as a multicultural international hub with a tattered history of segregation and injustices; when tackling issues of climate change, environmental justice, and displacement, these decisions must be made as a collective community.

126 Laura Sivels

There is the opportunity to learn from the past that has shaped the community. The early Jamaican settlers once built and incorporated the city only to be seg-regated into undesirable neighborhoods. Cuban migrants arrived in droves during the mid-20th century and carved the iconic community of Little Havana. Stadiums like the Orange Bowl provided a place of refuge during refugee crises and natural disasters. Ultimately, there is the opportunity to work as a community to establish joyful centers of sport and recreation that can benefit the whole community. The stressors that accompany climate change, like chronic inundation and the increased frequency of hurricanes and extreme heat, will be felt deep within the city of Miami. As cities grapple with these issues, they may look to sport as a resource to support communities through climate adaptation. In this capacity, sport has the duty to not disproportionately pass the financial, emotional, and physical burdens on to the most vulnerable members of the community.

References

Aalbers, M. B. (2020). Redlining. In A. Kobayashi (Ed.), *Encyclopedia of human geography* (2nd ed.). Elsevier Science & Technology.

Associated Press. (2005, October 26). *Slowly cleaning up after Wilma.* https://www.cbsnews.com/news/slowly-cleaning-up-after-wilma/

Associated Press. (2011, September 26). *Players won't miss Marlins' old home.* https://www.espn.com/mlb/story/_/id/7022128/players-miss-florida-marlins-games-sun-life-stadium

Boswell, T. D. (1987). Racial and ethnic change and Hispanic residential segregation patterns in metropolitan Miami, 1980–1990. *Southeastern Geographer, 33*(1), 82–109. https://www.jstor.org/stable/44371255

Bucuvalas, T. (2013). Little Havana. In S. J. Bronner (Ed.), *Encyclopedia of American folklife* (pp. 738–741). Routledge.

Bullard, R. D. (Ed.). (2007). *Growing smarter: Achieving livable communities, environmental justice, and regional equity.* MIT Press.

Burgess, G. (2009, March 23). *Baseball stadium financing* [Memorandum]. Miami-Dade County Board of County Commissioners. https://www.miamidade.gov/Govaction/Legistarfiles/Matters/Y2009/090732.Pdf

D'Angelo, T. (2012, December 28). For Florida State assistant James Coley, old Orange Bowl stadium was childhood 'playground. *Palm Beach Post.* https://www.palmbeachpost.com/story/sports/college/2012/12/28/for-florida-state-assistant-james/7923417007/

Davis, C. (2014, May 3). Stadium bill passes; Beckham benefits. *South Florida Sun-Sentinel,* C2.

Delgallo, A. (2017, January 28). Orlando, Miami and Tampa in different stages of MLS expansion. *Orlando Sentinel.* https://www.orlandosentinel.com/sports/os-sp-mls-expansion-0128-story.html

Dunn, M. (1997). *Black Miami in the twentieth century.* University Press of Florida.

Feldman, M. & Jolivet, V. (2014). Back to Little Havana: Controlling gentrification in the heart of Cuban Miami. *International Journal of Urban and Regional Research, 38*(4), 1266–1285. 10.1111/1468-2427.12097

FEMA. (2019). *National flood insurance program: Flood hazard mapping.* https://www.fema.gov/flood-maps#

Flechas, J. (2019, March 21). City of Miami wins lawsuit challenging referendum on Beckham soccer stadium. *Miami Herald.* https://www.miamiherald.com/news/local/community/miami-dade/article228256674.html

Flechas, J. (2022, January 30). From L.A. Galaxy to Miami Freedom Park: Beckham's long, winding path to a stadium deal. *Miami Herald.* https://www.miamiherald.com/news/local/community/miami-dade/article257754368.html

Florida House of Representatives. (2018). *Final report.* Select Committee on Hurricane Response and Preparedness.

Florida, R. & Pedigo, S. (2019). *Miami's housing affordability crisis.* Florida International University, Miami Urban Future Initiative. https://digitalcommons.fiu.edu/mufi-reports/6/

Hanks, D. (2013, January 24). How a $91 million loan on the Marlins ballpark will cost Miami-Dade $1.2 billion. *Miami Herald.* http://www.miamiherald.com/2013/01/24/3199018/how-a-91million-loan-on-the-marlins.html

Hanks, D. (2016, March 25). Beckham group pays almost $19 million for private land in soccer site. *Miami Herald.* https://www.miamiherald.com/news/local/community/miami-dade/article68227347.html

Hanks, D. (2018, February 1). David Beckham got team, but some don't want stadium. *Miami Herald.* https://www.miamiherald.com/news/local/community/miami-dade/article197640879.html

Hanks, D. (2021, March 16). Miami-Dade raises doubts about traffic study for David Beckham's Miami soccer stadium. *Miami Herald.* https://www.miamiherald.com/news/local/community/miami-dade/article249982234.html

Huang, G. & London, J. K. (2012). Cumulative environmental vulnerability and environmental justice in California's San Joaquin Valley. *International Journal of Environmental Research and Public Health, 9*(5), 1593–1608. 10.3390/ijerph9051593

Keenan, J. M., Hill, T., & Gumber, A. (2018). Climate gentrification: From theory to empiricism in Miami-Dade County, Florida. *Environmental Research Letters, 13*(5), 054001. 10.1088/1748-9326/aabb32

Kellison, T. & Orr, M. (2021). Climate vulnerability as a catalyst for early stadium replacement. *International Journal of Sports Marketing and Sponsorship, 22*(1), 126–141. 10.1108/IJSMS-04-2020-0076

Kelly, O. (2005, December 1). Orange Bowl's destiny uncertain. *South Florida Sun-Sentinel.* https://www.sun-sentinel.com/news/fl-xpm-2005-12-01–0511301507-story.html

Kim, S. K. (2020). The economic effects of climate change adaptation measures: Evidence from Miami-Dade County and New York City. *Sustainability, 12*(3), 1097. 10.3390/Su12031097

Klas, M. & Caputo, M. (2007, February 1). Governor boosts ballpark funding formula. *Miami Herald*, 1A.

Koh, E. (2017, September 7). Some Miamians want to park in Marlin's garages before Irma, but two will stay empty. *Miami Herald.* https://www.miamiherald.com/news/weather/hurricane/article171902907.html

Kollin, J. & Talalay, S. (2005, September 20). Weston pair pitch stadium with a twist: Facility could house Marlins and evacuees. *South Florida Sun-Sentinel*, 1B.

Larzelere, A. (1988). *The 1980 Cuban boatlift.* National Defense University Press.

Marquez, M. (2009, March 4). Marlins as demanding as Spence-Jones. *Miami Herald*, B1.

McAlpine, S. , & Porter, J. (2019, August 8). *State by state analysis: Property value loss from sea level rise* [Press release]. https://firststreet.org/press/property-value-loss-from-sea-level-rise-state-by-state-analysis/

McLeman, R. (2018). Migration and displacement risks due to mean sea-level rise. *Bulletin of the Atomic Scientists, 74*(3), 148–154. 10.1080/00963402.2018.1461951

Miami Marlins. (2022a). *Marlins Park information.* https://www.mlb.com/marlins/ballpark/information

Miami Marlins. (2022b). *Orange Bowl site history.* https://www.mlb.com/marlins/ballpark/orange-bowl

Orr, M. & Inoue, Y. (2019). Sport versus climate: Introducing the climate vulnerability of sport organizations framework. *Sport Management Review, 22*(4), 452–463. 10.1016/j.smr.2018.09.007

Plusurbia, & The National Trust for Historic Preservation. (2019). *Little Havana: Me importa - Revitalization master plan.* Plusurbia & The National Trust for Historic Preservation.

Spanger-Siegfried, E. (2017). *When rising seas hit home: Hard choices ahead for hundreds of US coastal communities.* Union of Concerned Scientists.

Tomer, A. & Kulkarni, S. (2012, December 17). Other viewpoints - Deal should end era of publicly funded stadiums. *Sun Sentinel*, 14A.

U.S. Census Bureau. (2020). *2020 census results.* https://www.census.gov/programs-surveys/decennial-census.html

U.S. Census Bureau. (2021). *S0501 – Selected characteristics of the native and foreign-born populations.* https://factfinder.census.gov/bkmk/table/1.0/en/ACS/16_1YR/S0501

U.S. Environmental Protection Agency. (2021). *Climate change and social vulnerability in the United States: A focus on six impacts.* https://www.epa.gov/cira/social-vulnerability-report

Veiga, C. & Smiley, D. (2015, November 24). David Beckham plans for Little Havana stadium in question. *Miami Herald.* https://www.miamiherald.com/news/local/article46343840.html

Viglucci, A. (2019, April 22). Miami-Dade's tale of two cities: 30 billionaires and the economic inequality of Colombia. *Miami Herald.* https://www.miamiherald.com/news/local/community/miami-dade/article229441144.html

9

STADIA AND COMMUNITY STEWARDSHIP: COMMUNITY BENEFITS AND PUBLIC FINANCE FOR NEW YORK'S YANKEE STADIUM

Austin H. Thompson and Kyle S. Bunds

Stadia exist as actualities and potentialities. In actuality, stadiums and the cities within which they reside are a reflection of historical social, economic, and political decisions (Bunds et al., 2019). The infrastructure that underlies urban areas and their sports teams exists as visible markers of existing decisions that tend to influence future decisions. While stadiums are costly infrastructure projects that must be balanced against a multitude of city wants and needs, the political, economic, and social bargaining power of influential sport clubs can result in inequities in the costs and benefits of stadium agreements and capital projects. The stadium, for as long as it exists, stands as a monument and memory of these decisions.

The stadium also exists as a potentiality. When the building of a new facility is discussed, designed, and constructed, the decisions made are often created through a discourse on the potentiality of that stadium and stadium site. Stadium project proponents often discuss the stadium as congruent with economic potentiality. Conversely, opponents will point to the potential gentrification and negative aspects of the stadium. This was evidenced in the decision of the city of Detroit, fresh off a bankruptcy filing, to fund the construction of Little Caesars Arena with the promise of economic development for the area (Bunds et al., 2020).

In this chapter, we argue that these potentialities and actualities result from conscious decision making and leave a lasting monument and memory of that decision making. We focus specifically on public subsidy, economic impact, and community benefits through the lens of environmental justice to explain the process behind Yankee Stadium receiving 22 acres of parkland, the organization promising to rebuild that parkland, and the subsequent modification of that promise.

DOI: 10.4324/9781003262633-11

Public Subsidy, Economic Impact, and Community Benefits

When deciding if a government should intervene in a market, the prevailing reason a government *should* intervene is a market failure. That is, a market does not provide the optimal level of a good or service. There are many examples of market failures, including, but not limited to, public goods, externalities, and monopolies (Gruber, 2019). Public goods are typically not provided by the private sector because they cannot exclude individuals that do not pay for a good or service. Externalities include costs or benefits that are not included in the price of a good or service, and thus may result in the overproduction or underproduction of that good or service. Monopolies are cases where there is only one seller and the market is not competitive, which influences the market price paid by consumers.

Government subsidy for stadium construction is an example of government intervention (Bland & Overton, 2019). Proponents of public financing for stadiums argue that stadiums are public goods that provide positive externalities to the degree that the total benefits provided by stadiums exceed total costs (Johnson & Whitehead, 2000; Schwester, 2007). As private investors cannot capture the benefits of those positive externalities, they will not provide stadiums in the absence of government intervention (Johnson & Whitehead, 2000). But, in the case of sports stadiums, the economic spillover effects are small (Gayer et al., 2016). Recognizing the shortcomings in the economic argument for public subsidies for professional sports stadiums, academics have attempted to explain the community benefits of stadiums, drawing on social capital and social network theories to explain that the benefits cannot all be monetized (see Crompton, 2004). According to Schwester (2007), examples of these externalities are often noneconomic, including "civic pride, city reputation and national identity, and patrimony" (p. 90). In a similar fashion, Seifried and Clopton (2013) used social anchor theory to explain how sports stadiums lead to community development. As a result, the authors argue that government subsidies for sports stadiums should not be viewed solely for their economic benefits, as social benefits cannot be easily quantified but may be valuable.

Nevertheless, the public good argument weakens when evaluating the monopolistic structure of professional sports teams in the United States. Indeed, professional leagues cap the number of franchises, and, typically, if one city has a team, then no other city in the region will also have a team (Jakar & Rosentraub, 2021). This creates a competitive system for a franchise that can result in a "race to the bottom" of tax incentives. Further, sports teams tend to have political power that allows them to play one subsidy offer against another to attain the lowest rent. As a result, despite the public good argument that is commonly used to support stadium subsidies, many economists agree that public subsidies for sports stadiums should be eliminated (Coates & Humphreys, 2008).

Environmental Justice

The environmental justice movement gained widespread attention in the 1980s, underscoring the racial and income-based divides in exposure to environmental harms (Holifield et al., 2018). According to Cutter (1995), the movement has focused on drawing attention to the localized impacts of pollution on low-income communities and communities of color and calling for measurable improvements in environmental and social outcomes. Environmental justice is rooted in three pillars: justice in the distribution of environmental goods and bads, recognition of the experiences of affected communities, and the procedures through which planning decisions are made (Schlosberg, 2004). Since the movement began, the distributional focus has grown from justice in exposure to harms to include justice in access to benefits. Nevertheless, historical planning decisions and modern economic drivers result in the retention of distributional injustices. In the United States, these environmental injustices look different between and within cities, including inequities in the distribution of Superfund sites or hazardous waste sites (Cutter, 1995) and inequitable access to green-spaces (Jennings et al., 2012), trees (Heynen et al., 2006; Perkins et al., 2004), or quality parks (Rigolon et al., 2018).

Stadiums are major infrastructure projects that often utilize scarce resources (e.g., public monies, land). As a result, stadium projects can be connected to the three pillars of environmental justice. On a distributional basis, stadiums require large plots of land and major redevelopment. They can both increase exposure to harm by creating flooding issues and increasing urban heat and decrease access to environmental goods by removing mature trees for construction or re-purposing greenspace for stadium construction. On a procedural basis, stadium decisions, particularly those that utilize public funds and require redevelopment, directly impact neighboring communities. Finally, in terms of sense of justice, stadium projects have been evaluated based on their impacts on surrounding communities. Though the rationale for stadium decisions is often that the economic and social community benefits provided by the stadium outweigh the costs to the taxpayers, evaluations of stadium projects suggest that they can result in an inequitable distribution of social and economic costs to proximate communities (Kellison, 2022).

In addition to the challenges in quantifying the full scope of stadium benefits, there are costs to stadiums *outside* of the direct subsidy that can be equally challenging to quantify. Such is the story of Yankee Stadium, a facility built on public parkland in a low-income, high-pollution exposure neighborhood of the Bronx using local, state, and federal subsidies. While the Yankees eventually replaced the 22 acres of parkland with 25 acres of parks, the conversion exchanged contiguous parkland for a few disconnected parks and left the community without its parkland for six years (McClure, 2012). Through the Yankee Stadium case, we will illustrate the economic, social, and environmental costs of stadiums to local communities. We close by calling for sports teams to consider their negative impacts and move toward a better model of community stewardship before and after the construction is complete (Locke, 2021).

FIGURE 9.1   Yankee Stadium and Macombs Dam Park in 2011. ("Yankee Stadium" by randreu is licensed under CC BY 3.0)

Case Study: Yankee Stadium

Background

When Rudy Giuliani was mayor of New York City, he assured the Yankees and the Mets that new stadiums in the city would be a top priority. When Mike Bloomberg was elected mayor in 2002, his administration had different priorities. Nevertheless, the Yankee Stadium deal remained in deliberation, with officials from the city, state, and team working to build a modern stadium (Harrington, 2011). In a city with limited space and a strong desire to keep the stadium in the South Bronx, the final plan called for the new Yankee Stadium to be built on 22 acres of city-owned parkland adjacent to the existing stadium (Kozlowski, 2007).

These 22 acres of parkland, though owned by New York City, were funded in part using money from the Land and Water Conservation Fund (LWCF) Act, a federal grant program. In 1979, the city received a $302,000 grant to supplement the creation of parks in the South Bronx. LWCF monies, like most federal grants, have stipulations. Namely, LWCF "prohibits any property acquired or developed with LWCF assistance from being converted from public outdoor recreational use unless the Secretary of the Interior approves the conversion" (Kozlowski, 2007, p. 30). With this in mind, the Yankees designated 24.56 acres of land, including the old stadium site, to be converted into parkland to serve as a substitute for the lost acreage. The substitute acreage, unlike the parkland slated for the new stadium, would be segmented into a few parks. The National Parks Service approved the conversion in 2006 (Kozlowski, 2007).

Shortly after, Save Our Parks, an organization of residents who opposed the new stadium, brought a lawsuit to state court and eventually federal court, arguing that the stadium project violated section 6 of the LWCF Act (Kozlowski, 2007). The federal court dismissed the lawsuit, and the project moved forward (Williams, 2006).

Nevertheless, the Yankee Stadium project has raised further questions about the politics of large stadium projects, the environmental justice impact of stadiums, the governance of community benefits, and public finance for large stadium projects.

The South Bronx and Environmental Justice

Both the old and new Yankee stadiums are located in the South Bronx neighborhood of New York City. The two properties are adjacent, occupying considerable acreage along Interstate 87 by the Macombs Dam Bridge, which connects the Bronx and Harlem. In 2010, the South Bronx was named the poorest county in the United States. At that time, 28% of residents lived under the poverty line (Maroko et al., 2014). In the South Bronx district of Bronx County, the number was even higher, with 38% of residents living below the poverty line. In an area of more than a million people, this equated to over 250,000 people living in poverty. As of 2019, not much has changed. U.S. Census Bureau American Community Surveys estimates 26.4% of residents in Bronx County live under the poverty line. Additionally, the Bronx has the highest percent minority population of New York City's five boroughs. According to the 2020 Decennial Census, 1.47 million people reside in the Bronx. Of those 1.47 million residents, 806,463 are Hispanic or Latino (54.8%), and 419,393 (28.5%) are Black or African American.

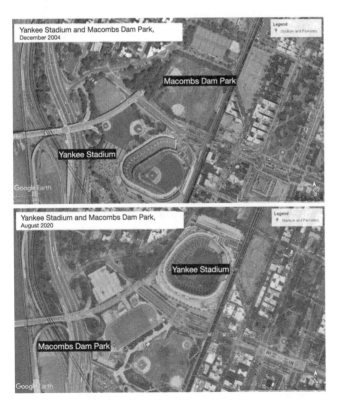

FIGURE 9.2 Satellite imagery of the Yankee Stadium site in 2004 (top) and 2020 (bottom). (Map data: Google, Maxar Technologies)

The South Bronx is bounded on three sides by interstate highways and has several large, pollution-generating waste transfer stations and trucking-intensive food distribution facilities (Maciejczk et al., 2004; Shearston et al., 2020). As a result, residents are often subject to high concentrations of air pollutants like black carbon (Maciejzck et al., 2004) and $PM_{2.5}$ (Spira-Cohen et al., 2009). Indeed, the area is known for its high asthma rates, with higher asthma death rates than anywhere else in New York City. The disparity is especially notable among children. According to NYC Health (2021), in 2016, asthma-related emergency room visits for Bronx children were twice the rate of the other four boroughs combined. The same report found an even greater prevalence of asthma among children in South Bronx neighborhoods.

Community Benefits Agreement

Community benefits agreements (CBAs) are a newer form of development agreements, having come about roughly 20 years ago (Korngold, 2018; Salkin & Lavine, 2007). Inspired by social justice and environmental justice concerns around large development projects, CBAs are a written agreement, *a contract*, between a private developer and the community (Salkin & Lavine, 2007; Wolf-Powers, 2010). The negotiations vary based on the project in question, but typically the contract outlines benefits the community will receive from a development project (e.g., higher wages, greenspaces, affordable housing) in exchange for community support, or at least community acceptance (Salkin & Lavine, 2007). CBAs give the community a seat at the negotiating table, allowing community groups to advocate for project benefits that align with the specific neighborhood goals or interests (Wolf-Powers, 2010). CBAs still do not have clear statutory guidelines, and thus relative power of community groups versus developments and the resulting agreements can, and do, vary in their success. In the United States, CBAs have been a popular component of stadium projects like Cypto.com Arena in Los Angeles, PPG Paints Arena in Pittsburgh, and Yankee Stadium in the South Bronx (Salkin & Lavine, 2007).

When the Yankee Stadium CBA was signed in 2006, it was met with criticism and questions of its legitimacy. Namely, the Yankee Stadium CBA was missing a key component in its signing and negotiation: the community. The CBA was signed by the Yankees, the Bronx delegate to NYC Council, and the Bronx borough president. The CBA outlined a trust fund for ongoing community funding but gave the signees the power to appoint the fund's trustee. The trustee determines who is awarded funding, and to what degree (Salkin & Lavine, 2007). The CBA also called for the 20 acres of lost greenspace for Yankee Stadium to be replaced but put that responsibility in the hands of the city and the pockets of the taxpayers.

In 2008, two years after the CBA was signed, no community funding had been distributed. *The New York Times* published an article detailing the hold-up in fund distribution, and just a few weeks later, the first grants were issued (Salkin & Lavine, 2007). Though it is impossible to determine the effect, if any, that the *Times* article had on the distribution of funds, the delay in funding illustrates that a signed agreement is not a guarantee of immediate benefits. Based on an inquiry into the trust fund grant distribution between 2008 and 2015, the benefit of the CBA and its trust fund to the community remains in question. The analysis suggested that most funding goes to nonprofits from the wealthier zip codes in the Bronx (Hauser, 2017). Further, the replacement greenspace was not completed until three years after new Yankee Stadium opened (McClure, 2012).

Public Finance

Yankee Stadium is not unlike other major stadiums in the United States, subsidized through a series of tax incentives and public funds. Stadiums are costly, and, like other major infrastructure projects, there are not a wealth of options available to pay for their construction. Additionally, the Tax Reform Act of 1986 complicated the use of publicly issued tax-exempt financing for stadiums by removing them from activities that qualified for said exemptions. So, in the case of the Yankees, there were two primary options: pay-as-you-go or debt-finance.

The first option, pay-as-you-go, does not increase the total debt service for the issuer. In the case of New York City in the early 2000s, this was desirable. The city's debt service had grown considerably in years prior, and carrying a larger debt service can have ripple effects on bond ratings and the total cost of future municipal capital projects. Conversely, stadium construction is expensive, and to find nearly $1 billion in a short period of time requires directing a funding source almost entirely to the Yankees. The second option, debt financing, is really a series of sub-options: the stadium could be financed using publicly issued taxable bonds, publicly issued tax-exempt bonds, or private financing by the team. Taxable bonds, because they are taxed, are typically subject to a higher interest rate to accommodate the tax losses by investors. Thus, the total cost of capital may be higher over the length of the bond. Tax-exempt bonds tend to be popular for constructing stadiums because they offer a lower interest rate. But the public is on the hook for repaying the bonds and, because of the Tax Reform Act of 1986, reliant on the team to pay rents that refund the taxpayer dollars financing its construction. Finally, private financing remains an option. To pay for private financing requires creative revenue generation by the stadium, like selling naming rights or connecting directly with investors (Mark et al., n.d.).

In 2006, Yankee Stadium was debt-financed using publicly issued tax-exempt PILOT (payment in lieu of taxes) revenue bonds. The New York City Industrial Development Agency (NYCIDA) sold the tax-exempt bonds on behalf of the City of New York (Savader, 2008). The NYCIDA is charged with economic development in the city, supporting "business growth, relocation, and expansion across the five boroughs by lowering the cost of capital investment" (NYCIDA, n.d.). To do this, NYCIDA offers tax incentives, and in the case of the Yankees, tax-exempt bond issuances, that lower the total cost of capital. To finance the construction of the new Yankee stadium, NYCIDA issued $942 million in PILOT revenue bonds in 2006. In addition to these revenue bonds, the Yankees agreed to a cash payment of $77 million and contributions of $225.5 million from new revenue streams such as sponsorships and suite sales. Meanwhile, the city agreed to contribute its interest earnings ($46.4 million) from the period after the bonds were sold but before construction was completed (Brown et al., 2017).

The stadium PILOT revenue bonds are backed by the stadium's expected revenues, including admissions. After construction is completed and the stadium is operational, the Yankee Stadium LLC, an agent operating on behalf of the baseball team, issues annual payments to the NYCIDA sufficient to cover the revenue bond debt service. Should revenues not be sufficient to cover debt service, the NYCIDA is not obligated to pay debt service. Similarly, given that the arrangement involves the NYCIDA and the Yankee Stadium LLC, the Yankees (i.e., the team) organization is not tied to the debt issuance. It is, therefore, not subject to any financial risk or debt obligations (Savader, 2008).

When issued in 2006, the bonds were rated at BBB- by Standard & Poor's Rating Services but were upgraded to BBB in 2012 (Reuters, 2012). In 2020, when interest rates were extremely low and ticket sales questionable due to the COVID-19 pandemic, the NYCIDA refinanced the stadium's bonds (Ozanian, 2020). The refunding bonds were rated BBB+ by Fitch Ratings (2020), reflecting a delicate balance between a deep fanbase for the Yankees and uncertain revenue generation during and after the pandemic. According to an NYCIDA cost-benefit analysis on the bond refundings, the lower interest rates could save the city $71 million over the length of the bonds (Yankee Stadium LLC, 2020).

This arrangement worked because of the land ownership structure underlying Yankee Stadium. The land under the stadium remained publicly owned by the city, thus exempting the stadium from property taxes. So, during the 40 years of debt service on the stadium, the Yankees would pay a payment in lieu of taxes to cover the debt service. In 2006, the NYC Internal Budget Office (IBO) estimated that this arrangement would save the Yankees $84 million in property taxes over 30 years and $10.6 million annually in interest savings from the bonds' tax exemption. The new stadium was being built on parkland, so no property tax revenue was ever generated on the land. Nevertheless, in order to uphold the agreement with the National Parks Service, the city would need to spend $149 million to demolish the existing stadium and convert the land and surrounding area into parkland. Unlike the revenue bonds issued by NYCIDA for the stadium, the parks project debt was issued through the city's general capital improvement program, thus drawing on the city's debt service and, in theory, allocating valuable capital funding that could be needed for other projects. Additionally, upon completion of the stadium construction, the city and state each agreed to a one-time, $4.7-million payment into the stadium's reserve fund (NYC IBO, 2006).

The subsidies and costs detailed above are not the only ones associated with the project. According to the NYC IBO (2006), the Yankee Stadium project financing arrangement saved the Yankees $276 million, largely at the expense of the state and local government. The subsidy for the stadium was distributed across local, state, and federal taxpayers. The local property tax exemption, park-conversion debt-financing, and one-time reserve payment fell on local taxpayers; the state reserve payment fell on state taxpayers; and the interest savings on the tax-

Stadia and Community Stewardship 137

exempt bonds fell on federal taxpayers. In short, taxpayers in New York City, New York State, and the United States as a whole contributed to the Yankees and their new stadium. But did the Yankees return the favor?

Greenspace

As mentioned previously, Yankee Stadium was built on public land that received federal LWCF grant dollars. To get permission from the National Parks Service to use the land for construction of the new stadium, the city agreed to replace the lost 22 acres of parkland with 25 acres of parks along the Harlem River, on the existing stadium site, and around the surrounding area (Kozlowski, 2007). When construction began on the new stadium in 2006, the South Bronx lost the majority of its greenspace and 377 mature trees. Rather than starting demolition of the old stadium when construction for the new stadium began, the city chose to wait. When the new Yankee Stadium was completed in 2009, none of the new greenspace had been completed. Finally, in 2010, the track was completed. Two years later, in 2012, the remaining greenspace was available for use. The area, known for air quality issues, poverty, and environmental injustices, lost its largest tract of greenspace for six years (McClure, 2012).

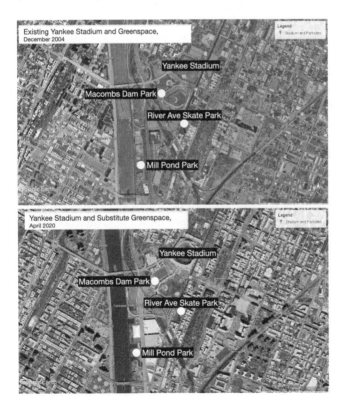

FIGURE 9.3 Comparison of greenspace near the Yankee Stadium site in 2004 (top) and 2020 (bottom). (Map data: Google, Maxar Technologies)

FIGURE 9.4 Joseph Yancey Track and Field at Macombs Dam Park. ("Joseph Yancey Track and Field" by Tdorante10 is licensed under CC BY-SA 4.0)

When the new greenspace was completed, it differed from the existing space in a number of ways. First, the new greenspace was not contiguous. The 25 acres were split across Mill Pond Park, an old Superfund site that had been remediated along the Harlem River, Macombs Dam Park on the old Yankee Stadium site, and the River Avenue Skate Park and pocket park. Second, the previously grass fields were replaced with turf, sitting atop a parking garage with one side at grade and the others above grade. The field, unlike its natural grass predecessor, can be incredibly hot. Third, and on a positive note, the new greenspace replaced aging parklands that were in desperate need of maintenance.

In the end, albeit in an altered way, the Yankees did pay their debt. However, the question remains whether the added benefit of new facilities has been worth the costs: six years from the loss of the existing greenspace to completion of the new greenspace; the replacement of a single 22-acre space with a few spaces that collectively provide 25-acres; and the replacement of grass with turf. Perhaps the most significant cost is the first one: six years without a complete replacement in an area where greenspace is essential to the health of residents. According to the EPA's EJScreen database, the South Bronx is in the highest percentile for cancer risk, traffic proximity, and diesel exposure. Additionally, a 2016 NYC OpenData map of greenspaces within the five boroughs suggests that the majority of the greenspace in the South Bronx is around Yankee Stadium and at Saint Mary's Park. For a child in an area with extremely high rates of childhood asthma, six years of even lower levels of greenspace is a further environmental injustice.

Conclusion: Toward More Sustainable Stadiums

Can stadiums be community stewards? The argument in favor of their construction typically includes a lengthy discussion of the economic benefits provided to nearby communities after construction and to the sense of place and community that comes from being home to a professional sports team. And, though the Yankees' delivery on the individual components of community stewardship has left many questioning the politics, economics, and social benefits of sport stadiums, the economic windfall from new stadiums, rising property values in urban areas, continued increases in debt service by municipal governments to finance capital projects in the city, and increased competition for land equate to a greater push from sports teams to get new stadiums and a greater challenge by governments to make it happen.

Community benefits agreements seem to be a way to address some issues, but they are clearly not a fix-all given that the Yankees had an agreement. As Saito and Truong (2015) stated, "Critics note that the Yankee Stadium CBA was negotiated by city officials rather than a community coalition, the Atlantic Yards CBA coalition contained only eight organizations, and the weak enforcement provisions for both CBAs" (p. 282). Including the stakeholders impacted by decisions is the exact issue that environmental justice advocates argue must change. As we noted in the beginning, two of the three pillars of environmental justice—recognition of the experiences of affected communities and the procedures through which planning decisions are made (Schlosberg, 2004)—seem to be lacking in the case of Yankee Stadium. Therefore, what we witnessed was, quite bluntly, the antithesis of justice for the South Bronx community.

But the Yankees do not have to be the model. Other sports stadium projects have engaged in much stronger and more equitable community benefits agreements, have been privately financed, and have been constructed on the same site as the existing stadium. Further, stadiums have begun electing to take on an increasingly "green" stance, recognizing the impact they can have on proximate communities and the global climate system. For example, Mercedes-Benz Stadium in Atlanta has a rainwater collection system on its roof that prevents stormwater runoff from the facility into the Proctor Creek Watershed, which has chronic flooding issues in historically Black neighborhoods of Atlanta. Similarly, Climate Pledge Arena in Seattle has committed to buying verifiable carbon offsets to offset emissions on-site and provides incentives for arena visitors to take public transportation to the site, thus reducing total carbon emissions and reducing the need for additional parking on site.

Better stewardship requires accountability. Accountability, especially in the delivery of community benefits, can be part of an outcomes-based contract designed by the individuals living in that community. Outcomes-based contracting has been used by local governments in similar public-private partnerships and could be applied to stadium financing. The application of the model could include, for example, disclosing measurable community outcomes, accountability in delivery, monitoring of outcomes, and program evaluation. Win or lose, economic windfall or downfall, the community is a written partner and beneficiary, not a contingency.

References

Bland, R. L., & Overton, M. R. (2019). *A budgeting guide for local government* (4th ed.). ICMA.

Brown, M., Rascher, D., Nagel, M., & McEvoy, C. (2017). Facility financing. In M. T. Brown, D. A. Rascher, M. S. Nagel, & C. D. McEvoy (Eds.), *Financial management in the sport industry* (2nd ed., pp. 215–252). Routledge.

Bunds, K. S., McLeod, C. M., & Newman, J. I. (2020). Political ecologies and environmental considerations in stadium development. In B. Wilson & B. Millington (Eds.), *Sport and the environment* (pp. 123–136). Emerald Publishing Limited.

Bunds, K. S., McLeod, C. M., Barrett, M., Newman, J. I., & Koenigstorfer, J. (2019). The object-oriented politics of stadium sustainability: A case study of SC Freiburg. *Sustainability, 11*(23), 6712. 10.3390/su11236712

City of New York Independent Budget Office. (2006). *Testimony of Ronnie Lowenstein before the City Council Finance Committee on financing plans for the new Yankee Stadium, April 10, 2006.* https://ibo.nyc.ny.us/iboreports/Yankstadiumtestimony.pdf

Coates, D., & Humphreys, B. R. (2008). Do economists reach a conclusion on subsidies for sports franchises, stadiums, and mega-events? *Econ Journal Watch, 5*(3), 294–315. http://journaltalk.net/articles/5584

Crompton, J. (2004). Beyond economic impact: An alternative rationale for the public subsidy of major league sports facilities. *Journal of Sport Management, 18*(1), 40–58. 10.1123/jsm.18.1.40

Cutter, S. L. (1995). Race, class and environmental justice. *Progress in Human Geography, 19*(1), 111–122. 10.1177/030913259501900111

Fitch Ratings. (2020, September). *Fitch rates Yankee Stadium's Series 2020 PILOT Bonds "BBB+"; Outlook stable.* https://www.fitchratings.com/research/infrastructure-project-finance/fitch-rates-yankee-stadium-series-2020-pilot-bonds-bbb-outlook-stable-15-09-2020

Gayer, T., Drukker, A. J., & Gold, A. K. (2016). *Tax-exempt municipal bonds and the financing of professional sport stadiums.* Brookings.

Gruber, J. (2019). *Public finance and public policy* (6th ed.). Worth Publishers.

Harrington, A. G. (2011). The house that cultural capital built: The saga of the new Yankee Stadium. *NINE: A Journal of Baseball History and Culture, 19*(2), 77–92. 10.1353/nin.2 011.0022

Hauser, M. (2017, June 28). Grants for Yankees' neighbors stray far away from stadium. *The New York Times*, A1.

Heynen, N., Perkins, H. A., & Roy, P. (2006). The political ecology of uneven urban green space: The Impact of political economy on race and ethnicity in producing environmental inequality in Milwaukee. *Urban Affairs Review, 42*(1), 3–25. 10.1177/1 078087406290729

Holifield, R., Chakraborty, J., & Walker, G. (2018). Introduction. In R. Holifield, J. Chakraborty, & G. Walker (Eds.), *The Routledge handbook of environmental justice* (pp. 1–11). Routledge.

Jakar, G. S., & Rosentraub, M. S. (2021). From public goods theory to municipal capitalism: Evaluating investments in sport venues from an urban entrepreneurial perspective. *Journal of Urban Affairs*. Advance online publication. 10.1080/07352166.2021.1881406

Jennings, V., Gaither, C. J., & Gragg, R. S. (2012). Reviews promoting environmental justice through urban green space access: A synopsis. *Environmental Justice, 5*(1), 1–7. 10.1089/env.2011.0007

Johnson, B. K., & Whitehead, J. C. (2000). Value of public goods from sports stadiums: The CVM approach. *Contemporary Economic Policy, 18*(1), 48–58. 10.1111/J.1465-7287.2000.TB00005.X

Kellison, T. (2022). An overview of Sustainable Development Goal 11. In B. McCullough & T. Kellison (Eds.), *The Routledge handbook of sport and sustainable development* (pp. 261–275). Routledge.

Korngold, G. (2018). Community benefits agreements: Flexibility and inclusion in U.S. zoning. In A. Lehavi (Ed.), *One hundred years of zoning and the future of cities* (pp. 95–120). Springer.

Kozlowski, J. C. (2007). Law review: New Yankee Stadium replaced parkland. *Parks & Recreation, 42*(4), 35.

Locke, M. (2021). *The stakes are high: Reinventing the private sport sector as a catalyst for good in communities* [Doctoral dissertation, University of Ottawa]. https://ruor.uottawa.ca/handle/10393/41635

Maciejczyk, P. B., Offenberg, J. H., Clemente, J., Blaustein, M.Martin, Thurston, G. D., & Chi Chen, L. (2004). Ambient pollutant concentrations measured by a mobile laboratory in South Bronx, NY. *Atmospheric Environment, 38*(31), 5283–5294 10.1016/j.atmosenv.2004.02.062

Mark, S., Belkin, D., & Cortell, J. (n.d.). *Double play: The economics and financing of stadiums for the Yankees and Mets.* City of New York Independent Budget Office. https://ibo.nyc.ny.us/iboreports/doubleplay.html

Maroko, A. R., Weiss Riley, R., Reed, M., & Malcolm, M. (2014). Direct observation of neighborhood stressors and environmental justice in the South Bronx, New York City. *Population and Environment, 35*(4), 477–496. 10.1007/S11111-013-0197-5/TABLES/7

McClure, R. (2012). *Kids wait six years for ballfields taken over by Yankee Stadium.* InvestigateWest. https://www.invw.org/2012/06/11/explaining-yankee-stadium-1282/

Ozanian, M. (2020, September). *New Yankee Stadium bonds will save team and city millions in debt payments.* Forbes. https://www.forbes.com/sites/mikeozanian/2020/09/16/new-yankee-stadium-bonds-will-save-team-and-city-millions-in-debt-payments/?sh=779a781e4eea

Perkins, H. A., Heynen, N., & Wilson, J. (2004). Inequitable access to urban reforestation: The impact of urban political economy on housing tenure and urban forests. *Cities, 21*(4), 291–299. 10.1016/J.CITIES.2004.04.002

Reuters. (2012). *S&P raises Yankee Stadium bonds to "BBB".* https://www.reuters.com/article/idUSWNA239120120731

Rigolon, A., Browning, M., & Jennings, V. (2018). Inequities in quality urban park systems: An environmental justice investigation of cities in the United States. *Landscape and Urban Planning, 178*, 156–169. 10.1016/j.landurbplan.2018.05.026

Saito, L., & Truong, J. (2015). The L.A. Live community benefits agreement: Evaluating the agreement results and shifting political power in the city. *Urban Affairs Review, 51*(2), 263–289. 10.1177/1078087414527064

Salkin, P. E., & Lavine, A. (2007). Negotiating for social justice and the promise of Community Benefits Agreements: Case studies of current and developing agreements. *Journal of Affordable Housing & Community Development Law, 17*(1/2), 113–144. https://www.jstor.org/stable/25782806?seq=1

Sanderson, A. R., & Shaikh, S. L. (2017). Economics, sports, and the environment: Incentives and intersections. In B. P. McCullough & T. B. Kellison (Eds.), *Routledge handbook of sport and the environment* (pp. 36–53). Routledge.

Savader, M. (2008). Yankees versus Mets: A subway series. In S. Feldstein & F. Fabozzi (Eds.), *The handbook of municipal bonds* (pp. 1233–1236). John Wiley & Sons, Ltd.

Schlosberg, D. (2004). Reconceiving environmental justice: Global movements and political theories. *Environmental Politics, 13*(3), 517–540 10.1080/0964401042000229025

Schwester, R. W. (2007). An examination of the public good externalities of professional athletic venues: Justifications for public financing? *Public Budgeting and Finance, 27*(3), 89–109. 10.1111/J.1540-5850.2007.00884.X

Seiffied, C., & Clopton, A. W. (2013). An alternative view of public subsidy and sport facilities through social anchor theory. *City, Culture and Society, 4*(1), 49–55. 10.1016/j.ccs.2013.01.001

Shearston, J. A., Johnson, A. M., Domingo-Relloso, A., Kioumourtzoglou, M.-A., Hernández, D., Ross, J., Chillrud, S. N., & Hilpert, M. (2020). Opening a large delivery service warehouse in the South Bronx: Impacts on traffic, air pollution, and noise. *International Journal of Environmental Research and Public Health, 17*(9), 3208, 10.3390/ijerph17093208

Spira-Cohen, A., Chen, L. C., Kendall, M., Sheesley, R., & Thurston, G. D. (2009). Personal exposures to traffic-related particle pollution among children with asthma in the South Bronx, NY. *Journal of Exposure Science & Environmental Epidemiology, 20*(5), 446–456. 10.1038/JES.2009.34

U.S. Census Bureau. (2019). *ACS 5-Year estimates subject tables.* https://www.census.gov/programs-surveys/acs

U.S. Census Bureau. (2020). *DEC redistricting data (PL 94–171).* https://www.census.gov/programs-surveys/decennial-census/data/datasets.html

Walters, S., Wilson, L., Konty, K., Day, S., Agerton, T., & Olson, C. (2021). *Disparities among children with asthma in New York City.* http://www1.nyc.gov/assets/doh/downloads/pdf/ah/zipcodetable.pdf

Williams, T. (2006, November 17). Bronx: Stadium objection dismissed. *The New York Times.* https://www.nytimes.com/2006/11/17/nyregion/17mbrfs-BRONXSTADIUM_BRF.html

Wolf-Powers, L. (2010). Community benefits agreements and local government: A review of recent evidence. *Journal of the American Planning Association, 76*(2), 141–159. 10.1080/01944360903490923

Yankee Stadium LLC. (2020). *NYCIDA project cost/benefit analysis.* https://edc.nyc/sites/default/files/2020-03/NYCIDA-Yankees-PHP-2020.pdf

10

THE ANACOSTIA WATERFRONT INITIATIVE, NATIONALS PARK, AND ENVIRONMENTAL JUSTICE IN WASHINGTON, D.C.

Michael Friedman

In 2018, travel writer Ann Abel identified Washington D.C.'s Navy Yard area as one of the twelve "coolest neighborhoods around the world." Discussing "its waterfront location, industrial infrastructure and historic roots," Abel quotes travel website Indagare founder Melissa Biggs Bradley, who states "the Navy Yard—or 'the Yards'—has a cool factor that most other D.C. neighborhoods lack." As the article identifies "up-and-coming neighborhoods where local creatives are settling in and setting up shop," the area, also known as the "Near Southeast" and "Capital Riverfront," is Washington's fastest growing neighborhood with 6.2 million square feet of development and 10,000 new residents since 1995 (Friedman, in press).

Abel (2018) labels Nationals Park, home of the Washington Nationals since 2008, as the neighborhood's main attraction. While the city's commitment to build the $670-million stadium was necessary to secure Major League Baseball's (MLB) return to the nation's capital, Mayor Anthony Williams used the stadium to advance the Anacostia Waterfront Initiative (AWI), his signature planning project. Focusing on one of the country's most polluted rivers, the AWI sought $8 billion of public and private investment over 25 years to clean up the Anacostia River and improve surrounding neighborhoods. Enumerating several environmental and social justice goals, the AWI promised to transform the Anacostia River from a symbol of the city's historic political, economic, and racial divisions into a source of economic opportunity and civic unity (District of Columbia Office of Planning [DCOP], 2003). In these efforts, Nationals Park has been described as "perhaps the defining element of the revitalization of the Anacostia Waterfront" (Amirtahmasebi et al., 2016, p. 327).

Despite being one of the most successful urban redevelopment projects of the 21st century, the AWI's accomplishments are tempered by unintended consequences as many people have been displaced by soaring property values and rental prices (Friedman, in press). Since 2003 when Williams announced a goal of

DOI: 10.4324/9781003262633-12

144 Michael Friedman

FIGURE 10.1   Nationals Park. (Photo by Jeremy Bishop is licensed by Unsplash)

bringing 100,000 new residents into a city of 572,000, people have been moving into long-neglected neighborhoods east of the Anacostia River that have been reshaped by the AWI and other planning efforts. Yet, as D.C.'s population reached 689,545 in 2020, questions relating to gentrification and the distributions of benefits and costs from development are increasingly shaping the city's politics (Gibson, 2015).

To explore problems of environmental justice in the development of Nationals Park, this chapter first examines the long-entrenched, structural disparities in planning and governance that have intentionally denied democratic participation to D.C. residents and ignored their needs. The chapter then discusses Williams' mayoral administration, the AWI, and redevelopment in the Near Southeast. Thus contextualized, the chapter assesses the fit and impact of Nationals Park on the AWI and concludes by discussing the impacts and implications of Nationals Park and AWI on environmental justice in Washington.

Histories and Geographies of Injustice in Washington D.C.

Washington, D.C. was founded with a fundamental contradiction: a city designed to symbolize democratic ideals denies residents full participation in democracy. Governed by a Congress lacking D.C. representatives, disparities between neighborhoods show the inequities produced by government officials and planners unaccountable to residents for most of the city's history. According to Gillette (2006), "as [the Federal Government] created an aesthetically pleasing monumental core at the heart of Washington, it allowed many of the surrounding neighborhoods to fall into the social and physical decay now considered endemic in urban areas" (p. x).

Established by the Constitution, the city was intended to serve as the functional center of the U.S. government and to represent the democratic ideals enshrined in the country's founding documents (Gutheim & Lee, 2006). Commissioned to design a city in the style of European capitals, French architect Pierre L'Enfant determined locations for major governmental buildings, created ceremonial spaces for celebrating national events, and identified monumental spaces to honor national leaders and heroes. Though neglected for much of the 19th century, L'Enfant's design inspired the McMillan Plan of 1903 that produced the city's federal core around the National Mall, built memorials to Abraham Lincoln and Thomas Jefferson, proposed the Federal Triangle to concentrate the headquarters of government agencies, and identified locations for future monuments and museums (Gutheim & Lee, 2006).

Despite the city serving as the functional and symbolic center of American democracy, the Constitution simultaneously gives Congress exclusive jurisdiction over the Federal District and denies Congressional representation to its residents (Friedman & Andrews, 2011). As a result, appointed commissioners answering only to Congressional committees rather than elected officials answerable to residents have governed the city for most of its history. Moreover, committees were frequently led by Southerners committed to segregation and generally opposed to initiatives and spending benefitting the city's large Black community or providing residents with meaningful political power. South Carolina Congressman John McMillan's[1] tenure as chairman of the House District Committee between 1948 and 1972 exemplified this dynamic (Smith, 1974). Essentially Washington's *de facto* mayor, McMillan ruled the city "with courtly indifference to the demands and concerns of the city's residents," once claiming "no one seems to object to the work performed by this committee except the public" (Smith, 1974, p. 142).

With no one in Congress accountable to D.C. residents representing the city's interests, this history of disenfranchisement retarded development beyond the Federal core. Throughout the 19th century, Congress generally avoided funding the public works projects needed for the city to achieve L'Enfant's vision (Gutheim & Lee, 2006; Hyra, 2017). During most of the 20th century, residents had little power to impact planning efforts initiated by Congress or delegated to the National Capital Planning Commission (NCPC; Gillette, 2006). With the NCPC focused on executing elements of McMillan Plan before World War II and broader regional concerns after the war, the city's neighborhoods received relatively little attention.

The most significant exception to this neglect was the NCPC-led redevelopment of Southwest D.C. between the 1950s and 1970s. Considered one of America's most ambitious urban renewal projects, the plan sought to transform 400 acres located within one-half mile of Capitol Hill and inhabited by 23,500 mostly poor residents (Ammon, 2009). As 80% of displaced residents were Black, community leaders criticized the project as "Negro removal" as planners sought to

146 Michael Friedman

slow suburban White flight. Despite high expectations, Southwest redevelopment failed as developers did not deliver the promised affordable housing, community facilities, and commercial projects; new modernist buildings were esthetically unappealing; and community life was irreparably shattered (Friedman, 2010; Gillette, 2006). This failure helped discredit large-scale raze-and-rebuild comprehensive urban renewal programs in the United States.

As demonstrated in the redevelopment of Southwest D.C., issues surrounding race have been significant in Washington's histories of governance and planning. Despite representing liberty and self-governance, slavery was legal in the city and the White House and U.S. Capitol were built with Black slave labor. Yet, D.C.'s proximity to the South has made it a magnet for Blacks throughout its history (Hyra, 2017). This status made Washington a center for Black education, culture, and employment, especially as a growing Federal bureaucracy during the mid-20th century that offered quality job opportunities denied to Blacks in other parts of the economy. As White residents moved to suburbs after World War II, in 1957, Washington became the first major American city to have a majority Black population (Gillette, 2006).

Pressured by civil rights activists, in 1973, Congress granted Home Rule to D.C. residents by allowing them to elect a mayor and city council but imposed significant constraints (Friedman & Andrews, 2011; General Accounting Office [GAO], 2003). First, Congress must approve the city's budget and all its laws, which has led to the imposition of conservative social programs and micromanagement of city affairs (Friedman, in press). Second, with nearly half of the city's real estate exempt from property taxes, Congress further restricts the D.C. government's ability to raise revenue by barring a commuter tax and diminishing property values through the 1910 Height of Buildings Act that imposes a 130-foot limitation on new construction (GAO, 2003). Finally, the city has additional financial burdens for transportation, justice, and welfare services typically managed by states and the unique costs of being the capital. The GAO (2003) estimated these factors produce annual structural deficits between $470 million and $1.1 billion and result in D.C. residents bearing one of the country's largest local tax burdens despite receiving below-average public services and utilizing decaying infrastructure.

Anthony Williams and the Anacostia Waterfront Initiative

As structural deficits, governance restraints, and corruption under Mayor Marion Barry placed Washington onto the edge of bankruptcy by the mid-1990s, Congress installed an independent Financial Control Board (FCB) and stripped Barry and the D.C. Council of most of their authority (Jaffe & Sherwood, 2014). To stabilize the city's financial situation, the FCB was given sweeping powers to restructure contracts, fire city employees, and enforce budgetary discipline (GAO, 2003). Williams, who was serving as Chief Financial Officer for the U.S. Department of Agriculture, was appointed to same role at the FCB.

In contrast to the flamboyant Barry, Williams was much more of a technocrat than a politician (Jaffe & Sherwood, 2014). Using the FCB's powers, Williams quickly turned a $772-million deficit into a surplus (Hyra, 2017). He so impressed the city's business community that, when Barry chose not to run for reelection, political activists from Northwest D.C. drafted him to run for mayor. Running a campaign essentially promising boring competence, Williams won the Democratic primary for mayor[2] in 1998 with 50% of votes in a race that included three councilmembers (Jaffe & Sherwood, 2014). Recognizing the city's progress and trusting Williams continued management, Congress ended the FCB in 2001.

Although recruited by D.C.'s wealthiest residents and businesses, Williams announced his mayoral campaign on the banks of the Anacostia River to signal his intention to create "a more inclusive city" (DCOP, 2003). Considered the city's dividing line and symbolic of its inequalities, communities east of the river were largely populated by Black residents and generally received fewer public resources and less attention from Congress and city planners. This disparity was evident within the development of the Metro subway system, which served suburban areas when opened in 1976 but not neighborhoods in Southeast D.C. until the 1990s (Avni & Fischler, 2019). The city's divisions impacted the Anacostia River directly as, despite D.C. never developing extensive heavy industry, general neglect and abuse allowed untreated overflows of sewage, stormwater, garbage, and fertilizer to produce one of the country's most polluted rivers (Friedman & Andrews, 2011).

Intending to address the economic, environmental, social, and transit injustices associated with the Anacostia River, Williams announced the AWI in 2000. Described as an effort on "par with the McMillan Commission Plan," project manager Uwe Brandes promised the AWI "will completely overhaul the quality of life in the District" (as quoted in Santana, 2003, p. T3) by targeting seven riverside neighborhoods for intensive redevelopment and expanding public access to the river. Anticipated to cost $8 billion over 25 years, the AWI's goals included 20,000 new housing units, 20 million square feet of commercial, office, and retail development, 10 new tourist destinations, and an integrated river-park system along the 6.8 miles of waterfront (Friedman & Andrews, 2011). Guided by five major principles, the AWI sought to:

- Restore "a clean and active river" by mitigating pollution, controlling run-off, restoring streams and wetlands, and promoting aquatic activities (DCOP, 2003, p. 21). In addition to the $2.7 billion D.C. Clean Rivers Project that is anticipated to reduce combined sewer overflows by 98% when finished in 2023, the AWI's environmental agenda incorporates sustainable development and design practices as part of its overall effort to enhance environmental justice.
- Connect the city by "breaking down barriers and gaining access" through improving transportation infrastructure and public transportation (DCOP, 2003, p. 21). While transportation design in other parts of the city produced a "memorable and engaging waterfront," the Anacostia River was cut off by highways that favored "regional mobility over neighborhood accessibility and

148 Michael Friedman

livability" (DCOP, 2003, p. 37). Rather than perpetuating racial, economic, and social divides, the AWI would enhance transit justice for underserved residents by expanding private and public transportation options, improving and upgrading existing roads (including a replacement for the deteriorating Frederick Douglass Bridge), building sidewalks, increasing connections across the river, and providing better access to the restored river.

- Produce "a great riverfront park system" by developing open spaces and providing continuous pedestrian and bicycle access to the waterfront (DCOP, 2003, p. 21). With the NCPC's resource allocation practices historically disadvantaging areas outside the federal core, the differences in quality between Rock Creek Park in Northwest D.C. and Anacostia Park served as "a stark reminder of the inequities that persist in the nation's capital" (DCOP, 2003, p. 59). As the AWI addressed inequalities by providing resources to improve existing parks, create new parks and recreational facilities, and expand recreation programming, it would also secure access to the waterfront from the multiple government agencies that controlled it.
- Build "strong waterfront neighborhoods" through encouraging development in neighborhoods on the eastern side of the river (DCOP, 2003, p. 21). Recognizing that an improved waterfront would attract investment, the AWI promised "equal effort at revitalizing and preserving existing neighborhoods" toward reducing the dislocation associated with gentrification (DCOP, 2003, p. 93). To support equitable development, policies sought to create mixed-income communities through affordable housing mandates, incentivize retail and commercial development, expand job training programs, build new schools, and create partnerships with existing community organizations.
- Create "cultural destinations of distinct character" that could provide residents with shared experiences and attract visitors to areas beyond the National Mall (DCOP, 2003, p. 21). The AWI identified more than "25 waterfront sites for museums, concert venues, fairs and commemorative places, among other cultural amenities" (DCOP, 2003, p. 79) and noted two sites identified for a potential baseball stadium were along the Anacostia River. Planners believed that these amenities would help reduce the city's historic divisions between the federal core and neighborhoods.

Explicitly recognizing the injustices perpetuated within D.C.'s history of planning, the AWI promised to transform the Anacostia River from a symbol of division into a source of economic opportunity and social unity (DCOP, 2003). Yet, Avni and Fischler (2019) suggest environmental and social justice goals, though usually complementary, can possess contradictory elements. This is especially evident within waterfront redevelopment projects that promise environmental improvements, enhanced access, and new amenities. However, as these projects prioritize economic development, benefits often are enjoyed by wealthy consumers who move into improving areas and dislocate previous residents (Avni & Fischler, 2019). Such tensions are evident within the development of Nationals Park.

Revitalizing the Near Southeast through Nationals Park

As one of the targeted neighborhoods within the AWI, the Near Southeast had long been recognized for both its development potential and repeated development failures (Friedman, 2008). Despite its status as one of the city's few industrialized areas, the presence of the Washington Navy Yard, and a location within one mile of Capitol Hill, multiple developers have lost fortunes investing in the neighborhood. In one example from the 1790s that seemingly set a two-century pattern, three speculators accumulated $13 million of debt (nearly $300 million in 2022 inflation-adjusted figures) in a complex land deal that first required them to build and sell 20 buildings in the Near Southeast. When poor construction failed to attract buyers, the investors declared bankruptcy and were incarcerated in a debtor's prison (Arnebeck, 2004).

As investors repeatedly failed, the Near Southeast neighborhood developed a unique character with a mix of light industrial uses, government buildings, and sexually oriented businesses serving the LGBTQ+ community. Besides 1,853 residents, most of whom lived in the Arthur Capper/Carrollsburg public housing projects, 16,500 people worked in the neighborhood (NCPC, 2006). With few retail options and no cultural or entertainment centers, Jacqueline Dupree, whose JDLand blog has chronicled changes in the Near Southeast since 2002, explained, "I think that it was a pretty common feeling among the people [living] on Capitol Hill, that unless you went to the nightclubs or to the Navy Yard ... there's just nothing there and really probably best to stay away" (Friedman, 2008, p. 147).

Three decisions by the Federal government launched the Near Southeast's transformation before the start of the AWI (Friedman, in press). The Naval Seas Systems Command, the Navy's procurement division, announced in 1997 that it would relocate to the Washington Navy Yard. This created demand for nearby Class A office space as procurement regulations include proximity requirements for contractors. In 2001, Congress authorized private development on the vacant 55-acre Southeast Federal Center site. With the U.S. Department of Transportation claiming 13 acres for a new headquarters, Forest City Enterprises secured rights to develop the remainder into "the Yards"—a $1-billion, 18-year project that would produce 2,600 housing units and 2 million square feet of office, retail, and cultural space (Hsu, 2005). Finally, the D.C. Housing Authority received a Federal Hope VI grant in 2001 to replace 707 public housing units at the Arthur Capper/Carrollsburg projects with 1,562 units of mixed-income housing (Friedman, 2008). With development underway, neighborhood business leaders formed the Capitol Riverfront Business Improvement District (CRBID) in 2007. The CRBID's initial estimates at buildout in 2040 anticipated a residential population of 18,000 and 80,000 workers and included 12–15 million square feet of office space, 9,000 residential units, 1,200 hotel rooms, 800,000 square feet of retail, and four public parks (Capitol Riverfront Business Improvement District, 2022).[3]

A baseball stadium was not originally part of Williams' mayoral agenda or the AWI. However, recognizing the impact of Capital One Center on the

FIGURE 10.2 Nationals Park, under construction in 2007. (Photo by Aude is licensed under CC BY-SA 3.0)

redevelopment of Penn Quarter in Northwest D.C., Williams believed a baseball stadium could provide similar benefits to another neighborhood (Friedman, in press; Hyra, 2017). With Williams instructing negotiators to "slightly overpay" to reach an agreement with MLB for the relocation of the Montreal Expos, the city promised to pay the entire cost of a new stadium (Friedman & Andrews, 2011, p. 189). As alternative sites were rejected due to security, price, environmental, or development concerns, construction in the Near Southeast would enable the city to justify additional infrastructure spending for the neighborhood, exert more influence on its development, and with its location at the end of the Frederick Douglass Bridge on South Capitol Street, produce an attractive gateway to the neighborhood and city (Friedman & Andrews, 2011).

The design of Nationals Park itself was expected to be inclusive, consistent with the planning and design principles of the AWI, and produce "an environmentally friendly ballpark" (D.C. Sports and Entertainment Commission [DCSEC], 2005, p. 3). Toward being inclusive, HOK Sport lead designer Joseph Spear sought to represent "the transparency of democracy" within the stadium's architecture (Friedman, 2010). This transparency would be achieved with spaces where the field could be seen from the sidewalk, the extensive use of glass both inside and outside the stadium and a modernist design suggestive of the National Gallery's East Building on the National Mall (Friedman, 2010).

By anchoring the 60-acre "Ballpark District," Nationals Park would contribute to the neighborhood's economic development as a "vibrant mixed-use waterfront destination" attracting visitors to cafés, bars, restaurants, boutique shops, hotels, offices, and apartments throughout the year (Friedman & Andrews, 2011). Moreover, the estimated $100 million annual revenues from increased property and sales tax collections would help justify the stadium's $670-million public cost (ROMA Design Group et al., 2005). As stadium construction began in 2006, Monument Realty announced it would develop 1.5 million square feet along Half Street and Akridge announced its plans for two office buildings and one residential building (O'Connell, 2014).

To meet environmental concerns, Nationals Park became the first major league sports stadium to meet Leadership in Energy and Environmental Design (LEED) standards (Friedman, 2008). Besides 95% of the stadium's steel having been recycled, green construction techniques reduced gaseous emissions and resulted in the recycling of 5,500 tons of construction waste. Recognizing stormwater control as necessary for cleaning the Anacostia River, Nationals Park includes a 6,300-square-foot green roof and a state-of-the-art filtration system to capture solid waste and chemicals (Friedman, 2008).

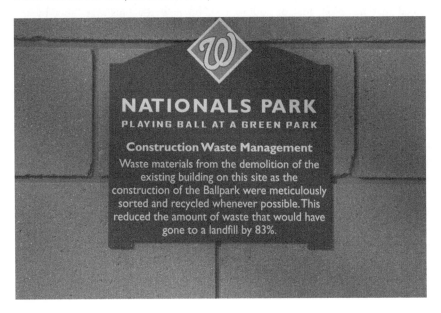

FIGURE 10.3   Sustainable design at Nationals Park

Assessing Justice in Nationals Park

Issues of social and environmental justice in Nationals Park cannot be separated from the stadium's position within the redevelopment of the Near Southeast and use within the AWI. Deeply embedded in both of these efforts, Nationals Park is

152 Michael Friedman

implicated within Avni and Fischler's (2019) critique that "it is clear from the AWI's master plan that the AWI is first and foremost a growth-oriented project and that the goal of fostering justice, though primary at the onset, became gradually more secondary as the project progressed" (p. 1781). First, Nationals Park is the most expensive and highest-profile project in the AWI, which has produced and intensified gentrification around the Anacostia River. Second, despite perceptions of driving economic growth in the Near Southeast, Nationals Park has been much less effective than people believe. Third, Nationals Park's construction displaced various users and uses from the neighborhood while its operations tend to be highly exclusionary despite the inclusionary rhetoric of its designers.

The AWI, Gentrification, and Justice

Although civic leaders proclaimed the AWI would pursue justice goals alongside economic development, these intentions were overwhelmed by the city's rapid growth. This is, in part, due to the unexpected success of the AWI and other planning initiatives in reversing Washington's population decline that had begun in the 1950s. Negative expectations were so pervasive that Mayor Williams described that his 2003 goal of adding 100,000 new residents was "met by indifference [as] nobody took me seriously" (personal communication, April 22, 2021). Yet, as Washington's population has increased by nearly 25% over the past two decades, the city's housing stock has been overwhelmed, which has caused prices to soar. The AWI's 18,000 new housing units built between 2003 and 2018 have been insufficient to meet rising demand as D.C. has the country's third highest rental prices with one-bedroom apartments costing an average of $2,223 per month (Chaplin & Warnock, 2021). Median prices for owner-occupied housing have increased from an inflation-adjusted $234,000 in 2006 to $580,000 in 2020 (U.S. Census Bureau, 2008, 2020). With housing increasingly unaffordable for households with annual income below $75,000, 36% of the people moving out of D.C. between 2000 and 2014 claimed to have done so for housing-related reasons (Taylor, 2015).

The AWI's successes contain a deep irony. Before the AWI, people living east of the Anacostia River had unequal access to a clean environment, grocery stores and fresh food options, health care facilities, convenient and reliable public transportation, and well-maintained public parks. As the city has addressed these inequities by producing a clean and accessible Anacostia River, attracting new housing, incentivizing retail and commercial development, improving public safety, expanding transit links to other parts of the city, and increasing recreational opportunities, the AWI's seven target neighborhoods are now desirable places to live. The resulting increases in consumer demand and housing prices have displaced many previous residents who can no longer afford to live there, despite the intentions of the AWI to pursue equitable development. Essentially, efforts to address previous injustices have produced new injustices: gentrification and displacement.

Development in the Ballpark District

Identified in the AWI for its development potential, activity in the Near Southeast has been remarkable with combined investment by public and private actors exceeding $3.3 billion (RCLCO Real Estate Advisors, 2019). Since 2000, development has produced 14 million square feet of mixed-use space and the entire neighborhood generated $287 million in tax revenues for the city's general fund in 2018 (3.5 times higher than in 2007). Although 2007 estimates anticipated 18,000 residents and 80,000 workers when the neighborhood was fully developed in 2040, changes in the area's development mix now suggest that the area will contain 30,000 residents and 45,000 workers at buildout (Friedman, in press).

Despite media proclamations that Nationals Park has been "an urban redevelopment triumph" (Boswell, 2016), deeper analyses suggest a more complicated picture as the Ballpark District lagged substantially behind the rest of the neighborhood. One cause was the 2008 financial crisis that was precipitated in part by the bankruptcy of Lehman Brothers, which was a partner in Monument Realty's Half Street project. With construction stalled due to bankruptcy proceedings, the building site became "Washington's most infamous hole in the ground" by 2013 (O'Connell, 2014). However, the financial crisis offers limited explanation because development activity in other parts of the Near Southeast quickly rebounded with 23 projects completed between 2009 and 2016 as compared to two in the Ballpark District (Friedman, in press).

Development patterns suggest the delay may be attributable to Nationals Park's intermittent usage. Despite more than 20 million people attending games at Nationals Park since 2008, the baseball schedule includes only 81 regular season home games between April and October. Such a schedule cannot sufficiently sustain businesses that are required to maintain payrolls, pay rent, and use utilities throughout the year (Friedman, in press). However, once other projects were completed and the Near Southeast achieved a critical mass of workers and residents, development of the Ballpark District proceeded with 12 projects being completed since 2016. Many key stakeholders in the Near Southeast seem to recognize this relationship. Rather than crediting Nationals Park for having direct impacts on development, Williams, CRBID executive director Michael Stevens, and Forest City Washington President Deborah Ratner Salzberg all describe the stadium as an "accelerant" that demonstrated the city's commitment to revitalizing the Anacostia River and for the visitors and attention the stadium brought to the Near Southeast (Friedman, in press). Yet, as costs for major league sports venues in the United States now exceed $1 billion, it is important to ask whether such indirect benefits represent a sufficient economic return or if resources can be better spent on other projects with much greater impact.

Nationals Park as an Exclusionary Space

As the AWI's most expensive public project, Nationals Park's questionable economic and development impacts may be problematic, but Williams suggests that these should not be the only metrics by which to judge the stadium. Rather, governments should have "some freedom to spend some money on entertainment, even if there's no [economic] benefit to it … it's a quality-of-life issue, but there's agency to the public. We have to consider that too. It's not all economic" (personal communication, April 22, 2021). In some regards, Nationals Park could be seen as an inclusive space serving as a focal point for communal identity and civic cohesion (especially during the team's 2019 World Series winning season). Nationals Park adds to regional cohesion as 80% of attendees live in D.C. suburbs (Friedman, in press). Yet, the stadium's social benefits have been produced on inequitable foundations within the displacement required for its construction and the highly exclusionary aspects of its design, operations, and symbolic representations of democracy.

The city seized much of the land to build Nationals Park through eminent domain and displaced many different individuals and groups from the neighborhood. Along O Street, there were several sexually oriented businesses, bars, and nightclubs that had served the LGBTQ+ community since the 1970s. In "a kind of 24-hour mini-mall of prurience" (Schwartzman, 2005, p. A1), patrons explored and expressed their sexual identities, and marginalized people found opportunities to work, find acceptance, and form communities within emotionally safe spaces as they faced social rejection and the AIDS crisis (Seymour, 2008). Beyond O Street, people like Ken Wyban and the operators of the Washington Sculpture Center were denied opportunities to be part of an up-and-coming neighborhood. Wyban, who was planning his retirement from the Army, purchased a pre-Civil War townhouse in 1998 that he intended to convert into a Bed-and-Breakfast catering to tourists (Morton, 2004). In 2003, Patricia Ghiglino and Reinaldo Lopez established the WSC to teach sculpture using glass, metal, and stone; to promote and place sculptures in D.C. public spaces; and to facilitate cultural and artistic exchange (Washington Sculpture Center, 2012). Losing the building due to eminent domain, Lopez described the situation as being "like reverse Robin Hood to me. They are taking from the poor and giving it to the rich" (Knott, 2004, p. C1). As most of the O Street businesses and WSC have not reopened and Wyban has moved out of the area, they have been permanently erased from the neighborhood and the city.

While the design and operation of Nationals Park may not take from the poor to give to the rich, the stadium provides significantly divergent price-differentiated experiences to attendees such that the rich are comfortable and the poor are virtually absent as spectators. In addition to private restrooms, air-conditioned clubs, gourmet buffets, and concierge service, premium seats offer padded seats that are three inches wider with greater legroom than seats in non-premium areas (Friedman, 2008). While such luxuries are expected within premium areas of sports facilities built since the 1990s, non-premium seats are narrower than those in RFK Stadium (opened in 1961), where the Nationals played for three seasons. Additionally, when Nationals Park opened, concourses provided non-refrigerated and non-filtered water fountains for patrons unwilling or unable to purchase beverages at concession stands (Friedman, 2008). Such disparate experiences are especially problematic as, in 2019, Nationals Park had MLB's sixth-highest Fan Cost Index[4] at $338 per game for a family of four (Hartweg, 2020). This cost significantly exceeds the monthly entertainment budget of the average American household, which makes attendance difficult for middle-class families and virtually unaffordable for those in lower socio-economic groups (Friedman, in press).

Finally, the symbolic representation of the "transparency of democracy" in the design of Nationals Park mirrors the city's contradictory representations and practices of democracy as visibility is not synonymous with access (Friedman, 2010). Although HOK Sport architects used glass to express transparency, they seemed to fail to appreciate that glass is an impermeable material separating viewers from the objects being viewed. Just as the residents of Washington, D.C. can see democracy while being barred from full participation in it, the transparency of Nationals Park only enables people to see spaces they cannot afford to access.

Conclusion

Questions of social and environmental justice around Nationals Park and the Anacostia Waterfront Initiative are complex and often contradictory. As Mayor Williams recognized the injustices represented by and perpetuated through the Anacostia River, he decided that his administration would focus unprecedented attention and resources through the AWI to create a more inclusive city. Building support from disparate public stakeholders and private investors, the AWI is cleaning up the river and making it accessible, has provided new parks and re-creational opportunities, enhanced transportation links, and attracted billions of dollars to build new housing, office buildings, and retail options in underserved areas of the city. However, despite its successes in addressing many long-term inequities, the AWI has produced new inequalities and exclusionary practices that detract from its promotion of social and environmental justice. Through its disconnections between inclusionary rhetoric and exclusionary practices, Nationals Park both symbolizes and contributes to this new problem.

Notes

1 South Carolina Congressman John McMillan was not related to Michigan Senator James McMillan of the McMillan Plan.
2 The Democratic Party primary is essentially the mayoral election. D.C. voters have supported Democratic presidential candidates with more than 80% of votes all but two times in 15 elections since 1961 when the 23rd Amendment to the Constitution gave D.C. three Presidential electors.
3 As a point of reference, the downtowns of midsized U.S. cities such as Memphis, St. Louis, and San Antonio possess between 6 and 8 million square feet of office space.
4 The Fan Cost Index consists of average-priced tickets for 2 adults and 2 children, 2 small beers, 2 small soft drinks, 4 regular hot dogs, parking for 1 car, 2 game programs, and 2 least expensive adult-sized caps.

156 Michael Friedman

References

Abel, A. (2018). The 12 coolest neighborhoods around the world. *Forbes*. https://www.forbes.com/sites/annabel/2018/06/22/the-12-coolest-neighborhoods-around-the-world/#5c74e4486eb1

Amirtahmasebi, R., Orloff, M., Wahba, S., & Altman, A. (2016). *Regenerating urban land: A practitioner's guide to leveraging private investment*. World Bank.

Ammon, F. R. (2009). Commemoration amid criticism: The mixed legacy of urban renewal in Southwest Washington. D.C. *Journal of Planning History, 8*(3), 175–220. 10.1177/1538513209340630

Arnebeck, B. (2004, October 22). *Green acres: Major land schemes on South Capitol Street have a shady history*. Washington City Paper. https://www.washingtoncitypaper.com/news/article/13029904/the-big-whiff

Avni, N., & Fischler, R. (2019). Social and environmental justice in waterfront redevelopment: The Anacostia River, Washington, D.C. *Urban Affairs Review, 56*(6), 1779–1810. 10.1177/1078087419835968

Boswell, T. (2016, September 14). Nationals Park has become an urban development triumph. *Who knew?* Washington Post. https://www.washingtonpost.com/sports/nationals/nationals-park-has-become-an-urban-development-triumph-who-knew/2016/09/14/7cf60e3c-7a80-11e6-bd86-b7bbd53d2b5d_story.html

Capitol Riverfront Business Improvement District. (2022). *Neighborhood dynamic*. www.capitolriverfront.org/neighborhood

Chaplin, J., & Warnock, R. (2021). *Average rent in Washington DC & rent price trends*. Apartment List. https://www.apartmentlist.com/renter-life/average-rent-in-washington-dc

DC Sports and Entertainment Commission. (2005). *Request for proposals: D.C. major league baseball park architectural and engineering services*. http://www.dcsec.com/dcsec_rfp/DesignServices.pdf

District of Columbia Office of Planning. (2003). *The Anacostia Waterfront framework plan*. http://planning.dc.gov/planning/cwp/view,a,1285,q,582200,planningNav_GID,1708.asp.

District of Columbia Office of Planning. (2018). *Resurgence of the Anacostia Waterfront: 15 years of progress along the Anacostia River, 2003–2018*. https://planning.dc.gov/sites/default/files/dc/sites/op/publication/attachments/Anacostia%20Waterfront%2015%20Year%20Progress%20Report_web.pdf

Friedman, M. T. (2008). *The transparency of democracy: A Lefebvrean analysis of Washington's Nationals Park*. University of Maryland.

Friedman, M. T. (2010). "The transparency of democracy": The production of Washington's Nationals Park as a late capitalist space. *Sociology of Sport Journal, 27*(4), 327–350. 10.1123/ssj.27.4.327

Friedman, M. T. (in press). *Baseball's mallparks: Producing contemporary cathedrals of consumption*. Cornell.

Friedman, M. T., & Andrews, D. L. (2011). The built sport spectacle and the opacity of democracy. *International Review for the Sociology of Sport, 46*(2), 181–204. 10.1177/1012690210387540

General Accounting Office. (2003). *District of Columbia: Structural imbalance and management issues*. http://www.gao.gov/new.items/d03666.pdf

Gibson, T. A. (2015). The rise and fall of Adrian Fenty, Mayor-Triathlete: cycling, gentrification and class politics in Washington DC. *Leisure Studies, 34*(2), 230–249. 10.1080/02614367.2013.855940

Gillette, H., Jr. (2006). *Between justice and beauty: Race, planning and the failure of urban policy in Washington, D.C.* University of Pennsylvania.

Gutheim, F., & Lee, A. J. (2006). *Worthy of the nation: Washington DC from L'Enfant to the National Capital Planning Commission (Vol. 2)*. Johns Hopkins.

Hartweg, C. (2020). What could have been: 2020 pre-pandemic MLB Fan Cost Index® up 3.2% to $242.02; Average ticket climbed 3.3% to $34.04: A look at game day fan revenue impact. *Team Marketing Report*. Retrieved https://teammarketing.com/fci/2020-mlb-fan-cost-index-pre-pandemic/

Hsu, S. S. (2005, July 21). Envisioning SoHo at the Southeast waterfront: Government partners with developer on $1 billion project. *Washington Post*, T01.

Hyra, D. (2017). *Race, class and politics in the cappuccino city*. University of Chicago Press.

Jaffe, H. S., & Sherwood, T. (2014). *Dream city: Race, power, and the decline of Washington, D.C.* Simon & Schuster.

Knott, T. (2004, October 1). Goodbye, yellow brick dream. *Washington Times*, C1.

Morton, D. (2004, October 22). No'doze: Proponents of baseball by the Anacostia must answer one question: What about the Garden of Love? https://washingtoncitypaper.com/article/247105/the-big-whiff/

National Capital Planning Commission. (2006). *Comprehensive plan for the National Capital: District Elements*. http://www.planning.dc.gov/planning/cwp/view.asp?a=1354&q=639789&PM=1

O'Connell, J. (2014, October 2). The saga behind Washington's most infamous hole in the ground nears a close. *Washington Post*. https://www.washingtonpost.com/news/digger/wp/2014/10/02/the-saga-behind-washingtons-most-infamous-hole-in-the-ground-nears-a-close/

RCLCO Real Estate Advisors. (2019). *Riverfront recaptured: How public vision & investment catalyzed long-term value in the Capitol Riverfront*. Capitol Riverfront Business Improvement District. https://ctycms.com/dc-capitol-riverfront/docs/riverfrontrecaptured2018.pdf

ROMA Design Group, 360 Architects, & Chan Krieger & Associates. (2005). Ballpark district urban development strategy: Draft Summary, September 23, 2005. http://www.anacostiawaterfront.net/pdfs/Summary%20Final.pdf

Santana, A. (2003, April 3). Time to change course: Anacostia waterfront holds big hopes for city's future. *Washington Post*, T03.

Schwartzman, P. (2005, June 8). D.C. gay clubs' vanishing turf: City earmarks block of O Street SE for stadium. *Washington Post*, A1.

Seymour, C. (2008). *All I could bare: My life in the strip clubs of gay Washington, D.C.* Atria.

Smith, S. (1974). *Captive capital: Colonial life in modern Washington*. Indiana University Press.

Taylor, Y. Y. (2015, May 30). Residents move into the city for jobs, move out for housing. *District, Measured*. https://districtmeasured.com/2015/06/08/residents-move-into-the-city-for-jobs-move-out-for-housing-2/

U.S. Census Bureau. (2008). *State & county QuickFacts: District of Columbia*. http://quickfacts.census.gov/qfd/states/11000.html

U.S. Census Bureau. (2020). *QuickFacts: District of Columbia*. https://www.census.gov/quickfacts/DC

Washington Sculpture Center. (2012). *Mission statement*. http://www.dcsculpture.org/mission.html

11

CAPE TOWN'S 2010 FIFA WORLD CUP STADIUM LOCATION AND ITS SPATIAL AND ENVIRONMENTAL JUSTICE IMPLICATIONS

Aadil Engar and Jacques du Toit

Sport stadiums, particularly those built for mega tournaments such as the FIFA World Cup, often pose a major burden on public revenues. As one example, the South African government, despite its agenda of socioeconomic upliftment following political transition in 1994, was heavily burdened with stadium construction for the 2010 FIFA Men's World Cup (Alegi, 2007, 2008; Gunter, 2011; Maharaj, 2011; Molloy & Chetty, 2015). Given the costs associated with these stadiums, a pivotal but less researched question is where to locate these stadiums considering their intended impacts. More recently, the question extends to whether impacts resulting from stadiums built for mega tournaments are environmentally justifiable, especially considering socioeconomic inequalities not just in South Africa but in many parts of the world.

While there is a noticeable body of literature on sport stadium costs and impacts, literature regarding the rationale behind the location of stadiums is more limited. Nelson (2001, 2002) argued that it is not so much a question of whether using public revenue to build stadiums is worthwhile from an economic development perspective (considering that stadiums continue to be built anyhow), but *where* to locate stadiums to ensure the greatest return on investment in public infrastructure. Using a time-series analysis of 25 metropolitan areas in the United States, Nelson found that central business districts (CBDs), the edge of CBDs, or other central locations appear to be best for Major League stadiums because economic gain generally comes from spectators spending money on other leisure activities when visiting a stadium, and that such activities tend to be found in more central locations. Therefore, suburban or peripheral locations are not preferable, as spectators spend less money in these locations. Moreover, stadiums located in suburbs are often associated with blight. Residents often view stadiums as a nuisance, while parking lots that stand empty for most of the week deter retailers.

DOI: 10.4324/9781003262633-13

Coupled with the question of whether to locate stadiums in CBDs or suburbs is whether the rationale behind the location of stadiums should be urban regeneration or commercial profit (see, e.g., Thornley, 2002, and Tarazona Vento, 2016). One such example is the debate whether the New York Yankees professional baseball team should have stayed with their existing stadium in the economically depressed South Bronx or built a new ballpark in upmarket Manhattan. Both sides of the debate claimed, among other things, that its respective location would result in greater economic gain for the city. Chanayil (2002) evaluated each sides' claims and found that they both employed weak political arguments and had little evidence to support their economic claims. Like Nelson, Chanayil maintained that economic gain is generally limited to leisure spending by spectators, but, unlike Nelson, the effect of this spending would be felt more in the South Bronx. Chanayil concluded that upgrading the existing stadium would have better served New York's urban planning policy and objectives.

Whether located in CBDs or suburbs, or whether the rationale is urban regeneration or commercial profit, the intended effect of stadiums on both commercial and residential property values has also been questioned. Davies (2008) points out that although stadiums can have tangible and intangible impacts on commercial property values in the UK, these are highly variable across different sectors and are rather inconclusive. While stadiums often solicit a "not-in-my-backyard" response from residents (see, e.g., Ahlfeldt & Maennig, 2012), Davies also points out that stadiums can eventually increase residential property values, as well as contribute indirectly to values through the creation of pride, confidence, and the enhanced image of an area.

Although the literature is limited regarding the location of sport stadiums, current literature suggests that the pivotal questions are whether to locate centrally or peripherally, whether the rationale should be urban regeneration or commercial profit, and whether property values can be increased. These questions still require further research. Moreover, further research about the environmental justice implications of locations (i.e., implications for the quality of life of residents living close to stadiums) is necessary.

Cape Town's 2010 FIFA Men's World Cup stadium offers a unique case to study some of the questions above, perhaps not in-depth, but more holistically. The city initially opted for a stadium upgrade in Athlone, a suburb in the economically depressed "Cape Flats" area, for purposes of urban regeneration. FIFA, however, opted for a new mega stadium to be built in the more scenic suburb of Green Point next to the Cape Town CBD and the Table Mountain heritage site. Eventually, the Athlone stadium was upgraded to incorporate a fan park and training facility for the tournament. In contrast, a mega stadium was built in Green Point, now known as Cape Town Stadium. Figure 11.1 shows the locations of these two stadiums.

The aim of this chapter is to describe and compare the spatial and environmental justice implications of both the Athlone and Green Point stadium sites. Adopting a critical realist perspective and a comparative case study approach using

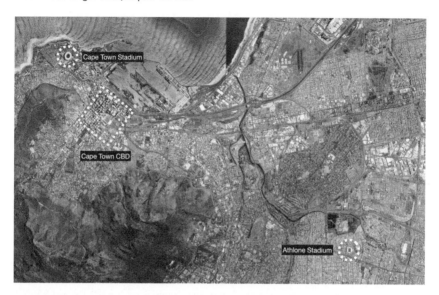

FIGURE 11.1 Aerial view of Cape Town. (Map data: Google, CNES/Airbus)

secondary sources and field observations, we first outline Cape Town's urban development priorities and objectives prior to 2010, then chronicle the decision-making dynamics behind the Green Point stadium location. Against this background, we then describe and compare both locations and stadiums in terms of their possible implications. The chapter contributes to the literature on the rationale, processes, and possible impacts behind stadium location and provides qualitative observations for further studies.

Cape Town's Urban Development Priorities and Objectives Prior to 2010

Cape Town currently has a population of about 4 million people (Statistics South Africa, 2016). Around 2010, the population was about 3.7 million given the last census count in 2011 (Statistics South Africa, 2011). The demography then included people of mixed-race (42.4%), African (38.6%), Caucasian (15.7%), and Indian, Asian, or other (3.3%). The gross domestic product in 2011 was approximately $13.5 billion, with much of the economy made up of finance, property, insurance, and business services (Statistics South Africa, 2011). Other sectors included manufacturing, wholesale, retail, and accommodation. With Mediterranean-like weather conditions, the areas surrounding the city have a large agricultural economy, which is serviced through the Port of Cape Town, making it one of the busiest in Africa. The city also has an airport with many direct routes to and from international destinations.

Typical of South African cities, Cape Town is spatially fragmented along class and racial divides following apartheid. Since political transition in 1994, various pieces of legislation have been passed to redevelop and integrate South African cities. The local provincial ordinances predating 1994 were used alongside the Development Facilitation Act (Act 67 of 1995; Republic of South Africa, 1995) to empower provincial governments to make certain planning decisions at a provincial level. The Act intended to fast-track the redress of apartheid spatial planning through the enforcement of the following basic principles:

- Promoting efficient and integrated land development;
- Integrating social, economic, institutional, and physical aspects of land development;
- Promoting residential and employment opportunities close to each other;
- Optimizing use of existing resources such as bulk infrastructure, roads, transportation, and social facilities;
- Contributing to the correction of historically distorted settlement patterns. (Republic of South Africa, 1995)

The Western Cape Provincial Spatial Development Framework (SDF) informed the planning and development of the city prior to 2010 (Western Cape Government, 2009). The SDF places sustainable development as the preeminent guiding principle with ecological integrity, social equity, and economic efficiency as its three pillars. At a municipal level, the South African planning system derives its powers and functions primarily from the Municipal Systems Act (Act 32 of 2000; Republic of South Africa, 2000), which provides the basis for an integrated development plan (IDP), incorporating also a municipal-level SDF. The IDP is the city's overall "business plan" and guides planning and budgeting at a local level. Stemming from the SDF, more detailed development plans for specific areas that require intervention are produced. These policies and planning instruments guide and direct planning and development within the South African city (Van Wyk & Steyn, 2015).

The Cape Town IDP for 2007 included seven focus areas for intervention. Three areas had direct implications for preparing the city for the 2010 FIFA Men's World Cup stadiums (City of Cape Town, 2007). The first focus area included *shared economic growth and development*, which focused on attracting investors, businesses, and visitors, and leveraging their financial impact to assist small business and skills development. This focus area of economic growth was dedicated to preparing for the World Cup in terms of the influx of investment that would also require a suitable environment to enable business to grow. The second focus area included *sustainable urban infrastructure and services*, which centered on universal access to basic services through eradicating backlogs in municipal services, preserving ecological resources, and managing infrastructure effectively. The third focus area included *public transport systems*, which could restructure the city through corridor development and improve public transport.

Considering this legislative and policy framework in the runup to the World Cup, it can be concluded that Cape Town would have been on a strong trajectory toward equitable development and resource allocation to redress apartheid spatial planning.

162 Aadil Engar and Jacques du Toit

Planning instruments at the time, however, did not provide a clear directive in terms of stadium development at Athlone or Green Point. These instruments in fact aimed to protect social facilities and greenspaces, especially in Green Point. As demonstrated below, the policy and planning void around stadium development in Cape Town, and unrealistic expectations placed around the World Cup, arguably contributed toward decision-making influenced by power and politics.

Decision-making Dynamics Behind the Cape Town Stadium Location

The World Cup Local Organising Committee (LOC), mandated by FIFA to organize the tournament, and an official subcommittee of the South African Football Association (SAFA), initially identified the Newlands rugby stadium as the preferred venue considering its optimal seating capacity and minimal upgrades that would have been required. Provincial and local officials, however, indicated their preference for the Athlone stadium because it was closer to the fanbase of the sport and was strategically located along the Klipfontein Corridor as means toward spatial integration. In a 2009 interview with Gert Bam, then-Head of Sport and Recreation in Cape Town, it was indicated that decision-makers "chose Athlone Stadium not just because of football ... but it would turn the city around, it [would] impact on this tale of two cities." The strategy was to leverage development for a blighted area in line with the city's IDP (Schoonbee & Brummer, 2010). Based on this reasoning, various government departments within the province began allocating large budgets toward the Athlone stadium in the hope that it would eventually become the official venue for the World Cup.

At the official bid presentation to FIFA on September 30, 2003, the Newlands rugby stadium was still the proposed venue for the Western Cape leg of the tournament. A FIFA delegation subsequently visited South Africa and found that the Newlands stadium was "easily suitable" for hosting a quarterfinal match that required a seating capacity of 40,000. South Africa was officially awarded host nation for the 2010 Men's World Cup on May 15, 2004, with Newlands as the confirmed venue. In July 2005, just over a year after the official announcement, FIFA sent a technical delegation to South Africa to view the prospective sites. After visiting the Newlands rugby stadium, the delegation visited the Athlone stadium (pictured in Figure 11.2) with the then-City Manager of Cape Town, who indicated the city's preference for Athlone. FIFA then indicated that a process would need to be undertaken to change the venue (Schoonbee & Brummer, 2010).

The LOC, however, seemed undeterred by the developmental ambitions of the province and city. Their continued confidence in the Athlone site was apparent in a letter from then-Premier of the Western Cape, Ebrahim Rasool, to the Chief Executive Officer of the LOC, Danny Jordaan:

> It is clear from what I am able to gather that there is some form of miscommunication between ourselves and the Local Organising

FIGURE 11.2 Athlone Stadium. (Courtesy of the City of Cape Town)

> Committee. The province and the City of Cape Town have always felt that the development of a dedicated football stadium in Athlone will leave a legacy for generations to come. In addition, the building of the stadium will allow us to leverage much needed transport and other socio-economic developments in the surrounding area ... we are expressing a strong preference in this regard. (Rasool, 2005)

During an official meeting between provincial and city officials on September 30, 2005, members of the meeting resolved that Athlone be investigated in terms of FIFA requirements, while it remained the preferred venue. Green Point would be the second option, as mentioned by some FIFA officials during their previous visit, while Newlands would be the third ("Record of the Meeting," 2005). This declaration was the first time Green Point was officially raised as a potential venue. Existing sporting facilities at Green Point were previously earmarked as a possible training venue only.

A feasibility study stemming from previous meetings with officials underestimated construction costs of the proposed stadiums and predicted low tourism benefits for Newlands and Athlone and high benefits for Green Point (Standish, 2005). These predictions opened the door for lobbyists to actively pursue the Green Point site while ignoring the local needs and objectives of the province and the city. Technical objections to the Athlone stadium became more pronounced, citing that seating behind the goalposts would be less valuable in terms of ticket sales. FIFA favored Green Point, citing that Cape Town would be underselling the potential for a world-class venue if Athlone or Newlands was selected (Platzkey, 2007).

164 Aadil Engar and Jacques du Toit

During November 2005, then-FIFA President Sepp Blatter visited Cape Town for the first time and had subsequent meetings with the Premier and President of South Africa, Thabo Mbeki. The day after meeting with Blatter, the Premier was informed that the Presidency proposed that Cape Town host a semifinal match in a 65,000-seat stadium at Green Point (Platzkey, 2007). It appears FIFA intended to sway government officials by offering a semifinal match for Cape Town to justify a new stadium at Green Point built according to technical specifications. Officials subsequently signed the host city agreements shortly before local government elections.

Following the elections, the more centrist Democratic Alliance took over the leadership of Cape Town through a coalition government and supported the leftist proposals to regenerate Athlone. Newly elected Mayor Helen Zille stopped all contracting in respect of the Green Point site and commissioned a new feasibility study comparing Green Point to five other locations. On a current affairs television show, *You be the Judge*, Mayor Zille explained:

> I assumed that if we're going to go into something like this, all the studies would be there, all the mathematics would have been done, all the costings and sums would be there. That has not happened. I really think that we are going into Green Point because Sepp Blatter says: "I like Green Point," not because it is the best thing for South Africans. (eTV, 2006)

A subsequent feasibility study looked at six venues, including Athlone, Green Point, and Newlands. Stadium construction cost estimates escalated to roughly three times what was forecasted just a year earlier (Standish, 2005). Predicted tourism benefits were highest for Newlands, followed by Athlone, then Green Point. Developmental need was highest for Athlone, followed by Newlands, then Green Point. All three sites were considered timeous and ready for implementation in terms of statutory approvals (Bayette Development Consulting, 2006). The final push, however, was the imposition of the requirement of a 65,000-seat stadium for the semifinal. This effectively made the construction of a new mega stadium at Green Point the only "feasible" option. It appears that the technical imposition of Cape Town hosting a semifinal match was the deciding factor tying officials to Green Point, despite the city's development objectives and contrary findings from the latest feasibility study. At significant cost to South African taxpayers, the Athlone stadium was upgraded to a fan park and training facility as a compromise, while a new world-class mega stadium was built at Green Point, known today as Cape Town Stadium. Considering the cost, what are some of the spatial and environmental justice implications of these two stadiums?

Spatial and Environmental Justice Implications of the Athlone and Cape Town Stadiums

After briefly introducing each stadium, we assess the stadiums along three themes: local planning policy, infrastructure upgrades, and possible social impacts. Stadium costs are indicated in U.S. dollars and at the time of construction.

The Athlone Location and Resulting Fan Park and Training Facility Upgrade

Athlone Stadium is owned by the City of Cape Town and is located approximately 10 km from the CBD. Originally earmarked by provincial and local authorities to serve as the home base of football in the Western Cape, the city spent approximately $43 million on the stadium before the World Cup and directed further provincial and local budgeting toward upgrades in preparation for the World Cup (Bob & Swart, 2009).

Local Planning Policy

The Cape Flats District Plan indicated no substantial development plans for Athlone Stadium at the time, with the stadium zoned as public open space (City of Cape Town, 2012). The district plan merely elevated the stadium's role to a district-level sports facility that was meant to be enhanced. A popular planning concept at the time to address spatial fragmentation in South African cities was "corridor development." The stadium is located next to the Klipfontein Corridor, while the district plan aimed to prioritize the corridor through the following: (1) maximizing nodal and corridor opportunities, (2) facilitating better access, (3) improving public transport, (4) intensifying development around nodes, and (5) facilitating the development of a range of economic opportunities.

Infrastructure Upgrades

Athlone Stadium was upgraded to a training facility and accommodated the temporary fan park for the duration of the tournament. The upgrades included two new stands, fencing, lighting, media facilities, changing rooms, and a pitch upgrade, all at an estimated cost of $54.5 million (Host City Cape Town, 2011). Considering that the upgrades were within the stadium site and not accompanied by surrounding upgrades to the same extent as in Green Point, benefit to surrounding communities was limited. Released shortly after the tournament, the *FIFA Green Goal Legacy Report* outlined the environmentally friendly upgrades undertaken at the Athlone and Green Point stadiums. At Athlone Stadium, these upgrades included the installation of energy-efficient and water-saving technologies, waste minimization, and branding of recycling signage and bins (Host City Cape Town, 2011).

Possible Social Impacts

While the literature debates the extent to which stadiums positively impact surrounding communities, an indicator of possible social impact is the perceptions communities have of stadiums. Positive perceptions may foster a sense of ownership, belonging, and willingness to remain invested socially and economically in the surrounding neighborhood. Bob and Swart (2009) surveyed residents around the Athlone and Cape Town stadiums in 2006—four years before the World Cup. Most respondents in Athlone were mixed-race middle-aged males. Respondents experienced World Cup euphoria, were looking forward to the stadium upgrades and the tournament itself, and had high expectations for the upgrades and the tournament bringing economic and social benefits to the community. Post-tournament surveys, however, may still be conducted to gauge current perceptions and any lasting social impacts. Ideally, such a survey ought to have been followed up with a post-tournament study among the same target population.

With the stadium located next to the Klipfontein Corridor, the stadium is strategically placed between the Cape Town International Airport, the Cape Flats, the former African township of Langa, and former "white" suburbs. Athlone Stadium is therefore highly symbolical of South African demography and diversity. Its greater accessibility relative to Green Point also makes it more affordable for lower-income communities relying on public transport, especially in the Cape Flats area. In terms of the Cape Flats District Plan, the stadium may also be a catalyst for economic development along the Klipfontein Corridor. However, further research is necessary to determine any such impact.

The Green Point Location and Resulting Cape Town Mega Stadium

The Green Point Commons was granted to the Cape Town City Council in 1923 by King George and the Union Government as public land for recreation and sport and to officially become a commonage (van Papendorp, 2010). While the city has spread significantly since, the commonage remained and became a popular public feature along the Sea Point promenade. Green Point has exceptional real estate value due to its panoramic view of the Atlantic Ocean and the nearby Victoria & Alfred Waterfront—one of Africa's most valuable retail centers. Figure 11.3 shows the newly constructed Cape Town Stadium, located approximately 2.5 km from the CBD.

Local Planning Policy

Upon the announcement of the Green Point Commons as the official site for a new stadium, residents and other stakeholders raised several objections. Residents mainly used the commons for its golf course and bowling field and arguably had little interest in a football stadium (De Vries, 2016). Residents formed the Green Point Common Association (GPCA) in 2006 to oppose the construction of the project. The majority white and affluent constituency argued that resources should instead be directed to poverty eradication programs, addressing unemployment and the fight against HIV/AIDS. The GPCA also advocated for the protection of a "last remaining green lung" of the city, which the proposed stadium would adversely affect. Residents directly affected by the stadium were concerned that a

FIGURE 11.3 Cape Town Stadium. (Courtesy of the City of Cape Town)

change in council policy would have negative impacts on their quality of life by virtue of the Green Point Park deteriorating and their property values subsequently decreasing. The strongest opposition to the stadium, however, came from the Cape Town Environmental Protection Association (CEPA), which threatened high court action and protests to stop the commons from becoming the official site. CEPA shared Mayor Zille's sentiments concerning the selection of a site, alluding to a top-down decision-making process from a foreign entity as opposed to a sovereign decision-making process in terms of local planning policy. The affidavit in their High Court interdict stated: "It is thus scarcely an exaggeration to say that the entire process has been stampeded to an undignified consummation, in the interest of satisfying a deadline arbitrarily imposed in distant Zurich" (Jarvis, 2007). As a compromise, the city eventually included the development of an "urban park" as part of getting approval for the stadium. A portion of the Green Point Commons was then rezoned from public open space to a designation that would allow for the development of the stadium, associated infrastructure, and the urban park as required by the community (Essop, 2007). Apart from the rezoning, the city had little in terms of other planning policies or instruments to guide the development of the new stadium.

Infrastructure Upgrades

The newly constructed Cape Town Stadium cost approximately $586 million at the time, and an urban park built to satisfy residents added another $77 million. A further $993 million was spent on the precinct, including upgrades to local roads and sporting facilities, and to the CBD road and public transport network (Host

City Cape Town, 2011). While these upgrades formed part of the 2010 Tournament Legacy projects, many were probably accelerated toward completion due to the new stadium in Green Point. City officials arguably did their best leveraging the new stadium to improve the inner city as well. With environmental activists having kept a close eye on developments in Green Point, the *FIFA Green Goal Legacy Report* outlined several more environmentally friendly upgrades for Green Point compared to Athlone. These included installing energy-efficient and water-saving technologies; identifying alternative sources of water for the commons; minimizing waste and creating branding of recycling signage and bins; establishing recycling drop-off points in the CBD and along the Atlantic seaboard; developing pedestrian, cycling, and public transport infrastructure; and several other eco-friendly and landscaping projects (Host City Cape Town, 2011). These environmental upgrades were certainly a step in the right direction to help mitigate the tournament's carbon footprint considering Cape Town's water scarcity and unique and sensitive biodiversity. Moreover, the new stadium and associated upgrades appear to have increased residential property values around Green Point, with average increases after the tournament approximately 5–6% higher than the rest of the city (Engar, 2016).

Possible Social Impacts

As indicated above, a pre-tournament survey was conducted among residents around the Athlone and Green Point stadium sites in 2006. Most respondents in Green Point were Caucasian middle-aged males. While respondents perhaps did not experience the same level of World Cup euphoria compared to those in Athlone, perceptions of the new stadium developments were nevertheless positive, although the tournament itself was perceived as incurring wasteful expenditure. Concerns were also raised about a possible increase in traffic and noise pollution. Furthermore, perceptions around economic and social benefits were unrealistically high (Bob & Swart, 2009).

As far as we could find, two post-tournament surveys have been conducted in Cape Town. First, Tichaawa and Bama (2012) surveyed residents in Green Point three months after the tournament and found that most respondents had a positive perception of the World Cup and were satisfied that it had a legacy of improved infrastructure. Thus, while there was fierce objection to the construction of a new stadium initially (De Vries, 2016), the compromise of an urban park and associated infrastructure upgrades—despite their massive cost—seemed to have turned perceptions toward a positive sense of place. Second, Swart and Jurd (2012) conducted a survey among residents in informal settlements in Cape Town three months after the tournament. These residents had a positive perception of the tournament in terms of its perceived impact on local sport and social development. Still, the economic benefit of the tournament was not perceived to be shared across the socioeconomic spectrum.

Conclusion

In Cape Town, the spatial and environmental justice around the 2010 FIFA Men's World Cup centered around the location of the official stadium. International literature prior to 2010 argued that locations near CBDs offered the best returns in terms of leisure spending by spectators. Considering South Africa's segregated past, Cape Town's city development priorities and objectives, however, had a strong redistributive, restorative, and developmental trajectory prior to the World Cup. City officials, therefore, identified the Athlone stadium as the preferred venue considering its symbolic and strategic location in the Cape Flats and along the Klipfontein Corridor. FIFA, however, insisted on a new mega stadium in Green Point next to the CBD and Table Mountain heritage site, despite objections by city officials and residents. Eventually, the Athlone stadium was upgraded and included a fan park and training facility for the tournament, while the official Cape Town stadium was built in Green Point. The Green Point stadium development included an urban park to satisfy residents and major infrastructure upgrades in and around the precinct, enabling city officials to leverage the construction of the stadium as best they could. An environmental report lists various eco-friendly initiatives for both the Athlone and Green Point venues and especially for the latter. Post-tournament surveys among residents in informal settlements suggest a positive symbolic impact but skepticism around shared economic benefits. Residents in Green Point felt the tournament was a success and appreciated the urban park and infrastructure upgrades. Residential property values in Green Point were also impacted positively.

While these findings suggest a degree of environmental justice, the gains are arguably very small compared to the costs involved, especially considering the developmental challenges that the country and city faced at the time and still face today. The city acquired a world-class stadium, but it was placed in neither the football nor rugby heartland of Cape Town, and that in addition to the original construction is now posing a major cost in terms of maintenance. Subsequent scholarship on the World Cup's impact on host cities in South Africa has also pointed out that infrastructure upgrades served little to integrate marginalized areas, while inequalities in the housing sector more likely worsened (Steinbrink et al., 2011). Although the literature suggests that central stadium locations offer better economic gains, the location of Cape Town Stadium on the more secluded side of the CBD places it further from most of the city's population and at least two or more public transport modal switches away from lower-income communities. Its spatial justice is therefore questionable.

References

Ahlfeldt, G. M., & Maennig, W. (2012). Voting on a NIMBY facility: Proximity cost of an "iconic" stadium. *Urban Affairs Review, 48*(2), 205–237. 10.1177/1078087411423644

Alegi, P. (2007). The political economy of mega-stadiums and the underdevelopment of grassroots football in South Africa. *Politikon, 34*(3), 315–331. 10.1080/02589340801 962635

Alegi, P. (2008). 'A nation to be reckoned with': The politics of World Cup stadium construction in Cape Town and Durban, South Africa. *African Studies, 67*(3), 397–422. 10.1080/00020180802505038

Axelson, E. (2022). *Cape Town.* https://www.britannica.com/place/Cape-Town

Bayette Development Consulting. (2006). *Evaluation of alternative venues.* Bayette Development Consulting.

Bob, U., & Swart, K. (2009). Resident perceptions of the 2010 FIFA Soccer World Cup stadia development in Cape Town. *Urban Forum, 20*(1), 47–59. 10.1007/s12132-009-9052-2

Chanayil, A. (2002). The Manhattan Yankees? Planning objectives, city policy, and sports stadium location in New York City. *European Planning Studies, 10*(7), 875–896. 10.1 080/0965431022000013275

City of Cape Town. (2007). *5 year plan for Cape Town: Integrated development plan (IDP) 2007/8–2011/12.* City of Cape Town.

City of Cape Town. (2012). *Cape Flats District plan: Spatial development plan and environmental management framework technical report.* City of Cape Town.

City of Johannesburg Metropolitan Muncipality v. Gauteng Development Tribunal and Others, ZACC 11 (Constitutional Court of South Africa, 2010). http://hdl.handle.net/20.500.12144/3594

Davies, L. E. (2005). Not in my back yard! Sports stadia location and the property market. *Area, 37*(3), 268–276. 10.1111/j.1475-4762.2005.00630.x

Davies, L. E. (2008). Sport and the local economy: the role of stadia in regenerating commercial property. *Local Economy, 23*(1), 31–46. 10.1080/02690940801906718

De Vries, L. (2016). *A 'paradox of the commons'? The planning and everyday management of Green Point Park.* University of Cape Town.

eTV. (2006, April 30). *Interview with Helen Zille* [Interview].

Engar, A. (2016). *The economic impact of Green Point Stadium on surrounding residential property values* [Master's thesis, University of Pretoria].

Essop, T. (2007). *Decision on appeals: Green Point Common development.* https://www.westerncape.gov.za/news/decision-appeals-green-point-common-development

Gunter, A. (2011). Stadium upgrades as local economic development: The fallacy of the Ellis Park Sports Precinct upgrade as LED. *South African Geographical Journal, 93*(1), 75–88. 10.1080/03736245.2011.572474

Host City Cape Town. (2011). *2010 FIFA World Cup Host City Cape Town Green Goal legacy report.* Host City Cape Town.

Jarvis, P. K. (2007). *Founding Affidavit (Case no. 4051) presented in the High Court of South Africa in the matter between Cape Town Environmental Protection Association (Applicant) and Western Cape Provincial Department of Environmental Affairs and Development Planning (First Respondent), Minister for Environmental Affairs, Planning and Economic Development, City of Cape Town, Building and Planning Development Management City of Cape Town, Federation Internationale Football Association, FIFA 2010 World Cup Organizing Committee South Africa, Metropolitan Golf Club.*

Maharaj, B. (2011). 2010 FIFA World Cup: (South) 'Africa's time has come'?. *South African Geographical Journal, 93*(1), 49–62. 10.10520/EJC93357

Molloy, E., & Chetty, T. (2015). The rocky road to legacy: Lessons from the 2010 FIFA World Cup South Africa stadium program. *Project Management Journal, 46*(3), 88–107. 10.1002/pmj.21502

Nelson, A. C. (2001). Prosperity or blight? A question of Major League stadia locations. *Economic Development Quarterly, 15*(3), 255–265. 10.1177/089124240101500305

Nelson, A. C. (2002). Locating Major League stadiums where they can make a difference: Empirical analysis with implications for all major public venues. *Public Works Management & Policy, 7*(2), 98–144. 10.1177/108772402236952

Platzkey, L. F. (2007, July 4). *Affidavit on behalf of the Director: Integrated Environmental Management (Region B), Western Cape Provincial Department of Environmental Affairs and Development Planning and the Minister for Environmental Affairs, Planning and Economic Development, Western Cape.*

Rasool, E. (2005, August 17). Letter from Premier to Chair of LOC. *Annexure LFP1 of Platzky affidavit in Environmental Appeal.*

Record of the meeting between the cabinet of the provincial government of the Western Cape and the mayoral committee of the City of Cape Town. (2005, September 30). *Annexure LFP3 of Platzky's affidavit in environmental appeal.*

Republic of South Africa. (1995). *Development Facilitation Act.* Republic of South Africa.

Republic of South Africa. (2000). *Local government: Municipal Systems Act.* Republic of South Africa.

Schoonbee, K., & Brümmer, S. (2010). Public loss, FIFA's gain: How Cape Town got its "white elephant". In C. S. Herzenberg (Ed.), *Player and referee: Conflicting interests and the 2010 FIFA World Cup* (pp. 133–167). Institute for Security Studies.

StadiumDB.com. (2022). *Athlone Stadium.* http://stadiumdb.com/stadiums/rsa/athlone_stadium

Standish, B. (2005). *2010 soccer World Cup: Financial and socio-economic analysis of three potential venues for 2010 matches in Cape Town.*

Statistics South Africa. (2011). *Census 2011.* https://www.statssa.gov.za/publications/P03014/P030142011.pdf

Statistics South Africa. (2016). *Community Survey 2016.* http://cs2016.statssa.gov.za/?page_id=270

Steinbrink, M., Haferburg, C., & Ley, A. (2011). Festivalisation and urban renewal in the Global South: Socio-spatial consequences of the 2010 FIFA World Cup. *South African Geographical Journal, 93*(1), 15–28. 10.1080/03736245.2011.567827

Swart, K., & Jurd, M. C. (2012). Informal residents' perceptions of the 2010 FIFA World Cup: A case study of an informal settlement in Cape Town. *African Journal for Physical Health Education, Recreation and Dance, 18*(1), 42–52.

Tarazona Vento, A. (2016). Mega-project meltdown: Post-politics, neoliberal urban regeneration and Valencia's fiscal crisis. *Urban Studies, 54*(1), 68–84. 10.1177/0042098015625025

Thornley, A. (2002). Urban regeneration and sports stadia. *European Planning Studies, 10*(7), 813–818. 10.1080/0965431022000013220

Tichaawa, T. M., & Bama, H. K. (2012). Green Point residents' perceptions of the 2010 FIFA World Cup: A post-event analysis. *African Journal for Physical Health Education, Recreation and Dance, 18*(2), 22–33.

van Papendorp, J. (2010). *Reconstruction of Green Point Common* [Paper presentation]. ILASA Conference, Johannesburg, South Africa.

Van Wyk, J., & Steyn, P. (2015). *Planning law casebook* (3rd ed.). Juta.

Western Cape Government. (2009). *Provincial spatial development framework.* Department of Environment and Development Planning.

World Bank. (2002). *Inequality in Southern Africa: An assessment of the Southern African Customs Union.* The World Bank Group.

12

SETTLER COLONIALISM AS ENVIRONMENTAL INJUSTICE: ROGERS PLACE AND EDMONTON

Chen Chen and Judy Davidson

This chapter discusses how the recent construction of a downtown sport arena in a major city on the Canadian Prairies (Rogers Place in Edmonton, Alberta) in the second decade of the 21st century is deeply entangled within the longue durée and ongoing process of capitalist settler colonialism on Indigenous territory. Drawing upon literature in environmental justice and Indigenous environmental studies, we explore how settler colonialism itself should be understood as a profound environmental justice issue in the context of Global North settler colonial states like Canada, wherein sport arenas such as the Rogers Place contribute to enduring forms of environmental injustice. Importantly, we invite scholars and educators concerned with environmental and ecological issues to confront and engage with the following definition of settler colonialism offered by Potawatomi scholar Kyle Powys Whyte (2017):

> As an injustice, settler colonialism refers to complex social processes in which at least one society seeks to move permanently onto the terrestrial, aquatic, and aerial places lived in by one or more other societies who already derive economic vitality, cultural flourishing, and political self-determination from relationships they have established with the plants, animals, physical entities, and ecosystems of those places. (p. 158)

The chapter is structured as follows: we first describe the context of our case before we briefly review the history and development of the environmental justice movement. After introducing "settler colonialism as environmental injustice" as the theoretical framework that guides our case study, we then draw from the insights of two empirical studies (Davidson et al., 2019; Scherer et al., 2021) to guide our readers toward a preliminary understanding of the role played by Rogers Place in perpetuating environmental injustice in the process of settler colonialism.

DOI: 10.4324/9781003262633-14

Case Context: The Conventional Story of Rogers Place in the City of Edmonton

A multiuse indoor arena located in downtown Edmonton, Alberta, Canada, Rogers Place is best known for replacing the Northlands Coliseum (previously known as Rexall Place) as the new home rink for the NHL's Edmonton Oilers and the Western Hockey League's Edmonton Oil Kings at the start of the 2016–17 season. Edmonton is the fifth-largest municipality in Canada and the largest, northernmost metropolitan area in North America, with a metropolitan population of over 1.4 million as of 2021 (Government of Alberta, 2021). Due to its proximity to the oil and mining development in northern Alberta and western Canada, Edmonton's local economy follows a boom–bust cycle that fluctuates with demand in the broader oil and gas industry (Cake et al., 2018).

The Edmonton Oilers was one of the founding franchises of the World Hockey Association in 1971 and later joined the NHL in 1979. It won the Stanley Cup five times in the 1980s. In 2005, it was reported that the Oilers' ownership group became concerned with how the franchise's then home venue, Rexall Place, one of the oldest in use by an NHL team (located in a city that is one of the smallest markets in the entire league), had hindered the franchise's revenue-generating ability (Sant et al., 2019). The franchise was purchased in 2008 by the Katz Group, a local, privately-owned company operating in film, sport and entertainment, and real estate development. Its owner, billionaire Daryl Katz, is one of the wealthiest individuals in Canada (Dykstra, 2013).

Thereafter, the City of Edmonton and the Katz Group started negotiations concerning a proposed new facility for the Oilers and reached an agreement after a prolonged period. The "arena debate" was, at times, heated and highly divisive amongst the city residents. There was some organized resistance to the public funding of the entertainment district. For instance, the grassroots community group "Voices for Democracy" intervened in the debate to oppose the public subsidization of the Oilers and their billionaire owner (Scherer, 2016). However, as reflected in the agreement, the entire project cost $613.7 million CAD ($483.5 million for the arena, with an additional $130.2 million for associated infrastructure; City of Edmonton, n.d.). To finance the construction, the City of Edmonton contributed $279 million in total, with the remaining $39 million coming from other forms of government (Sant et al., 2019). The proposed new arena anchors the center of the "Ice District," a multibillion-dollar sports and entertainment development in downtown Edmonton. The purpose of these developments was to ensure the profitability of the Oilers and to "revitalize" the downtown core as a "spectacular center of consumption" (Scherer et al., 2021). The construction of the new arena started in March 2014, and the building officially opened on September 8, 2016. On December 3, 2013, Rogers Communications announced a 10-year naming rights deal for the new arena, henceforth known as Rogers Place (Canadian Press, 2013). With a seating capacity of 18,500 as a hockey venue, the arena can host 20,734 as a concert venue (Salz, 2014).

FIGURE 12.1 Rogers Place and the Edmonton Ice District in 2016. ("ICE district Edmonton" by Jason Woodhead is licensed under CC BY 2.0)

Theoretical Framework: Environmental Justice and Settler Colonialism

Environmental Justice

The term "environmental justice" first emerged in response to movements in low-income, racialized (predominantly Black and Hispanic) minorities in the United States in the 1980s when these communities started to actively resist the disproportionate pollution exposure and challenged both state agencies and corporations' role therein (Murdock, 2020; Pulido, 2018). Early academic research on environmental justice identified "environmental racism" as the central concern that rose into prominence in the public sphere and policy discourses (Pulido, 1996). "Environmental racism" describes the disproportionate exposure to environmental pollution that racial minorities face as well as the low level of environmental benefits they enjoy, that is, the "unequal distribution of environmental benefits and pollution burdens based on race" (Sze & London, 2008, p. 1332), notably manifest in industries' siting practices driven by the logic of "paths of least resistance" (Bullard, 1990).

While early environmental justice movement and scholarship was primarily concerned with pollution and toxic waste disposal practices that affected low-income communities of color, it has since broadened its scope to address environmental inequalities manifest in a multiplicity of other areas such as transportation, access to health care, housing quality, homelessness, land use, water, energy, incarceration, redevelopment of brownfields, militarization, and sustainable development in both domestic and international contexts (Pellow, 2018; Sze & London, 2008). It is increasingly acknowledged that environmental injustice solidifies and reinforces other axes of injustices and inequitable conditions (e.g., gender, age, location) that are already affecting marginalized communities locally and globally (Main & Ryder, 2018; Murdock, 2020).

Settler Colonialism as Environmental Injustice

While environmental racism remains an important concern, newly incorporated theoretical constructs and frameworks such as decolonization, settler colonialism, and intersectionality further broadened the principles underlying the mobilizations of environmental justice in the Western hemisphere in recent decades (Álvarez & Coolsaet, 2020; Murdock, 2020). For example, highlighting the limitations of the *distributive justice* paradigm in environmental justice, Figueroa (2011) argued for a conceptualization of environmental injustice as beyond the unequal distribution of environmental harms and amenities but with deep and far-reaching physical, psychological, and existential consequences (Figueroa, 2011). Notably, Dina Gilio-Whitaker (2019) elaborated on an Indigenous environmental justice framework and argued that for Indigenous peoples, environmental justice *cannot* be possibly achieved without fundamentally challenging the structure and processes of settler colonialism.

In this chapter, we draw from Whyte's (2017, 2018) conceptualization of *settler colonialism as environmental injustice*. Currently, settler colonialism is defined as an enduring structure of domination predicated upon the dispossession of Indigenous peoples' land and the infringing of the political authority and jurisdiction that govern relationships therein (e.g., Coulthard & Simpson, 2016; Wolfe, 2006). The centrality of land (and its dispossession) and its governance (and the erasure and marginalization of knowledge about governance and relationship building) in this definition have profound implications for developing a critical understanding of settler colonialism as deeply affecting the "environment." In many Indigenous communities across the world, conceptualizations of relationships to land are built on reciprocity, respect, and responsibility not only between humans but also extended to the non-human/more-than-human life forms (McGregor, 2009). This relationship has been violently disrupted by settler colonialism, particularly the transfiguration of land into private property (Whyte, 2018).

As observed by Murdock (2020), settler societies not only hold an instrumental attitude toward the land to be "developed," but also lack an existential recognition of Indigenous peoples' occupancy and deep relationship with the land. With settler colonialism being a structural, continuous violence (Wolfe, 2006), its consequences go beyond the treatment of the physical environment but extend to the alternation of the identity and very existence of its original inhabitants.

Highlighting the enormous environmental consequences created by the agricultural, military, transportation, and extractive industries as part of the U.S. settler colonial project (e.g., broken treaty agreements, allotment, and boarding schools), Whyte (2017) critiqued that after centuries of occupation, settlers managed to "have transformed the ecological conditions in ways that are not sustainable for settlers, Indigenous peoples, or anyone else" (p. 165).

Concurring with the critiques of settler colonial disruption of human-to-human and human-to-land relationships in other academic fields (Davis & Todd, 2017; TallBear, 2016), environmental studies scholar Whyte (2018) highlighted the environmental/ecological underpinnings of settler colonialism. For Whyte (2018), settler colonialism manifests as environmental injustice in that it is "a social process by which at least one society seeks to establish its own collective continuance at the expense of the collective continuance of one or more other societies." In other words, from an ecological perspective, settler colonialism damages the "qualities of relationships that are constitutive of collective continuance and that facilitate social resilience or adaptive capacity" (p. 136).

Vicious Sedimentation

Whyte's (2018) discussion of *vicious sedimentation* is of particular relevance to contemporary urban contexts in settler North America, including that of Edmonton, a settler city. Resonating with Mishuana Goeman's (2014) notion, "settler grammars of place," which describes "repetitive practices of everyday life that give settler place meaning and structure" (p. 237), Whyte (2018) uses *vicious sedimentation* to name the process wherein "constant ascriptions of settler ecologies onto Indigenous ecologies fortify settler ignorance against Indigenous peoples over time" (p. 138). The sedimentation, exemplified by urban gentrification, is "vicious" because it works to prevent settler populations from accepting Indigenous peoples as adaptive people with long and continuing living histories in North America, further diminishing settlers' inclination to enter consensual decision-making with Indigenous peoples (Whyte, 2018). Therefore, for Whyte (2018), a critical discussion of environmental (in)justice should include not only the manifest aspects of violence, such as the imposition of environmental destruction and pollution but also the undermining of "qualities of relationships" that are crucial to Indigenous people's social resilience or collective continuance within settler states.

However, despite the historical and ongoing oppression, many Indigenous communities and communities of color have accumulated intergenerational knowledge and experience in resisting the global regime of power that aims at furthering the capitalist-colonial project, including the appropriation of land, the extraction of resources, processes at the expense of degrading the environment and people (Gilio-Whitaker, 2019; Murdock, 2020; Yazzie, 2018). As Goeman (2014) observed, Indigenous peoples continue to develop and sustain qualities of relationships among humans and nonhumans in environments that would otherwise be considered by settlers as absent of Indigenous ecologies.

Sport-related Gentrification and the Urban Environment

Within the "globalizing" economy of the 20th century and the advancement of transportation and media technologies, sport arenas have become a highly symbolic and central part of how cities and nations "brand" themselves in competition for status and capital (Chen & Mason, 2016; Whitson & Macintosh, 1996). Cities in Western Canada in general, and Edmonton in particular, are no exceptions: civic boosters have long utilized sport as an essential part of their strategies to champion the advantages of the city and region (e.g., Misener & Mason, 2008; Whitson & Macintosh, 1993). This should serve as an important backdrop to understand the complex role that sport arenas play in environmental issues, which will be elaborated on next.

Environment as Places to "Live, Work, Play and Belong"

As noted by Sze (2009), existing critical studies on the development of sport infrastructure in urban areas have adopted a more expansive definition of the environment as the place where people "live, work, play and belong" (e.g., Whitson & Macintosh, 1996). This complements the previous "wilderness preservationist" conceptions that limited the environment to Nature, where only the more privileged groups have access to escape to and recreate in (Sze, 2009). On the other hand, gentrification, which has recently been expanded beyond residential displacement to address issues of equitable access to public spaces, has been deemed an environmental justice issue (Mullenbach & Baker, 2020; see also Chapter 2 of this volume). In an analysis that is particularly resonating with the settler colonial context of our chapter, Canadian scholar Liza Kim Jackson (2017) describes the contemporary process of urban gentrification in Toronto, Canada, as a heightened reinforcement of colonial relationalities that "discipline on poor and Indigenous bodies, spaces and lands, through the capitalist way of life" (p. 43). In the remainder of this chapter, we situate sport-related gentrification (Scherer et al., 2021) taking place during the construction and operation of Rogers Place in Edmonton within the longue durée of Canadian capitalist settler colonialism. We hope that this discussion provides a useful lens for interested readers to deepen their understanding toward the nexus of sport, environmental (in)justice, and settler colonialism.

The Other "Side" of the Story: Edmonton as a Settler City

To better grasp the extent of the environmental injustice that settler colonial cities perpetuate with the development of sport stadia complexes, it is crucial to provide a detailed historical reckoning of how colonial capital has systematically displaced Indigenous peoples, their cosmologies, and the connection to the land over the last 300 years in the place now called Edmonton in Treaty 6 territory. The building of the new Edmonton hockey arena is the logical outcome of decades of settler urban planning decisions that are driven almost exclusively by white patriarchal capital accumulation. Framing Rogers Place in environmental justice terms shows how sport stadia contribute to the displacement and removal of (now urban) Indigenous community members and disavows (even/indeed at times criminalizes) Indigenous claims to environment and place (see also Chapter 3).

Amiskwaciwâskahikan (Nêhiyawak/Cree for Beaver Hills, or what is now known as Edmonton) has long been the traditional territory for the Nêhiyawak Plains Cree, the Stoney Nakota Sioux, and it is also one of the homelands of/for the Métis. It has been a gathering place for multiple nations to engage in trade and ceremony for thousands of years (Donald, 2017; Todd, 2013). Much more recently, as the first contact with Europeans happened in the 19th century, British fur traders set up competing and then later consolidated forts along the North Saskatchewan River. Enabled by the Doctrine of Discovery, the Hudson's Bay Company was empowered by British Royal Charter to exclusive trading rights in Rupertsland—a massive amount of territory comprising the drainage of the Hudson's Bay, including central Alberta, where Edmonton is located. Fur trading was the first of several subsequent extractive resource industries that Europeans initiated in this place, which was facilitated for hundreds of years in a relationship with various Indigenous nations (Tobias, 1991).

As the fur trade waned in the mid-19th century, the occupying colonial state was developing legal, business, and policy frameworks to unilaterally make way for the next extractive industry—that of agricultural settlement by white European immigrants. To do this, sacred buffalo herds were decimated, inducing starvation and disease (Daschuk, 2019). Treaty 6 was entered into by several Indigenous nations under inequitable conditions of manufactured desperation. The 1869 Indian Act was (and continues to be) the basis of a genocidal national settler strategy, which attempted to assimilate vast and varied Indigenous peoples by suppressing and forbidding any expression of Indigenous sovereignty, governance, and cultural expression. The Indian Act "legally" incarcerated Indigenous people on tiny reserves away from the growing town of Edmonton over the next decades, severely limiting their mobility and ability to engage in their customary practices and/or to participate in the newly emerging capitalist economy. Indigenous children were involuntarily placed in Indian Residential Schools, often forcibly taken there by the North-West Mounted Police and later, the Royal Canadian Mounted Police. This police force was created for the express purpose of creating settler "order" and to control any Indigenous resistance (Carleton, 2020). As we will see, this carceral system continues to surveil and contain Indigenous peoples today, as Rogers Place private security and the Edmonton Police Service secure "safe" settler space for Oilers fans.

In 1891, the Calgary and Edmonton Railway, an early pioneer railway in Western Canada, was completed to Edmonton. Between 1892 and 1914, the settler population explosion in Edmonton was truly extraordinary—going from 700 people in 1892 to over 70,000 in 1914, a 100-fold increase in a generation (Goyette & Roemmich, 2004). As part and parcel of the vicious sedimentation of

Settler Colonialism as Environmental Injustice   **179**

settlement practices, modern sport organizations contributed to the settler colonial apparatus. Venues for settler sport and leisure entertainments participate in establishing the permanent white European claim to the river's valley flats and northern banks. Hockey and its arenas played a particular role in this displacement during this time. Originally played on the frozen river, local business and political boosters/elites sponsored organized men's teams. The unpredictability of weather meant that promoters could not dependably schedule games. In 1902, funded by fur magnate and land developer Richard Secord, the Thistle Rink opened downtown, just above the river valley flats (Scherer et al., 2019). The barn-like wooden structure held the gala celebration for the inauguration of the province of Alberta in 1905 and was where the fledgling province's legislative assembly met in 1906. Hockey, capitalist local elites, and Anglo-Saxon sovereignty were symbolically linked in this moment of setter colonial assertion.

As the first half of the 20th century progressed, settler agriculture flourished on stolen Indigenous territory, comprising the next wave of the extractive resource economy. In this timeframe, Indian Residential Schools were in their ascendancy, the Pass system severely limited Indigenous mobility and ability to engage economically, and an apartheid state on reserves was realized. Edmonton became an important regional settler hub supporting rural agriculture and related industry. The third wave of Alberta's racial capitalist economy was kicked off when oil was struck in 1949 just south of Edmonton. As the post-war economic boom privileged the primarily white population, a burgeoning middle-class left Edmonton's central neighborhoods for a growing suburbia. Housing in the downtown and surrounding communities became more affordable. Concomitantly, with the gradual abolition of the Pass system and the federal government's policies encouraging urban migration from Indian Reserves (Peters, 2001), an identifiable urban Indigenous community emerged in central Edmonton. Alongside an earlier established Chinatown and the Black community, a racially diverse community formed in the city's downtown, in an otherwise hostile prairie settler city.

There is now a considerable houseless population that calls this neighborhood home. It is a vibrant and diverse community. This (counter)public, who are primarily Indigenous, has been the focus of biopolitical state management techniques that involve de facto forms of containment and elimination for most of the last seven decades. This has included the proliferation of many social service agencies from within the non-profit industrial complex, working-class bars, and "low-income" housing. As we overview below, a two-year ethnography by Scherer, Davidson, Kafara, and Koch (2021) demonstrates how the building of Rogers Place has exacerbated the surveillance and harassment of preexisting community members in downtown Edmonton. This is another outcome of the latest iteration of gentrifying extractive capitalism. Bourgeois sport promoters, civic booster elites, and land developers came together to recolonize the space of Edmonton's city center, culminating with the building of Rogers Place in the early decades of the 21st century. However, as the study notes, city center community members have also adapted in some ways to these punitive conditions.

Carceral Redlining at Rogers Place

The development of the arena prompted widespread concerns about the displacement of the houseless community in Edmonton's downtown area, one that is "decidedly Indigenous" (Koch et al., 2018). Between 2016 and 2018, Scherer et al. (2021) conducted a two-year ethnography to understand changes in this community ("the Ice District study"). The project explored how different kinds of classed and racialized people are differentially supported along biopolitical lines—some extravagantly supported in life, and others literally left to die in heightened conditions of coercive surveillance and policing. It showed that the presence of the new arena and its associated processes of gentrification sent shock waves to the downtown core—a place where different people's possibility to live, work, play, and belong are concomitantly altered.

As outlined in the Ice District study, keeping affluent, predominantly settler fans separated from less affluent, predominantly Indigenous community members was an explicit policing mandate for "securing" Rogers Place. During the construction of the arena, Edmonton Police Service (EPS) met with central social service agencies to discuss how to keep preexisting community members away from Oilers' ticket-holding fans. Fans were clearly characterized by both the Katz group and the EPS as the only legitimate citizens with a right to the space around the arena during the game hours. This attitude was reinforced by ongoing media representation of the city center as a "dangerous" and "seedy" area, perpetuating racist colonial discourses that are used repeatedly in settler cities to make the case for increased policing and security. The EPS's tactics for policing the arena district:

> focused on ensuring the arena's success as a positive economic force for Edmonton. With the "reputation of the city on the line," the EPS representative explained, police efforts would center on keeping patrons visiting the arena separate from residents of the adjacent "shelter district." (Scherer et al., 2021, p. 112)

On game nights, extra EPS officers, hired at public expense, conducted traffic (vehicular and pedestrian) at busy intersections around the arena and patrolled transit stations. Private security hired by Rogers Place would often encourage community members to seek shelter and assistance at any one of a number of social service agencies near the arena. Differential policing was observed along racialized and classed lines. On one particular night in the playoff season of 2017, an Indigenous woman had been cheering "let's go Oilers!" with a huge crowd of settler fans, all in jerseys, preparing to go inside the arena for the game. Rogers Place security singled her out, removed her from the crowd of paying fans, and escorted her to a bench in front of the Boyle Street Community Services entrance, over two blocks away (Scherer et al., 2021). This is but one

Settler Colonialism as Environmental Injustice **181**

example of the new forms of profiling and policing of who is and who is not allowed to belong in the recently developed Ice District.

Punitive policing was practiced in a variety of ways to clear the area around Rogers Place of almost all visible Indigenous presence. In the Ice District study, the authors describe how community members seeking warmth in the transit train station directly behind Rogers Place were regularly ticketed and/or forcibly removed by EPS officers on very cold winter nights. On other occasions, visibly Indigenous folks who dared to join in fan revelry by loudly chanting for a team were targeted by police, detained, and threatened with arrest if they did not leave the area. In another instance, two young Indigenous men were detained for over 20 minutes while EPS officers ticketed them for not having appropriate lights on their bicycles. There is a clear double standard in police treatment of people on game nights. Settler Oiler fans regularly made excessive noise by singing and chanting (often in an inebriated state), walked on city sidewalks with open alcohol, and illegally jaywalked across city streets in front of EPS officers (Scherer et al., 2021). These activities are clearly differentially policed when performed by different kinds of bodies. In Edmonton, poor people, people of color, and people who are houseless are statistically more often ticketed, detained, and/or arrested (Huncar, 2017). This channels proportionately more Indigenous folks into the ever-expanding carceral prison-industrial complex (Sylvestre et al., 2020), which has been conceptualized as a clear arm of ongoing settler colonialism in Canada (Nichols, 2020).

However, the men who survive on and through the streets in downtown Edmonton have developed various forms of localized knowledge and embodied practices to navigate their communities in the aftermath of the building of Rogers Place (Scherer et al., 2021). For some folks, panhandling opportunities have to some extent increased on game nights, albeit often farther away from the arena or through an increasing bodily docility that never impedes the flow of fan traffic. Bottle picking had become less worthwhile and hanging around in one's community almost impossible. In the Ice District study, all residents with whom the researchers interacted indicated that police presence, surveillance, and harassment had increased with the arrival of the arena.

All of these practices point to carceral redlining, that is "the systemic ways in which incarceration practices are operationalized by the redlining of racialized communities as a tool for social control. There are effectively red lines drawn around certain communities to be criminalized and as such, targeted for incarceration" (Reece, 2020, para. 12). The development of Rogers Place has redrawn some of the earlier redlines that have contoured the spaces available to community members in Edmonton's downtown. "Sport-related gentrification and the dividends reaped by both private capital and state interests exacerbates deadly systems of carcerality, resedimenting the next iteration of 21st century settler colonial dispossession" (Scherer et al., 2021, p. 118).

Pillars of the Community

The City of Edmonton and the Edmonton Oilers have used multiple strategies in their quest to mobilize Rogers Place as an apparatus of gentrification in downtown Edmonton. As the previous section outlined, some of these tactics are explicit and literal attempts to erase particular people from the area through racialized policing and displacement. As Davidson et al. (2019) have outlined, the structure of ongoing settler colonialism in Edmonton is also produced through the development of "socially conscious" public art projects. We revisit Whyte's (2018) observation that urban gentrification here "erases any traces of Indigenous origins of the area. Gentrification processes often commodify highly selective memories and legacies of other groups, often people of color, who lived there before the most recent gentrification process" (p. 138). More than a decade ago, Sze (2009) observed the increasingly nuanced strategies deployed by corporate actors to co-opt elements from progressive social movements for advancing urban development projects that aligned with corporate interests. This can be similarly seen in the case we examine here. Public art has been used in and around Rogers Place to "represent" contemporary Indigenous presence and other marginalized communities. We end this chapter by briefly overviewing the *Pillars of the Community* art installation and the ways in which it perpetuates highly selective images to make way for a neoliberal assuaging of social difference in a city space of radical disjuncture and inequity.

In November of 2016, the *Pillars of the Community* public art installation was unveiled behind Rogers Place. The project has been championed as a socially conscious initiative, working in close collaboration with the inner-city community. As one of the artists said, "*Pillars of the Community* mirrors the diversity and reality of Edmonton. We wanted to celebrate the unsung heroes, daily faces, and the less heard or underpraised people who call this city home" (Edmonton Arts Council, 2016, para. 2). Five large portraits of inner-city community members—Brian, Noah, Fatima, Mike, and Vanessa—grace each of the 10-meter-high concrete slabs that cover a large public transit air vent, near the community rink in the Roger's Place development (Davidson et al., 2019).

The mural is part and parcel of the processes and practices of neoliberal gentrification. Davidson et al. (2019) mobilized Rory Crath's (2017) identification of three governance strategies: "1. creative city urbanism, 2. heightened securitization and penal governance of spaces and populations deemed threatening to a city's economic competitiveness, and 3. cultivation of neoliberal consumer citizenship" (p. 1267). The *Pillars of the Community* project dovetails with these three strategies in Edmonton's new Ice District, in how these portrait murals of "disenfranchised" people further ideals of "community engagement" while ensuring that a certain type of urban sport consumer will be made to feel comfortable, welcomed, and reassured by sanitized, individualized representations of the "diversity" of the preexisting neighborhood. Difficult difference is aesthetically managed and diffused through these representations. The entrepreneurial assemblage composed of corporate capital, public-private partnerships, arms-length municipal councils, and front-line social service providers comprises the non-profit industrial complex—a powerful juggernaut in Edmonton.

As Davidson et al. (2019) point out, murals have become a popular means of marking public space—engaging communities, particularly communities "at risk" (read: structurally disadvantaged and systematically disempowered by the legacies and active workings of capitalist settler colonialism) to build capacity, develop skills, and beautify neighborhoods. In this case, five photos of community members were chosen by the artists that represented a "spectrum of experiences, genders, ethnicities, ages, and lives" ("Celebrating Pillars," n.d.) that comprised several central neighborhoods. It is important to critically assess this purportedly benevolent community art initiative. Following the first of Crath's (2017) three strategies, *Pillars of the Community* was a creative venture that characterized community experience in a very particular way, "according to normative regimes of the politics of difference, an economy prefiguring the representational limits to what can be understood and visualized about targeted populations and spaces deemed other, and thus problematic, to the project of urban transformation" (p. 1264).

The images depicted work in the service of creating "safe" spaces for monied sport consumers. As our foregoing conversation indicates, the area around Rogers Place has repeatedly been depicted as "dangerous," and this was used as the justification for increased policing and security presence. Removing any formal representation of so-called threatening or disruptive individuals is entirely congruent with this policing strategy. Therefore, all embodied versions of uncontrollable difference must be removed from the area around the arena, and the static mural representations stand in, in that space of the arena, as individualized stories of quiet legible success (Davidson et al, 2019).

This leads to Crath's third point—that of cultivating neoliberal consumer citizenship. Only one of the five images in the *Pillars of the Community* installation depicts a visibly white man. "Brian" is described as a man with a troubled past, but he is "recuperated" by the Edmonton Arts Council as a "joyous example of positive self-reclamation through community engagement" ("Celebrating Pillars," n.d.). The only white man embodies the individualized success story of the settler neoliberal citizen. He has overcome involvement in illegal drug culture, kicked his addiction, and his mural image has been picked up as part of a social justice marketing campaign by the bank ATB Financial (Davidson et al., 2019). Brian got lucky—in the right place at the right time and was rewarded for "performatively displaying his compliance as a self-responsivised, global city participant and collaborator in realizing creative city aspirations" (Crath, 2017, p. 1269). This political sensibility is "restricted to practices of one's own self-care, non-state dependency, and understandings of community as a localized mechanism for securitization and productivity" (Crath, 2017, p. 1270). What mural projects like *Pillars of the Community* do is participate in this pacified political sensibility, neatly aligning with a particular form of aesthetic engagement that is clearly linked with creative city entrepreneurialism, the most recent form of extractive racial capitalism in this place called Edmonton.

FIGURE 12.2 Portrait from *Pillars of the Community* mural collection

Conclusion

In this chapter, we have endeavored to carefully situate the development of a contemporary sport-entertainment complex (Rogers Place in Edmonton, Canada) within the history of colonial settlement in Alberta, Canada. Our contribution to the emerging literature on sport and environmental justice is to highlight ongoing settler colonialism as a form of environmental injustice. In the wake of the construction of Rogers Place, we overviewed how increased private security and policing have brought adverse changes to a city center community for its residents. In addition, we did a critical reading of a public art installation associated with this arena and its role in sanitizing the arena area for suburban ticket-holding sports fans. In doing so, we hope to draw attention to the workings of settler colonialism. Analyzing these deliberately raced and classed strategies that are mobilized by the settler state, the police, and the professional sport industry is a crucial first step in working toward any form of environmental justice (Chen, 2022). As we briefly noted earlier, there was minor civic opposition to the public subsidization for

Rogers Place in Edmonton. However, we argue that "environmental justice" on occupied Indigenous land will not be possible without collective mobilizations and movement building that fundamentally unsettle racial capital.

References

Álvarez, L., & Coolsaet, B. (2020). Decolonizing environmental justice studies: A Latin American perspective. *Capitalism Nature Socialism, 31*(2), 50–69. 10.1080/10455752.2018.1558272

Bullard, R. D. (1990). *Dumping in Dixie: Race, class, and environmental quality*. Westview Press.

Cake, S., Jackson, E., Pineault, E., & Hussey, I. (2018). *Boom, bust, and consolidation: Corporate restructuring in the Alberta oil sands*. Parkland Institute. https://www.parklandinstitute.ca/boom_bust_and_consolidation

Canadian Press. (2013, December 3). Rogers snaps up naming rights to future downtown home of Edmonton Oilers. *The Globe and Mail*. https://www.theglobeandmail.com/sports/hockey/rogers-snaps-up-naming-rights-to-future-downtown-home-of-edmonton-oilers/article15739948/

Carleton, S. (2020, February 21). Might is not right: A historical perspective on coercion as a colonial strategy. *Canadian Dimension*. https://canadiandimension.com/articles/view/might-is-not-right-a-historical-perspective-on-coercion-as-a-colonial-strategy

Celebrating Pillars of the Community. (n.d.). https://yegarts.tumblr.com/post/153483588428/celebrating-pillars-of-the-community

Chen, C. (2022). Naming the ghost of capitalism in sport management. *European Sport Management Quarterly*. Advance online publication. 10.1080/16184742.2022.2046123

Chen, C., & Mason, D. S. (2016). Professional sports franchises and city status: Los Angeles and the National Football League. In V. Fletcher (Ed.), *Urban and rural developments: Perspectives, strategies and challenges* (pp. 133–150). Nova Science Publishers.

City of Edmonton. (n.d.). The Agreement. https://www.edmonton.ca/attractions_events/rogers_place/the-agreement

Coulthard, G., & Simpson, L. B. (2016). Grounded normativity/place-based solidarity. *American Quarterly, 68*(2), 249–255. 10.1353/aq.2016.0038

Crath, R. (2017). Governing youth as an aesthetic and spatial practice. *Urban Studies, 54*(5), 1263–1279. 10.1177/0042098015625034

Daschuk, J. (2019). *Clearing the plains: Disease, politics of starvation, and the loss of Indigenous life*. University of Regina Press.

Davidson, J., Kafara, R., & Scherer, J. (2019, November 6–9). *Pillars of the community: Public art and professional sports arenas* [Paper presentation]. North American Society for the Sociology of Sport, Virginia Beach, VA, United States.

Davis, H., & Todd, Z. (2017). On the importance of a date, or, decolonizing the Anthropocene. *ACME: An International Journal for Critical Geographies, 16*(4), 761–780. https://www.acme-journal.org/index.php/acme/article/view/1539

Donald, D. (2017, April). *Edmonton as traditional gathering place: A walking tour* [Walking tour commentary]. Edmonton, AB, Canada.

Dykstra, M. (2013). Edmonton Oilers owner Daryl Katz jumps in Forbes magazine wealthiest Canadian rankings. *Edmonton Sun*. https://edmontonsun.com/2013/03/04/edmonton-oilers-owner-daryl-katz-jumps-in-forbes-magazine-wealthiest-canadian-rankings

Edmonton Arts Council. (2016). *Urban mural takes shape at Rogers Place*. https://www.edmontonarts.ca/static_media/pdfs/files/eac_misc/MEDIA_RELEASE_Urban_Mural.pdf

Figueroa, R. M. (2011). Indigenous peoples and cultural losses. In J. S. Dryzek, R. B. Norgaard, & D. Schlosberg (Eds.), *The Oxford handbook of climate change and society* (pp. 232–250). Oxford University Press.

Gilio-Whitaker, D. (2019). *As long as grass grows: The Indigenous fight for environmental justice, from colonization to Standing Rock*. Beacon Press.

Goeman, M. (2014). Disrupting a settler-colonial grammar of place: The visual memoir of Hulleah Tsinhnahjinnie. In A. Smith (Ed.), *Theorizing Native studies* (pp. 235–265). Duke University Press.

Goyette, L. & Roemmich, C. J. (2004). *Edmonton: In our own words*. University of Alberta.

Government of Alberta. (2021). *Edmonton*. https://regionaldashboard.alberta.ca/region/edmonton/#/

Huncar, A. (2017, June 27). *Indigenous women nearly 10 times more likely to be street checked by Edmonton police, new data shows*. CBC News. https://www.cbc.ca/news/canada/edmonton/street-checks-edmonton-police-aboriginal-black-carding-1.4178843

Jackson, L. K. (2017). The complications of colonialism for gentrification theory and Marxist geography. *Journal of Law & Social Policy, 27*, 43–71.

Koch, J., Scherer, J., & Holt, N. (2018). Slap shot! sport, masculinities, and homelessness in the downtown core of a divided western Canadian inner city. *Journal of Sport and Social Issues, 42*(4), 270–294. 10.1177/0193723518773280

Malin, S. A., & Ryder, S. S. (2018). Developing deeply intersectional environmental justice scholarship. *Environmental Sociology, 4*(1), 1–7. 10.1080/23251042.2018.1446711

McGregor, D. (2009). Honouring our relations: An Anishnaabe perspective on environmental justice. In J. Agyeman, P. Cole, & R. Haluza-Delay (Eds.), *Speaking for ourselves: Environmental justice in Canada* (pp. 27–41). University of British Columbia Press.

Misener, L., & Mason, D. S. (2008). Urban regimes and the sporting events agenda: A cross-national comparison of civic development strategies. *Journal of Sport Management, 22*(5), 603–627. 10.1123/jsm.22.5.603

Mullenbach, L. E., & Baker, B. L. (2020). Environmental justice, gentrification, and leisure: A systematic review and opportunities for the future. *Leisure Sciences, 42*(5–6), 430–447. 10.1080/01490400.2018.1458261

Murdock, E. G. (2020). A history of environmental justice: Foundations, narratives, and perspectives. In B. Coolsaet (Ed.), *Environmental justice* (pp. 6–17). Routledge.

Nichols, R. (2020). *Theft is property! Dispossession and critical theory*. Duke University Press.

Pellow, D. N. (2018). *What is critical environmental justice?* Polity.

Peters, E. J. (2001). Developing federal policy for First Nations people in urban areas: 1945-1975. *The Canadian Journal of Native Studies, 21*(1), 57–96. http://www3.brandonu.ca/cjns/21.1/cjnsv21no1_pg57-96.pdf

Pulido, L. (1996). A critical review of the methodology of environmental racism research. *Antipode, 28*(2), 142–159. 10.1111/j.1467-8330.1996.tb00519.x

Pulido, L. (2018). Historicizing the personal and the political: Evolving racial formations and the environmental justice movement. In R. Holifield, J. Chakraborty, & G. Walker (Eds.), *The Routledge handbook of environmental justice* (pp. 15–24). Routledge.

Reece, R. (2020, June 25). Carceral redlining: White supremacy is a weapon of mass incarceration for Indigenous and black peoples in Canada. https://yellowheadinstitute.org/2020/06/25/carceral-redlining-white-supremacy-is-a-weapon-of-mass-incarceration-for-indigenous-and-black-peoples-in-canada/

Salz, A. (2014, September 30). Edmonton media get sneak peek at downtown arena construction site. *Edmonton Sun*. https://edmontonsun.com/2014/06/02/edmonton-media-get-sneak-peek-at-downtown-arena-construction-site

Sant, S. L., Mason, D. S., & Chen, C. (2019). 'Second-tier outpost'? Negative civic image and urban infrastructure development. *Cities, 87*, 238–246. 10.1016/j.cities.2018.10.006

Scherer, J. (2016). Resisting the world-class city: Community opposition and the politics of a local arena development. *Sociology of Sport Journal, 33*(1), 39–53.

Scherer, J., Davidson, J., & Kafara, R. (2021, June 4–6). *The impacts of Rogers Place Arena on homelessness in Edmonton, Alberta* [Keynote address]. The Hockey Conference, Halifax, NS, Canada.

Scherer, J., Davidson, J., Kafara, R., & Koch, J. (2021). Negotiating the new urban sporting territory: Policing, settler colonialism, and Edmonton's Ice District. *Sociology of Sport Journal, 38*(2), 111–119. 10.1123/ssj.2020-0113

Scherer, J., Mills, D., & McCulloch, L. S. (2019). *Power play: Professional hockey and the politics of urban development.* University of Alberta Press.

Sylvestre, M. E., Blomley, N., & Bellot, C. (2020). *Red zones: Criminal law and the territorial governance of marginalized people.* Cambridge University Press.

Sze, J. (2009). Sports and environmental justice: "Games" of race, place, nostalgia, and power in neoliberal New York City. *Journal of Sport & Social Issues, 33*(2), 111–129. 10.1177/0193723509332581

Sze, J., & London, J. K. (2008). Environmental justice at the crossroads. *Sociology Compass, 2*(4), 1331–1354. 10.1111/j.1751-9020.2008.00131.x

TallBear, K. (2016). *Failed settler kinship, truth and reconciliation, and science.* http://www.kimtallbear.com/homeblog/failed-settler-kinship-truth-and-reconciliation-and-science

Tobias, J. L. (1991). Canada's subjugation of the Plains Cree, 1879–1885. In J. R. Miller (Ed.), *Sweet promises: A reader on Indian–White relations in Canada* (pp. 212–240). McGill Queen's University Press.

Todd, Z. (2013, July 10). *You call it Rossdale, we call it Pehonan.* Speculative fish-ctions. https://zoestodd.com/2013/07/10/you-call-it-rossdale-we-call-it-pehonan/

Whyte, K. P. (2017). The Dakota access pipeline, environmental injustice, and U.S. colonialism. *Red Ink: An International Journal of Indigenous Literature, Arts, & Humanities, 19*(1), 154–169.

Whyte, K. (2018). Settler colonialism, ecology, and environmental injustice. *Environment and Society, 9*(1), 125–144. 10.3167/ares.2018.090109

Whitson, D., & Macintosh, D. (1993). Becoming a world-class city: Hallmark events and sport franchises in the growth strategies of Western Canadian cities. *Sociology of Sport Journal, 10*(3), 221–240. 10.1123/ssj.10.3.221

Whitson, D., & Macintosh, D. (1996). The global circus: International sports, tourism and the marketing of cities. *Journal of Sport and Social Issues, 20*(3), 278–295. 10.1177/0193 72396020003004

Wolfe, P. (2006). Settler colonialism and the elimination of the native. *Journal of Genocide Research, 8*(4), 387–409. 10.1080/14623520601056240.

Yazzie, M. K. (2018). Decolonizing development in Diné Bikeyah: Resource extraction, anti-capitalism, and relational futures. *Environment and Society, 9*(1), 25–39. 10.3167/ares.2018.090103

13

MICRO LAND GRABBING OF SPORTING GROUNDS IN NAIROBI: A NEW FORM OF ENVIRONMENTAL JUSTICE AT PLAY

Stephanie Gerretsen

AUTHOR'S NOTE

I would like to thank Daniel Obunyasi and Caroline Gushu for providing their assistance in the data collection process by organizing and facilitating interviews and focus groups in each of the study's six sites, in addition to translating the interviews from Swahili and Sheng (the local dialect spoken in parts of Nairobi) into English for transcription. This study would not have been possible without their efforts in the field. I am grateful for their support in providing a voice to communities that are too often left voiceless.

In 2013, Kenya inaugurated its 4th President, Uhuru Kenyatta, since the country's independence in 1963. President Uhuru Kenyatta outlined in his *2013–2017 Jubilee Manifesto* that a new coalition would be formed, bridging together the country's four most prominent political parties to outline strategies to actualize *Kenya's Vision 2030* (Coalition, 2013). The ambitious promises outlined in the *Jubilee Manifesto* included tackling some of Kenya's greatest social challenges and required a strategy to generate more resources that could be reinvested back into the economy and address the country's immense challenges. This included reducing unemployment rates, poverty, food insecurity, and income inequality while improving the overall living standards and providing social benefits such as universal healthcare coverage and adequate and affordable housing. Of the 23 programs and initiatives outlined in the *Manifesto*, there were two important

DOI: 10.4324/9781003262633-15

infrastructure projects including the completion of the Standard Gauge Railway (SGR) that connects Mombasa to Nairobi and the expansion of the national electrical grid. A third important legacy project was the expansion of Kenya's sports infrastructure and securing Kenya's legacy as a sporting nation.

Kenya has been a sports powerhouse in Africa, dominating the international long-distance athletic events, culminating in several Olympic medals. In 2005, the government of Kenya presented a framework for sustainable growth and development of sport in the country, mainstreaming sport across all areas of development and playing a more significant role in public policy (Byron & Chepyator-Thomson, 2015). With government priorities shifting across various other social issues, from health to youth unemployment, sport policy has been of relative unimportance and deemed an "elusive political exercise" with few tangible results (Byron & Chepyator-Thomson, 2015, p. 309). This chapter begins with an overview of the Government of Kenya's strategy to construct 11 stadiums across the country to secure its legacy as a sporting nation and the various challenges involved in implementing these strategies. Of these challenges, this chapter emphasizes the disconnect between national strategies and local development practices, in which land designated for sport and recreational land uses is increasingly disappearing through various land grabbing practices, an important form of environmental injustice not often discussed.

Kenya's Jubilee Manifesto

The *Jubilee Manifesto* emphasized that the "collective love of sport and the arts is one of the strongest factors that unites" the country and that Kenya produces world leaders in athletics. Yet, despite the country's international success and recognition as a leader in sport, "successive governments have too often neglected sports and creative industries, and as a result, the potential in these sectors has not been accorded a chance to improve [Kenyan] quality of life or boost [the Kenyan] economy" (Coalition, 2013, p. 20). It was further stated that:

> Kenya should be a serious contender to host future regional and international sporting events …. and believe [the sport and creative industry] should be nurtured and supported to ensure they are able to flourish and contribute to [Kenya's] economic growth and general well-being as a nation. (p. 20)

A comprehensive list of solutions was provided, but some of the most noteworthy as it relates to sport and development include:

- Establish a National Lottery Scheme, boosted by National budget allocations to fund and support professionalization of local sporting leagues across the major sporting disciplines.

- Pursue tax incentives for individual and private sector investors in the Sport, Arts, and Entertainment sectors.
- Provide both the national teams and the domestic leagues with all the support they require while respecting their autonomy.
- Facilitate and encourage the better management of sports and facilitate the professionalization of sports through the introduction of professional coaches in schools.
- Build five new national sports stadia in Kisumu, Mombasa, Nakuru, Eldoret, and Garissa, while upgrading existing sporting facilities at the County level to accommodate swimming, tennis, basketball, and rugby.
- Bid to host the 2019 Africa Cup of Nations and the 2019 World Athletics Championships.

In 2013, as part of the *Jubilee Manifesto*, five national stadium construction projects were proposed for the cities of Kisumu, Eldoret, Mombasa, Garissa, and Nakuru. Kenya's Treasury released KSh.1.9 billion (US$16 million) to begin the ground-breaking process (Owino, 2019). By 2017, in the lead up to the general presidential elections, the promises for the five stadiums still had not been fulfilled. The Kenyan Auditor General estimates that KSh.830 million (US$7 million) allocated for the construction of those stadiums that were paid out to contractors across the country had been lost through corruption (Mwai, 2022). Despite these financial issues, the incumbent president and his administration committed to include additional stadium projects, both in new construction and renovation, as part of the sitting administration's reelection promise. This was largely to appease the youth population and secure the youth vote (Rintaugu et al., 2011). Many of the additional stadiums were not planned to be of the size and scale of the national stadiums and were designed for regional league competitions. A combination of national and regional funding allocated for the regional stadium construction was directed toward the following counties: Elgeyo Marakwet, Kiambu, Marsabit, Nyeri, Tharaka Nithi, and Uasin Gishu (Eldoret). The total construction and renovation costs for the 11 facilities increased to KSh.23.5 billion (US$215 million). Since 2019, the Jubilee government has made major strides to ensure that at least five national stadiums were built throughout the country to accommodate national and international sporting events, attract revenue, and create direct and indirect employment opportunities. Moreover, it was a priority to ensure Uhuru Kenyatta's presidential campaign promise was ultimately met, and he could end his tenure with legacy projects that were realized.

Over the past decade, sport in Kenya has received an immense amount of attention, as political parties and individual politicians solicited their political candidacy and reelection, leveraging the youth vote through sport (Rintaugu et al., 2011). To ensure the development of the venues, government land and funding were allocated for the stadium construction. Furthermore, the Sports, Arts, and Social Development Fund, a program managed under the Ministry of Sport, Culture, and Tourism, collected KSh.30.3 billion (US$260 million) through betting, gaming, and lottery (Republic of Kenya National Assembly, 2020). However, while these national and regional stadium construction projects received substantial public funding, sport and recreation at the county and city level is substantially less funded by the national, county, and city governments, despite its critical role in developing athletes for the national teams. Illustrated in the city of Nairobi's mismanagement of urban land development, open spaces for sport, recreation, and environmental protection are given low priority in the spatial planning and development pipeline in comparison to housing, commercial, and industrial land uses (Muiga, 2009). Since the country's independence in 1963, Kenya developed without a national land policy, which has largely led to the poor management of public spaces. In 2009, a policy was passed with specific aims of creating more equitable access to land, securing land ownership, imposing more regulation of land development, designating more sustainable land uses, and increasing access to land information (Republic of Kenya, 2009). The 2009 National Land Policy, however, did not address public open spaces nor open land designated for sport and recreational use.

Addressing these issues within the land-use policies and their late creation is pivotal to the consequential sport-related environmental (in)justices within Kenya. To address these land issues, this chapter highlights how Nairobi's complicated history of colonialism and management of land, and lack thereof, have resulted in substantial wage gaps, expanding informal settlements, and the disappearance of public land and greenspace allocated for sport and recreation at increasing rates for alternative land uses. As power brokers and other stakeholders illegally and illicitly grab more land, marginalized communities are exposed to environmental injustices due to the uneven access to land and the infringement on their "inherent right to a clean, safe, and healthy environment" (United Nations, 2022).

Nairobi's *1948 Master Plan* and Impact on Future City Development and Access to Recreational Spaces

The urban planning of many sub-Saharan African cities is grounded in colonial urban history, in which institutionalized racial segregation was a key strategy in urban land management. This was particularly notable in the development of Nairobi since the mid-1900s. Rooted in a racially segmented spatial order, the priorities of colonial urban planning were to serve the interests of Nairobi's white minority population and colonial administration. Nairobi started as an important rail depot during the British East Africa Company's construction of the Kenya–Uganda Railway in the late 1890s, which stretched from Mombasa, a port city on the eastern coast, to Kisumu, located on the banks of Lake Victoria. At the time, no urban settlement existed in the area. However, Nairobi quickly grew and by 1907, Nairobi replaced Mombasa as Kenya's capital city.

Nairobi's urban development was based on the neighborhood concept, in which estate models were planned and implemented by the British colonial state between 1918 and 1948. Many colonial cities were planned from Ebenzer

Howard's *Garden City Concept* (1898). The Garden City model was considered the cornerstone of modern urban planning and directed special attention to the importance of urban greenspaces. The overarching principles of the Garden City model aimed to solve issues of a congested industrial city and an undeveloped countryside. This would provide residents of towns the ability to "live in leafy, airy, and healthy environments" (Girardet, 1996, p. 54) in which an appropriate amount of shared open and agricultural space was provided to residents. The Garden City model emphasized urban greenspaces and their spatial layout as a critical part of development, integrating the natural environment of the countryside within urban neighborhoods. Surrounding greenbelts limited the city size, served as recreational areas, and created buffers between residential zones and areas designated for industry. The Garden City movement is now widely considered outdated due to the costly effects of urban sprawl and the higher density of cities. Despite the social, health, and ecological benefits that are provided through urban greenspaces, the Garden City model has received its fair share of criticisms. While it aimed to improve quality of life and create an even balance between nature and the built environment, the model has been criticized for "providing the means to institutionalize contemporary social cultural ideas and values of the dominant group [that being the British colonialists] onto the physical fabric of urban areas" (Simon & Christopher, 1984, as cited in Mbatia, 2006). It embodied an impractical ideal in city development (Zuraidi & Sawab, 2011; Pinder, 2005; Rapoport, 2014; Ward, 2005), and as a result, led to greater degrees of spatial polarization (Gandy, 2006) and segregation (LeGates & Stout, 2020).

Nairobi's *1948 Master Plan*, led by white South African planner and architect Thornton White, was originally developed for a city with a population of 250,000 and designed to guide the city's development until 1975. The *Master Plan* considered numerous factors, including Nairobi's urban form, its relationship to the railway, future industrialization and population growth, regional development, and demographics. In adopting the Garden City model, the *Master Plan* emphasized the importance of open spaces, allocating 24.96 sq km of land for public open spaces, which made up 27.5% of the municipality's total land area of 90.64 sq km (Makworo & Mireri, 2011). These open spaces were comprised of greenbelts and game and forest reserves. It has also been found that 10 sq m of local open space should be provided per household (but not located further away than a 100–150 m distance) in order to meet residential needs (Makworo & Mireri, 2011). The *1948 Master Plan* laid a foundation for town planning to be segregated by race, ethnicity, and socioeconomic status. European settlers formed their communities in areas such as Karen, Upper Hill, Kileleshwa, Kilimani, and Muthaiga, while Asians lived in Parklands, Ngara, Eastleigh, South C, Pangani, and Highridge. These areas had a relatively low density in population and sprawling estates in areas such as Karen and Muthaiga. Africans, on the other hand, were not permitted to permanently settle in Nairobi. The city was envisioned to be a European town; therefore, no housing, nor intention of providing housing, was accessible to Africans. As a result, spontaneously built housing formed around the city's peripheries, creating settlements that still exist today, such as Kibera and Pumwani (Martin & Bezemer, 2020). In Eastlands, the housing structures were deliberately small, "bachelor-housing" designed for temporary low-income African workers commuting into the central business district. These subdivisions served the interests of Nairobi's white minority population and colonial administration as it also outlawed indigenous and communal land ownership, despite the majority of the population being African (Myers, 2015). While the *1948 Master Plan* was not viewed as an apartheid tool, under British colonial rule and post-independence in 1963, Africans suffered colonial injustices with respect to their right to the city.

After Kenya gained independence in 1963, the city of Nairobi underwent rapid urbanization. While the city extended its geographic boundaries from 8 sq km in 1900 to 690 sq km in 1963 (Oyugi & K'Akumu, 2007), the city's administration was unable to effectively control the city's population growth and rural-to-urban migration. Both the *1973 Nairobi Metropolitan Urban Growth Strategy* and *the Five-Year Development Plan (1984–1988)* failed to manage rapid population influx, which grew an average of 8% a year, from 250,000 before independence, to 500,000 by 1969, to 828,000 by the 1980s (Macrotrends, 2022). From the 1980s to the 2000s, the annual growth rate dropped to an annual increase of 5% and then again to consistent annual growth of 4% over the last 20 years. Nairobi's most recent population count is approximately 4.9 million in 2021 (Myers, 2015). The *Growth Strategy* was not approved due to competing political interests and because some of the proposals for new development were presented in ad hoc fashion. Furthermore, unlike the *1948 Master Plan*—which provided a comprehensive plan for residential, industrial, and transportation land uses, including recreational space—open spaces were not prioritized in the *Growth Strategy*. As a result, the city's development has continued to be guided by a now outdated *1948 Master Plan*. Moreover, even though the city's geographic boundaries may have extended, there was no planning strategy implemented to ensure infrastructure and public services aligned with population growth (Makworo & Mireri, 2011).

Due to ineffective urban planning, post-independence Nairobi became an even more divided city as underserviced informal settlements expanded. Limited strategic urban planning led to a clear shift away from the ideals of the colonial city and its framing along the Garden City model, and toward addressing more imminent social issues, including housing, unemployment, and poverty (Makworo & Mireri, 2011).

The social and spatial inequalities in land use and access to urban greenspaces in Nairobi are grounded in the city's colonial urban history. Urban spaces serve multiple functions, including providing space for leisure, recreation, and physical activity, creating a vibrant culture while protecting visual character and heritage, beautifying cityscapes, and attracting and retaining businesses and jobs in close proximity to recreational spaces (Mandeli, 2019). The type and scale of public open spaces in a city typically affect a country's level of development (Kwon, 2021). As mentioned, Nairobi's *1948 Master Plan* allocated land for public space to support a population of 250,000. However, this land allocation did not increase in

194 Stephanie Gerretsen

tandem with the city's population. Today, only 5% of the total land area in the city is dedicated to recreational space, which is inefficient in supporting a city of 5 million (Ikawa, 2015). Public open spaces in the city of Nairobi have been increasingly under threat and disappearing due to rapid urbanization, poor planning, weak urban management, and illegal land grabbing. Land grabbing and land governance have played critical roles in allocating public and recreational spaces throughout Nairobi, have influenced the development of sport infrastructure and fields, and played a significant role within the environmental justice discourse.

Environmental Justice within an International Context

The discourse around environmental justice has evolved through a culmination of theories and practice that has mostly focused on the global North, and more specifically, on the United States (Agyeman, 2005; Bullard, 2005; Cole & Foster, 2001). Environmental justice sits at the nexus between structural inequalities, power imbalances, and environmental degradation (Robbins, 2014). The framing of environmental justice is largely based on the unique history of the United States, centered on the civil rights movement and the confluence of racial and spatial inequalities (Mohai et al., 2009; Ravi Rajan, 2014; Stretesky et al., 2011; Strong & Hobbs, 2002; Willett, 2015), in which low-income, racial and ethnic minority communities are disproportionately exposed to environmental harms and risks (Nixon, 2011; Sikor & Newell, 2014). This includes the location of waste sites and landfills and exposure to air pollution and radiation. Unequal social, economic, and political power dynamics cause low-income communities and communities of color to be more vulnerable to health and environmental threats compared to other racial and ethnic groups. In fact, a national study funded by the Commission for Racial Justice of the United Church of Christ found that race and ethnicity were the most significant factors in determining where waste facilities, landfills, and other environmental and chemical hazards should be located (Chavis & Lee, 1987; see also Mohai et al., 2009; Robbins, 2014).

The social and political aspects highlighted by the environmental justice movement in the US created a groundswell of global activism. For instance, greater focus was directed toward protests and social movements and how socially transformative action can increase awareness of environmental justice in different regions around the world (Busscher et al., 2020; Carruthers, 2008; Nixon, 2011; Schlosberg & Carruthers, 2010; Sebastien, 2017; Urkidi & Walter, 2011). This, in turn, has led to more proactive organizing around areas of community health and sustainability, and in the building of social capital (Hanna et al., 2016; Martínez-Alier, 2012; Mehmood & Parra, 2013). More specifically, with the increased prevalence of land-use changes across communities of differing regional contexts and their heightened awareness surrounding environmental justice issues, broader political action and activism can be enhanced (Hanna et al., 2016; Kollmuss & Agyeman, 2002; Narain, 2014; Nixon, 2011; Sebastien, 2017).

Conflicts over the distribution and exploitation of natural resources, such as land, and the unbalanced participation of those with decision-making authority, illustrate that the "core issues at the heart of environmental justice struggles are [both] universal" (Sikor & Newell, 2014, p. 151) and transboundary. While environmental injustices may stem from specific practices and policies that arise from uneven capitalist development in a specific location, when there is alignment among the practices and stakeholders involved, these issues evolve and become connected on a global scale (Holifield et al., 2009). This increases a broader understanding of how resource-specific environmental conflicts are embedded and shape global processes and policies (Sikor & Newell, 2014). Conflicts such as water scarcity, food insecurity, and the growing number of climate refugees stem from political mismanagement, uneven urban and economic development, and ecological ambivalence. The common narrative from these conflicts is that despite contributing the least to the proliferation of these social and environmental issues, the poorest and most vulnerable communities are the most adversely impacted and typically victimized by other injustices as well (Minkler et al., 2008; Mohai et al., 2009; Sikor & Newell, 2014). The movement around environmental justice has taken a new shape in highlighting the environmental and social inequities on a global scale, drawing a deep connection to the history of colonialism.

Early studies of environmental justice were centered around toxic and hazardous siting but have since expanded to other thematic areas such as air pollution, flood hazards, energy scarcity, water scarcity, access to public transportation, food insecurity, and lack of urban and greenspaces (Holifield et al., 2009). Issues related to land rights, such as involuntary displacement and land grabbing, can also be considered an environmental justice issue. Varying levels of poverty and consequent environmental conditions exacerbate the impacts of land grabbing (Busscher et al., 2020). Impoverished communities that tend to be more vulnerable to land grabs face other pressing issues, including meeting basic needs and accessing clean water, electricity, healthcare, and education. That said, these types of communities and individuals are more likely to "adapt their livelihoods and accommodate the environmental injustices" that result from land grabbing (Busscher et al., 2020, p. 503). This, however, continues the spread of land grabbing practices. Those who inadvertently accept land grabbing as a normal process are prime examples of individuals who are limited in the ability to engage in social and political movements proactively. Although the Kenyan Constitution has outlined the need for greater public participation in governance affairs Kenya's colonialist past, its oppressive legislation, and apparent disparities of access and opportunity as a result of socioeconomic class and politics, illustrate marginalized and vulnerable communities' hesitancies and challenges in engaging in a social justice campaign that combines land tenure issues with environmental justice.

Land Governance and the Link to Environmental Justice

Land grabbing is the act in which "individuals, corporations, or governments undertake large-scale acquisitions of land, by way of lease, allocation, concession or purchase, or private use" (Kariuki & Ng'etich, 2016, p. 80), which involves the displacement of families and individuals, but can also involve the illegal or irregular acquisition of large tracts of land by governments or private entities. These acquisitions often disregard the social, economic, and environmental impacts; are not based on free, prior, and informed consent of the affected land-users; do not entail transparent contracts; nor are based on meaningful participation by individuals or broader communities (National Academy of Public Administration, 2003). Land grabs have typically led to tenure insecurity, conflicts over land within and between communities, and resistance, protest, and violence (Busscher et al., 2020). Moreover, the "'global land grab' is an assessment of the economic and political policies that advocate for the privatization of land and resources for economic growth, jobs creation and food insecurity" (Gardener, 2012, p. 378). Land grabbing is likened to "control grabbing," which is the "grabbing of power to control land" (Borras et al., 2012). This is, in effect, a grab for control over resources. While obtaining a land title—a formal document that outlines the rights of an individual to own a piece of property—was meant to mitigate land grabbing practices, most individuals are unaware of their ownership rights. Yet, even if they were knowledgeable of their ownership rights, they are often incapable of registering the land because of various financial constraints (e.g., banks denying individuals credit). These existing social inequities benefit those with access to power, knowledge, and social networks in gaining rights to property at the expense of others (Zoomers, 2010). Hall et al. (2011) outline four concepts in which individuals are excluded from accessing land. These include:

1. Regulation: the use of rules and policies employed by states and other power groups, defining what and by whom land can be used for
2. Force: the use of violence or threats of violence to establish and maintain control over land
3. Legitimation: the use of principled arguments to discuss how, by whom, and for what, land is allocated or used
4. Market powers: the fluctuation in land pricing which creates barriers of entry in access and use of land (pp. 4–5)

The social and political power relations and historical and ecological dimensions of a place influence land governance issues and play a critical role in access to land. Land grabbing issues are often defined by the acquisition of large land tracts. For instance, it has been determined that land grabbing is any land acquisition that exceeds 1,000 hectares (approximately 2,500 acres; Kariuki & Ng'etich, 2016, as cited in Cotula, 2013, p. 44). This obscures the fact that land grabbing can also occur gradually and on a smaller scale. This process is known as micro land grabbing and directly impacts local communities around the world. Across a multi-country case study on micro land grabbing, Jahn (2022) found three consistent themes. First, micro land grabbing involves stakeholders, such as village leaders, local elites, chiefs, local, and regional traditional authorities or government officials, and regional companies, who are socially integrated within their communities. These stakeholders typically exude their power both within and over the community to fulfill their own self-interests. Second, those stakeholders are either financially supported or have strong relationships with local political leaders. And third, the process of micro land grabbing occurs gradually as piecemeal development, one plot of land disappearing after another.

Land grabbers can use illegal land ownership documents to force community members out, they can employ those working in private real estate firms to draw up documents for land plots through a legal privatization process, or they can instill violence by forcibly expelling families, tearing down their houses, cutting down fences and guard walls, and intimidating individuals and families by threatening, shooting, and killing community members. Micro land grabbing greatly impacts local communities by taking on diverse forms, which creates its own set of conflicts. For instance, land grabbing can occur within a community, between local communities, and between communities and government authorities, in which community leaders or chiefs act as intermediaries for land grabbers, such as private developers or local politicians, without community approval. Ultimately, these conflicts result from traditional hierarchies, power asymmetries, and income inequalities. For this reason, national and local governments, alongside the private sector, play an equally important role in perpetuating land grabbing schemes.

Kenya's land governance and prevalence of land grabbing have been shaped over three transformative periods in history. The first period is defined by the acquisition of land by British colonialists to establish their power and authority. Under the colonial administration, Africans were prevented from holding land interests. In fact, all land in Kenya was declared the "Crown Land" under the Crown Lands Ordinance of 1915 (Olima, 1997). Upon Kenya gaining independence in 1963, post-colonial Kenya was characterized by land grabs from new political elites, many of whom fostered political and economically viable relationships with the British, to retain their authority and ranks. Land designated for use of school grounds, cemeteries, playgrounds, parks, forests, recreation, and other public uses was often grabbed by individuals or private companies (Kariuki & Ng'etich, 2016). Finally, the third period derives from a new phenomenon in which foreign multinationals and governments are acquiring land across a slew of developing countries to invest in capital-intensive infrastructure projects such as large-scale farming, irrigation, and mining.

Kenya is in critical need of more effective urban land management. Kenya's land crisis is a combination of unsustainable urban growth and demographic patterns, limited knowledge on sustainable land use, the prevalence of social inequities and justice issues as the wealthy individuals buy up more urban land, and rife levels of corruption among government officials (Olima, 1997). The allocation of urban plots often yields inconsistent outcomes due to the interference of individuals in positions of authority. Simply put, Kenya's land policy has been controlled by influential politicians and the wealthy, with little consideration given to the urban poor. To ensure more effective urban land management, regulations

198 Stephanie Gerretsen

need to be reformed to better control the use, management, and ownership of land, and support efforts for the most marginalized and vulnerable populations to have greater access to land. Moreover, nearly half of Kenya's urban population does not have access to clean water, and three-quarters of Kenyans do not have access to functioning solid waste management systems (Willett, 2015). Many are also exposed to air pollution from unregulated vehicle emissions (Kinney et al., 2011). In sum, a large proportion of the Kenyan population is at high risk of environmental problems. Nairobi provides an important case study in illustrating the intersection of structural inequalities that stem from Kenya's colonial past, the degraded environment that is a result of poor urban land management, the gradual disappearance of open space dedicated for sport and recreation through power land grabs, and how these different factors combine to lend an international voice to the environmental justice literature.

Nairobi's Soccer Fields Under Siege

Nairobi County has 17 constituencies, the country's highest number, divided into 85 electoral wards. There are five wards in each constituency. The six wards listed in Table 13.1, Githurai 44, Kahawa West, Mwiki, Kayole, Huruma, and Babadogo, were selected to analyze micro land grabbing practices of sporting grounds, the impact land grabs have had on the communities at large, and how the lack of protection over the limited number of existing sport and recreational spaces exacerbates environmental injustices in informal and semi-informal communities that are vulnerable to systemic social and environmental issues that are often associated with environmental justice. These wards were selected either because of any former or current involvement in ongoing land ownership debates of sports grounds. The social, economic, and environmental conditions of the six wards are poor, defined by insecurity, overcrowding, poor garbage collection and waste and sewage management, high rates of unemployment, and poverty.

The average population across the six wards is approximately 35,000, concentrated in small, high-density areas. Githurai 44, for example, is one of the largest growing informal settlements in Nairobi; its population is close to 50,000,

TABLE 13.1 Sample of Nairobi County's Wards and Their Areas' Population and Size

Ward	Constituency	Population (2021)	Area Size (km²)
Githurai	Roysambu	47,193	2.0
Kahawa West	Roysambu	39,994	13.9
Mwiki	Kasarani	39,156	18.8
Kayole	Embakasi Central	37,590	1.2
Huruma	Mathare	36,247	0.35
Baba Dogo	Ruaraka	30,741	1.95

Source: Smith, 2021.

concentrated over a mere 2 sq km. Overcrowding and high-density living can create intense living conditions, leading to insecurity and violence. The expansion of Nairobi's informal settlements is a result of years of poor urban land management, rapid urbanization, and population growth. The organized yet segregated form of colonial masterplanning that prioritized open spaces and greenspaces is forepassed The conflict over land in Nairobi is volatile because of overcrowding and lack of space. Any vacant plot of land or land that is open and designated for sport and recreation is under threat of being grabbed. Once grabbed, the land is cornered off and converted for industrial, commercial, or residential use. Despite the clear need and social and economic benefits of sports grounds, they are vulnerable to micro land grabbing. The sports grounds identified in each of the wards are often the only form of available open space. As a result, they are highly contested locations. Neighboring wards may not even have space allocated for sport, which means that within a constituency composed of five wards, one sports ground will need to serve upward of 250,000 people.

Amenities such as quality streets, public squares, and well-designed public spaces should not just be amenities found in affluent communities. These amenities are critical to the well-being of individuals and for the development of communities. In poor and marginalized communities, public spaces become the extension of one's living room, providing a place for social interaction and economic activities, and vital in increasing productivity and human capital. Living in high-density and confined spaces leads to public health issues and low quality of life standards, but it can also negatively impact economic activities, increase environmental pollution, and increase insecurity. International governmental organizations recognize the basic right to public space as a fundamental aspect of their human-rights development agenda: public space creates safe spaces, offers a sense of inclusion, and is an essential component of sustainable urban development (Smithsimon, 2015).

The ongoing land conflict over the municipal sports fields, taking the form of a complete land grab overnight or a slow, gradual process of encroachment, illustrates the fragility of vacant land and the powerlessness of communities in protecting their community assets. Surveys, field notes, ethnographic interactions and observations, and formal interviews were conducted in Githurai 44, Kahawa West, Mwiki, Kayole, Huruma, and Babadogo to better understand the contested land rights of the local sporting grounds and the environmental injustices these communities are challenged with as key spaces are gradually taken. Formal interviews were conducted with the various sport community leaders across the six communities who have substantial knowledge or have played a role in leading protests against land grabbing practices of their constituency's sports grounds. Through the support from the Mathare Youth Sports Association and the contacts from the sport coaches and community leaders, snowball sampling and focus groups were organized to complete a survey with questions related to the importance of public space, environmental justice, and the current state of sports grounds being land grabbed. Twenty formal interviews were conducted, which lasted between

45 minutes and 1 hour, along with the completion of 75 surveys, which consisted of 30 questions that included a combination of multiple choice, Likert scale, open-ended, and demographic questions.

Survey respondents and interviewees were unanimous in their belief that it is their human right to have access to a clean, healthy, and sustainable environment. Limited public space is an infringement of this fundamental human right. Bold, actionable change is required to ensure communities have access to a healthy environment, as it is the foundation for transformative economic, social, and environmental change (United Nations, 2022). Ninety-seven percent strongly agreed that every community or neighborhood should have a recreational space or social hall that community members can access and use; 85% strongly agreed that the lack of open space for sport and recreational use harms the community and its surrounding environment; and 97% strongly agreed that sport contributes to community cohesion, cooperation, and sense of belonging. Community members believe public space is critical to have in their communities as it "engages the youth and prevents them from being idle and engaging in criminal activities" and "gives [them] a greater sense of security over [their] children's welfare and/or the welfare of the children in [their] community." A community leader who has lived in Githurai for over 20 years mentioned that because of the lack of facilities and sporting grounds:

> We don't have spaces for kids to engage themselves, the youths don't have areas to engage and thus at the end of the day they engage in unhealthy behaviors—they form gangs and end up in the wrong hands of the police and can risk losing their lives. We lack the continuity of generations.

A social activist from Githurai explained that due to the high unemployment rates among families, children have little access to education due to financial constraints. As a result:

> You have a lot of young people with nothing to do. They say an idle mind is the devil's workshop. I do not know what the devil's workshop looks like, but [the Githurai Sports Ground] has nurtured so many youths who even play on the national and international teams now.

In Baba Dogo for instance, protecting the sports grounds has been instrumental in developing future talent, including players who have played for regional teams including Ulinzi, Mathare United, Tusker, Gor Mahia, and AFC Leopards.

The lack of community spaces and sporting fields also contributes to foundational environmental justice issues. Discussions on environmental and climate justice issues are integral and interrelated with those oriented to social justice issues. A social activist from Githurai explained that:

> The political decisions that have been made affect the environmental decisions that are made, that then affect social decisions. There is

interconnectivity of all these rights. We've really been part of trying to advocate for justice, environmental justice, and also trying to link the land question and the environment, [which can be seen in how] our laws are in Kenya ... environment and law go hand in hand. [This is demonstrated in the] Environmental Lands Courts. Anytime that land comes into a conversation, you cannot avoid talking about the environment.

Each of the six wards is exposed to systemic environmental issues that contribute to concerns over water scarcity, frequent power outages and electrical blocks, food insecurity, and different forms of pollution such as air, chemical, and waste. Compounding these environmental conditions can lead to insecurity and violence, and in some cases, increase police brutality. The Githurai social activist further explained that because Githurai is designated as a semi-informal settlement,

There is so much pressure for space and trying to find where people will live, that there is not a lot of emphasis on how to take care of the environment. You will realize that our drainage systems are so bad, that you will find people releasing raw sewage at night into the roads, playgrounds and sporting fields where the youth play. Also, because the county [Nairobi County] has slacked on garbage collection ... you will find a lot of garbage around. People just do not have a place to take their garbage, so they start garbage sites wherever they please.

In effect, some of the sports grounds become garbage dumping sites simply because the land is vacant. Since Nairobi County does not properly manage waste and garbage collection in its informal settlements, youth groups will collect garbage at a small fee, which creates temporary employment opportunities. Situations like these bring youth groups together to solve a common cause, in which they advocate to community chiefs for greater accountability and report improper dumping to NEMA, Kenya's national environmental agency. In such instances, this empowers the youth to become informed and advocate for their rights. However, allowing one of the only vacant spaces in a ward to become an active dumpsite can also be leveraged by land grabbers (Figure 13.1).

A similar situation occurred around Kisumu's national stadium, Moi Stadium, located in the center of Kenya's third-largest city. On the west side of the national stadium lies the city's major dumpsite, Kachok. The Kachok dumpsite has been a point of contention for a long time. It was on the Governor of Kisumu's agenda to relocate the dumpsite in his first 100 days in office back in 2017. Four years later, it still has not been removed and has directly impacted the ability to host matches and other athletic events. In 2021, the county government purchased a 207-acre piece of property 35 km away to relocate the dumpsite; however, the stadium has still not recovered and must undergo environmental remediation at an immense cost in order to recover and repurpose the land outside of the facility. As spaces become recognized as regular dumping sites and trash collection is managed ad

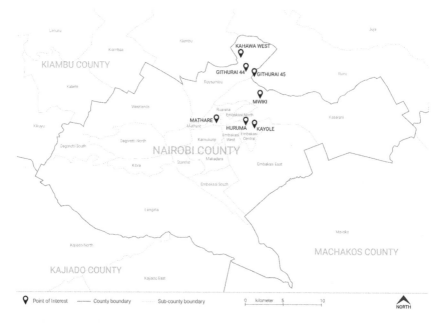

FIGURE 13.1 Map of Nairobi County

hoc, land grabbers take advantage of the "undesirable" land and claim it at night by installing fences and other barricades. Due to the lack of government oversight, community members' limited familiarity with reporting land grabbing issues, and fear of retribution from community chiefs, police officers, and local officials most likely involved in similar undercover operations, sporting grounds and access to greenspaces disappears.

Eighty-eight percent of respondents agreed that powerful or well-connected people in their ward and community are responsible for amassing land and resources. Sixty-four percent believed elected officials are most involved in land or resource grabbing in their immediate communities, followed by 61% who believe it is the business community (including private developers), 45% government agencies, and 35% religious groups. Eighty-three percent strongly agreed that as a community member, it is their responsibility to raise awareness about land grabbing issues that have or are currently occurring within their ward. Both in Githurai and Kahawa West, the burgeoning number of churches has also posed an issue on land titling and encroachment on the sports fields. Over the past several years, many churches and been built and have attempted to gradually impose their presence onto the fields. Official complaints were filed with the Ministry of Lands, while a legal team has organized to determine ways in which future conflicts can be appropriately handled.

Eighty-one percent also stated that they had never reported a land grabbing issue over a sports ground to a community organizing group. Some reasons for not reporting include a lack of proper and protected channels to discuss grievances, limited knowledge of reporting procedures, and fear of political interference. Most community residents do not understand how to hold local government officials and ward administrators accountable for providing basic and necessary public utilities. Limited knowledge of these processes impacts public participation. It was indicated that because of the lack of transparency over government budgeting, requesting for a community needs assessment, and facilitating open dialogue between government and residents, citizens are unable to advocate for their needs and rights. For example, one respondent noted:

> Public utilities are supposed to actually help the citizen and since they actually pay for these services through their taxes, they need to be able to hold these people [local politicians and ward administrators] accountable. It is not enough for them to tell the citizens they built the community a hospital. For how much was the hospital built? Did [the community] need a hospital, or was a school needed instead? Did they ask?

Another respondent asked:

> Because no one has come to inform or educate the community around what is [designated as] public land or government land, when land grabbers come with documents who will know if they are not authentic? You can have idea that the sports field is public land but without evidence you keep quiet … community leaders need to empower the community with proper information so that community can be proactive.

In Baba Dogo, intermediaries between the community and a private developer have taken the debate over land titling of the field to court. While a fence had been put up and there had been an attempt to build a national office on the grounds, through court order it was stopped and removed. Details, however, on the land titling and deeds are still under consideration. Similarly, in Mwiki, a protesting group also filed a complaint with the court and with the Ministry of Lands:

> Nothing has happened to date. A portion of lands [around the field] have been development. We don't have the capacity to go and remove them. We have tried our best. We have demonstrated. We have had people get arrested. We were teargassed. It has not been an easy battle, but we have tried to raise the complaints and waiting for authorities to maybe one day serve justice.

As a result of these power asymmetries and drastic income inequalities, speaking out on contentious issues, such as those related to land, can have costly consequences. Disclosure of these private groups who are leading on the land grabbing tactics is impossible. However, it is important to note that it is a collective of

204 Stephanie Gerretsen

individuals who come together, identify the public spaces, conspire with county offices to develop new land documents or change the existing ones, and proceed to grab them. The most cited reason for lack of reporting is the fear of instigating life-and-death consequences. For example:

> Issues with land always involves wealthy people and the police and people lose their lives so [they] don't want to participate in such issues ... these issues involve people with money and influence so [they] won't have any impact at all ... reporting matters related to land grabbing makes [them] a target ... issues with land grabbing are rampant, but still don't want to lose [their] life for such a cause unless it's [their own] land.

All six wards have been challenged with the same narrative. The existing sports grounds in question are the last remaining open spaces in their respective constituencies. All other public spaces and playgrounds have been grabbed. Community organizing around these remaining grounds is paramount to ensure their protection for future generations. Furthermore, obtaining original title deeds and ensuring they are not accessed or altered will also provide safeguards over land ownership.

Kenya Vision 2030

Kenya's *Vision 2030*, a development blueprint for the country's future, lays out an ambitious proposal to reimagine Nairobi as a "world class African metropolis" and an "iconic and globally attractive city" (Republic of Kenya, 2008). Visionary plans include massive improvements to infrastructure, the development of satellite cities, the transformation of governance structures, and substantive investments in commercial, industrial, and residential real estate financed by conglomerates of private capital managed by private partnerships (Myers, 2015). These transformative ideas, however, illustrate an immense disconnect between how the government's lofty urban development strategies benefit the interests of multinational corporations and global elites and those of the broader urban population. The perceived success in adopting a brand of global city masterplanning has led to "corporate-led urban development, spectacular skylines, and exclusive urban living" (Smith, 2017, p. 32). Abandoning the "messier urban reality" (De Cauter, 2004), this new mode of development seeks vacant land to create enclaves for the global elite. These spaces consist of privatized urban security, infrastructure, waste management, and other public services to serve the urban elite, while the remaining urban population is left to Nairobi's urban spaces that are congested, polluted, insecure, and densely populated (Myers, 2015). While *Vision 2030* is a strategy to position Nairobi, and Kenya more broadly, in becoming the commercial gateway and regional hub of East Africa, in which pro-business reforms were instituted to boost business investments and an enabling environment was created to grow the ICT services, the new level of infrastructure development reproduces the spatial logistics and urban planning of colonial cities and perpetuates the spatial and economic injustices of local citizens.

Kenya's *Jubilee Manifesto* outlined strategies to tackle some of the country's greatest social challenges, including reducing unemployment rates, poverty, food insecurity, and income inequality. It also outlined an ambitious plan to secure its legacy as a sporting nation by constructing 11 national stadiums across the country. While these plans and ambitions are well formulated on paper, the reality on the ground tells a very different narrative, both from a national and local perspective. Most of the budgets for each national stadium construction or upgrading project have been disbursed, yet by 2021, completion rates have not even reached 50% (Figures 13.2 and 13.3).

Likewise, existing stadiums such as in Kisumu are underutilized because the city's dumpsite has developed on vacant land next to the stadium. Large budgets were allocated for these national sports projects. However, in local cases such as in Nairobi, in which local sporting grounds are instrumental in developing the talents of athletes who will eventually compete in these national stadiums, little-to-no support is being provided by the national and local governments. In fact, public spaces allocated for sport and recreation are quickly disappearing, and their uses converted for industrial, commercial, or residential use. Informal and semi-informal settlements are systematically more vulnerable to environmental impacts such as the lack of access to clean drinking water, increased exposure to air and

FIGURE 13.2 Front façade of Kirigiti Stadium in Kiambu County, under construction in January 2022

FIGURE 13.3 Interior of Kirigiti Stadium, under construction in January 2022

noise pollution, and poor wastewater and sewage management. The loss of public land is also an environmental concern. By way of unregulated growth and poor land management, the gradual loss of Nairobi's inter-regional sporting grounds is a direct infringement on the community's right to a clean, safe, and healthy environment and a core element of environmental injustice. This chapter has demonstrated that sport ambitions at the national level have failed to translate to the regional and local levels in Nairobi and illustrates the growing environmental injustices communities are challenged with as public spaces and sport are under-prioritized compared to more profitable land uses.

References

Agyeman, J. (2005). *Sustainable communities and the challenge of environmental justice*. New York University Press.

Ako, I. R. (2011). Resource exploitation and environmental justice: The Nigerian experience. In F. N. Botchway (Ed.), *Natural resource investment and Africa's development* (pp. 74–76). Edward Elgar Publishing.

Borras, S. M., Cristóbal, K., Gómez, S., & Wilkinson, J. (2012). Land grabbing and global capitalist accumulation: key features in Latin America. *Canadian Journal of Development Studies*, *33*(4), 402–416. 10.1080/02255189.2012.745394

Bullard, R. D. (2005). *The quest for environmental justice: Human rights and the politics of pollution*. University of California Press.

Busscher, N., Parra, C., & Vanclay, F. (2020). Environmental justice implications of land grabbing for industrial agriculture and forestry in Argentina. *Journal of Environmental Planning and Management, 63*(3), 500–522. 10.1080/09640568.2019.1595546

Byron, K., & Chepyator-Thomson, J. R. (2015). Sports policy in Kenya: Deconstruction of colonial and post-colonial conditions. *International Journal of Sport Policy and Politics, 7*(2), 301–313. 10.1080/19406940.2015.1023823

Caldeira, T. (2000). *City of walls: Crime, segregation and citizenship in Sao Paulo.* University of California Press.

Carruthers, D. V. (2008). Popular environmentalism and social justice in Latin America. In D. V. Carruthers (Ed.), *Environmental justice in Latin America: Problems, promise, and practice* (pp. 1–22). MIT Press.

Centre for Minority Rights Development (Kenya) and Minority Rights Group International on behalf of Endorois Welfare Council v. Kenya, No. 276 (2003).

Chavis, B. F., Jr., & Lee, C. (1987). *Toxic wastes and race in the United States: A national report on the racial and socio-economic characteristics of communities with hazardous waste sites.* United Church of Christ Commission for Racial Justice.

Coalition Between the National Alliance [TNA], the United Republican Party [URP], the National Rainbow Coalition [NARC], and the Republican Congress Party [RC]. (2013). *Transforming Kenya: Securing Kenya's future.* https://s3-eu-west-1.amazonaws. com/s3.sourceafrica.net/documents/119133/Jubilee-Manifesto-2013.pdf

Cole, L. R., & Foster, S. R. (2001). *From the ground up: Environmental racism and the rise of the environmental justice movement.* New York University Press.

Cotula, L. (2013). *The great African land grab? Agricultural investments and the global food system.* NBN International.

Cotula, L., Vermeulen, S., Leonard, R., & Keeley, J. (2009). *Land grab or development opportunity? Agricultural investment and international land deals in Africa.* United Nations Food and Agriculture Organization.

De Cauter, L. (2004). *The capsular civilization: On the city in the age of fear.* NAI Publishers.

Gandy, M. (2006). Urban nature and the ecological imaginary. In N. Heynen, M. Kaika, & E. Swyngedouw (Eds.), *In the nature of cities: Urban political ecology and the politics of urban metabolism* (pp. 63–75). Routledge.

Gardner, B. (2012). Tourism and the politics of the global land grab in Tanzania: Markets, appropriation and recognition. *Journal of Peasant Studies, 39*(2), 377–402. 10.1080/03066150.2012.666973

Girardet, H. (1996). *The Gaia atlas of cities: New directions for sustainable urban living.* Gaia.

Grain, M.-A. J., Temper, L., Munguti, S., Matiku, P., Ferreira, H., Soares, W., Porto, M. F., Raharinirina, V., Haas, W., Singh, S. J., & Mayer, A. (2014). The many faces of land grabbing. Cases from Africa and Latin America. *EJOLT Report, 10.* http://www.ejolt. org/wordpress/wp-content/uploads/2014/03/140305_EJOLT10.pdf

Guha, R., & Martínez-Alier, J. (1999). Political ecology, the environmentalism of the poor and the global movement for environmental justice. *Kurswechsel, 3,* 27–40.

Hall, D., Hirsch, P., & Murray, L. (2011). *Powers of exclusion: Land dilemmas in Southeast Asia.* University of Hawai'i Press.

Hanna, P., Vanclay, F., & Langdon, J. (2016). Conceptualizing social protest and the significance of protest action to large projects. *Extractive Industries and Society, 3*(1), 217–239. 10.1016/j.exis.2015.10.006

Holifield, R., Porter, M., & Walker, G. (2009). Introduction: Spaces of environmental justice: Frameworks for critical engagement. *Antipode, 41*(4), 591–612. 10.1111/j.1467-8330.2009.00690.x

Ikawa, J. V. O. (2015). *The impact of policies on the development and management of recreational spaces in Nairobi, Kenya* [Unpublished doctoral dissertation]. University of Nairobi.

Jahn, T. M. (2022). *Micro land grabbing and local communities: Comparative analysis of important actors, effects, and reactions for a basic understanding of a gradual process*. Kassel University Press. 10.17170/kobra-202112215294

Kariuki, F., & Ng'etich, R. (2016). Land grabbing, tenure security and livelihoods in Kenya. *African Journal of Legal Studies*. 9(2), 79–99. 10.1163/17087384-12340004

Kinney, P. L., Gichuru, M. G., & Volavka-Close. (2011). Traffic impacts on $PM_{2.5}$ air quality in Nairobi, Kenya. *Environmental Science & Policy*, *14*(2), 369–378. 10.1016/j.envsci.2011.02.005

Kollmuss, A., & Agyeman, J. (2002). Mind the gap: Why do people act environmentally and what are the barriers to pro-environmental behavior? *Environmental Education Research*, *8*(3), 239–260. 10.1080/13504620220145401

Komesha Ufisadi. (2021, September 21). *Taxpayers looking at loss of KSHS. 830 million in stadia projects*. Komesha Ufisadi. https://komeshaufisadi.com/taxpayers-looking-at-loss-of-kshs-830million-in-stadia-projects

Kwon, O.-H., Hong, I., Yang, J., Wohn, D. Y., Jung, W.-S., & Cha, M. (2021). Urban green space and happiness in developed countries. *EPJ Data Science*, *10*, 28. 10.1140/epjds/s13688-021-00278-7

LeGates, R. T., & Stout, F. (2020). Editors' introduction: Frank Lloyd Wright: "Broadacre City: A new community plan." In R. T. LeGates & F. Stout (Eds.), *City reader* (7th ed., pp. 401–406). Routledge.

Macrotrends. (2022). *Nairobi, Kenya metro area population 1950–2022*. https://www.macrotrends.net/cities/21711/nairobi/population

Makworo, M., & Mireri, C. (2011). Public open spaces in Nairobi City, Kenya, under threat. *Journal of Environmental Planning and Management*, *54*(8), 1107–1123. 110.1080/09640568.2010.549631

Mandeli, K. (2019). Public space and the challenge of urban transformation in cities of emerging economies: Jeddah case study. *Cities*, *95*, 102409. 10.1016/j.cities.2019.102409

Martin, A. M., & Bezemer, P. M. (2020). The concept and planning of public native housing estates in Nairobi/Kenya, 1918–1948. *Planning Perspectives*, *35*(4), 609–634. 10.1080/02665433.2019.1602785

Martínez-Alier, J. (2012). Environmental justice and economic degrowth: An alliance between two movements. *Capitalism Nature Socialism*, *23*(1), 57–73. 10.1080/10455752.2011.648839

Mbatia, T. W. (2016). *Social-political analysis of urban greenspaces in Nairobi: Perspectives on the (re)production and (re)construction of spatial injustice in the consumption of public nature reserves in the city: A critical inquiry into outcomes of non-state actors interventions in the management and conservation of urban protected areas* [Unpublished doctoral dissertation]. Université Bordeaux Montaigne.

Mehmood, A., & Parra, C. (2013). Social innovation in an unsustainable world. In F. Moulaert, D. MacCallum, A. Mehmood, & A. Hamdouch (Eds.), *The international handbook on social innovation: Collective action, social learning and transdisciplinary research* (pp. 53–66). Edward Elgar.

Minkler, M., Vásquez, V. B., Tajik, M., & Petersen, D. (2008). Promoting environmental justice through community-based participatory research: The role of community and partnership capacity. *Health Education & Behavior*, *35*(1), 119–137. 10.1177/10901981 06287692

Mohai, P., Pellow, D., & Roberts, J. T. (2009). Environmental justice. *Annual Review of Environment and Resources, 34*, 405–430. 10.1146/annurev-environ-082508-094348

Muiga, J. G. (2009). *Provision of recreational facilities within Kasarani neighborhood-Nairobi* [Unpublished master's thesis]. University of Nairobi.

Mwai, M. (2022, June 16). *Auditor-General questions exaggerated costs of stadia renovations and delays in completion.* People Daily. https://www.pd.co.ke/sports/auditor-general-questions-exaggerated-costs-of-stadia-renovations-and-delays-in-completion-132752/

Myers, G. (2015). A world-class city-region? Envisioning the Nairobi of 2030. *American Behavioral Scientist, 59*(3), 328–346. 10.1177/0002764214550308

Narain, V. (2014). Whose land? Whose water? Water rights, equity and justice in a peri-urban context. *Local Environment, 19*(9), 974–989. 10.1080/13549839.2014.907248

National Academy of Public Administration. (2003). *Addressing community concerns: How environmental justice relates to land use planning and zoning.* Environmental Protection Agency. https://www.epa.gov/sites/default/files/2015-02/documents/napa-land-use-zoning-63003.pdf

Nixon, R. (2011). *Slow violence and the environmentalism of the poor.* Harvard University Press.

Olima, W. H. A. (1997). The conflicts, shortcomings, and implications of the urban land management system in Kenya. *Habitat International, 21*(3), 319–331. 10.1016/S0197-3975(97)00010-6

Owino, S. (2019, October 27). *Kenya: Government officers to inspect 11 stadiums.* Daily Nation. October 27. https://allafrica.com/stories/201910270024.html

Oyugi, M. O., & K'Akumu, O. A. (2007). Land use management challenges for the city of Nairobi. *Urban Forum, 18*(1), 94–113. 10.1007/BF02681232

Pinder, D. (2005). *Visions of the city: Utopianism, power and politics in twentieth century urbanism* (2nd ed.). Routledge.

Rapoport, E. (2014). Utopian visions and real estate dreams: The eco-city past, present and future. *Geography Compass, 8*(2), 137–149. 10.1111/gec3.12113

Ravi Rajan, S. (2014). Environmental justice in India. *Environmental Justice, 7*(5), 115–116. 10.1089/env.2014.7502

Republic of Kenya. (2008). *Kenya Vision 2030: A globally competitive and prosperous Kenya.* Government of the Republic of Kenya.

Republic of Kenya. (2009). *Sessional Paper No. 3 of 2009 on National Land Policy.*

Republic of Kenya National Assembly. (2020). *Departmental Committee on Sports, Culture, and Tourism: Report on the inquiry into the status of stadiums in Kenya.* http://www.parliament.go.ke/sites/default/files/2020-10/Report%20on%20Inquiry%20into%20the%20Status%20of%20Stadia%20in%20Kenya.pdf

Rintaugu, E. G., Munayi, S., Mwangi, I., & Ngetich, E. D. K. (2011). The grand coalition government in Kenya: A recipe for sports development. *International Journal of Humanities and Social Science, 1*(18), 305–311.

Robbins, P. (2014). Cries along the chain of accumulation. *Geoforum, 54*, 233–235. 10.1016/j.geoforum.2012.12.007

Schlosberg, D., & Carruthers, D. (2010). Indigenous struggles, environmental justice, and community capabilities. *Global Environmental Politics, 10*(4), 12–34. 10.1162/GLEP_a_00029

Schroeder, R., St. Martin, K., Wilson, B., & Sen, D. (2008). Third world environmental justice. *Society & Natural Resources, 21*(7), 547–555. 10.1080/08941920802100721

Sebastien, L. (2017). From NIMBY to enlightened resistance: a framework proposal to decrypt land-use disputes based on a landfill opposition case in France. *Local Environment, 22*(4), 461–477. 10.1080/13549839.2016.1223620

Sikor, T., & Newell, P. (2014). Globalizing environmental justice? *Geoforum, 54*, 151–157. 10.1016/j.geoforum.2014.04.009

Simon, D., & Christopher, A. J. (1984). The apartheid city. *Area, 16*(1), 60–62.

Smith, C. (2017). "Our changes'? Visions of the future in Nairobi." *Urban Forms and Future Cities, 2*(1), 31–40. 10.17645/up.v2i1.834

Smithsimon, G. (2015). *The right to public space.* Metropolitics. https://metropolitics.org/The-Right-to-Public-Space.html

Stretesky, P. B., Huss, S., Lynch, M. J., Zahran, S., & Childs, B. (2011). The founding of environmental justice organizations across U.S. counties during the 1990s and 2000s: Civil rights and environmental cross-movement effects. *Social Problems, 58*(3), 330–360. 10.1525/sp.2011.58.3.330

Strong, D., & Hobbs, K. A. (2002). Administrative responses to environmental racism. *International Journal of Public Administration, 25*(2–3), 391–417. 10.1081/PAD-120013242

United Nations. (2022). *Right to healthy environment.* Office of the High Commissioner for Human Rights. United Nations. https://www.ohchr.org/en/statements-and-speeches/2022/04/right-healthy-environment

Urkidi, L., & Walter, M. (2011). Dimensions of environmental justice in anti-gold mining movements in Latin America. *Geoforum, 42*(6), 683–695. 10.1016/j.geoforum.2011.06.003

Walker, G., & Bulkeley, H. (2006). Geographies of environmental justice. *Geoforum, 37*(5), 655–659. 10.1016/j.geoforum.2005.12.002

Ward, S. V. (2005). *Planning and urban change* (2nd ed.). SAGE.

Willett, J. (2015). Exploring the intersection of environmental degradation and poverty: Environmental injustice in Nairobi, Kenya. *Social Work Education, 34*(5), 558–572. 10.1080/02615479.2015.1066326

Zoomers, A. (2010). Globalisation and the foreignisation of space: Seven processes driving the current global land grab. *Journal of Peasant Studies, 37*(2), 429–447. 10.1080/03066151003595325

Zuraidi, E., & Sawab, H. (2011). Garden City: The suitability of its principles as a model to the contemporary planning. *NALARs, 10*(1), 18–28.

14

POLITICS AND DECISION-MAKING IN THE TAIPEI DOME COMPLEX PROJECT

Chun-Chieh Lin

Taipei Dome Complex, alternatively referred to as Taipei Cultural and Sports Park or simply Taipei Dome Complex, is arguably the most balanced public-private stadium project in Taiwan. Although this project has yet to be completed at the time of this writing, the planning of the Taipei Dome Complex intertwines with the hegemonic discourse of Taiwan baseball nationalism, the public-private partnership in response to financial austerity, and the national policy against international isolation.

Despite Taipei Dome's cultural and political representation and significance in Taiwan, it also details the project's externalities, including the loss of public parklands, the impact on the living environment, and safety concerns. This refers to the contentious decision-making process that ensued as a result of an environmental injustice affecting surrounding neighborhoods and the entire Taipei population. Taipei Dome is viewed in this light as a contested field in which collective actions taken by stakeholders or interest groups that have an effect on not only the process, evaluation, and implementation of the Taipei Dome project but also jeopardize the natural and living environment in the process of pursuing, contending, and negotiating their concentrated interests.

This chapter integrates the aforementioned perspectives within the framework of the urban regime to provide a holistic analysis of the political and decision-making processes in the Taipei Dome project. This chapter argues that the policy initiation, decision-making process, and dynamic politics surrounding Taipei Dome have profoundly affected the natural, social, and living environment. To illustrate this point, I begin below by reviewing recent scholarship related to urban regimes in the context of sports stadiums.

Urban Regime and Sports Stadium: A Brief Overview

Urban regime theory has articulated an analytical framework for examining the political process of urban land-use changes as it relates to the formation-, capacity-,

DOI: 10.4324/9781003262633-16

agenda-, agency-, and identity-building in a governing coalition in which mobilized actors exercise their power to interact with broader structural conditions in particular local and national contexts (Dowding, 2002; Imbroscio, 1998; Stone, 1989). The role of sport in urban politics has been critically discussed in the regime-related analysis in terms of (i) how various types of governing coalitions can be identified in sustaining sport-city relationships (Jakar et al., 2018); (ii) how place-based stadium constructions become a contested field between public and private sectors in order to shape urban politics toward a local development end (Sullivan, 2008); and (iii) how urban regimes use sport-centered development strategies to achieve their social, cultural, and political interests (Riess, 2001).

Stadium construction, in the context of urban planning, should be structurally understood as what Hall (1980) defined as a decision-making process for implementing a physical plan in a geographical space. Urban geographers asserted that entrepreneurial governance results in the commodification of urban land use, transforming the spatial dimension of urban projects into a point of contention between local and global communities, displacing the authentic, pluralistic, and organic daily practices of urban spaces (Harvey, 1989; Zukin, 2011). Additional studies have examined the relationship between displacement and stadium construction (Gustafson, 2013; Smith & Himmelfarb, 2013).

Nonetheless, little research has been conducted outside of Western settings on the implementation process of sports stadiums using a regime analytical framework (Koch, 2016). East Asian developmental states have developed a similar state-led model, collaborating with the private sector to build stadiums for mega-events (Ahn, 2002; Tagsold, 2020). Such a top-down development strategy has the potential to reconstruct a closed-border coalition that restricts civic participation during the stadium construction process (Kellison et al., 2019). In light of these considerations, the following section discusses the social implications and decision-making process in the Taipei Dome Complex.

Who Wants the Domed Stadium? More Than Just a Game

On November 10, 1991, a sudden downpour in downtown Taipei forced the umpire to suspend Game 7 of the Taiwan Series between the Wei-Chuan Dragons and Uni Lions due to flooding at the 32-year-old Taipei Municipal Stadium. Thousands of enraged spectators responded by repeatedly shouting toward the press box, where former Taiwanese Premier Pei-Tsun Hau stood, with the catchphrase "Premier! We demand a dome-shaped stadium!" (Chow, 1991). Hau did not commit until the Chinese Taipei baseball team won a silver medal in the 1992 Summer Olympics, prompting parliament members to urge Hau to declare baseball as Taiwan's national pastime officially and include such a domed stadium project in Taiwan's Six-Year National Development Plan (Yan & Yang, 1992). On August 28, 1992, Hau then directed Da-Zhou Huang, Mayor of Taipei (1990–1994), to initiate the domed stadium project (Taipei Municipal Government, 2015a), raising the curtain on the 32-year-long Taipei Dome saga.

This ambitious project appeared to be motivated by the suspended game in 1991, but it was also in response to Kuomintang's (KMT)—the nationalist party that fled to Taiwan in 1949 after being defeated by communist China—governing discourse about baseball that penetrates Taiwan's development history. Taiwan baseball nationalism is a discourse that combines collective memories of suppression under Japanese colonialism (1895–1945), perseverance of commitment to legitimate China against Communist China since the 1950s, measurement of building Taiwanese confidence through international baseball tournaments victories against international isolation since the late 1960s, and the niche of regaining recognition from other countries in Asian and Olympic games for shaping and ruling Taiwan's domestic and national identity to support KMT's governance (C.-C. Chan, 2012; Yu, 2007). Thus, this persuasive discourse assists the KMT in establishing patron–client relationships within society, political parties (C.-S. Wang, 1996), and in growth coalition operation of this domed stadium project.

Taipei Dome was also the successor of a suspended project entitled *Building an Indoor Stadium within Minimum 50,000 Seating Capacity in Taipei* in 1979. Ching-Kuo Chiang, Taiwan's last dictator and President (1978–88) commanded this project as a sport-for-all policy after observing that Taipei residents were highly engaged in regular sports activities in 1979 (Taipei Municipal Government, 1984a). In 1980, the Taipei Municipal Government selected two potential sites, the No. 7 greenfield site and Guandu Plain, but they were halted due to a lack of funding for processing the compulsory purchase of the land (Taipei Municipal Government, 1984b). After South Korea successfully elevated its international profile by hosting the 1986 Asian Games and 1988 Olympic Games, Teng-Hui Li (President of Taiwan, 1988–2000), Premier Hau, and the Chinese Taipei National Olympic Committee (CTNOC) supported the Taipei Municipal Government's relaunch of this suspended project as part of their bid for the 1998 and 2002 Asian Games (Lai, 1989; W.-J. Wang, 1990).

Taipei lost its 1998 Asian Games bid to Bangkok because of suppression from China (Feng, 1990). Rather than frustrating KMT politicians, this result encouraged them to pursue their dream of hosting mega-sport events by completing this domed stadium project in some form. The Taipei Dome project thus is not merely motivated by a suspended baseball match but also by a state apparatus seeking to shine a light on its governance legacy.

Building Taipei Dome: Briefing the Decision-making Stage and its Core Issue

An overview of the decision-making process of the Taipei Dome complex is necessary to appreciate its political and administrative complexity. The decision-making process of the Taipei Dome complex can be divided into five stages: site selection (1992–99), stadium plan preparation (2000–03), invitation to tender (2004–06), design review (2007–11), and the commencement of construction works (2011–). Each thematic stage highlights specific issues and controversies within the political context, aligning with the project's broader problematic development agenda.

The first stage examines the flipped process of site selection decisions for Taipei Dome. Three former Taipei mayors were discussed: Da-Zhou Huang (1990–94), Shiu-Bien Chen (1994–98), and Ying-Jeou Ma (1998–2006). This was prompted by their disparate political positions, levels of support from the central government, and perceptions of the financial feasibility of land acquisition in reserved options for Taipei Dome, which included Guandu Plain, Taipei Municipal Stadium, and Songshan Tobacco Factory. An identified externality is the land politics that resulted in soaring property prices in those areas, increasing Taipei Municipal Government's financial burden and compelling developers to flip properties in those areas.

In deciding on a location for Taipei Dome, the second stage specifies the contentious preparation process (2000–03) of preparing Songshan Tobacco Factory, the historic industrial building with expansive greenspaces located in one of the ritziest and heavily trafficked neighborhoods in central Taipei, for a domed stadium under Mayor Ma's directive to make Taipei a global city and attract the 2008 Asian Games and 2009 East Asian Games. Ma's proposal to build a 40,000-seat domed baseball stadium was later accepted by the Democratic Progressive Party (DPP) central government in 2000 via a build–operate–transfer (BOT) contract. Nevertheless, this project disregarded the opposition and voices of experts, scholars, and local neighborhoods concerned about negative environmental externalities.

The third stage emphasizes the dubious invitation to tender; the selection of the best applicant; and the BOT contract negotiation process between the best applicant, the consortium led by the Farglory Group, and Taipei Municipal Government from 2004 to 2006. Throughout this process, the Taipei Municipal Government was suspected of (i) unequally unraveling the definition of the building's total gross floor area for each tender, (ii) violating conflict of interest standards during the applicant selection process, and (iii) recklessly deciding not to charge development royalty, which was estimated to be NT$28.7 billion[1] (Taipei Municipal Government, 2015a). Following the agreement between the Taipei Municipal Government and the Farglory Group aggreged the BOT contract in 2006, this resulted in a reputational externality for Taipei Dome, exacerbating the design disputes.

The focus of the fourth stage is the administrative review process (2006–11) of the Taipei Dome design proposal. This period specifically focuses on Lung-Pin Hau, successor of Mayor Ma, and more specifically on the tensions and power dynamics between pro- and anti-construction groups regarding the project scale in the Urban Design Review (UDR) and Environmental Impact Assessment (EIA) Committees. Both parties engaged with issues about the (i) rationale for adding commercial properties to this project, (ii) loss of greenspace, (iii) possible damage to Songshan Tobacco Factory, (iv) safety and evacuation plan, and (v) traffic congestion and light pollution. After Mayor Hau was reelected in 2010, the government retook the initiative to approve the Taipei Dome project and fulfill Hau's political commitment to bid for the 2017 Summer Universiade, 2018 Asian Games, and 2019 East Asian Youth Games.

Since 2012, the Farglory Group has been expediting Taipei Dome Complex in order to prepare for the upcoming 2017 Taipei Universiade until Wen-Je Ko, a rising populist politician who reviewed Taipei Dome as a scandal, was elected as Taipei's mayor in 2014. Ko's strongman-like influence over the decision-making process is central to the fifth stage, particularly his administration's approach to pressuring the Farglory Group for contract negotiation and design amendment.

Struggling with the Promised Land for Taipei Dome: The Politics of Site Selection

Finding the ideal location for Taipei Dome has been a matter of geography and politics. As part of the Six-Year National Development Plan, the KMT government identified Guandu Plain, a natural reserve and prospective sub-city center in suburban Taipei, as a potential site for the Asian Games. Nonetheless, Mayor Huang's ambition necessitated the acquisition of over 1 million sq ft of private land and more than $53 billion for stadium construction (S.-Y. Chan, 1994). Although the Huang administration was successful in getting this bill approved by the City Council in January 1994, the Chen administration later dropped this intolerable burden in December 1994 (Kung, 1994).

After reconsidering the budget bill's use, the Chen administration proposed three alternative plans for Taipei Dome in order to keep land acquisition costs down. The initial proposal, made in December 1994, was to redevelop the Zhongshan football stadium, a publicly owned facility located within 1.1 million sq ft of the hinterland, but it fell short of meeting the 704-ft building height restriction and the traffic impact assessment (Chin, 1995). Chen's second proposal, made in 1995, was to form a consortium with the Taiwan Provincial Government to redevelop nearly 3.8 million sq ft of the Songshan Tobacco Factory, which was owned by the provincial government (C.-Y. Yang, 1996). Although both parties had reached an agreement following a 17-month negotiation, Governor Soong, a KMT power figure, halted the plan in May 1996, ending the negotiation (Chin, 1996). Mayor Chen was then forced to reconsider the use of Taipei Municipal Stadium and the surrounding 1.1 million sq ft of public-owned land for the construction of Taipei Dome. However, this plan encountered the same obstacles as the first plan (J.-C. Chen, 1997), thus making this plan die on the vine prior to Chen leaving office in December 1998.

Ying-Jeou Ma was elected Mayor of Taipei in December 1998, and as a descendant KMT power figure, he revived the idea of building the Taipei Dome in Songshan Tobacco Factory to host mega-sports events. Due to the Taiwan province's downsizing, the National Property Administration, a central government agency, took over all province-owned properties (Chu, 1998). Such a re-organization of government measurement facilitated administrative efficiency in

216 Chun-Chieh Lin

reevaluating the aforementioned options, ultimately leading to the selection of Songshan Tobacco Factory as the promised land for Taipei Dome (Chin, 1999).

From Mayor Huang to Ma, the hidden agenda of land politics and the legacy of hosting mega-sport events have played dominant roles in deciding the location of Taipei Dome. Neither local neighborhoods nor local retailers benefited from these changes. Between 1980 to 1996, average property prices in Guandu Plain rose 30 times from $1,820 to $54,600 per sq m (Economy Daily News, 1991; Hung, 1996). From 1995 to 1996, local retailers surrounding either Songshan Tobacco Factory or Taipei Municipal Stadium faced rent increases of 60% and 20%, respectively (Hung, 1996). Nevertheless, this was only the beginning of the butterfly effect, let alone the subsequent conflicts during the preparation process.

Planning the Domed Stadium in a Tobacco Factory? Voices of Doubt and Certainty

The voice of doubt has never been silent during the Taipei Dome's preparation and planning stages. Previously reserved sites for Taipei Dome had elicited repeated complaints about property flipping, environmental disruptions, and degraded neighborhood quality of life (C.-K. Chen, 1994; Niu, 1994). Indeed, Taipei residents are sensitive to those externalities, as the city has consistently had the highest population density and property prices in Taiwan, but lacks greenspace. Experts, scholars, and residents questioned the project's rationale, procedure, and assessment for displacing such scarce greenspace in Songshan Tobacco Factory with a multi-purpose, domed-stadium complex. These doubters were howling at the moon because governments were pursuing political gains from Taipei Dome rather than addressing public concerns.

In July 1999, the Ma administration presented the BOT proposal to the Executive Yuan's review board (the executive branch of government). The Ma administration proposed establishing superficies for 70 years and requesting a gratuitous appropriation of nearly 3.8 million square feet of land, valued at $48 billion, from the central government in order to attract private sector investment of $18.34 billion for the construction of a hotel, department store, international conference center, and a domed stadium with a capacity of 25,000 seats (Hsiao, 1999). Following party alternations in 2000, the DPP central government amended the Ma administration's proposal in March 2002 into a 50-year BOT project that requested the Taipei Municipal Government to purchase 1.9 million sq ft of land in Songshan Tobacco Factory with $25 billion (Li & Wang, 2002). In 2003, the Ma administration used A21, which is located in the ritziest Xinyi District and is worth $10.5 billion, with $14 billion cash as an exchange (C.-Y. Yang, 2003), together with entrusting Taipei Dome's planning and feasibility study to Shau-Yu Hsu's Architects and completing *Advance Taipei Cultural and Sports Park*'s master plan and EIA (Taipei Municipal Government, 2015a), thereby wrapping up the whole preparation and planning process.

Despite such a top-down perspective promoting win-win cooperation between the DPP and the KMT, grassroots voices of doubt were drowned out by political commitment, rendering the entire decision-making process a democratic façade. In 1999, eight village leaders, scholars, and experts identified the cultural, historical, and environmental significance of Songshan Tobacco Factory, urging the Ma administration and the KMT central government to reconsider the site's logistical suitability (W.-T. Chien, 1999). These concerns were later addressed during three public hearings held between May and August 2000. Despite the fact that Songshan Tobacco Factory was designated a monument in 2001, there was no agreement or consensus regarding the impact on the environment and quality of life during the discussion (Taipei Municipal Government, 2000a, 2000b, 2000c), leaving behind the externalities raised by the local residents.

It's difficult to say that the Taipei Dome's preparation and planning processes were inclusive. Rather than that, it was exclusively those in positions of authority, including politicians and urban decision-makers, who demonstrated their influence over the development process by outperforming public doubt. Although this was common in Taiwan, the development of Taipei Dome demonstrated the act first–ask later agenda dynamically negotiated by power figures in regime politics between the central and municipal governments, eclipsing the public demand for environmental justice.

FIGURE 14.1 Songshan Tobacco Factory historic site and Taipei Dome Complex under construction in June 2015. National Sun Yat-sen Memorial Hall is visible behind the stadium and to the left

218 Chun-Chieh Lin

Selecting the Dream Builder: Process of Tender and Beyond

Before delving into specifics about controversies, it is necessary to outline the tender process. When the Ma administration issued a 90-day invitation to tender for Taipei Dome on December 26, 2003, this 50-year BOT project requiring $17 billion in private investment offered concessional taxes, loans, and rents, attracting the interest of hundreds of multinational corporations (W.-C. Yang & Huang, 2003). Surprisingly, only the Taipei Dome Entrepreneurial Consortium (TDEC), led by the Farglory Group and comprised of Takenaka Corporation and Ricky Liu Architects, submitted their investment proposal prior to the April 30, 2004 deadline. This consortium was later selected as the exclusive tenderer in May 2004, but it was contentiously dissolved prior to contracting with the Ma administration in October 2004 due to a conflict in project design and liquidating distribution (Shih, 2004). To process the BOT application, the Farglory Group regrouped with Obayashi Corporation and Populous in January 2005 (W.-C. Yang, 2005). After eight contentious selection meetings and eleven contract negotiations, the selection committee approved the new consortium in June 2006 (W.-C. Yang, 2006a), thus finally becoming the builder of Taipei Dome in October 2006 (I.-C. Lin, 2006).

To begin, TDEC was the sole tenderer because the Ma administration was inconsistent in its responses to Ricky Liu Architects and Proma Group's inquiries about the tender period's limit and definition of total floor area (TFA; Taipei Municipal Government, 2015a). The Ma administration replied to Proma Group with numbers addressed in the Tender Document (Taipei Municipal Government, 2003a), which established a development limit of 3.41 million sq ft for TFA and a minimum floor area of 1.24 million sq ft for the domed stadium (Taipei Municipal Government, 2003c); the reply to Ricky Liu Architects (Taipei Municipal Government, 2003a) implied that the TFA should adhere to Articles 1 and 162 of the Building Technical Regulations, which exempted parking lots, electromechanical, and other evacuation-related equipment from the TFA. The former interpretation may create the false impression that builders should reduce commercial space to accommodate the aforementioned facilities, thereby decreasing the interest of other potential tenderers and vice versa.

Second, the consortium's dissolution was related to the administrative conflict between the DPP-led central government and the Ma administration, not just to the conflict among members of the growth coalition. When Ricky Liu Architects and Takenaka Corporation withdrew from the consortium in October 2004, the Farglory Group was forced to find new subcontractors. Nonetheless, the selection committee disagreed twice on whether this new consortium possessed comparable or superior technical competence to previous ones, thus waiving the Farglory Group's best applicant from July 2005 to January 2006 (Taipei Municipal Government, 2005, 2006a). On three occasions, the Farglory Group filed for administrative remedy to the Public Construction Commission (PCC) in

Executive Yuan (W.-C. Yang, 2006b). PCC overturned the selection committee's arbitrary administrative disposition three times due to procedural flaws (W.-J. Lin, 2006). The Ma administration, on the other hand, never accepted such charges and urged the DPP central government to respect local autonomy. In June 2006, this controversy was resolved by reconvening the selection committee and conducting a review of the applicant's qualifications and subcontractors (Taipei Municipal Government, 2006b).

Another source of contention was the 11-time contract negotiation process that occurred between June and September 2004. To begin, Shu-Te Lee, the selection and negotiation committee's Chief Commissioner, waived the development royalty on September 23, 2004, claiming Mayor Ma and the Farglory Group had reached an agreement prior to September 20, 2004 (Taipei Municipal Government, 2015a). This top-down directive influenced both the neutral roles and decision-making mechanisms of both committees during the tender process. Second, the negotiation committee did not renegotiate the BOT contract after the Farglory Group controversially regrouped the consortium and redesigned Taipei Dome Complex, which increased the profitability to $116.9 billion (Taipei Municipal Government, 2015a). Without the contract's royalty and feedback provisions, there was no compensation for environmental externalities to surrounding neighborhoods or financial externalities to the Taipei Municipal Government, which had spent $14.8 billion on land acquisition.

All of the tender processes' identified controversies do not simply concern the interests of various enterprises, political parties, or governments. As a result of these disagreements, externalities such as environmental impact have shifted from a single sector to multi-level tensions within the administrative system, parliamentary system, and local communities, as discussed in greater detail in the following section.

Mobilization, Communication, and Negotiation: Tensions in Taipei Dome Complex's Design Review

The total floor area of the Taipei Dome Complex and the proportion of commercial properties were central issues during the review process, particularly the Farglory Group's 2008 alternate plan to the UDR and EIA. In comparison to the Ma administration's 2003 BOT plan, the Farglory Group's 2008 alternate plan increased the total floor area from approximately 3.9 million sq ft to more than 6.3 million sq ft. Additionally, it decreased the proportion of the domed stadium from 27% to 21%, as illustrated in Table 14.1 (Taipei Municipal Government, 2003b, 2011b). Residents expressed outrage at this revision due to the anticipated impact on daily life. As a result, local communities and environmental groups joined forces with members of the Taipei Municipal Council to investigate the decision-making process that resulted in the malpractices, closely monitor the Hau administration's reevaluation of the project's feasibility, and press both the UDR and EIA committees for a thorough review of the Taipei Dome Complex.

TABLE 14.1 Square Footage of Taipei Dome Complex Plan at Selected Stages of Environmental Impact Analysis Review

	Original Plan	Alternate Plans				Final Plan
	Aug 2003	Jan 2008	Jun 2010	Feb 2011	May 2011	Jun 2011
Domed stadium	1,054,324	1,344,734		1,317,329	1,317,329	1,317,329
Department store	579,098	1,441,243		1,376,272	1,376,272	1,239,011
Office building	1,141,673	550,197		543,308	543,308	370,935
Hotel	–	771,126		721,397	721,397	570,928
Parking lot	1,112,169	2,102,825		2,012,473	170,146	1,623,271
Other facilities	–	141,653		159,370	182,598	182,598
Total area	**3,887,264**	**6,351,777**		**6,130,149**	**4,311,050**	**5,304,072**
Result of review	**Approved**	**Continue**	**Rejected**	**Continue**	**Revision**	**Approved**

Source: Converted from sq m and rounded to the nearest whole number.

Between 2008 and 2009, both the UDR and EIA committees, in response to public concern about the Taipei Dome Complex BOT project and dissatisfaction with the project's negative impact on traffic and the natural environment, repeatedly directed the Farglory Group to clarify their position on the Taipei Dome Complex (Taipei Municipal Government, 2008b), to provide the committee with documents pertaining to the Taipei Dome Complex BOT project (Taipei Municipal Government, 2009), and to propose solutions to local community concerns, including but not limited to tree transplantation, fire evacuation, construction noise prevention, and traffic congestion measurement (Taipei Municipal Government, 2008a). To address these concerns, the Farglory Group was delayed by a year, resulting in an increase in construction spending from $18 billion to $26 billion in 2008 (W.-C. Yang & Huang, 2008).

The Farglory Group maintained communication with the Taipei Municipal Government and local communities to expedite the review process. Nonetheless, Yi Yu, a member of a protest group, appealed to the government's watchdog Control Yuan, and Control Yuan censured the decision to change PCC's subcontractors in 2006, as well as 39 problematic clauses in the Taipei Dome Complex BOT contract, in September 2009 (Control Yuan, 2009). As a result of the Hau administration's decision to halt the dome project, the Farglory Group was forced to regroup with the previous consortium (C.-Y. Chien, 2009), but was later revoked by PCC in May 2010, providing the Farglory Group with a silver lining in the June 2010 review process.

The 97th EIA committee, however, vetoed the 2008 alternate plan due to its massive building mass and unresolved traffic impact and recommended that the Farglory Group resubmit another alternate plan (Taipei Municipal Government, 2010a). After revising the alternate plan, the 296th UDR committee approved the alternate plan in December 2010 with significant changes, including reducing building mass and proposing solutions for traffic and environmental impacts (Taipei Municipal Government, 2010b). The Farglory Group then revised its alternate plan, which was approved in May 2011 by the 107th EIA committee (Taipei Municipal Government, 2011a), obtaining a building permit in a record-setting 14 days on June 30 (Ho, 2011) and completing a $16-billion syndicated loan agreement on November 15 (Lu, 2011). Construction work finally commenced in April 2012.

In comparison to the twists and turns of the 2006–2009 review process, the 2010 review process took place in a different setting. As the Farglory Group reached successive agreements with the UDR, the EIA, and the Hau administration, public and Municipal Council members expressed reservations about such an efficient review and administrative work that the Hau administration might defend (Taipei Municipal Government, 2011c) in order to avoid contract breach and disregard those environmental externalities. This uncertainty developed as a result of an internal power imbalance, particularly between the Hau administration and other stakeholders, which resulted in information asymmetry and harmed the decision-making process.

Throughout the design process, Municipal Council members from various parties accused the Hau administration of municipal council contempt for refusing to reevaluate the project's feasibility, disclose key decision-making factors, and provide Taipei Dome Complex documents for close scrutiny (Taipei Municipal Government, 2010c). Rather than that, the Hau administration agreed to an extension of the Farglory Group's building permit and syndicated loans agreement in August 2010 and March 2011, respectively, as well as an additional extension in July 2011 for syndicated loans agreement (Ho, 2011).

Rather than overturning national policy in favor of a domed stadium, the UDR and EIA committees served as a forum for discussion and alignment of expectations between builders, municipal government, municipal council members, and local communities. Although the case of Taipei Dome Complex exemplified civic mobilization in the name of environmental justice to engage the decision-making process, a critical impediment to inclusive communication is the municipal government's entrenched power imbalance. Having said that, decisions regarding the Taipei Dome Complex were highly centralized and reserved for elected officials. Thus, the Taipei Dome Complex is not only a matter of sport, land, environment, community, or institutional system but also a social issue with political implications.

FIGURE 14.2 Construction of Taipei Dome Complex in April 2015. During this time, civic organizations staged a protest, legally closing one-way lanes on Guangfu South Road to simulate traffic congestion during events at the stadium. The banner reads, "Once the domed stadium is completed, this area will experience bumper-to-bumper traffic"

Scandal, Construction, and Public Safety: Taipei Dome Complex as Bargaining Chips

On November 29, 2014, newly elected non-partisan Taipei Mayor Wen-Je Ko pledged to conduct a thorough investigation into five high-profile, contentious projects. Taipei Dome Complex was on the list two years after construction began. Following its December 25, 2014 inauguration, the Ko administration boldly declared its intention to renegotiate those pragmatic 39 clauses in the BOT contract with the Farglory Group. As a result, it established a Clean Government Committee (CGC)—an anti-corruption agency—to conduct a reinvestigation of the Taipei Dome Complex project, as well as an ad hoc Safety Review Committee (SRC) to conduct the project's safety inspection. On the one hand, the Ko administration leveraged this high-profile tripartite structure to garner media attention and support from constituencies in Taipei. On the other hand, such an approach may reveal evidence or information against the Farglory Group that was overlooked during the previous decision-making process. Both were used by the Ko administration to safeguard the public interest and establish command at the negotiating table.

SRC determined in April 2015 that the Taipei Dome Complex was a high-risk area due to the following: (i) the entire complex, which includes a department store, an office building, a hotel, and a parking lot, is expected to accommodate 140,000 people, but the current design can accommodate only 59,833 people; (ii) the underground interconnectedness of the main buildings could result in the uncontrolled and rapid spread of fire; (iii) the evacuation plan, open-air space, and emergency ladder placement were all designed inappropriately; and (iv) an implausible plan for medical and fire services in the event of a disaster (Taipei Municipal Government, 2015b). Following the seven safety standards proposed by SRC, SRC recommended that the Farglory Group increase open space by demolishing either the department store connected to the domed stadium (Alternate Plan A), which would increase capacity to 88,638 people, or the domed stadium itself (Alternate Plan B), which would increase capacity from 59,833 to 78,927 people (Taipei Municipal Government, 2015b).

Following that, CGC released its Taipei Dome investigation report, recommending that the Ko administration pursue legal action against Mayor Ma and Shu-Te Lee, reevaluating the BOT's utility for infrastructure development, and involving civil society in public project decision-making (Taipei Municipal Government, 2015a). Although this report served as a reference for the Ko administration in gaining a better understanding of the Taipei Dome Complex's context, its ad hoc nature limited its impact on reviewing BOT in public infrastructure development and promoting civic participation in the Taipei Dome project.

In May 2015, the Taipei City Government ordered a halt to construction on the Taipei Dome Complex due to violations of the approved blueprint, as well as damage to adjacent historic buildings and the MRT blue line (Taipei Municipal Government, 2016c). Given the low quality of construction and design, the Ko administration considered terminating the BOT contract with the Farglory Group. To expedite decision-making, members of the cross-party Municipal Council filed a motion on May 28, 2015, urging the Municipal Government to immediately terminate the contract and take over the Taipei Dome Complex (Y.-C. Wang, 2015). The Ko administration rejected the council's proposal but continued to look for a silver lining toward contract termination, averting the worst-case scenario in which the government would have to repurchase Taipei Dome Complex from the Farglory Group for $37 billion (Wei, 2016a).

Despite contract termination, the Ko administration amended the design to comply with seven safety standards. Chou-Min Lin, the Department of Urban Development's commissioner from 2014 to 2018, incorporated the concept of urban disaster prevention and the seven safety standards into the scope of the EIA and UDR reviews after inquiring with the Ministry of the Interior's Construction and Planning Agency about review gaps between multiple government regulatory standards (Taipei Municipal Government, 2016b). It then assisted the Ko administration in discussing the design amendment with the Farglory Group, resulting in the submission of a feasible alternate plan on July 15, 2016, that suggested reducing the building's mass and increasing (semi-)outdoor space (Taipei Municipal Government, 2016a).

However, the Ko administration opted out of both proposed resolutions. On June 8, 2016, the Ko administration issued an ultimatum to the Farglory Group to resolve safety concerns by September 8, 2016 (Wei, 2016b); in the event that these issues are not resolved, the contract will be terminated. Both parties reached an agreement on the due date (Liberty Times, 2016a), provoking public outrage and criticism from members of the Municipal Council (Liberty Times, 2016b), requiring Taipei Dome Complex to undergo another review of its safety concerns via EIA and UDR committees. Commissioner Lin, chair of the UDR committee, insisted that the Farglory Group amend the design to comply with seven safety standards, and from 2016 to 2018, they rigorously reviewed Farglory's alternate plan (Taipei Municipal Government, 2018a, 2018b), while Ching-Mao Huang, Lin's successor, controversially approved the revised design in October 2019 without reviewing all safety standards (Taipei Municipal Government, 2019). Farglory's alternate plan was later reapproved by the EIA committee in March 2020 (Taipei Municipal Government, 2020) and received a new building permit in July 2020. After a five-year suspension, work resumed in August 2020.

Throughout this decision-making phase, the Ko administration's actions spoke louder than words—with the exception of a contentious start to contract negotiations and design amendments with the Farglory Group, the administration largely exhausted the patience of citizens, council members, and Farglory over a five-year period. Additionally, the Ko administration's reckless decision-making significantly harmed the government's credibility and diminished private sector interest in public infrastructure development. Without defending or pursuing the public interest, the Ko administration fell short of public expectations, deferring to neighboring areas and Taipei residents to address safety and development externalities.

Conclusion: An Unfinished Saga

Throughout the 32-year development process of the Taipei Dome Complex, residents, environmental groups, and Municipal Council members have raised the same environmental concerns on each occasion, including the displacement of greenspace, damage to historic buildings, traffic congestion, safety concerns, and reflecting light from the stadium. Nonetheless, those in positions of power have failed to take these issues seriously. At the time of this writing, the Farglory Group intended to seek user license approval from the Taipei Municipal Government in order to complete construction work before Mayor Ko's tenure ends in 2022. However, in August 2021, the Taipei Dome Complex's construction encountered another setback when the Construction and Planning Agency discovered problems with the building's refuge floor plan (Liberty Times, 2022). Taipei Dome Complex has not yet scheduled an opening ceremony date.

In a broader sense, the political significance of Taipei Dome is linked to collective memories of Taiwan baseball (Yu & Bairner, 2008), the East Asian state's neoliberal land politics (Chou & Chen, 2014), and its struggle for recognition by the international community following its withdrawal from the United Nations in 1971 (Yu, 2007). In a narrow sense, it exhibits the stunning local politics shaped by client politics and the systematic failure of urban planning (C.-C. Lin, 2020). This failure resulted in a heavy reliance on administrative support from the central government, depriving the municipal government of the autonomy to assess feasibility and suitability in advance, resulting in unexpected externalities at a later stage. At the moment, nothing is guaranteed except that those issues mentioned earlier will remain controversial, and the dreams of bidding for the 2025 East Asian Games and 2030 Asian Games will keep shining.

From a dictator's decree to a sports mega-project, this chapter examined the dynamic decision-making process within a selective account of the historical and political context to demonstrate how this butterfly effect developed to affect the natural, social, and living environments of neighboring areas. Unlike current stadium studies, which employ a regime analysis framework in which sport serves as a powerful discourse that outweighs other voices, politicians associated with the Taipei Dome Complex have politicized sport in order to advance their own interests. Thus, Taipei Dome is a political arena in which politicians' governing agendas have a strong influence on the decision-making stage and snowball issues, affecting Taiwan society's quality of life, public safety, and civic trust.

Note

1 All cost figures in this chapter are listed in New Taiwan dollar (NT$).

References

Ahn, M.-S. (2002). The political economy of the World Cup in South Korea. In J. Horne & W. Manzenreiter (Eds.), *Japan, Korea and the 2002 World Cup*. Routledge.

Chan, C.-C. (2012). *Exploring spatial justice: A case of Taipei Dome Complex* [Master's thesis, National Taiwan University]

Chan, S.-Y. (1994, January 26). It costs nearly 50 billion to build Guandu Park and the domed-stadium. *United Daily News*.

Chen, C.-K. (1994, May 14). Who benefits from land acquisition? *United Daily News*.

Chen, J.-C. (1997, August 23). Where is the dome built? full of political wrangling. *China Times*.

Chien, C.-Y. (2009, September 2). Farglory is requested to change subcontractors by Taipei Municipal Government.

Chien, W.-T. (1999, August 6). To protest against the construction of the domed-stadium, the villagers have to complain to the chief executive. *China Times*.

Chin, F.-J. (1995, January 5). Zhongshan Football Stadium builds a domed-stadium within doubts. *United Evening News*.

Chin, F.-J. (1996, May 9). The location of Taipei Dome is changed. *United Evening News*.

Chin, F.-J. (1999, March 17). Taipei Municipal Government evaluated Songshan Tobacco Factory as most suitable for building a domed-stadium. *United Evening News*.

Chou, T.-L., & Chen, T.-C. (2014). Multi-scalar governance challenge of neo-liberalist urban development strategy: A case study of New Taipei Metropolis. *Journal of Geographical Science*, *72*, 31–55. 10.6161/jgs.2014.72.03

Chow, D.-Y. (1991, November 11). Spectators shouted at PM Hau within the slogan—We want a domed-stadium. *United Daily News*.

Chu, H.-H. (1998, December 31). The domed stadium will be built in Songshan Tobacco Factory. *Central Daily News*.

Control Yuan. (2009). *Censure on Taipei Dome Cultural and Sports Park BOT tender process*.

Dowding, K. (2002). Explaining urban regimes. *International Journal of Urban and Regional Research*, *25*(1), 7–19. 10.1111/1468-2427.00294

Economy Daily News. (1991, March 6). The value of farmland has soared.

Feng, C.-H. (1990, October 5). Failing the 1998 Asian Game Bid; stadium project will go on. *United Daily News*.

Gustafson, S. (2013). Displacement and the racial state in Olympic Atlanta: 1990–1996. *Southeastern Geographer*, *53*(2), 198–213. https://www.jstor.org/stable/26229061

Hall, P. (1980). *Great planning disasters*. University of California Press.

Harvey, D. (1989). From managerialism to entrepreneurialism: The transformation in urban governance in late capitalism. *Geografiska Annaler: Series B, Human Geography*, *71*(1), 3–17. 10.1080/04353684.1989.11879583

Ho, H.-P. (2011, July 3). The Coordination Committee agreed an extension. *United Daily News*.

Hsiao, C.-H. (1999, July 24). Taipei Municipal City will have a domed-stadium. *Economic Daily News*.

Hung, W.-C. (1996, January 9). The rent of shops next to the domed-stadium has increased by an average of 20%. *China Times*.

Imbroscio, D. L. (1998). Reformulating urban regime theory: The division of labor between state and market reconsidered. *Journal of Urban Affairs*, *20*(3), 233–248. 10.1111/j.1467-9906.1998.tb00420.x

Jakar, G. S., Razin, E., Rosentraub, M. S., & Rosen, G. (2018). Sport facility development: Municipal capital and shutting out the private sector. *European Planning Studies*, *26*(6), 1222–1241. 10.1080/09654313.2018.1451826

Kellison, T., Sam, M. P., Hong, S., Swart, K., & Mondello, M. J. (2019). Global perspectives on democracy and public stadium finance. *Journal of Global Sport Management*, *5*(4), 321–348. 10.1080/24704067.2018.1531680

Koch, N. (Ed.). (2016). *Critical geographies of sport: Space, power and sport in global perspective*. Routledge.

Kung, T.-S. (1994, December 26). Guandu Plain will not be developed for the time being. *United Daily News*.

Lai, C.-K. (1989, August 29). Hosting 1998 Asian Games. *China Times*.

Li, S.-T., & Wang, Y.-C. (2002, March 20). Taipei Dome will be built in Songshan Tobacco Factory. *Economic Daily News*.

Liberty Times. (2016a, September 8). Farglory Group backs down, Taipei Municipal Government will not terminate the BOT contract for the time being. *Liberty Times*. https://news.ltn.com.tw/news/focus/paper/1029885

Liberty Times. (2016b, September 8). KMT and DPP Municipal Council Members bombard Wen-Je Ko. *Liberty Times*. https://news.ltn.com.tw/news/politics/breakingnews/1819973

Liberty Times. (2022, March 9). It is reported that the construction and planning agency refused to issue the approval. Wen-Je Ko may be difficult to cut the ribbon during his tenure. *Liberty Times*. https://news.ltn.com.tw/news/politics/breakingnews/3853522

Lin, C.-C. (2020). Understanding the controversy of sport, city, and environment: A case of Taipei Dome Complex construction [Master's thesis, Seoul National University]. https://s-space.snu.ac.kr/handle/10371/170011

Lin, I.-C. (2006, October 2). Taipei Dome will be completed in 2011. *United Daily News*.

Lin, W.-J. (2006, April 22). PCC finds Farglory reasonable. *United Daily News*.

Lu, S.-M. (2011, November 15). Farglory obtained syndicated loans agreement. *United Daily News*.

Niu, C.-F. (1994, May 5). The Guandu Park Self-Help Organization was established, and no environmental damage should be allowed. *United Daily News*.

Riess, S. A. (2001). Historical perspectives on sports and public policy. In W. C. Rich (Ed.), *The economics and politics of sports facilities*. Praeger.

Shih, W.-N. (2004, October 13). Subcontractors left the Consortium. *China Times*.

Smith, C. J., & Himmelfarb, K. M. G. (2013). Restructuring Beijing's social space: Observations on the Olympic Games in 2008. *Eurasian Geography and Economics*, *48*(5), 543–554. 10.2747/1538-7216.48.5.543

Stone, C. N. (1989). *Regime politics: Governing Atlanta, 1946–1988*. University Press of Kansas.

Sullivan, N. J. (2008). *The diamond in the Bronx: Yankee Stadium and the politics of New York*. Oxford University Press.

Tagsold, C. (2020). Symbolic transformation: The 1964 Tokyo Games reconsidered. *The Asia-Pacific Journal*, *18*(5), 1–8. https://apjjf.org/2020/5/Tagsold.html

Taipei Municipal Government. (1984a). *Taipei Municipal Council gazette*.

Taipei Municipal Government. (1984b). *Taipei Municipal Council gazette*.

Taipei Municipal Government. (2000a). *Minutes of the first forum at SongShan Tobacco Factory*.

Taipei Municipal Government. (2000b). *Minutes of the second forum at SongShan Tobacco Factory*.

Taipei Municipal Government. (2000c). *Minutes of the third forum at SongShan Tobacco Factory*.

228 Chun-Chieh Lin

Taipei Municipal Government. (2003a). *Answered inquiries during Taipei Sport and Cultural Park 90-day tender.*

Taipei Municipal Government. (2003b). *Taipei Cultural and Sports Park environmental impact statement.*

Taipei Municipal Government. (2003c). *Taipei Sport and Cultural Park BOT document.*

Taipei Municipal Government. (2005). *Meeting minutes of 7th Taipei Sport and Cultural Park BOT Project Selection Committee.*

Taipei Municipal Government. (2006a). *Meeting minutes of 7th Taipei Sport and Cultural Park BOT Project Selection Committee (first extension).*

Taipei Municipal Government. (2006b). *Meeting minutes of 8th Taipei Sport and Cultural Park BOT Project Selection Committee.*

Taipei Municipal Government. (2008a). *Meeting minutes of 65th Environmental Impact Assessment Committee.*

Taipei Municipal Government. (2008b). *Meeting minutes of Urban Design Review Committee on Taipei Cultural and Sports Park Project.*

Taipei Municipal Government. (2009). *Meeting minutes of 81st Environmental Impact Assessment Committee.*

Taipei Municipal Government. (2010a). *Meeting minutes of 97th Environmental Impact Assessment Committee.*

Taipei Municipal Government. (2010b). *Meeting minutes of 296th Urban Design Review Committee.*

Taipei Municipal Government. (2010c). *Taipei Municipal Council gazette.*

Taipei Municipal Government. (2011a). *Meeting minutes of 107th Environmental Impact Assessment Committee.*

Taipei Municipal Government. (2011b). *Taipei Cultural and Sports Park environmental impact statement.*

Taipei Municipal Government. (2011c). *Taipei Municipal Council gazette.*

Taipei Municipal Government. (2015a). *Investigation report of Taipei Dome.*

Taipei Municipal Government. (2015b). *Taipei Dome safety review.*

Taipei Municipal Government. (2016a). *Mayor Ko's briefing to Taipei Municipal Council.*

Taipei Municipal Government. (2016b). *Safety resolution of Taipei Dome Complex.*

Taipei Municipal Government. (2016c). *Taipei Dome Complex safety review report.*

Taipei Municipal Government. (2016d). *Taipei Municipal Council gazette.*

Taipei Municipal Government. (2018a). *Meeting minutes of 506th Urban Design Review Committee.*

Taipei Municipal Government. (2018b). *Meeting minutes of 510th Urban Design Review Committee.*

Taipei Municipal Government. (2019). *Meeting minutes of 538th Urban Design Review Committee.*

Taipei Municipal Government. (2020). *Meeting minutes of 221st Environmental Impact Assessment Committee.*

Wang, C.-S. (1996). *Faction politics in Taiwan: A perspective on patron-client theory* [Doctoral dissertation, University of Kansas].

Wang, W.-J. (1990, September 17). PM Hau supports bidding 1998 Asian Games. *United Evening News.*

Wang, Y.-C. (2015, May 28). *DPP Council Member proposed 'take-over Taipei Dome' motion to pressure the Taipei Municipal Government.* The Storm Media. https://www.storm.mg/article/51026

Wei, S. (2016a, April 13). *Terminating the BOT contract? Farglory Group: repurchase it back with*

37 billion NTD. Central News Agency. https://www.cna.com.tw/news/firstnews/201604135027.aspx

Wei, S. (2016b, June 8). *An ultimatum to Farglory Group*. Central News Agency. https://www.taiwannews.com.tw/ch/news/2934950

Yan, C.-C., & Yang, J.-C. (1992, August 6). PM Hau instructs to initiate a baseball domed-stadium; Parliament Members urges to entitle baseball as the National Game. *United Daily News*.

Yang, C.-Y. (1996, January 21). Idea of building a domed-stadium at Songshan Tobacco Factory reached consensus. *United Daily News*.

Yang, C.-Y. (2003, March 6). The land exchange will be completed in April, and the domed-stadium's construction will start next year. *United Daily News*.

Yang, W.-C. (2005, January 13). New Taipei Dome Consortium. *Economic Daily News*.

Yang, W.-C. (2006a, June 20). Farglory group retakes the best applicant. *Economic Daily News*.

Yang, W.-C. (2006b, March 13). Retender for Taipei Cultural and Sports Park in February. *Economic Daily News*.

Yang, W.-C., & Huang, C.-Y. (2003, November 4). Taipei Dome BOT with a total investment of 17 billion NTD. *Economic Daily News*.

Yang, W.-C., & Huang, J.-C. (2008, June 5). Taipei Dome is expected to commence of construction work in the end of 2008. *Economic Daily News*.

Yu, J. (2007). *Playing in isolation: A history of baseball in Taiwan*. University of Nebraska Press.

Yu, J., & Bairner, A. (2008). Proud to be Chinese: Little League Baseball and national identities in Taiwan during the 1970s. *Identities, 15*(2), 216–239. 10.1080/10702890801904636

Zukin, S. (2011). *Naked city: The death and life of authentic urban places*. Oxford University Press.

15

SEATTLE AND CLIMATE PLEDGE ARENA: A PROGRESSIVE AND SUSTAINABLE ARENA THAT MUST INTEGRATE EQUITY AND INCREASE ACCOUNTABILITY

Alex Porteshawver

Seattle's Climate Pledge Arena has demonstrated its commitment to building the most sustainable arena in professional sports. Sustainability means "net zero carbon," the arena generates more renewable energy than it uses, reducing water consumption and waste generation by eliminating single-use plastics and composting and encouraging patrons to use public transit when attending events. Sustainability must also mean addressing, integrating, and reporting about equity—these are interconnected issues. Climate Pledge Arena's commitments should be applauded, and it must hold itself accountable to those pledges by creating transparent and frequent reporting opportunities that deepen connection to nearby communities.

Climate Pledge Arena: A Symbol That We Must Address Climate Change Now

Climate Pledge Arena (the "Arena") is located at Seattle Center and is home to the NHL's Seattle Kraken, the WNBA's Seattle Storm, and also hosts live music performances and events (Climate Pledge Arena, 2022a). The arena was originally built for the 1962 Seattle World's Fair and now is the first net-zero certified arena in the world. Its new name is linked to the "The Climate Pledge" (the "Pledge"), which was founded by Amazon and Global Optimism in 2019. The Pledge is a commitment from companies to achieve net-zero carbon greenhouse gas (GHG) emissions by 2040.

This chapter will examine the Arena's environmental and social commitments and the connection between those commitments and equity. This chapter explains the connections between sports, climate, and equity and discusses accountability frameworks used by the private sector and local governments to track progress on

DOI: 10.4324/9781003262633-17

FIGURE 15.1 Construction of the Space Needle and Coliseum (later KeyArena and ultimately Climate Pledge Arena) in 1961. The pyramid shape of the arena roof's supporting structure can be seen near the center of the photo. ("Century 21 from top of the Grosvenor House" courtesy of the Seattle Municipal Archives, item number 165665)

climate and equity goals. Then, the chapter suggests specific frameworks the Arena can use to hold itself accountable to its goals. The Arena serves as a symbol that society must address climate change, and specifically that large companies like Amazon must take the lead. The symbol is important, and so is whether the Arena meets its laudable goals.

What About Equity?

Equity and climate change are interconnected. Frontline communities suffer first and worst from climate disasters because these communities, which are often disproportionately made up of low-income people and people of color and who are often the least responsible for producing GHG emissions, are frequently located in areas that lack basic infrastructure to respond to climate change. These same communities can live in or near industrial zoned land, and therefore, they bear the brunt of pollution and poor air quality and may also be displaced as industrial areas are redeveloped for other uses, such as arenas.

The Greenlining Institute defines racial equity as:

> transforming the behaviors, institutions and systems that disproportionately harm people of color. Racial equity means increasing access to power, redistributing and providing additional resources, and eliminating barriers to opportunity in order to empower low-income communities of color to thrive and reach full potential. (Creger, 2020, p. 4)

Racial equity and climate equity are interconnected concepts. It is imperative that the public and private sectors work together to "design climate policies that are transparent and give agency to socially and economically marginalized groups" (World Resources Institute, 2022, para. 6).

This imperative applies to the design, construction, and operation of sports facilities. For example, arena owners often interact with nearby communities, including community-based organizations and businesses, when building a new stadium, renovating an existing stadium (as is the case with the Arena), or as part of ongoing community relations. The Arena recognizes this imperative through the One Roof Foundation. This Foundation works to "[center] diverse voices, experiences, and perspectives in all interactions internal and external to our organization, and leveraging our platforms to advance equity and opportunity in the sports and entertainment industries" (One Roof Foundation, 2022, para. 2).

Governments Address Equity and Climate Change

Governments are also working to meaningfully address and integrate equity into their climate change planning and implementation efforts. Fifty-one percent of proceeds from the California Cap and Trade Program benefit the state's most disadvantaged populations (California Climate Investments, 2022). This means funds are allocated to projects and programs statewide that not only reduce GHG emissions but provide tangible benefits in "disadvantaged communities."[1] This funding trickles down to the local level and impacts how and where GHG reduction projects are implemented. Additionally, it is now best practice to address and integrate equity in any climate change effort. For example, several local governments have developed or adopted justice, equity, diversity, and inclusion guidelines that must be considered as climate plans are developed (City and County of San Francisco, 2021; County of Marin, 2020).

Local governments have also created task forces and working groups to address and integrate equity in climate action planning efforts. King County (Washington) first focused on building partnerships with frontline community organizations, supporting and investing in community leadership development, collaborating on co-created translated (in multiple languages) climate communications materials, conducting youth workshops, and building capacity both internally and externally around community-driven climate policy-making (King County, 2022). Additionally, King County convened a Climate Equity Community Task Force (CECTF). The CECTF "is a group of leaders who represent frontline communities and organizations across greater King County, bringing multi-ethnic and multi-racial cross-sector experiences to climate-related community building" (para. 5). This group met over two years, "using an interactive, collaborative visioning process that valued long-term and transformative relationships, acknowledged power dynamics, worked to remove barriers to participation, and compensated community members for their time and expertise" (para. 6).

Organizations Address Equity and Climate Change

Additionally, many organizations that work directly with local governments and their representative communities are actively addressing climate and equity. Based in Oakland, California, The Greenlining Institute works to ensure that the future is being built where communities of color thrive (The Greenlining Institute, 2022). To that end, it conducts research and develops reports, participates in regulatory and legislative proceedings, and actively supports community-based organizations (CBOs) to advance health, economic, energy, environmental, and technology equity. GRID Alternatives is headquartered in Oakland, California, and it works across the nation to bring the benefits of solar technology to communities that would otherwise not have access to it (GRID Alternatives, 2022). It participates in regulatory and legislation proceedings at the state and national levels, actively supports CBOs, advances solar and energy services technologies in low-income communities, and develops and implements a variety of workforce development programs.

Front and Centered is a Seattle-based organization that "envision[s] a Just Transition to a future where our communities and the earth are healed and thriving, our people have dignified work, and our government values, respects, and represents us" (Front and Centered, 2022a, para. 2). Front and Centered supports a growing coalition of communities of color-led groups and activates change by amplifying those groups' voices (Front and Centered, 2022b). The organization conducts research and develops policy, advocates at the legislature, convenes communities at the regional and state levels, and provides grants and technical assistance to help build community capacity.

Finally, the Washington Climate Alliance for Jobs and Clean Energy, also based in Seattle, is "committed to building a resilient climate justice movement and passing equitable solutions to the climate crisis" (Climate Alliance, 2022, para. 1). It also organizes at the community level and participates in legislative processes by advocating for policies that center frontline communities, accelerate the transition from fossil fuels to cleaner energy sources, and create a resilient future for all.

Climate and Equity at Climate Pledge Arena

Like local governments and organizations working to meaningfully address and integrate climate and equity work, the Arena has pledged to achieve a Net Zero Carbon certification from the nonprofit International Living Future Institute and committed to engaging and partnering with nearby communities during renovations and operation of the facility (Nelson, 2020).

Climate Pledges

In anticipation of Climate Pledge Arena's reopening in 2021, several media reports focused on the venue's ambitious sustainability goals. As Nelson (2020) noted:

> Rather than simply joining the ranks of the 300-plus sports venues around the world that had achieved some level of LEED certification from the U.S. Green Building Council ..., the joint venture between Amazon, entertainment investment firm Oak View Group, and NHL Seattle's ownership aims to be the first arena in the world to achieve a Net Zero Carbon certification from the nonprofit International Living Future Institute (ILFI). This would eclipse the LEED Platinum certification first earned by Atlanta's Mercedes-Benz Stadium in 2017 and set a new gold standard. (para. 3)

Similarly, Belson (2021), while recognizing the Arena's contemporary features and technological advanced, highlighted its lofty environmental aspirations:

> Climate Pledge Arena is indeed state-of-the-art. It includes the latest LED scoreboards, grab-and-go food stands and ticketless technology. But the operators of the $1.2 billion arena are also trying to set a new standard in green building by reducing and offsetting all of the planet-warming emissions that they, their vendors and even their fans produce. (p. B10)

The name itself indicates its focus on a cause rather than a company. To achieve carbon neutrality, many building features were preserved and many new, sustainable features were added. As Obando (2021) observed, "Underway since December 2018, the renovation led by Minneapolis-based Mortenson included interiors and walls but preserved the original roof. The windows system was salvaged, as well as the curtain wall system" (para. 3). The renovation included a "Rain to Rink" system that uses rainwater to supply the ice for the NHL's Kraken and the Zamboni uses natural refrigerants (typically a potent source of GHG emissions), all-electric, and powered by on- and off-site renewable energy (Fouts, 2021).

The Arena has identified four primary sustainability goals:

1. Carbon Zero

    - No fossil fuel consumption in the arena for daily use: mechanical systems, gas combustion engines, heating, dehumidification, and cooking—all converted to electric.
    - Solar Panels on the Alaska Airlines Atrium and 1st Ave. Garage

combined with off-site supplementary renewable energy for 100% renewable energy power.

- Reducing all carbon emission activities and offsetting all those we can not—like transportation—by purchasing credible carbon offsets.

2. Zero Single-Use Plastic

- We are the first arena and NHL Team to announce our intention to eliminate single-use plastics, which we are committed to being 100% free of by 2024.

3. Water Conservation

- Our "Rain to Rink" system harvests water off the roof, collects it into a 15,000-gallon cistern, and turns it into the greenest ice in the NHL.
- Waterless urinals and ultra-efficient showers.
- Significant on-site retention tanks reduce stormwater runoff.
- Water bottle filling stations throughout the arena.

4. Zero Waste

- Consumer education, beautiful and simple infographics, and on-site sorting allows us to reach this unprecedented level of performance.
- We compost our waste and recycle extensively throughout the arena.
- Removing single-use plastics from the arena by 2024. (Climate Pledge Arena, 2022c, para. 3–6)

As Belson (2021) reported, the Arena's "mission is expensive, time-consuming and risky, and has never been tried at a sports venue before. Calculating emissions is complex and imprecise, and exposes the arena operators to accusations of 'greenwashing'—providing misleading information about the building's environmental attributes" (p. B10). According to the Arena's website, they have made several commitments that will help them meet the above-stated goals while being transparent and accountable to the public, including establishing an Advisory Committee "made up of partners at Amazon" to "deepen our commitment to be the most progressive and sustainable arena in the world" (Climate Pledge Arena, 2022c, para. 7). Other commitments include creating transparency through public reporting, hosting events that celebrate the environment, and forming educational partnerships to "utilize the arena as a classroom for environmental education" (para. 10).

Connections to Equity

A sustainable arena must mean a carbon-neutral and equitable arena. At the very least, equity in the context of arenas means that building or operating an arena does not cause nearby communities—often low-income communities of color living in areas near industrial zoned land—environmental harm or increased health

FIGURE 15.2 Climate Pledge Arena. ("Climate Pledge Arena in Kraken configuration" by Bruce Englehardt is licensed under CC BY-SA 4.0)

risks. For example, an arena should not negatively impact local air quality or reduce accessible greenspace. It also means that nearby communities, including individuals, businesses, and organizations, are part of the decision-making process from the very beginning, conceptual phases of work related to sports facilities, and that their input is acted on and they are meaningfully involved long-term.

The Arena's commitments touch on the imperative links between climate and equity. For example, it has committed to establishing an Advisory Committee that could create a space where partners—corporate, private, and community-based—are given equal decision-making power and the opportunity to collaborate on decisions affecting the arena and nearby communities. It has also committed to being transparent and reporting progress on its pledges, which can help build trust between the arena and the community. Finally, its promise to celebrate nearby educational institutions and local businesses also presents an opportunity to create events and conversations where the community regularly participates in events and other collaborative efforts that may lead to the empowerment of communities typically not included. As an example of how community involvement was utilized during renovations of the venue:

> Populous and Swift Company met regularly with nearby residents and community groups to understand needs and gather input, such as the desire to enhance the pedestrian circulation around the arena. This feedback influenced a 360-degree park surrounding the Arena that brings people up to the historic façade and under the shelter of the roofline. It connects the north side of the arena plaza to adjacent building tenants, providing spaces and access routes for new events that were previously unattainable in the confined courtyards. (Populous, 2021, para. 12)

Arena owners have already committed to sourcing at least three-quarters of the Arena's food from local farmers and producers, with viable unused food diverted to local community food programs (Nelson, 2020). Additionally, the website prominently features a Land and Peoples Acknowledgment statement (see Chapter 3).

Finally, the Arena established the One Roof Foundation. This Foundation centers diverse voices and perspectives from within and outside the Arena organization and leverages the Arena's resources to advance equity (One Roof Foundation, 2022). The Foundation's stated purpose is to address climate and environmental justice, focusing on Black, Indigenous, and persons of color (BIPOC) communities by elevating and supporting those communities disproportionately impacted by climate change. For example, it partners with the Duwamish to host the Duwamish River Festival to increase awareness of the river that runs through Seattle; it is a very contaminated site, and together, they are working to make sure the standards of the current clean-up align with community expectations. Additionally, the Foundation is listening to the nearby Southpark Community to understand how they can address some of the worst air quality in Seattle. On April 13, 2022, the One Roof Foundation hosted a virtual panel discussion to talk about environmental justice initiatives to address pollution in South Park and Duwamish Valley (Condor, 2022). Recognizing they were not experts in this work, One Roof Foundation partnered with frontline community leaders to better understand local climate change impacts and how to address them. In Fall 2021, a Climate Equity Fund was launched to fund community-identified projects that addressed health inequities, climate change, pollution, and other environmental issues.

Accountability: A Pledge is Not Enough

The Arena has made many climate- and equity-related pledges, and they should be commended for making the arena about a cause and not just a corporate identity. That being said, the Arena needs to make good on its promises. There are several existing accountability, reporting, and transparency platforms that the Arena may use or draw from as it discloses its progress on its goals and commitments.

Local Government Accountability Frameworks

Many U.S. local governments have adopted climate action plans, and those plans require that they report annually on GHG emissions trends, community resilience, and equity. Below are samples of climate- and equity-specific accountability frameworks used by local governments.

Climate

The Climate Registry (TCR) is a "non-profit organization that empowers North American organizations to do more in the fight against climate change by providing services and tools that help them reduce their emissions" (The Climate Registry, 2022a, para. 1). TCR drives climate action on the road to net zero by recognizing and showcasing sub-national leadership through reporting and partnership building. According to TCR's website, "The disclosure of climate risks and environmental performance is rapidly becoming the norm in many sectors. Reporting and verifying a GHG inventory with TCR can help [organizations] convey [their] climate efforts to stakeholders" (The Climate Registry, 2022c, p. 4). A GHG inventory can set a baseline and track environmental performance over time, inform broader sustainability and corporate social responsibility reporting, and provide metrics and performance indicators for water, energy, and waste management. Nearly 300 organizations voluntarily report to TCR, including many local governments, utility companies, Kaiser Permanente, Delta Airlines, United States Postal Service, and The Hershey Company (The Climate Registry, 2022b).

CDP is a "not-for-profit charity that runs the global disclosure system for investors, companies, cities, states and regions to manage their environmental impacts" (CDP, 2022a, para. 1). CDP helps investors, companies, and governments measure and act on their environmental impact. Disclosing data through CDP can improve engagement, centralize data and tracking progress, and benchmark performance against other similar entities (CDP, 2022c). Unlike TCR, CDP's reporting does not prescribe a methodology, and using the platform is free and voluntary, and cities can disclose publicly or privately (CDP, 2022b). There are 812 cities across 85 countries that disclosed their climate and environmental data through the CDP-ICLEI[2] Unified Reporting System in 2020 (CDP, 2022c). CDP publishes actions these cities are taking to rapidly cut emissions and build resilience against climate threats for populations now and in the future.

Local governments use a variety of other ways to report their progress on climate goals. For example, some conduct GHG inventories on an annual basis, calculate GHG emissions reductions associated with project and program implementation, post the results on their websites, and report them to their respective governing bodies (e.g., city councils or boards of supervisors). Local governments may also share data via newsletters, social media, and directly with community-based organizations or individuals at local events and meetings. If a local government has adopted a climate action plan, that plan likely contains reporting requirements, which are legally binding if the government's administrative body has adopted the plan. Some of the plans proscribe what reporting platform will be used, and others do not.

Equity

Unlike more well-established third-party and internal climate reporting systems, many local governments are still experimenting with frameworks that allow them to report on their equity efforts. Numerous local governments participate in the Local and Regional Government Alliance on Race and Equity (GARE):

> In communities across the US, public and private sector organizations are working to advance racial equity and social justice. Governments, in particular, are seeking to ensure that their constituents have equitable opportunities for education, employment, access to healthy foods and affordable health care, as well as safe housing options. (Government Alliance on Race and Equity, 2022a, para. 1)

GARE offers tools and resources that help local governments operationalize equity, establish transparent reporting processes, and eliminate inequities in their communities. For example, the County of Marin (California) used the GARE Racial Equity Toolkit's "Normalize, Organize, and Operationalize" framework to understand if it was meeting its equity goals in the context of a countywide initiative to address climate change (Drawdown: Marin Equity Task Force, 2021). GARE supports work in hundreds of state, regional, and local governments and special districts as well as public corporations (Government Alliance on Race and Equity, 2022b). GARE suggests that local governments explicitly address racial equity as they develop plans, programs, and policies (Nelson, 2016).

Local governments may also be required to address equity when applying for grant funding that supports climate change-related projects. For example, the California State Coastal Conservancy has developed justice, equity, diversity, and inclusion (JEDI) guidelines to articulate guiding principles about its role in promoting equity, inclusion, and diversity and addressing environmental justice (State of California Coastal Conservancy, 2022). These guidelines emerged after conducting surveys "of people working in Environmental Justice to get their perspectives on which priorities are most important for the guidelines to encompass, and a series of targeted interviews and focus groups throughout the state to obtain more in-depth feedback" (para. 5). The guidelines cover six areas: Partnerships, Funding Programs, Meaningful Community Engagement, Working with California's Tribes, Coastal Conservancy Staff and Board, and Accountability and

240 Alex Porteshawver

Transparency (State of California Coastal Conservancy, 2020). Example guidelines include the following:

- Build relationships with community-based organizations that are rooted in and serve underserved and/or frontline communities
- Prioritize funding for projects that benefit underserved and/or frontline communities
- Ensure underserved and/or frontline communities have a decision-making role in the development of Coastal Conservancy-funded projects. (State of California Coastal Conservancy, 2020, p. 2)

When local governments apply for grant funding, they must indicate if and how their proposed project addresses the JEDI Guidelines. Furthermore, additional points are given for projects that benefit frontline and underserved communities.[3]

Local governments may also address equity in comprehensive plans (e.g., General Plans[4]). In 2016, California adopted Senate Bill 1000, which requires local governments to identify environmental justice communities (called "disadvantaged communities") in their jurisdictions and address environmental justice in their general plans (An Act to Amend Section 65302 of the Government Code, Relating to Land Use, 2016). This law aims to facilitate transparency and public engagement in local governments' planning and decision-making processes, reduce harmful pollutants and health risks, and promote equitable access to healthy food options, housing, public facilities, and recreation.

There are other voluntary and mandatory equity frameworks, guidelines, and principles that local governments may follow as they work to meaningful address equity and integrate equity and climate change. Many of these frameworks are informed by best practices (e.g., those developed by GARE or expert organizations like The Greenlining Institute).

Accountability Frameworks for Climate Pledge Arena

The Arena has promised to report progress on its environmental goals quarterly and maintain a live dashboard. While these efforts are a good start, there are other activities that could lead to increased accountability on climate and equity goals and promises while deeply engaging and empowering the community to actively participate in Arena operations. The following sections elaborate on existing accountability activities (previously described above) and propose additional opportunities to increase transparency and empower the community.

Existing: Reporting and Sharing Sustainability Metrics

The Arena wants to create a public-facing dashboard to provide insights into the arena's environmental performance. Chris Roe, Amazon's Head of Sustainable Operations, said,

Now that the arena is operating, we're starting to collect performance data and are excited to share that with the public. The arena is launching a public facing dashboard to provide more insight into the arena's sustainability commitments around carbon, energy, waste, food and many other areas, and we hope this provides a measurement mechanism to identify and track additional improvement opportunities so the arena continues to reduce its impact over time. (as quoted in Fouts, 2021, para. 17)

Furthermore, "Climate Pledge Arena will share sustainability performance data on a quarterly basis, incorporating data points around energy and water use, as well as how much of the arena's waste is diverted from landfills" (Nelson, 2020, para. 8). Additionally, hockey and soccer tickets double as free public transit passes, allowing the Arena to track the number of fans using public transportation (Fouts, 2021). Details on how, where, and when these reports will be released are not posted on the Arena's website. That being said, the Arena has promised to achieve Net Zero Carbon certification from the ILFI. This certification requires that 100% of the operational energy use be offset by new on- or off-site renewable energy and 100% of the embodied carbon emissions impacts must be disclosed and offset (International Living Future Institute, 2022). At the very least, its quarterly reporting is likely to include data that demonstrate the Arena's compliance with the certification requirements.

Additionally, as referenced above, the Arena has committed to creating an Advisory Committee to realize its goal of being "the most progressive and sustainable arena in the world" (Climate Pledge Arena, 2022c, para. 7). There are no additional details about this committee on the website including who will be a part of it, how often it will meet, or what its responsibilities will be.

New: Reporting and Sharing Sustainability Metrics

It remains unclear the level of detail that will be included in the Arena's quarterly reports and what will be posted on a public dashboard. At the very least, it should publish data related to its ILFI Net Zero Carbon certification. ILFI requires entities seeking net-zero carbon certification to provide several data points over the course of 12 months (International Living Future Insitute, 2022). For example, existing buildings must demonstrate a 30% reduction of energy use intensity (EUI) from a typical existing building of an equivalent type, size, and location. ILFI does allow existing buildings to continue using non-renewable energy (e.g., natural gas) but requires that the usage be offset by on- or off-site renewable energy. Additionally, ILFI requires that projects calculate all embodied emissions using an approved life-cycle assessment tool. These data can be complex and highly technical. The Arena must develop a way to clearly explain this information to the public and make it part of its quarterly reporting. Further discussion regarding the role of the Advisory Committee is provided below.

In addition to publishing its building performance data linked to its Net Zero Carbon certification, the Arena should opt to report to at least one third party voluntarily. Amazon does not currently report to The Climate Registry, but it did complete a CDP 2021 Climate Change Report (CDP, 2022b). However, that report has not been scored and is not publicly available. Additionally, CDP requested that Amazon submit the following reports: Water Security 2021, Forests 2021, Climate Change 2020, and Forests 2020. It failed to submit any of these reports and therefore received an *F* grade.[5] Even if Amazon.com continued to report to CDP, it should complete a separate report for the Arena to increase transparency and accountability of this specific facility.

The Arena should consider an online platform that would allow it to report data at least quarterly. This platform should be easy to understand and use and provide information relevant to the public and nearby communities. For example, it should include total energy and water used, total waste generated, total food scraps composted, number of local farms supplying food and other products, number of people taking public transit, local air quality, and so on. All data should be reported in "equivalents" that are easy to understand (e.g., "5,000 people took public transit to today's game; that is the equivalent of taking 300 cars off the road for one year"). There should be a visual component that displays these data in ways that are exciting and easy to understand. For example, the Marin Climate and Energy Partnership is a group of 11 Marin towns and cities, the County of Marin, and three public agencies that serve Marin (Marin Climate and Energy Partnership, 2022a). They developed an online tracker that allows the community to clearly track each jurisdiction's progress as it works to meet GHG reduction goals (Marin Climate and Energy Partnership, 2022b). Members of the public can see how much energy and water each community has used, how much solar photovoltaic (PV) has been installed, and the number of electric vehicles registered in its geographic boundaries.

Another example is Transparent Richmond (California), an open data and performance reporting system that allows the community to explore the City's data, strategic goals, and progress toward meeting those goals (City of Richmond, 2022a). The platform has a Sustainability and Health Equity section that explains Climate Action Plan Goals and Initiatives. (City of Richmond, 2022b). Each initiative has a separate page where goals and evaluation metrics are clearly explained, and data are updated regularly. The City tracks many data points, which include but are not limited to GHG emissions trends, the tonnage of waste diverted from landfills, and the number of people that received hands-on training related to solar PV panel installation. Finally, the City indicates that it is committed to ensuring equitable access to the platform.

Equity is defined here as using public information in a way that reduces disparities, helps to meet service needs of vulnerable communities, ensures that low-income communities and communities of color will not be negatively impacted by City programs and policies, and works to acknowledge and correct disparities caused by a history of systemic inequitable policy decisions (City of Richmond, 2022c).

The Arena must work closely with the Advisory Committee to design and maintain its own platform that ensures equitable access to Arena information.

Existing: Reporting and Sharing Equity Metrics

The Arena has acknowledged the importance of centering diverse voices, experiences, and perspectives internal and external to its organization and indicates it will leverage its platforms to advance equity (One Roof Foundation, 2022). It has not made clear how it will track progress on this work. The One Roof Foundation may report on its initiatives, but its website does not make clear if and how often it will publish its progress.

The One Roof Foundation commits to focusing on BIPOC communities by elevating and supporting these communities. A report should explain what efforts it has taken, how many BIPOC communities have been engaged and supported and in what ways, what lessons it has learned, and how it will change its approach because of those experiences. Additionally, the Arena has indicated it is listening to the Southpark Community to understand how it can bring about much-needed change. There should be increased transparency around this effort. Listening how? How often? What is the Arena doing with the information it receives? What projects or initiatives result from this listening? Finally, the Arena has indicated it is committed to partnering with the Duwamish Tribe and increasing awareness that the sacred river needs to be cleaned. More specificity is required, and similar questions as stated above must be asked in the context of this relationship. Finally, it is unclear whether the proposed Advisory Committee will also monitor and report outcomes related to the Arena's equity and community commitments.

New: Reporting and Sharing Equity Metrics

Generally, the Arena needs to significantly deepen its equity and community engagement work, link those efforts to its climate pledges, and transparently report on those efforts. As a starting point, it should revisit how it interacts with nearby communities and co-develop (with those communities) a framework for continued discussion and shared decision-making. Communities affected by the Arena must have a seat at the table and be empowered to share input and make decisions with Arena staff. Their direct-lived experience must be prioritized as the Arena works to achieve its climate and equity goals.

There are several frameworks for community engagement, which are not examined in great detail. However, it is important to note that arena owners, designers, operators, and staff must consider the spectrum of engagement opportunities. If the community is to have a real impact on decisions affecting the arena and their neighborhoods, they must be *empowered* to make the final decisions related to projects that affect their communities. Other engagement options include (in order of least impactful to most impactful on decision-making): inform, consult, involve, collaborate, and empower. No matter what engagement

244 Alex Porteshawver

approach is used, the Arena must be clear about its promise to the community and be accountable. For example, the Arena has committed over $70 million to support community-driven efforts (Climate Pledge Arena, 2022b). The website does indicate approximately how much money will go to each effort. This commitment is a great opportunity to engage the community. For example, the community could co-design grant guidelines or grant reporting, help identify specific causes and projects to donate money, and identify ways to measure the impacts of the Arena's philanthropic investment. As stated above, it is possible that the proposed Advisory Committee could include community members, and it could be the group that leads co-design and decision-making with the Arena.

Additionally, any effort to work with and support the community should involve *multisolving*, in which groups "pool expertise, funding, and political will to solve multiple problems with a single investment of time and money" (Sawin, 2018, para. 2). Multisolving is challenging, and there is no one-size-fits-all approach. There are three key principles of multisolving that the Arena should commit to: (1) Everyone matters; everyone is needed; (2) We can succeed by addressing tough problems in an integrated fashion; and (3) Large solutions start small; growth results from learning and connecting. These principles can be meaningfully addressed if the Arena welcomes the community, wants to learn and document what communities share, and is committed to amplifying the stories they hear. Finally, and important to note, this work is hard and requires dedication and the willingness to iterate approaches over time.

Another important framework that requires a deep commitment and additional time is *deep democracy*. As defined by the International Association of Practitioners of Process Oriented Psychology (2022), deep democracy is an attitude and a principle:

> Deep Democracy is an attitude that focuses on the awareness of voices that are both central and marginal …
>
> Unlike "classical" democracy, which focuses on majority rule, Deep Democracy suggests that all voices, states of awareness, and frameworks of reality are important. Deep Democracy also suggests that the information carried within these voices, awarenesses, and frameworks are all needed to understand the complete process of the system. … Deep Democracy is a process of relationship, not a state-oriented still picture, or a set of policies. (paras. 2–3)

In the context of the Arena, this means raising awareness of community voices typically not included, honoring those voices by considering them as important as internal staff voices or investor voices, and understanding that by inviting those voices in, it is starting and needs to nurture a real relationship with those communities.

One way of honoring those voices and increasing the ability of Arena staff and decision-makers to act based on what they hear is by offering ongoing diversity, equity, inclusion, and belonging (DEIB) training to its staff and developing shared training opportunities between staff and the community. For example, there are many community-based organizations and nonprofits that offer this type of training, and there are many different approaches to deepening understanding of DEIB concepts. The County of Marin created the "Safe Space, Brave Space" series, which is "an open forum for employees to participate in discussions focused on healing, critical conversations, and to provide a space to receive racial equity resources that offer opportunities for learning, healing, and deepening understanding of the County's equity work" (County of Marin, 2022). It has offered 12 multi-hour sessions featuring guest speakers on a variety of topics, including Gender Identity, Unconscious Bias, and Restorative Justice. This is just one example. Many large corporations also offer this type of training for their employees (e.g., Fluker, 2021).

Another way of honoring and including these voices is by offering community leaders positions on the Advisory Committee. This is a very visible way of showing that the Arena is committed to diversifying perspectives on the Committee, comfortable shifting decision-making power to the community, and interested in being accountable to its sustainability and equity goals. Community leaders should be invited at the same time as Amazon and other Arena staff to avoid tokenism[6] and to ensure these individuals participate in group decision-making and goal setting from the very beginning. The Arena should plan to make the necessary accommodations to ensure community leaders can participate in Committee meetings. For example, leadership could schedule meetings after working hours, provide childcare, offer food if meeting at meal time, offer stipends for participation, and consider technological barriers to participating. Inviting community leaders is just as important as creating a space where those leaders want to participate. The Committee should develop group agreements including parameters around how each member participates so that everyone has an opportunity to participate.

Finally, the Arena could regularly report its co-developed equity metrics (perhaps through the Advisory Committee). This reporting could be integrated with its sustainability reporting as outlined above. The metrics should closely link to the Arena's and One Roof Foundation's existing goals and clearly indicate when it falls short of those goals and how it will address those shortcomings. This type of reporting can go a long way toward cultivating relationships with nearby communities and can invite ongoing dialogue around how best to achieve the Arena's and communities' goals collectively. Additionally, it can help build trust between the Arena and communities and may help attract additional resources (e.g., grants, private donations, foundation funding) to support and expand community-driven efforts.

Conclusion

Climate and equity are interconnected issues, and sports arenas have an incredible opportunity to commit to addressing these issues. Climate Pledge Arena has set loften environmental goals and aspires to engage and support nearby communities. These commitments should be applauded and the Arena's ability to raise awareness of these issues celebrated. However, commitments or pledges are not enough. The Arena must go beyond to create climate and equity accountability frameworks and systems that increase transparency and help build trust with the public. There are several reporting mechanisms, community engagement frameworks, and principles that the Arena can refer to and use as it develops its public reporting mechanisms. If it is able to not only meet its goals but also meaningfully address equity by integrating the community into decision-making at the Arena, it will serve as a symbol that society in general, and specifically large companies like Amazon, must do better.

Notes

1 The State of California Office of Environmental Health and Hazards Assessment (2022) provides guidance on how "disadvantaged communities" are defined and mapped.
2 ICLEI – Local Governments for Sustainability is "a global network of more than 2500 local and regional governments committed to sustainable urban development. Active in 125+ countries, [they] influence sustainability policy and drive local action for low emission, nature-based, equitable, resilient and circular development" (ICLEI, 2021, para. 1).
3 As evidence of the State of California Department of Justice's claim that the state is "a leader in enacting laws specific to environmental justice," it cites "laws directing funding to environmental justice communities (SB 535 and AB 1550), a law creating a community air quality protection program (AB 617), and another that requires environmental justice to be addressed in local government planning (SB 1000)" (State of California Department of Justice, 2022, para. 2).
4 The State of California Governor's Office of Planning and Research (2022) notes a general plan is "each local government's blueprint for meeting the community's long-term vision for the future" (para. 1).
5 As CDP (2022b) notes, "An F does not indicate a failure in environmental stewardship." Instead, it means the entity failed to submit requested reports, and therefore, they could not be scored.
6 Tokenism is the practice of inviting someone to participate just to avoid criticism (Sherrer, 2018).

References

An act to amend Section 65302 of the Government Code, relating to land use. Cal. Gov. Code, § 65302 (2016).
Belson, K. (2021, October 30). Shooting at a big goal in the Kraken's new home. *New York Times*, B10.
California Climate Investments. (2022). *Background*. https://www.caclimateinvestments.ca.gov/about-cci
CDP. (2022a). *About us*. https://www.cdp.net/en/info/about-us
CDP. (2022b). *Search and view past CDP responses*. https://www.cdp.net/en/responses/658
CDP. (2022c). *Why your city should disclose*. https://www.cdp.net/en/cities-discloser
City of and County of San Francisco. (2021). *San Francisco's Climate Action Plan 2021*. https://sfenvironment.org/sites/default/files/cap_fulldocument_wappendix_web_220124.pdf

City of Richmond. (2022a). *Transparent Richmond*. https://www.transparentrichmond.org/

City of Richmond. (2022b). *Transparent Richmond sustainability and health equity*. https://www.transparentrichmond.org/stories/s/Sustainability-and-Health-Equity/fe48-z44c

City of Richmond. (2022c). *Transparent Richmond user guide*. https://www.transparent-richmond.org/stories/s/6y4r-3rdy

Climate Alliance. (2022). *Homepage*. https://waclimatealliance.org/

Climate Pledge Arena. (2022a). *About us*. www.climatepledgearena.com/about

Climate Pledge Arena. (2022b). *Community*. https://climatepledgearena.com/community/

Climate Pledge Arena. (2022c). *Sustainability*. https://climatepledgearena.com/sustainability/

The Climate Registry. (2022a). *About us*. https://www.theclimateregistry.org/who-we-are/about-us/

The Climate Registry. (2022b). *List of members & profiles*. https://www.theclimateregistry.org/our-members/list-of-members-profiles/

The Climate Registry. (2022c). *Starter kit reporting FAQs*. https://www.theclimateregistry.org/starterkit/reporting-faqs/

Condor, Bob. (2022). *Marking Earth Month, One Roof Foundation and partners launch environmental justice initiatives to address pollution in South Park and Duwamish Valley*. One Roof Foundation. https://onerooffoundation.org/2022/04/11/air-fair/

County of Marin. (2020). *Drawdown: Marin strategic plan*. https://www.marincounty.org/-/media/files/departments/cd/planning/sustainability/climate-and-adaptation/drawdown-marin/strategic-plan/drawdownmarinstrategicplan120820.pdf?la=en

County of Marin. (2022). *Safe space, brave space*. County of Marin.

Creger, H. (2020). *Making racial equity real in research*. The Greenlining Institute. https://greenlining.org/wp-content/uploads/2020/10/Greenlining-Making-Racial-Equity-Real-2020.pdf

Drawdown: Marin Equity Task Force. (2021). *Equity progress report*. https://www.marincounty.org/-/media/files/departments/cd/planning/sustainability/climate-and-adaptation/drawdown-marin/drawdown-marin-equity-progress-report.pdf?la=en

Fluker, D. (2021, May8). *12 companies ramping up their diversity & inclusion efforts—and how you can too*. Glassdoor. https://www.glassdoor.com/employers/blog/inspiration-for-ramping-up-diversity-inclusion-efforts/

Fouts, F. (2021, December 21). *How Climate Pledge Arena is on track to become the world's first net-zero carbon arena*. GreenBiz. https://www.greenbiz.com/article/how-climate-pledge-arena-track-become-worlds-first-net-zero-carbon-arena

Front and Centered. (2022a). *About us*. https://frontandcentered.org/about-us/#our-purpose

Front and Centered. (2022b). *Action*. https://frontandcentered.org/action/

Government Alliance on Race and Equity. (2022a). *Tools and resources*. https://www.racialequityalliance.org/tools-resources/

Government Alliance on Race and Equity. (2022b). *Where we work*. https://www.racialequityalliance.org/where-we-work/jurisdictions/

The Greenlining Institute. (2022). *Homepage*. http://www.greenlining.org

GRID Alternatives (2022). *Who we are*. http://www.gridalternatives.org

ICLEI. (2021). *About us*. https://iclei.org/en/About_ICLEI_2.html

International Association of Practitioners of Process Oriented Psychology. (2022). *Definition of deep democracy*. https://iapop.com/deep-democracy/

International Living Future Institute. (2022). *Zero carbon certification*. https://living-future.org/zero-carbon-certification/

King County. (2022). *Climate Equity Community Task Force (CECTF).* https://kingcounty.gov/services/environment/climate/actions-strategies/strategic-climate-action-plan/equity-task-force.aspx

Marin Climate and Energy Partnership. (2022a). *About us.* https://marinclimate.org/about-us/

Marin Climate and Energy Partnership. (2022b). *Marin tracker.* http://www.marintracker.org/

Nelson, J., & Brooks, L. (2016). *Racial equity toolkit.* Government Alliance on Race and Equity. https://racialequityalliance.org/wp-content/uploads/2015/10/GARE-Racial_Equity_Toolkit.pdf

Nelson, T. (2020, July 21). How Amazon plans to revolutionize green stadium design. *Architectural Digest.* https://www.architecturaldigest.com/story/how-amazon-plans-revolutionize-green-stadium-design

Obando, S. (2021, October 21). *On site: An inside look at the construction of Seattle's $1.15B Climate Pledge Arena.* Construction Dive. https://www.constructiondive.com/news/climate-pledge-arena-seattle-mortenson-construction/607484/

One Roof Foundation. (2022). *Diversity, equity, and inclusion.* https://onerooffoundation.org/about-us/diversity-equity-inclusion/

Populous. (2021). *Climate Pledge Arena revolutionizes sustainable public assembly design.* https://populous.com/climate-pledge-arena-sustainable-design

Sawin, E. (2018). The magic of "multisolving." *Stanford Social Innovation Review.* 10.48558/W5D4-6430

Sherrer, K. (2018, February 26). *What is tokenism, and why does it matter in the workplace?* Vanderbilt University Owen Graduate School of Management. https://business.vanderbilt.edu/news/2018/02/26/tokenism-in-the-workplace/

State of California Coastal Conservancy. (2020). *Justice, equity, diversity, and inclusion (JEDI) guidelines.* https://scc.ca.gov/files/2020/09/JEDI_Guidelines_FINAL.pdf

State of California Coastal Conservancy. (2022). *Justice, equity, diversity, and inclusion (JEDI).* https://scc.ca.gov/justice-equity-diversity-and-inclusion-jedi/

State of California Department of Justice. (2022). *SB 1000 – Environmental justice in local land use planning.* https://oag.ca.gov/environment/sb1000

State of California Governor's Office of Planning and Research. (2022). *General plan information.* https://opr.ca.gov/planning/general-plan/

State of California Office of Environmental Health Hazard Assessment. (2022). *SB 535 disadvantaged communities.* https://oehha.ca.gov/calenviroscreen/sb535

World Resources Institute. (2022). *Climate equity.* https://www.wri.org/initiatives/climate-equity

INDEX

A21 216
Abel, Ann 143
Abell Foundation 110
accountability 139, 237–245
acknowledge principle 34
activism: environmental justice 5, 11;
environmental racism 5
Advance Taipei Cultural and Sports Park 216
Agua Caliente Clippers 50
Air Canada Centre 60
air pollutants 4, 14
air quality 4
Allen, Ivan 96–97
American Indian Nations 34
Amiskwaciwaskahikan 178
Amway Arena 62
Anacostia River 143–144, 147, 152
Anacostia Waterfront Initiative: description
of 143–144; gentrification and 152; goals
of 147–148, 152; housing units 152;
Nationals Park. *See* Nationals Park; Near
Southeast neighborhood 149, 153;
Williams' involvement with 143–144,
146–148, 153
Arizona Coyotes 47
assaults 9
Astrodome 65–66
Athlone Stadium 159, 162–166, 168–169
Atlanta: Mercedes-Benz Stadium in 139;
Olympic Games in 98; Peoplestown
neighborhood of 91–92, 99–100; sewage
system in 98–100; stormwater in 98–102;

Summerhill neighborhood of 91–92,
99–100
Atlanta Braves 44
Atlanta-Fulton County Stadium 91, 98
Atlanta Journal-Constitution 91, 93
Atlanta Regional Commission 101
Atlanta Stadium 96–98
Atlanta's southside: Black housing in 91;
eminent domain in 100; environmental
injustices in 101; flooding in 91–102,
139; Girls' High in 96; Hebrew Orphans'
Home property 94–96, 100; Loyd Street
sewer 93–94, 102; Rawson-Washington
Urban Redevelopment Area 96–97;
sewers in 92–96, 98, 100; stadium
construction in 91, 96–98, 102; stadium
neighborhoods in 91–93; stormwater in
98–102; urban renewal in 96
Atlantic Yards project 7, 57, 139
AWI. *See* Anacostia Waterfront Initiative

ballot box loophole, of California
Environmental Quality Act 82–84
Ballpark District 153
Baltimore: Black population in 109; civil
rights and 107–108; demographics of
109; discrimination in 108; Ednor
Gardens-Lakeside neighborhood of 106,
113; environmental discrimination in
108–114; environmental injustices in
108–114; gentrification of 109–111;
Inner Harbor 114; Jim Crow laws in

250 Index

108; Memorial Stadium in 106–107, 111–114; racial segregation in 110; stadium relocation in 105–107; tax increment financing in 112; urban decay and renewal in 112–113; urban gentrification in 109–111; urban revival in 111; White flight in 109, 112; World War II and 109
Baltimore Colts 106
Baltimore Orioles 105–107, 110, 114
Baltimore Ravens 105–107, 110–111, 114
Baltimore Sun 109
Barclays 46
Barry, Marion 146–147
Bayview-Hunters Point Shipyard 60
Bean v. Southwestern Waste Management, Inc. 5
Becker, mark 101
Beckham, David 124–125
Biber, Eric 81–82
BIPOC neighborhoods and communities 119, 237, 243
Black, Indigenous, and persons of color communities. *See* BIPOC neighborhoods and communities
Black Lives Matter 20
Black neighborhoods: eminent domain effects on 11; in Miami 119; redlining in 4–5
Blatter, Sepp 164
Bloomberg, Mike 132
Bradley, Melissa Biggs 143
Brandes, Uwe 147
Bronx 132–134
Brown v. Board of Education 108
Building an Indoor Stadium with Minimum 50,000 Seating Capacity in Taipei 213
build–operate–transfer contract 214, 218, 221

Cahuilla Indians 50
Calgary and Edmonton Railway 178
California: Cap and Trade Program 232; stadium development in 82–83
California Environmental Quality Act: ballot box loophole of 82–84; description of 73, 78–79; environmental review under 79; goals of 83; legislative exemptions from 81; reform 81; stadium projects exempt from 79–80; stadium-specific legislative exemptions from 79–82
Calls to Action Report 41–42
Camden Yards 106–107, 110, 112, 114

Canada. *See also* Edmonton; land acknowledgments in 38, 41–43; naming rights in 47–48; stadiums in 36
Canadian Football League 42, 49
Candlestick Park 59–60, 64–65
Cape Flats District Plan 165–166
Cape Town: aerial view of 160; apartheid influences on 160–161; Athlone Stadium 159, 162–166, 168–169; coalition government of 164; demographics of 160; Development Facilitation Act 161; economic growth and development in 161; environmental justice in 159, 164–169; FIFA Men's World Cup stadium in 159, 162; integrated development plan for 161–162; population of 160; public transport systems in 161; sustainable urban infrastructure of 161; urban development in 160–162
Cape Town Environmental Protection Association 167
Cape Town Stadium 166–167, 169
Capital One Center 149
Capitol Riverfront Business Improvement District 149, 153
carceral system 178
Cardinal, Douglas 49
Carter USA 100–101
CBA. *See* community benefits agreement
CBD. *See* central business districts
CBOs. *See* community-based organizations
CDP 238
CECTF. *See* Climate Equity Community Task Force
Centennial Olympic Stadium 91, 99
Centerfire Energy Group 47–48
central business districts 158–159, 167, 169
CEPA. *See* Cape Town Environmental Protection Association
CEQA. *See* California Environmental Quality Act
CFL. *See* Canadian Football League
CGC. *See* Clean Government Committee
Chen, Shiu-Bien 214
Chiang, Ching-Kuo 213
Chicago Blackhawks 39–40
Chicken or Egg hypothesis 14
China 213
Chinese Taipei National Olympic Committee 213
civil rights, in Baltimore 107–108
Civil Rights Movement 108
Clean Government Committee 223

Clean Rivers Project 147
Clean Water Act 72, 98
Cleveland Browns 107
climate change: equity and 231–233, 236, 245; governments and 232–233; local government accountability frameworks for 238–239; organizations and 233
climate equity 232
Climate Equity Community Task Force 232
climate gentrification 119–120, 124
Climate Pledge Arena: accountability frameworks for 240–245; Advisory Committee of 245; climate at 233–235; commitments by 236–237; community engagement by 243–244; deep democracy 244; description of 40–41, 139, 230–231; diversity, equity, inclusion, and belonging training for staff of 244–245; equity at 233, 235–237, 243–245; illustration of 236; multisolving by 244; Net Zero Carbon certification pledge by 233–234, 242; One Roof Foundation 237, 243, 245; public reporting mechanisms used by 246; sustainability 230, 234–235, 240–243
Climate Vulnerability of Sport Organizations 122
colonialism 33, 35, 39, 50, 172, 175–176
Comerica Park 36
Commission for Racial Justice 194
Communist China 213
communities of color: air quality in 4; definition of 14; environmental hazards in 5; environmental justice barriers in 11; environmental racism in 4–5
community-based organizations 233
community benefits agreement 134–135, 139
community engagement, with Indigenous Nations: in Canada 45–46; description of 43–44; environmental injustices managed with 46; in United States 44–45
community engagement principle 34
community facilities redevelopment, of shadow stadia 64–65
composite gentrification index 26
Connally Street sewer 94–95, 102
Connecticut Sun 49, 51
consumerism 21
control grabbing 196
Control Yuan 221
corporatization 23

COVID-19 42
Crath, Rory 182
CRBID. See Capitol Riverfront Business Improvement District
Creative Village 62
crime 9
Crist, Charlie 121
Crypto.com Arena 46, 134
CTNOC. See Chinese Taipei National Olympic Committee
Cuban Refugee Emergency Center 120
CWA. See Clean Water Act

Dakota Access Pipeline 47
dead zones 9
debt financing, of Yankee Stadium 135–137
deep democracy 244
DEIB training. See diversity, equity, inclusion, and belonging training
Department of Homeland Security 24
Despa-Szto, Courtney 44
Detroit Tigers 35–36
Development Facilitation Act 161
Dickens, Andre 101
discrimination: in Baltimore 108; environmental 108–114
displacements: Nationals Park as cause of 154; stadium development as cause of 23, 26, 28, 154
distributive justice 33, 49, 175
diversity, equity, inclusion, and belonging training 244–245
Doctrine of Discovery 178
Du Bois, W.E.B. 91
Dumping in Dixie: Race, Class, and Environmental Quality 5
Dupree, Jacqueline 149

Edmonton: history of 178; homeless population in 179–180; Rogers Place in 172–173, 184–185; as settler city 177–183; settler colonialism in 172, 175–176, 182
Edmonton Arts Council 183
Edmonton Elks 45
Edmonton Eskimos 43, 45
Edmonton Oil Kings 173
Edmonton Oilers 173, 182
Edmonton Police Service 180
Ednor Gardens-Lakeside neighborhood 106, 113
EIA. See Environmental Impact Assessment
EIR. See environmental impact report
EIS. See environmental impact statement

252 Index

eminent domain 11, 100, 154
Endangered Species Act 72
energy use intensity 241
environment: definition of 177; as places for "live, work, play and belong" 177; sport and 3
environmental amenities 7
environmental disamenities 72
environmental discrimination 108–114
environmental hazards: in communities of color 5; stadiums as 8–10, 21
Environmental Impact Assessment committee 214, 219, 221
environmental impact report 75–76, 78
environmental impact statement 75–78
environmental inequity 6–7, 11
environmental injustice: in Atlanta's southside 101; in Baltimore 108–114; community engagement for 46; origins of 195; settler colonialism as 175–176
environmental justice: achieving of 57; activism 5, 11; in communities of color 11; definition of 4; description of 194–195; distributive justice in 175; early studies of 195; environmental racism and 57, 174; as frame 4–7; gentrification as issue of 177; history of 130–131, 174; Indigenous 32–34, 38, 50, 185; in international contexts 194–195; land grabbing and 195–197; as movement 4–7, 174–175; Nationals Park and 151, 155; organizations seeking 5; overview of 3–4; pillars of 131; principles of 5; requirements for 32; Rogers Place and 178; scope of 174–175; shadow stadia 56–57; as social movement 5; in sport 7–12; state environmental policy acts and 73; theories regarding 6; in United States 56–57
Environmental Justice Demographic Index 111
environmental policies 7
environmental policy acts: national 73, 75, 77; state. *See* state environmental policy acts
environmental racism: academic studies of 5; activism against 5; in communities of color 4–5; description of 3–4, 174; environmental justice and 57, 174; legacies of 33
environmental sustainability 59
EPS. *See* Edmonton Police Service
equity: climate change and 231–233, 236, 245; at Climate Pledge Arena 233,

235–237; definition of 242; Government Alliance on Race and Equity 239; governments and 232–233; local government accountability frameworks for 239–240; metrics of 243–245; organizations and 233; racial 232
ESA. *See* Endangered Species Act
EUI. *See* energy use intensity
event-led regeneration 22
event-themed regeneration 22
exclusionary displacements 23

Fan Cost Index 155
Farglory Group 214–215, 218–219, 221, 223–224
federal environmental laws 72
FIFA Green Goal Legacy Report 165, 168
FIFA Men's World Cup stadium 159, 162, 169
FIFA World Cup 158
Financial Control Board 146
First National People of Color Environmental Leadership Summit 5
First Nations: in Canada 34; naming rights deals 47
Five-Year Development Plan (1984–1988) 193
flooding: in Atlanta's southside 91–102, 139; in Miami 119–120
Florida Panthers 118
football 9, 42, 49
Forest City Enterprises 149
Forsman, Leonard 41
Forsyth, Janice 41
Fort McMurray Oil Barons 47
Frederick Douglass Bridge 150
Front and Centered 233

GAO. *See* Government Accounting Office
Garden City Concept 192
GARE. *See* Government Alliance on Race and Equity
genocide 178
gentrification: Anacostia Waterfront Initiative and 152; in Baltimore 109–111; climate 119–120, 124; definition of 22; displacements caused by 22–23; as environmental justice issue 177; examples of 24–28; measurement of 24; Nationals Park as cause of 152; neighborhood demographics affected by 26, 28; positive 24; Rogers Place and 180, 182; sport-related 177, 181; stadiums and 20–29; trends in 26; urban

regeneration and 22; urban renewal as cause of 113
Georgia State University 99–101
Ghiglino, Patricia 154
Gila River Casinos 47
global land grab 196
Golden 1 Center 9
Government Accounting Office 146
Government Alliance on Race and Equity 239
GPCA. *See* Green Point Common Association
Gray, Freddie 107
Green Building Council 56, 59
Green Point 162–164, 166–168
Green Point Common Association 166
Green Point Commons 166–167
greenhouse gas emissions 230–231, 234, 238
greenhouse gas emissions inventory 238
Greenlining Institute 232–233
greenspace 135, 137–138
greenwashing 235
Grey Cup 42–43
GRID Alternatives 2337
grocery chain redevelopment, of shadow stadia 60–61
Guiliani, Rudy 132
Gwangju-Kia Champions Field 9

Hamilton Tiger-Cats 42–43
Harlem River 137
Hau, Lung-Pin 214
Hau, Pei-Tsun 212
Haudenosaunee Confederacy Chiefs Council 42, 48
hazardous waste 5
Hebrew Orphans' Home property 94–96, 100
Height of Buildings Act 146
Hill, Leroy 42
HKS, Inc 49
hockey 44
Home Owners Loan Corporation 120
Homeland Infrastructure Foundation-Level Data 24
homeless population, in Edmonton 179–180
Horita, Mari 40
Housing Act of 1949 96
Housing Justice League 101
Houston Astros 65
Houston Oilers 65
Howard, Ebenzer 191–192

Hsu, Shau-Yu 216
Huang, Ching-Mao 224
Huang, Da-Zhou 212, 214–216
Hudson's Bay Company 178
Hurricane Dorian 123
Hurricane Irma 123
Hurricane Katrina 66
Hurricane Wilma 121

Ice District 180–181
ICLEI - Local Governments for Sustainability 246
IDP. *See* integrated development plan
ILFI. *See* International Living Future Institute
Independent First Nations of Saskatchewan 49
Indian Act 34, 178
Indian Residential Schools 178–179
Indigenous athletes 45–46
Indigenous Environmental Justice 32–34, 48, 50
Indigenous Environmental Justice 32–33
Indigenous heritage nights 43
Indigenous Nations: colonialism of 35–36; community engagement with 43; environmental injustices against 32, 35, 48, 185; genocidal strategy against 178; Indian Act effects on 178; land loss by 34–37; land rights of 35; mascots and 40; Olympic Games relations with 41–42; partnerships with 46–48, 50; reclamation by 50; self-determination and sovereignty of 34–35; stadiums and 39–41; team ownership by 48–49; territory rights of 35; treaties in 34
Indigenous self-determination 34
informal settlements 205
integrated development plan 161–162
Inter Miami CF 118, 124–125
International Association of Practitioners of Process Oriented Psychology 244
international government organizations 199
International Living Future Institute 233–234, 241
Intrenchment Creek 93
Iroquois Nationals lacrosse team 48
Irsay, Robert 106

Jackson, Mattie 100
James Bays Girls at Bat program 45
JEDI guidelines. *See* justice, equity, diversity, and inclusion guidelines
Jim Crow laws 108

254 Index

Jordaan, Danny 162
Jubilee Manifesto 188–191, 205
justice: distributive 33, 49, 175;
environmental. *See* environmental
justice; procedural 33; recognition 33,
37, 39, 45
justice, equity, diversity, and inclusion
guidelines 239–240

Kasdin, Neisen 124
Katz, Daryl 173
Kenya: *Jubilee Manifesto* 188–191, 205; land
crisis in 197; land grabbing in 196–199,
202; Moi Stadium in 201; Nairobi.
See Nairobi; Sports, Arts, and Social
Development Fund in 190–191; sports in
189–190; stadium construction projects
in 190–191; stadiums in 205; urban
population in 198; *Vision 2030* 188,
204–206
Kenyatta, Uhuru 188, 190
Kenya–Uganda Railway 191
Key Arena 40
Kezar Stadium 64–65
King, Martin Luther Jr. 5
Kirigiti Stadium 205–206
Kisumu 205
Klipfontein Corridor 165–166, 169
Ko, Wen-Je 215, 223–225
Kuomintang 213, 215, 217

lacrosse 44, 48
land acknowledgments: in Canada 38,
41–43; definition of 37–38; mistakes
involving 42–43; as recognition justice
39; as reconciliation 41; in United States
38–41, 44
Land and Water Conservation Fund
132, 137
land grabbing 195–197, 199, 202
land loss, by Indigenous Nations 34–37
landfills 5
Lane (Lummi), Temryss 41
Latino population, in Miami 118–119, 124
Leadership in Energy and Environmental
Design 55–56, 59, 123, 151
Lee, Shu-Te 223
LEED. *See* Leadership in Energy and
Environmental Design
legitimation 196
Leiweke, Tod 40
L'Enfant, Pierre 145
Levi's Stadium 59–60
Lin, Chou-Min 224

Linklater, Michael 46
Little Caesars Arena 23, 129
Little Havana 120–121, 123, 126
Loblaws 61
LOC. *See* Local Organising Committee
local government accountability
frameworks 238–240
Local Organising Committee 162
locally undesirable land uses 10–11, 14, 21
long-term site vacancies, of shadow stadia
65–66
Lopez, Reinaldo 154
Los Angeles Clippers 50
low-income communities: environmental
hazards in 6; environmental justice
barriers in 11
Loyd Street sewer 93–94, 102
LULUs. *See* locally undesirable land uses
Lundberg, Dan 122
LWCF. *See* Land and Water Conservation
Fund

Ma, Ying-Jeou 214–216, 219
Macombs Dam Bridge 133
Macombs Dam Park 63, 132–133
Malerba, Lynn 49
mandates 78
Maple Leaf Gardens 60–61
Maple Leaf Sports and Entertainment 42, 60
marginalized communities 21
Marin Climate and Equity Partnership 242
market dynamics 14
market failures 130
Marlins Park 121–124
Maryland Baseball Park 111
Maryland Stadium Authority 114
mascots 40, 43–46
Mattamy Athletic Centre 61
Mbeki, Thabo 164
McFadden, David 109
MCFN. *See* Missaugas of the Credit First
Nation
McMillan, John 145
McMillan Plan 145
Melreese Country Club 124
Mercedes-Benz Stadium 139
metrics: equity 243–245; sustainability
240–243
Miami: BIPOC neighborhoods in 119;
Black population in 119; climate change
122–123; climate gentrification in
119–120, 124; flooding in 119–120;
Grapeland Heights 125; Haitians in 119;
hurricanes in 120–121, 123; Latino

Index **255**

population in 118–119, 124; Little Havana in 120–121, 123, 126; Marlins Park 121–124; as multicultural hub 118–119, 125–126; Orange Bowl 120–121, 123, 126; Overtown in 119, 121, 124; redlining in 120; sea-level rise in 119–120; sports teams in 118; summary of 125–126; weather-proof design for stadiums in 122–123
Miami Beach 119
Miami Dolphins 118, 120
Miami Freedom Park 125
Miami Heat 118, 124
Miami Herald 121, 124
Miami Hurricanes 120
Miami Marlins 118, 121–122
Miami Parking Authority 123
Michigan Strategic Fund 36
micro land grabbing 196–197
Mill Pond Park 138
Millbrook First Nation 49
minority communities: environmental hazards in 6; environmental justice barriers in 11; gentrification effects on 23
Minority Move-In Hypothesis 14
Missaugas of the Credit First Nation 42–43
mixed-use redevelopment, of shadow stadia 59–60
MLSE. *See* Maple Leaf Sports and Entertainment
Modell, Art 107
Mohegan Tribe 49, 51
Moi Stadium 201
monopolies 130
Montreal Expos 150
Mosaic Stadium 49
M&T Bank Stadium 111
multisolving 244
Municipal Systems Act 161
murals 183
Musqueam Nation 48

Nairobi. *See also* Kenya; amenities in 199; Baba Dogo ward 198, 203; constituencies of 198; environmental justice in 200; Garden City model for 192; Githurai ward of 200–201; informal settlements in 199; Kahawa West ward of 198, 202; land allocation for public space in 193–194; map of 202; *1948 Master Plan* 191–194; population of 198–199; soccer fields in 198–204; urban development in 191–192; urbanization of 193

naming rights: in Canada 47–48; description of 46; in United States 47
National Capital Planning Commission 145
national environmental policy acts 73, 75, 77
National Historical GIS 26
National Housing Act 120
National Indigenous Peoples Day 45
National Native American Boarding School Healing Coalition 44
National Parks Service 136
National Property Administration 215
National Truth and Reconciliation Day 45
Nationals Park: Ballpark District 153; description of 143–144; design of 150–151, 155; displacements caused by 154; eminent domain for obtaining land for 154; environmental justice in 151, 155; as exclusionary space 153–155; Fan Cost Index 155; gentrification caused by 152; intermittent usage of 153; justice and 151–152
Native Governance Center 37
Naval Seas Systems Command 149
Navy Yard 143, 149
NCPC. *See* National Capital Planning Commission
ND. *See* negative declaration
Near Southeast neighborhood 149, 153
negative declaration 76
neighborhood: demographics of 26–27, 29; gentrification effects on 26, 28; stadium 26
neoliberal consumer citizenship 183
NEPAs. *See* national environmental policy acts
Net Zero Carbon certification 233–234, 242
New York City Industrial Development Agency 135–136
New York Times 134
NHL 173
NIMBY ideology. *See* not in my backyard ideology
1973 Nairobi Metropolitan Urban Growth Strategy 193
North America, sport expansion in 34–37
North-West Mounted Police 178
not in my backyard ideology 10, 21
Nova Scotia 49
NYCIDA. *See* New York City Industrial Development Agency

Olympic Games 41, 98
One Roof Foundation 237, 243, 245

256 Index

Orange Bowl (Miami) 120–121, 123, 126
Orange Shirt Day 42
Oriole Park 106–107
Orlando Magic 62
outcomes-based contracting 139
Overtown (Miami) 119, 121, 124
ownership principle 34

Paralympic Games 99
Paris Climate Change Agreement 64
partnership(s) 46–48, 50
partnership principle 34
PCC. *See* Public Construction Commission
People of Color Population Index 111
Pillar of the Community 182–184
PILOT revenue bonds 135–136
Port of Cape Town 160
positive gentrification 24
poverty 92, 195
PPG Paints Arena 134
Premier Lacrosse League 44
Principles of Environmental Justice 5
procedural justice 33
Proctor Creek Watershed 139
Professional Women's Hockey Players
    Association 44
Public Construction Commission 218–219
public financing: for stadiums 130,
    135–137; for Yankee Stadium 135–137
public goods 130
public spaces: murals for marking of 183; in
    poor and marginalized communities 199
punitive policing 181
PWHPA. *See* Professional Women's
    Hockey Players Association
Pyramid Communications 40–41

race. *See also specific race*; hazardous waste
    and 5; socioeconomic status and 110;
    stadium areas and 27–28
racial equity 232
racial segregation, in Baltimore 110
racialized poverty 92
racism, environmental. *See* environmental
    racism
Rasool, Ebrahim 162
Rawson-Washington Urban
    Redevelopment Area 96
recognition justice 33, 37, 39, 45
reconciliation: description of 38; land
    acknowledgments as 41
redlining: in Black neighborhoods 4–5;
    carceral, at Rogers Place 180–183; in
    Miami 120

Reed, Kasim 101
Regan, Beth 49
replacement stadium or infrastructure on
    existing shadow stadia site 62–64
residential redevelopment, of shadow
    stadia 62
retail chain redevelopment, of shadow
    stadia 60–61
reverse migration 109
Rexall Place 173
Ricky Liu Architects 218
River Avenue Skate Park 138
Rock Creek Park 148
Roe, Chris 240
Rogers Place: carceral redlining at 180–183;
    description of 172–173; environmental
    justice and 178; gentrification and 180,
    182; punitive policing around 181;
    summary of 184–185
Royal Canadian Mounted Police 178
Rupertsland 178
Ryerson University 61

SAFA. *See* South African Football
    Association
Safety Review Committee 223
SAGII. *See* Southeast Atlanta Green
    Infrastructure Initiative
Saint Mary's Park 138
Salzberg, Deborah Ratner 153
Save Our Parks 132
Scotiabank Arena 42
Secord, Richard 179
segregation 7, 110
semi-informal settlements 205
Senate Bill 1000 240
SEPAs. *See* state environmental policy acts
SERQA. *See* State Environmental Quality
    Review Act
settler colonialism 172, 175–176, 182
settler grammars of place 176
SGR. *See* Standard Gauge Railway
shadow stadia: Amway Arena 62;
    Astrodome 65–66; Candlestick Park
    59–60, 64–65; classifying of 57–66;
    community facilities redevelopment of
    64–65; contributing factors 57; definition
    of 55; environmental justice approach
    56–57; grocery chain redevelopment of
    60–61; Kezar Stadium 64–65; long-term
    site vacancies of 65–66; Maple Leaf
    Gardens 60–61; mixed-use
    redevelopment strategies for 59–60;
    overview of 55–56; recommendations

for 67; replacement stadium or infrastructure on existing site of 62–64; residential redevelopment of 62; retail chain redevelopment of 60–61; "uber-planning" for 67; Yankee Stadium 63–64
Six-Year National Development Plan 212, 215
Snidal, Michael 109
social anchor theory 130
social movement, environmental justice as 5
socioeconomic status, race and 110
solid waste 5
Songshan Tobacco Factory 214–217
Sonn, Ralph A. 92–93
South African Football Association 162
South African government 158
South Bronx 132–134, 137, 159
Southeast Atlanta Green Infrastructure Initiative 100
Space Needle 232
Spear, Joseph 150
Spokane Indians 45
Spokane Tribe of Indians 45
sponsorship 46–48
sport: environment and 3, 8–10; environmental justice in 7–12; growth of 111; North America expansion of 34–37; in urban politics 212
sport colonialism 33, 35, 39, 50
sport industry, power relations in 11–12
sport-related gentrification 177, 181
sport stadiums. *See* stadium(s)
Sports, Arts, and Social Development Fund 190–191
sports betting 48
sports-driven apartheid 20
sports sponsorship 46–48
sports teams. *See also specific team*; Indigenous Nations and, partnerships between 46–48, 50; in Miami 118; ownership of 48–49
Squamish Nation 48
SRC. *See* Safety Review Committee
stadium(s). *See also specific stadium*; appeal of, for cities 10; biodiversity losses associated with 71; in Canada 36; colonialism caused by 33; as community stewards 139; construction of 212; consumerism and 21; costs of 153; dead zones caused by 9; description of 3; as environmental hazards 8–10, 21; gentrification and 20–29; geographic classification of 25; government subsidy for 130; indigenizing of 48–50; Indigenous

heritage nights at 43; Indigenous Nations partnerships with 46–48; land acknowledgements implemented by 38–39; legacy values of 22; multiplier effects associated with 22; naming rights for 46–48; neighborhood demographics affected by 26–27, 29; neighborhoods affected by 131; potentiality of 129; property values affected by 24; public financing for 130; racial demographics of areas near 27; shadow. *See* shadow stadia; in suburbs 158; tourism and 21; traffic congestion caused by 9; in United States 36; urban development and 22; urban regeneration led by 20–24, 28, 55; urban regime and 211–212; in urban spaces 3, 25; vacancy of 57. *See also* shadow stadia
stadium development: in California 82–83; California Environmental Quality Act exemptions 79–80; description of 20; displacements caused by 23, 26, 28; environmental impacts associated with 71; environmental review avoidance 79; gentrification and 20–21; law compliance 72; negative interaction associated with 10; neighborhood planning and 21; permeable surfaces affected by 71; politics of 10–12; urban 10–12
Stadium Place 113
Standard Gauge Railway 189
state environmental policy acts: in California 75; criticism of 73; description of 72–73; environmental impact statement 75–77; environmental justice and 73–74; environmental review model of 78; exemptions 75; lead agency in 75–77; legal challenges to 78; mandates imposed by 78; negative declaration 76; overview of 73–78; public participation requirements of 77; purpose of 73; state-specific statutory language in 76; state variations in 74–75; statutory exemptions 75; statutory scope of 74; summary of 84
State Environmental Quality Review Act 74
Stevens, Michael 153
sustainability 230, 234–235
sustainability metrics 240–243

Taipei Cultural and Sports Park 211
Taipei Dome Complex: administrative review stage of 214; building of 213–215; build–operate–transfer contract

258 Index

of 214, 218, 221; Clean Government Committee reinvestigation of 223; commencement of construction stage of 214–215; construction of 217, 222; contract negotiation process for 219; description of 211; design review stage of 214–215, 219–222; Environmental Impact Assessment committee 214, 219, 221; externalities of 211; Farglory Group 214–215, 218–219, 221, 223–224; invitation to tender stage of 214–215, 218–219; location of 215; origins of 212–213; political significance of 225; public safety issues 223–224; scandal regarding 223–224; site selection stage of 214–216; Songshan Tobacco Factory 214–217; square footage of 220; stadium plan preparation stage of 214–215; summary of 225; Urban Design Review committee 214, 219, 221
Taipei Dome Entrepreneurial Consortium 218
Taipei Municipal Council 219
Taipei Municipal Government 214, 216, 221, 223
Taipei Municipal Stadium 215
Taiwan 212–213
Takenaka Corporation 218
tax increment financing 112
Tax Reform Act of 1986 135
TCR. *See* The Climate Registry
TDEC. *See* Taipei Dome Entrepreneurial Consortium
territorial acknowledgments 41
The Climate Registry 238
Thistle Rink 179
Thompson, Lyle 44
Tim Hortons Field 42
tomahawk chop 44
Toronto Maple Leafs 42, 60
Toronto Raptors 42, 46, 60
tourism 21
toxic waste 5, 174
Toxic Wastes and Race in the United States 5
traffic congestion 9
Transparent Richmond 242
TRC. *See* Truth and Reconciliation Commission
Treaty 6 177–178
Tribal Nations 34
trickle-down economics 29
Truth and Reconciliation Commission 41–43
Tsleil-Waututh Nation 48

UCC. *See* United Church of Christ
UCC Commission for Racial Justice 5
UDR. *See* Urban Design Review
UNDRIP. *See* United Nations Declaration on the Rights of Indigenous Peoples
United Church of Christ 5
United Nations Declaration on the Rights of Indigenous Peoples 35
United Nations Sports for Climate Action Framework 63–64
United States: community engagement in 44–45; environmental justice in 56–57; Green Building Council 56, 59; land acknowledgments in 38–41, 44; naming rights in 47; sport team ownership in 49; stadiums in 36
Upper Chattahoochee Riverkeeper 98–99
urban decay: in Baltimore 112–113; definition of 112
Urban Design Review committee 214, 219, 221
urban regeneration: planning and policy for 28–29; stadium-led 20–24, 28, 55
urban regime theory 211–212
urban renewal 112–113
U.S. Bank 47

Vancouver Winter Games 41–42
vicious sedimentation 176, 178
Vision 2030 188, 204–206

Washington, D.C.: Clean Rivers Project 147; democracy and 144–145; disenfranchisement in 145; founding of 144–145; Home Rule 146; Housing Authority 147; housing in 152; National Capital Planning Commission redevelopment of 145–146; Navy Yard 143, 149; neighborhood disparities in 144; population of 144; Southwest 145–146; urban redevelopment projects in 143
Washington Climate Alliance for Jobs and Clean Energy 233
Washington Nationals 143
Washington Sculpture Center 154
water conservation 235
Wembley Stadium 9
Western Cape Provincial Spatial Development Framework 161
White, Thornton 192
White flight: in Baltimore 109, 112; definition of 109
White return 109

Whyte, Kyle Powys 172, 176
Williams, Anthony 143–144, 146–148, 153
WNBA 49, 51
women's professional sports 44
World Hockey Association 173
Wyban, Ken 154

Yankee Stadium: background on 132–133;
community benefits agreement 134–135,
139; debt financing of 135–137;
description of 63–64, 131;

environmental justice and 133–134;
greenspace 135, 137–138; land
ownership structure for 136; opposition
to 132; parkland for 132; PILOT
revenue bonds for 135–136; public
financing of 135–137; in South Bronx
132–134, 159

Zamboni 234
Zille, Helen 164, 167
Zirin, Dave 20